NOLO *Products & Services*

Books & Software

Nolo publishes hundreds of great books and software programs on the topics consumers and business owners want to know about. And every one of them is available in print or as a download at Nolo.com.

Plain-English Legal Dictionary

Free at Nolo.com. Stumped by jargon? Look it up in America's most up-to-date source for definitions of cutting edge legal terminology. Emphatically not your grandmother's law dictionary!

Legal Encyclopedia

Free at Nolo.com. Here are more than 1,200 free articles and answers to frequently asked questions about everyday consumer legal issues including wills, bankruptcy, small business formation, divorce, patents, employment and much more. As *The Washington Post* says, "Nobody does a better job than Nolo."

Online Legal Forms

Make a will or living trust, form an LLC or corporation or obtain a trademark or provisional patent at Nolo.com, all for a remarkably affordable price. In addition, our site provides hundreds of high-quality, low-cost downloadable legal forms including bills of sale, promissory notes, nondisclosure agreements and many more.

Lawyer Directory

Find an attorney at Nolo.com. Nolo's unique lawyer directory provides in-depth profiles of lawyers all over America. From fees and experience to legal philosophy, education and special expertise, you'll find all the information you need to pick a lawyer who's a good fit.

Nolo's Aim:
to make the law...

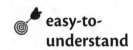

- easy-to-understand
- affordable
- hassle free

Keep Up to Date!

*Old law is often bad law. That's why Nolo.com has free updates for this and every Nolo book. And if you want to be notified when a revised edition of any Nolo title comes out, sign up for this free service at **nolo.com/ legalupdater.***

"Nolo is always there in a jam."
—NEWSWEEK

Please note

1st edition

Nolo's
Plain-English Law
Dictionary

**By the Editors of Nolo, Gerald N. Hill
and Kathleen Thompson Hill**

FIRST EDITION   MAY 2009

Editor   SHAE IRVING

Cover Design   SUSAN PUTNEY

Book Design   TERRI HEARSH

Proofreading   ROBERT WELLS

Printing   DELTA PRINTING SOLUTIONS, INC.

Nolo's plain-English law dictionary / by the editors of Nolo and Gerald and Kathleen Hill. -- 1st ed.
     p. cm.
  ISBN-13: 978-1-4133-1037-5 (pbk.)
  ISBN-10: 1-4133-1037-0 (pbk.)
  1. Law--United States--Dictionaries. I. Hill, Gerald N. II. Hill, Kathleen, 1941- III. Nolo (Firm) IV. Title: Plain-English law dictionary.
  KF156.N654 2009
  349.7303--dc22

                        2009011279

Quantity sales: For information on bulk purchases or corporate premium sales, please contact the Special Sales Department. For academic sales or textbook adoptions, ask for Academic Sales. Call 800-955-4775 or write to Nolo, 950 Parker Street, Berkeley, California 94710.

Your Legal Companion

Like it or not, legal terms are everywhere, demanding our attention. When you rent an apartment, are you the lessor or the lessee? When you read a newspaper article about a politician embroiled in scandal, what does it mean that a grand jury has been convened? If a state trooper pulls you over, and the speeding ticket says you must post bail, what is it talking about?

To make sense of words like these, turn to Nolo. It's our mission to put the law into everyday, understandable language. We've been doing it for almost 40 years— and now we're tackling legal language one word at a time. *Nolo's Plain-English Law Dictionary* includes nearly 4,000 legal terms, old and brand new.

Just a few years ago, legal terms like "cramdown," "phishing," "CSI effect," and "coho" didn't exist or were rarely used in everyday conversation. Here, you'll find clear definitions of these and many more

of the latest twists in legal language. We're committed to finding and defining the important terms that aren't contained in other legal dictionaries. And we'll keep adding new terms to the online version of this dictionary, which you can find at www.nolo.com. You can also use this dictionary on your iPhone—just check the iTunes Store.

Here's another quick tip to help you use this book: If you're looking for a term that starts with a number, like "410(k) plan" or "1031 exchange," you'll find it spelled out as a word. For example, to find "1031 exchange" look it up as though it's spelled "ten-thirty-one exchange."

More than 15 lawyers and a talented support staff have worked together to bring you *Nolo's Plain-English Law Dictionary*. We hope you'll find it both useful and entertaining.

Contributors

Keith Bauerle worked at Nolo and contributed to this dictionary while attending law school at UC Berkeley. After graduating, he clerked for the High Court of American Samoa and practiced environmental law with the Denver office of Earthjustice. He currently practices environmental and land use law in the San Diego City Attorney's office.

Ilona Bray Illona's legal background includes solo practice as well as experience in the nonprofit and corporate worlds. She has written or coauthored several Nolo titles, including *Effective Fundraising for Nonprofits, Becoming a U.S. Citizen*, and *Nolo's Essential Guide to Buying Your First Home.*

Catherine Caputo Before joining Nolo, Cathy was an attorney in private practice assisting start-up and small business clients with a wide range of legal needs. She edits small business books and software and also focuses on issues affecting seniors, such as Social Security benefits and retirement. Cathy received her law degree, with honors, from the University of San Francisco School of Law.

Emily Doskow Emily is a Nolo author and editor, and a mediator and attorney in private practice in Berkeley, California, specializing in adoption and family law,

especially for same-sex couples. She is the coauthor of several Nolo books, including *Nolo's Essential Guide to Divorce, Becoming a Mediator, Do Your Own California Adoption*, and *How to Change Your Name in California.*

Diana Fitzpatrick Diana worked on municipal finance issues at the San Francisco City Attorney's office before joining Nolo. She also worked at a law firm in New York for several years before moving to the Bay Area. Diana is a graduate of New York University School of Law and Barnard College.

Lisa Guerin During her years as a law student at the University of California at Berkeley, Lisa worked for Nolo as a research and editorial assistant. After a stint as a staff attorney at the U.S. Court of Appeals for the Ninth Circuit, Lisa has worked primarily in the field of employment law, in both government and private practice. Lisa rejoined Nolo in 2000 and is the coauthor of several employment titles, including *Create Your Own Employee Handbook* and *Dealing With Problem Employees.*

Gerald N. Hill and Kathleen Thompson Hill Gerald has practiced law in San Francisco's financial district and in a small town; has served as a pro tem judge, arbitrator, university law instructor, and executive director of a state agency; and has drafted legislation. He has a B.A. in political science from Stanford University and a J.D. from the University of California, Hastings College of the Law.

Kathleen is a journalist and language analyst, who writes a weekly newspaper column, was a Coro Fellow in Public Affairs, served on a grand jury, and chaired two municipal commissions. She earned a B.A. at the University of California, a degree from the Sorbonne, Paris, and an M.A. in political psychology from Sonoma State University.

Together, the Hills have coauthored 28 books, including *The Encyclopedia of Federal Agencies and Commissions, The Facts on File Dictionary of American Politics,* and *The Real Life Dictionary of the Law.* They have taught at the University of British Columbia, University of Victoria, and Sonoma State University, and were visiting scholars at the Institute of Governmental Studies at the University of California, Berkeley.

Shae Irving Shae graduated from Berkeley Law (Boalt Hall) in 1993 and began working for Nolo in 1994. She has written extensively on durable powers of attorney, health care directives, and other estate planning issues. She is the managing editor for *Nolo's Quicken WillMaker Plus* software.

Bethany K. Laurence Beth graduated from Hastings College of the Law at the University of California in 1993. She spent several years working for a corporate legal publisher before coming to Nolo. She joined Nolo's editorial staff in 1997 and has never been happier. Beth is the coauthor of Nolo's *Business Buyout Agreements* and the editor of many of Nolo's small business books.

Janet Portman Janet received undergraduate and graduate degrees from Stanford University and a law degree from the University of Santa Clara. She was a public defender before coming to Nolo. Janet is Nolo's managing editor, the author of *Every Landlord's Guide to Finding Great Tenants,* and the coauthor of many Nolo titles, including *Every Landlord's Legal Guide, Every Tenant's Legal Guide, Renters' Rights,* and *Negotiating the Best Lease for Your Business.*

Mary Randolph Mary has been editing and writing Nolo books and software for more than a decade. She earned her law degree from Berkeley Law (Boalt Hall), and her undergraduate degree at the University of Illinois. She is the author of *Deeds for California Real Estate, The Executor's Guide,* and other Nolo materials.

Alayna Schroeder Alayna graduated from the University of California, Hastings College of the Law. She is coauthor of several Nolo titles, including *Nolo's Essential Guide to Buying Your First Home*. Alayna currently practices employment law, focusing on advising employers on sound employment practices and investigating employment disputes.

Betsy Simmons-Hannibal Betsy is a Nolo editor specializing in estate planning books and software. She graduated with honors from Golden Gate University School of Law where she was research editor of the law review. Prior to joining Nolo, she trained at two private law firms as well as the San Francisco Superior Court and the Federal District Court of Northern California. When she's not working, you might find her playing soccer, traveling with her husband, or doting on her curious dog.

Marcia Stewart Marcia is an expert on landlord-tenant law, buying and selling houses, and other issues of interest to consumers. She is the coauthor of Nolo's *Every Landlord's Legal Guide*, *Every Tenant's Legal Guide*, *Renters' Rights*, and *Leases & Rental Agreements*, and editor of Nolo's *LeaseWriter* software for landlords.

Richard Stim Rich graduated from the University of San Francisco Law School and worked in private practice for 16 years until joining Nolo as an editor in 2000. He is the author of *Profit From Your Idea*, *Getting Permission*, and *Music Law*, and is the coauthor of *Patent Pending in 24 Hours*.

Ralph Warner Ralph is a cofounder of Nolo. He is the author (or coauthor) of a number of Nolo books, including *Every Landlord's Legal Guide*, *Everybody's Guide to Small Claims Court*, *Form a Partnership*, and *Get a Life: You Don't Need a Million to Retire Well*. Ralph is a lawyer who became fed up with the legal system and dedicated his professional life to making law more accessible and affordable to all Americans.

Drew Wheaton Drew received his undergraduate degree from Willamette University, where he studied philosophy. In 2004, he joined Nolo, where he now works in the editorial department as a legal researcher. In the near future, Drew plans to attend law school.

Table of Contents

A

ABA See: American Bar Association

abandon To intentionally and permanently give up, surrender, leave, desert, or relinquish all interest, obligations, or ownership in a house, apartment, or other property (such as a patent), a right of way, or a spouse or children. The word is often used when a tenant has left his or her rental unit and the property inside and does not intend to come back. State landlord-tenant laws typically regulate how the landlord may deal with abandoned property left behind by the tenant. To abandon a child or spouse means to have no contact and give no support for an extended period of time.

abandoned property To relinquish ownership and rights in real estate or other property—for example, a tenant who (by all outside appearances) has intentionally and permanently left an apartment with personal possessions. Abandoned property includes intellectual property rights—for example, if an inventor has not applied for a patent, others are legally permitted to use the invention.

abandonment 1) Giving up a right, generally of ownership, with the intention never to claim it again. 2) In family law, leaving a spouse or child(ren) with the intent not to return. In some cases, such as adoption, abandonment will be presumed if the parent fails to contact or support the child for a specified period of time.

abandonment (of residence) An immigration law term referring to situations where a permanent resident (green card holder) leaves the United States with the intention of making a permanent home in another country. Permanent residents who spend longer than six months outside the United States will, upon their return, face serious questions about whether they intended to abandon their residence. After one year away, an immigrant will be presumed to have abandoned residence, and will need to prove otherwise in order to reenter the United States.

abandonment (of trademark) A situation in which trademark rights are lost because the owner: does not use the mark for an extended period of time with the intent not to resume use; lets others use the mark without adequate supervision; or allows the mark to become a generic term. (See also: generic)

abate 1) To do away with or put an end to a problem. 2) To reduce or decrease in amount or value, usually proportionally. (See also: abatement)

abatement 1) The removal of a problem that is against public or private policy or that endangers others, including nuisances such as weeds that might catch fire in an otherwise empty lot. 2) An equal reduction of recovery of debts by creditors when there are not enough funds or assets to pay the full amount. 3) A partial or complete cancellation of a taxpayer's taxes, penalties, or interest by the IRS. 4) Reducing the sum owed under a contract, on the grounds that the other side did not deliver as promised. For example, rent may be abated when a landlord has failed to maintain a habitable premises. 5) After a death, an equal reduction in gifts to beneficiaries if the deceased person didn't leave enough property to fulfill all the bequests made in the will and meet other expenses, such as debts or taxes.

abduction Leading someone away by fraudulent persuasion or by force. In some states, the abductor must intend to marry or defile the person, the person abducted must be a child, or the abductor must intend to subject the victim to concubinage or prostitution. Kidnapping is more limited, requiring the use of force or the threat of force.

abet To help someone commit a crime, including helping the criminal escape from police or plan the crime. (See also: aid and abet)

abeyance A condition in which there is no clear legal owner to real estate. For example, after a property owner dies, it may take a while to determine who the new legal owner of the real estate is.

ab initio Latin for "from the beginning" —for example, "the contract was void ab initio."

abortion The termination of a pregnancy by the removal, by surgical or other means, of an embryo or fetus from a woman's uterus. Until 1973 abortion was considered a crime unless performed by physicians to protect the life of the mother. The Supreme Court ruled in the case of *Roe v. Wade* (1973) that a woman had the right to choose abortion to end a pregnancy through the first trimester. In the latter stages of pregnancy, danger to the life of the mother could still justify a legal abortion.

abrogate To annul or repeal a law or pass legislation that contradicts the prior law. Abrogate also applies to revoking or withdrawing conditions of a contract.

abscond To leave suddenly and in secret, usually to avoid arrest, prosecution, or service of process; or to leave with funds or goods that belong to someone else.

absentee ballot A paper ballot submitted by mail or in person by a voter who expects to be unable to get to his or her polling place on election day.

absolute Complete, without condition, and not subject to modification, as with "absolute ownership" or a "divorce absolute."

abstention doctrine The principle underlying a federal court's decision not to hear a case or controversy that is also being considered by a state court. Federal courts will abstain when they want to avoid the possibility that their decisions could conflict with a state's administration of its own affairs.

abstract In general, a summary of a record or document, such as an abstract of judgment, abstract of trust, or abstract of title to real property.

abstract of judgment A written summary of a court judgment stating how much money the losing defendant (the judgment debtor) owes to the person who won (the judgment creditor),

the rate of interest to be paid on the judgment amount, court costs, and any specific orders that the losing defendant must obey. The abstract is acknowledged and stamped so that it can be recorded and made official with the government. The purpose is to create a public record and create a lien or claim if necessary on any real property owned or later acquired by the defendant located in the county in which the abstract of judgment is recorded.

"The law must be stable, but it cannot stand still."

—Roscoe Pound,
The Philosophy of Law

abstract of title A short history of a piece of real estate that lists any transfers in ownership as well as any liabilities attached to it, such as mortgages, easements, liens, or property taxes. It is usually prepared by an abstracter or title insurance agent.

abstract of trust See: certification of trust

abstracter One who prepares a title report or abstract of title for real estate.

AB trust A trust that allows couples to reduce or avoid overall estate taxes. Each spouse puts property in the AB trust. When the first spouse dies, his or her half of the property goes to the beneficiaries named in the trust—commonly, the couple's grown children—with the crucial condition that the surviving spouse has the right to use the property for life and is entitled to any income it generates. The surviving spouse may even be allowed to spend principal in certain circumstances. When the surviving spouse dies, the property passes to the trust beneficiaries. It is not considered part of the second spouse's estate for estate tax purposes. Using this kind of trust keeps the second spouse's taxable estate half the size it would be if the property were left directly to the spouse. (See also: bypass trust, credit shelter trust)

abuse 1) Mistreatment, as in child abuse. 2) Excessive and wrongful use, as in substance abuse. 3) In bankruptcy, misuse of Chapter 7 bankruptcy by a debtor that has enough disposable income to fund a Chapter 13 repayment plan.

abuse excuse A type of self-defense claim with which defendants seek to justify their actions by proving that they were subjected to years of prolonged child or spousal abuse.

abuse of discretion A standard of reviewing a lower court's or other decision maker's judgment. To overturn a decision for abuse of discretion, the appellate court must find that the decision was wholly unsupported by the evidence, illegal, or clearly incorrect.

abuse of process Using a legal process in a civil or a criminal case, such as filing a lawsuit or taking a deposition, in order to inconvenience another party or otherwise use the process improperly. Some courts define the term to mean using litigation to pursue objectives other than those named in the suit. For example, filing a lawsuit over a certain debt, when the real reason for the suit is to force payment on another debt, would be abuse of process. Because of its chilling effect on the right of access to the courts, claims of abuse of process are difficult to win.

abut When two pieces of land or other parcels of real property touch each other or share a common border.

accelerated depreciation A method of deducting the cost of a business asset more rapidly than by using straight-line depreciation. There are several accelerated depreciation methods, often referred to as MACRS (modified accelerated cost recovery system).

acceleration To bring about at an earlier time. For example to advance the due date of a promissory note so the outstanding balance is immediately due. (See also: acceleration clause)

acceleration clause A contract clause that provides that the entire outstanding amount owed under the contract will become immediately due under certain circumstances. This clause is most often found in promissory notes with installment payments for purchase of real property and requires that if the property is sold then the entire amount of the note is due immediately (the so-called "due on sale clause").

accept See: acceptance

acceptance Agreeing to the terms of an offer, thereby creating a contract. (Compare: counteroffer)

acceptance of service Agreement by a defendant or the defendant's attorney to accept a complaint or other petition (like divorce papers) without having the sheriff or process server show up at the door (often, the papers are received by mail). Most states use a form entitled Receipt and Acknowledgment of Acceptance of Service (or similar language), which the person who is served signs, dates, and sends back to the attorney who sent the complaint or petition. Attorneys must be careful that they have written legal authority from clients to receive papers on their behalf. (See also: service)

access In the context of real estate, the right and ability to enter, approach, and pass to and from. In copyright law, a person who is accused of infringing upon another's copyrighted material may seek to refute the claim by showing that he had no opportunity to see, hear, or copy that work—that is, he had no access. In family law, a husband who disputes paternity of his wife's child might have argued that his wife had relations with other men—that is, others "had access"—but that claim is rarely relied upon in light of modern and highly accurate scientific paternity testing.

accessory Someone who intentionally helps another person commit a felony by giving advice before the crime or helping to conceal the evidence or the perpetrator. An accessory is usually not physically present during the crime. For example, hiding a robber who is being sought by the police might make someone an "accessory after the fact" to a robbery. (Compare: accomplice)

accommodation 1) A favor done without compensation (pay or consideration), such as a signature guaranteeing payment of a debt, sometimes called an accommodation indorsement. 2) Giving in to an adversary on a point to make a deal work. 3) A change in an employer's or landlord's policy or practice, made in order to allow a person with a disability to perform a particular job or live in a rental. (See also: reasonable accommodation)

accompanying relative A family member of someone who immigrates to the United States, who is legally allowed to immigrate at the same time. Most people who receive some type of visa or green card can also obtain green cards or similar visas for their accompanying relatives—that is, their spouses and unmarried children under the age of 21.

accomplice Someone who helps another person (known as the principal) commit a crime. Unlike an accessory, an accomplice is usually present when the crime is committed. An accomplice is guilty of the same offense and usually receives the same sentence as the principal. For instance, the driver of the getaway car for a burglary is an accomplice and will be guilty of the burglary even though he may not have entered the building. (See also: accessory)

accomplice witness A person who is a witness to a crime and also charged as an accomplice to the same crime.

accord and satisfaction An agreement to settle a contract dispute by accepting less than what's due. This procedure is often used by creditors who want to cut their losses by collecting as much money as they can from debtors who cannot pay the full amount.

accountant Someone who works with financial data. Usually a skilled professional trained in financial analysis rather than one who keeps the books. (Compare: bookkeeper)

accounting The process by which financial information about a business is recorded and analyzed.

accounts payable Money owed by a business to suppliers, vendors, employees, banks, landlords, and other creditors. On a company's balance sheet, accounts payable are categorized as liabilities.

accounts receivable Money due or owed to a business or professional by customers or clients for goods or services. Generally, accounts receivable refers to the total amount due to a business and is considered in calculating the value of the business.

account stated 1) A statement of the amount that parties to a transaction, loan, or settlement agree is owed by one to the other. 2) The name for a cause of action in a lawsuit brought to collect the amount the parties have agreed is owed.

accredited investor A high-net-worth investor who is permitted to invest in certain types of higher risk investments without the securities being registered with the U.S. Securities and Exchange Commission (SEC). Under federal securities law, a company that offers or sells its securities must register the securities with the SEC or find an exemption from the registration requirements. Selling to accredited investors is one such exemption. The term generally includes wealthy individuals and organizations such as corporations, endowments, or retirement plans.

accretion An out-of-the-ordinary increase in property that goes to the property owner. In real estate, accretion is an increase in land that results from the deposit of soil by a river or ocean. Accretion also occurs when someone who inherits assets receives more than expected because another beneficiary dies or doesn't accept a share, or when trust assets increase due to some unexpected and unusual event. (See also: alluviation)

accrual method of accounting A method of accounting in which income is accounted for when earned (not received) and expenses are accounted for when liability for paying them is incurred (not when they are paid). (Compare: cash method of accounting)

accrue To earn or accumulate over time, such as interest on an investment that grows or vacation time that is earned by working a certain number of hours.

accumulated earnings See: retained earnings

accumulation trust A trust in which the income is retained and not paid out to beneficiaries until certain conditions are met. For example, if Uncle Pierre creates a trust for Nick's benefit but directs that Nick not get a penny until he gets a PhD in French; Nick is the beneficiary of an accumulation trust.

accusation A formal assertion, by a prosecuting attorney, that a defendant has committed an illegal act.

The Accused. (1988) A victim of gang rape caught in the law enforcement/judicial system convinces a prosecutor to press for a conviction instead of settling for a plea bargain. Jodie Foster won an academy award. With Kelly McGillis, Bernie Coulson, Leo Rossi.

accused A person charged with a crime.

acknowledge 1) To admit something, whether bad, good, or indifferent. 2) To state to a notary public or other officer (such as a county clerk) that a document bearing your signature was actually signed by you. (See also: acknowledgment)

acknowledged father The biological father of a child born to an unmarried couple who has been established as the father either by his admission, by his signing a voluntary written acknowledgment of paternity, or by an agreement between him and the child's mother. An acknowledged father has parental rights and obligations, including the obligation to support the child.

acknowledgment A statement you make in front of a notary public or other person who is authorized to administer oaths stating that a document bearing your signature was actually signed by you.

acquisition of citizenship When a child born outside the United States becomes a U.S. citizen by virtue of having a U.S. citizen parent or parents. The exact legal requirements depend upon the year in which the child was born, and the laws that were in effect then.

acquit The finding by a judge or jury that a defendant is not guilty of a crime.

acquittal A decision by a judge or jury that a defendant in a criminal case is not guilty of a crime. An acquittal is not a finding of innocence; it is simply a conclusion that the prosecution has not proved its case beyond a reasonable doubt.

act A statutory plan passed by Congress or any state legislature which is a "bill" until enacted and becomes law.

action Another term for a lawsuit. For example, a plaintiff might say, "I filed this negligence action last fall after the defendant, Ms. Adams, struck me while I was crossing the street at Elm and Main."

actionable A situation where enough facts or circumstances exist to meet the legal requirements to file a legitimate lawsuit. If the facts required to prove a case cannot be alleged in the complaint, the case is not actionable. (See also: cause of action)

"America is the paradise of lawyers."
—Justice David J. Brewer

---

act of God An extraordinary and unexpected natural event, such as a hurricane, tornado, earthquake, tsunami, or even the sudden death of a person. An act of God may be a defense against liability for injuries or damages; insurance policies often exempt coverage for damage caused by acts of God. Under the law of contracts, an act of God often serves as a valid excuse if one of the parties to the contract is unable to fulfill his or her duties—for instance, completing a construction project on time.

act of nature See: act of God

actual controversy An actual dispute that can be legally resolved, as opposed to a hypothetical or theoretical conflict created for the sake of attaining an advisory opinion. It is a Constitutional requirement for federal jurisdiction.

actual damages In a lawsuit based on one party's injuries, the loss or harm suffered by the injured person, or the specific amounts of money that the person loses as a result of the injuries, including lost wages and medical expenses. (See also: damages)

actual notice Actual awareness or direct notification of a specific fact or proceeding. Actual notice occurs when an individual is directly told about something—for example, when a tenant notifies the landlord that a window is broken, the landlord has actual notice of the broken window. "Personal service" of court documents is another common method of delivering actual notice. Also called "express notice." (Compare: constructive notice)

actuarial tables Standardized life expectancy tables based on various human conditions such as age, sex, and health. Actuarial tables are widely accepted in courts as evidence of life expectancy.

actus reus Latin for a "guilty act." The actus reus is the act which, in combination with a certain mental state, such as intent or recklessness, constitutes a crime. For example, the crime of theft requires physically taking something (the actus reus) coupled with

the intent to permanently deprive the owner of the object (the mental state, or mens rea).

ADA See: Americans with Disabilities Act

addendum An addition to a contract or completed written document, such as a detailed explanation of a contract clause or a proposed change to a contract. House purchase agreements often included addenda (plural of addendum), covering subjects such as payment schedules and other financing terms, what appliances are included in the sale, and date of transfer of title. An addendum should be signed separately and attached to the original agreement so that there will be no confusion as to what is included or intended.

ADEA See: Age Discrimination in Employment Act

adeem See: ademption

ademption The failure of a bequest of property in a will. The gift fails (is "adeemed") because the person who made the will no longer owns the property when he or she dies. Often this happens because the property has been sold, destroyed, or given away to someone other than the beneficiary named in the will. If a bequest is adeemed, the beneficiary named in the will might be out of luck; it depends on state law. For example, say Mark writes in his will, "I leave to Rob my Honda Accord," but then trades in the Accord for a new hybrid. When Mark dies, Rob might get nothing or might receive the hybrid, depending on state law. States that have adopted the Uniform Probate Code generally allow a beneficiary to get something in this situation. (See also: ademption by satisfaction)

ademption by satisfaction When a person bequeaths specific property through a will and then gives that property to the beneficiary while still living. (See also: ademption)

adequate remedy A remedy that a court deems adequate under the circumstances. The remedy may be ordered by the court or arrived at by the parties to the lawsuit. For example, a court might consider it adequate for one party to compensate the other with money (damages) or to take some other action such as tearing down a shed that crosses a property line.

adhesion contract (contract of adhesion) A contract that so strongly favors one party or so unfairly restricts another, that it creates a presumption that one party had no choice when entering into it. If a court determines that the contract is overly unfair, it may refuse to enforce the agreement against the disadvantaged party. An example of a contract of adhesion might be a form contract provided by an unethical leasing company. Adhesion contracts are often evidenced by the comparative strength of the parties—for example, a giant corporation as compared to an average citizen.

ad hoc (ad-**hock**) Latin shorthand meaning "for this purpose only." Thus, an ad hoc committee is formed for a specific purpose, usually to solve a particular problem. An ad hoc attorney is one hired to handle one problem only, perhaps to analyze a specialized area of the law or argue a key point in court.

adjourn The final closing of a meeting, such as a meeting of the board of directors or any other official gathering. It should not be confused with a recess, meaning the meeting will break and then continue at a later time.

adjudicate To rule upon or decide in a judicial proceeding.

adjudication 1) In a judicial proceeding, the act of resolving a dispute or deciding a case. 2) A judicial ruling or decision.

adjustable rate mortgage (ARM) A mortgage loan with an interest rate that fluctuates in accordance with a designated market indicator—such as the weekly average of one-year U.S. Treasury Bills—over the life of the loan. To avoid constant and drastic fluctuations, ARMs typically limit how often and by how much the interest rate can vary.

Former San Francisco 49ers quarterback Steve Young is an attorney, as is baseball manager Tony LaRussa. Other sports figure attorneys include broadcasters Howard Cosell and Mel Allen, as well as Miller Huggins, who managed the Murderers' Row New York Yankees in the 1920s.

adjusted basis An owner's original tax basis in an asset, adjusted for various events during the period of ownership. The costs of capital improvements are added to the original basis (which is normally the price the owner paid for the asset). The costs of damage or deprecation are subtracted from the original basis. Adjusted basis is used to calculate the owner's capital gain or loss for income tax purposes if the property is sold, or an inheritor's tax basis if the asset passes at the owner's death.

adjusted gross income (AGI) Adjusted gross income (AGI) is gross income from taxable sources (including wages, interest, capital gains, income from retirement accounts, alimony received) minus allowable deductions, such as unreimbursed business expenses, some medical expenses, alimony

paid, and deductible retirement plan contributions. You calculate your AGI on the first page of your federal tax return and it serves as the basis for figuring the income tax you owe.

adjuster A person hired by an insurance company to negotiate and settle an insurance claim.

adjustment The settlement of how much is to be paid on a claim or debt. For example, an IRS-approved change to a tax liability as originally reported on a tax return. Or, an insurance company's settlement on a claim. Also includes deductions from an individual taxpayer's total income on Form 1040.

adjustment of status The procedure for applying for U.S. permanent residence (a "green card") while living in the United States. Applicants submit a written application and later attend an interview at a local USCIS (U.S. Citizenship and Immigration Services) office. Adjustment of status is available only to certain people. Not only does the immigrant have to be eligible for a green card in the first place, he or she must also (with some exceptions), be staying in the United States legally, with a visa or other status.

ad litem (ad-**light**-em) Latin, meaning "for the purposes of the legal action only." A person who files a lawsuit for a minor child or for a person who is incompetent acts as "guardian at litem" (guardian just for the purposes of the lawsuit). A person acting ad litem has the responsibility to pursue the lawsuit and to account for the money recovered for damages. (See also: guardian ad litem)

administer 1) To conduct the duties of a job or position. 2) To manage the affairs of the estate of a person who has died under supervision of the local probate court. 3) To give an oath to someone who is about to testify in court or assume governmental office, as in "administer the oath." (See also: executor, probate)

administration (of an estate) The court-supervised distribution of the probate estate of a deceased person. If there is a will that names an executor, that person manages the distribution. If not, the court appoints someone, who is generally known as the administrator. In some states, the person is called the "personal representative" in either instance.

administrative expenses In a Chapter 13 bankruptcy case, the trustee's fee, the debtor's attorney fees, and other costs of bringing a bankruptcy case, which the debtor must pay in full. Administrative costs are typically 10% of the debtor's total payments under the repayment plan.

administrative hearing A hearing before a governmental agency or an administrative law judge. There is no jury, but the agency or the administrative law judge has the authority to make a decision and issue a ruling.

administrative law The procedures created by administrative agencies (governmental bodies), including rules, regulations, opinions, and orders. These procedures are often unique to each agency and are usually not found in statutes.

administrative law judge (ALJ) A professional hearing officer who works for the government to preside over hearings and appeals involving governmental agencies. ALJs are generally experienced in the particular subject matter of the agency involved. Formerly called hearing officers.

Administrative Procedure Act A federal statute establishing the rules and regulations for applications, claims, hearings, and appeals involving governmental agencies. There are similar acts in many states which spell out the rules for dealing with state government agencies. (See also: administrative law)

administrator A person appointed by a probate court to handle the distribution of the property of someone who has died without a will, or with a will that fails to name someone to carry out this task. (See also: administrator ad litem, administrator ad prosequendum, administrator cum testamento annexo, administrator de bonis non, administrator de bonis non cum testamento annexo (DBNCTA), administrator pendente lite, administrator with will annexed, special administrator)

"It is far better to have less learning and more moral character in the practice of law than it is to have great learning and no morals."

—Vice President Thomas R. Marshall

---

administrator ad litem A person appointed by a probate court to represent an estate during a lawsuit. (Ad litem is Latin for "during the litigation.") An administrator ad litem is appointed only if there is no existing executor or administrator of the estate, or if the executor or administrator has conflicting interests. For example, Jerry's will leaves most of his property to his brother, Jeff, and also names Jeff as executor of the will. But Jerry's sister, Janine, feels that Jerry made the will under improper pressure from Jeff and brings a lawsuit to challenge it. The court appoints an administrator ad litem to represent Jerry's estate while the lawsuit is in progress. Also known as administrator ad prosequendum,

meaning administrator "during the prosecution."

administrator ad prosequendum See: administrator ad litem

administrator cum testamento annexo See: administrator with will annexed

administrator de bonis non Latin for "administrator of goods not administered." The person appointed by a probate court to finish probate proceedings when the executor or previous administrator can't finish the job.

administrator de bonis non cum testamento annexo An administrator appointed by a probate court to take over probate proceedings when the named executor dies, leaving the job unfinished.

administrator pendente lite Latin for "administrator pending litigation." The person appointed by a court to begin probate proceedings during a lawsuit that challenges the will. The administrator pendente lite takes an inventory of the deceased person's property and handles the business affairs of the estate until the dispute is settled. Also called a special administrator.

administrator with will annexed An administrator who takes the place of an executor under a will. The administrator steps in either when a will fails to nominate an executor or the named executor is unable to serve. Also called administrator cum testamento annexo or CTA.

administratrix An outdated term for a female administrator—the person appointed by a court to handle probate on behalf of someone who died without a will. Now, whether male or female, this person is called the administrator or, in some states, personal representative.

admiralty court See: maritime court

admiralty law See: maritime law

admissible evidence The evidence that a trial judge may allow in at a trial for the judge or jury to consider in reaching a decision. Evidence is admitted or deemed inadmissible based on the applicable rules of evidence in the place where the case is being heard. The basic rules of evidence are the same in almost all jurisdictions. There are also both federal and military rules.

admission 1) One side's statement that certain facts are true, or failure to respond to certain allegations, in response to a request from the other side during pretrial discovery. 2) An out-of-court statement by an adverse party that is against the interest of the party who said it, offered into evidence as an exception to the hearsay rule. (Compare: declaration against interest)

admission against interest An admission against interest is an exception to the hearsay rule which allows someone to testify to a statement by another person that reveals something incriminating, embarrassing, or otherwise damaging to the maker of the statement.

admission of guilt Admission by someone that he or she has committed acts that amount to a criminal offense.

admit To state something is true. 1) In civil cases, the defendants will admit or deny each allegation in their answers filed with the court. When the defendant admits an allegation, that claim need not be proved in trial. 2) In criminal law, to agree that a fact is true or to confess guilt. 3) To allow something to come in as evidence in a trial, as when the judge rules, "Exhibit D, plaintiff's letter, is admitted into evidence."

adopt 1) To approve or accept something—for example, a legislative body may adopt a law or an amendment, a government agency may adopt a regulation, or a party to a lawsuit may adopt a particular argument. 2) To assume the legal relationship of parent to another person's child. (See also: adoption)

adopted child Any person, whether an adult or a minor, who is legally adopted as the child of another in a court proceeding. (See also: adoption)

adoption A court procedure by which an adult becomes the legal parent of someone who is not the adult's biological child. An adoption decree creates a parent-child relationship recognized for all legal purposes—including child support obligations, inheritance rights, and custody. An adult can also adopt another adult under certain circumstances.

adoptive parent A person who completes all the requirements to legally adopt a child who is not his or her biological child. Generally, any single or married adult whom the court determines to be a "fit parent" may adopt a child. Some states have special requirements, such as requiring the adoptive parent to be at least a specified number of years older than the child, and requiring the parent to have resided in the county for a minimum amount of time. An adoptive parent has all the responsibilities of a biological parent.

ADR See: alternative dispute resolution

ad seriatim (add sear-ee-**ah**-tim) One after another, as in "The neighbors' lawsuits against my client were filed ad seriatim."

adult In most situations, any person 18 years of age or older.

adultery Consensual sexual relations by a married person with someone other than the person's spouse. In states that still allow fault grounds for divorce, adultery is always sufficient grounds for a divorce. In addition, some states factor in adultery when dividing property between divorcing spouses.

ad valorem tax A tax that is calculated "according to value" of property, based on an assigned valuation of a piece of real estate or personal property. Local property tax and sales tax are common examples. An ad valorem tax may be imposed annually or when an asset is sold, inherited, or transferred. (See also: millage)

advance A type of loan or payment in which money is paid ahead of time, in anticipation of repayment or other future adjustment. For example, paying for goods before they are shipped.

advance directive A legal document that allows you to set out written wishes for your medical care and to name a person to make sure those wishes are carried out. (See also: living will, durable power of attorney for health care)

advance parole In the immigration context, advance parole may be granted to a person who is already in the United States but needs to leave temporarily, without a visa. With advance parole, the applicant's pending immigration application will not be canceled while he or she is away. This helps preserve the person's right to return to the United States—though it does not guarantee entry.

advance sheets A looseleaf booklet comprising recent court decisions. (See also: reports)

advancement A gift made by a living person—usually from a parent to a child—with the intent that the amount will proportionately reduce the recipient's share of the gift-giver's estate. Gifts made shortly before death are more typically treated as advancements than those made years earlier.

adverse Contrary or opposed to one's own interests. For example, an adverse party would be the one suing you.

adverse interest A right or concern that's contrary to the interest or claim of another. An adverse interest in real property is a claim against the property, such as an easement.

adverse party The opposite side in a lawsuit. Sometimes when there are numerous parties in one lawsuit, they may be adverse to each other on some issues and in agreement on other matters.

adverse possession A means by which one can legally take another's property without paying for it. The requirements

for adversely possessing property vary between states, but usually include continuous and open use for a period of five or more years and paying taxes on the property in question.

adverse witness See: hostile witness

advisory opinion An opinion by a court, administrative agency, or attorney general that does not resolve a dispute between parties but instead states the legal rule on a particular matter.

affiant Someone who signs an affidavit and swears to its truth before a notary public or another person authorized to take oaths, such as a county clerk. (Compare: declarant)

"Laws grind the poor, and rich men rule the law."

—Oliver Goldsmith

affidavit Any written document in which the signer swears under oath before a notary public or someone authorized to take oaths (like a county clerk) that the statements in the document are true. In many states, a declaration under penalty of perjury, which does not require taking an oath, is the equivalent of an affidavit.

affirm An act by one court to agree with and confirm a lower court's decision.

affirmative action Policies of governments and other institutions, private and public, intended to promote employment, contracting, educational, and other opportunities for members of historically disadvantaged groups. Because they may favor some groups over others, affirmative action policies must be narrowly tailored to meet the institution's legitimate goals, such as remedying the effects of past discrimination or promoting full diversity in a school setting.

affirmative defense When a defendant in a civil lawsuit files a response, usually called an "answer," the answer will state the defendant's denials of the claims made. In addition, the defendant may state affirmative defenses that excuse or justify the behavior on which the lawsuit is based. For example, an affirmative defense of "unclean hands" argues that the person bringing the lawsuit has acted badly in a way that should preclude any finding against the defendant.

affix 1) To attach something to real estate in a permanent way, including planting trees, constructing a building, or installing a built-in bookshelf. 2) To add a signature or or seal to a document.

a fortiori (ah for-shee-**oh**-ree) Latin for "with even stronger reason," which applies to a situation in which if one thing is true then it can be inferred that a second thing is even more certainly true. Thus, if one party is too young to serve as administrator, then his younger brother certainly is too young.

after-acquired evidence In employment law, facts the employer learns after firing an employee for which the employer would have fired the employee anyway. After-acquired evidence may be used as a defense to a wrongful termination lawsuit or to limit the damages available to an employee who was wrongfully fired. For example, an employer may discover, after illegally firing an employee because of his age, that the employee stole from the employer. The employer may use this evidence to limit its damages for lost wages in an age discrimination lawsuit to what the employee would have earned between the time he was fired and the time the employer would have discovered his theft and fired him absent any age discrimination.

after-acquired property 1) Property that a person acquires after taking on a debt, which becomes additional collateral for the debt. Typically, this occurs when the debtor has signed an agreement pledging all property as security for the debt. 2) Property acquired by a debtor after filing for bankruptcy. 3) Property someone acquires after making a will.

after-acquired title Title to property acquired by someone after that person has purportedly transferred the property to someone else. As soon as the seller actually acquires title, it passes to the person to whom it was sold. For example, John signs, acknowledges, and records a deed of his late father's ranch to Sam, even though John has not yet received title from his father's estate. When John gets the title from his father's estate and records it, the after-acquired title goes automatically to Sam.

The Firm. (1993) Tale of a top-of-class neophyte lawyer caught in a law firm fronting for crooks—with deadly results. Tom Cruise, Gene Hackman, Jeanne Tripplehorn, Holly Hunter, Hal Holbrook.

---

after-discovered evidence (newly discovered evidence) Evidence found by a losing party in a civil or criminal case after a motion has been ruled upon or trial has been completed. To convince the judge to reopen the matter, the losing party must prove that the evidence absolutely could not have been discovered earlier. (See also: writ of coram nobis)

age discrimination Treating an employee or applicant for employment less favorably because of his or her age, if the employee or applicant is at least 40 years old.

Age Discrimination in Employment Act (ADEA) A federal law that prohibits discrimination based on age against employees or applicants who are at least 40 years old. (See also: Older Workers Benefit Protection Act (OWBPA))

agency The relationship of a person (called the agent) who acts on behalf of another person, company, or government, known as the principal. The principal is responsible for the acts of the agent, and the agent's acts bind the principal.

agent A person authorized to act for and under the direction of another person when dealing with third parties. The person who appoints an agent is called the principal. An agent can enter into binding agreements on the principal's behalf and may even create liability for the principal if the agent causes harm while carrying out his or her duties. Also called an attorney-in-fact.

agent for acceptance of service See: agent for service of process

agent for service of process The individual designated to receive legal documents and tax notices for a corporation or an LLC. The agent is responsible for ensuring that the business's owners receive important correspondence and legal notices in a timely manner. State law requires that the agent be designated in the corporation's articles of incorporation or the LLC's articles of organization.

age of consent See: legal age, age of majority

age of majority Adulthood in the eyes of the law. After reaching the age of majority, a person is permitted to vote, make a valid will, enter into binding contracts, enlist in the armed forces, and purchase alcohol. Also, parents may stop making child support payments when a child reaches the age of majority. In most states the age of majority is 18, but this varies depending on the activity. For example, in some states people are allowed to vote when they reach the age of 18, but can't purchase alcohol until they're 21.

aggravate To make more serious or severe.

aggravated assault The crime of physically attacking another person and causing serious bodily harm; or assault with a deadly or dangerous weapon such as a gun, knife, ax, or blunt instrument. Aggravated assault is usually a felony, punishable by a term in state prison. (See also: assault)

aggravated battery A crime in which someone has not only used force

against the victim, but did so using extreme force (such as a deadly weapon). Aggravated battery may also be charged on the basis of the seriousness of the victim's injuries. (See also: battery)

aggravating circumstances Circumstances that increase the seriousness or outrageousness of a given crime, which will increase the wrongdoer's penalty or punishment. For example, the crime of aggravated assault is a physical attack made worse because it is committed with a dangerous weapon, results in severe bodily injury, or is made in conjunction with another serious crime. Aggravated assault is usually considered a felony, punishable by a prison sentence.

AGI See: adjusted gross income

agreed statement of facts A statement of facts, agreed to by the parties to a lawsuit (at trial or on appeal) and submitted to the court in writing.

agreement A meeting of the minds. An agreement is made when two people reach an understanding about a particular issue, including their obligations, duties, and rights. While agreement is sometimes used to mean a contract—a legally binding oral or written agreement—it is actually a broader term, including understandings that might not rise to the level of a legally binding contract.

aid and abet To help someone else commit a crime. An aider and abettor is a helper who is present at a crime scene but in a passive role, such as acting as a lookout. In most situations, an aider and abettor faces the same punishment as the perpetrator of the crime.

a.k.a. An abbreviation for "also known as," usually used before alternate names for the same person. For example, "Elizabeth Simmons a.k.a. Betsy Simmons."

aleatory Depending on an uncertain event. Usually applied to insurance contracts in which payment is dependent on the occurrence of an uncertain event, such as injury to an insured person or fire damage to an insured building.

alias A name used that is not the given name of a person (such as Harry for Harold, initials, a maiden name, or a criminal's false name).

alibi A defense that asserts that the defendant could not have committed the crime because the defendant was somewhere else when the crime took place.

alibi witness A witness who confirms a defendant's alibi.

alien A foreign-born person in the United States who has not become a U.S. citizen and is still a citizen of another country. Can refer to legal immigrants as well as undocumented (or, in common parlance, "illegal") aliens.

alienation In real estate law, the complete and voluntary transfer of title to real estate from one person to another. The freedom to alienate property is considered essential to complete ownership.

alienation of affections Deliberate diversion of a person's affection away from someone—usually a spouse—who has a right to expect such affection. In most places, alienation of affection is no longer recognized as a legal claim.

alien registration card (ARC) The official name used in immigration law for a green card, indicating that the holder has U.S. permanent residence.

alimony The money paid by one ex-spouse to the other for support under the terms of a court order or settlement agreement following a divorce. Except in marriages of long duration (ten years or more) or in the case of an ailing spouse, alimony usually lasts for a set period, with the expectation that the recipient spouse will become self-supporting. Alimony is also called "spousal support" or "maintenance."

aliquot (**al**-ee-kwoh) A Latin term for a definite fractional share, usually applied when dividing and distributing the assets in a deceased person's estate or trust.

ALJ See: administrative law judge

allegation A statement by a party in a pleading describing what that party's position is and what that party intends to prove. Certain allegations are required for a plaintiff to maintain a lawsuit. (See also: pleading)

allege To claim a fact is true. A complaint, which plaintiffs file to commence a lawsuit, will allege certain facts. Civil defendants may allege their own facts in their answers.

Allen **charge** See: dynamite charge

alluviation The depositing of gravel or sediment by a river. (See also: accretion, alluvion)

alluvion An increase in one's land from soil deposited on the shoreline by natural action of a stream, river, bay, or ocean. (Compare: accretion)

alter ego A corporation, limited liability company, or other entity set up to provide a legal shield for the person controlling the operation. Proving that such an organization is a mere cover, or alter ego, for the business owner is one way to "pierce the veil" of the corporation or limited liability company, or take away the owners' limited liability protection.

alternate beneficiary A person, organization, or institution that receives property through a will, trust, or insurance policy when the first named beneficiary is unable or refuses to take the property. For example, in his will Jake leaves his collection of sheet music to his daughter, Mia, and names the local symphony as alternate beneficiary. If Mia dies before Jake or if Mia decides to disclaim the gift, the manuscripts will pass directly to the symphony. In insurance law, the alternate beneficiary, usually the person who receives the insurance proceeds because the initial or primary beneficiary has died, is sometimes called the secondary or contingent beneficiary.

William O. Douglas served the longest on the Supreme Court—36 years, from 1939–1975.

---

alternative dispute resolution (**ADR**) A catchall term that describes a variety of methods that parties can use to resolve disputes outside of court, including negotiation, conciliation, mediation, collaborative practice, and the many types of arbitration. The common denominator of all ADR methods is that they are faster, less formalistic, less expensive, and often less adversarial than a court trial.

alternative minimum tax (AMT) An IRS system created to ensure that high-income individuals, corporations, trusts, and estates pay a minimum amount of tax, regardless of deductions, credits, or exemptions. To arrive at AMT, certain items (such as passive losses from tax shelters) are added back to adjusted gross income. If the alternative minimum tax is higher than the regular tax liability for the year, then you must make up the difference by paying the alternative minimum tax.

alternative pleading A legal fiction in which a pleader alleges two or more legal claims which are inconsistent with each other. For example, someone hurt in an accident can plead that the other party was negligent or ran into him intentionally. Or in a criminal trial, a defendant may plead not guilty and not guilty by reason of insanity (in which there is the implied admission that the defendant committed the act). (See also: pleading)

Alternative reproductive technology (ART) A general term for a collection of methods for conceiving children through medical technology, including in vitro fertilization, ovum donation, donor insemination, and other techniques. Conception by ART can lead to legal conflict over who the parents of the resulting child are.

alternative writ of mandate (mandamus) A court order that requires a governmental agency, court, or officials to obey to take a certain action, or show cause at a hearing why it should not have to obey. (Compare: peremptory writ of mandate)

ambiguity When language in an agreement has more than one meaning. Patent ambiguity occurs when the language of the document itself is ambiguous. Latent ambiguity is not readily apparent, but arises in connection with external circumstances. When a contract is ambiguous, external evidence may be introduced to help determine the original intent of parties.

amend To alter or change by adding, subtracting, or substituting. One can amend a statute, a contract, or a written pleading filed in a law suit. The change is usually called an amendment.

amended complaint A second (or third, or fourth, etc.) version of a complaint submitted by the plaintiff or petitioner. A party may amend a complaint to correct facts, add new claims, substitute discovered names for persons sued as "Doe" defendants, or revise a cause of action after the court has found the complaint inadequate.

amended pleading A written pleading in a lawsuit that is changed and refiled as an amended pleading by the party who initially filed it. Pleadings are amended for various reasons, including correcting facts, adding claims, adding affirmative defenses, or responding to a court's finding that a pleading is inadequate as a matter of law.

amended tax return A tax return filed by an individual or entity to correct an error made on a previously filed return or to get a refund of taxes paid.

America's first woman admitted to the bar was Arabella Mansfield of Iowa on June 15, 1869, when the admitting judge ruled that the word "men" in the state law meant men and/or women. Mrs. Mansfield never actively practiced but served as a professor at Iowa Wesleyan and later DePauw.

American Bar Association (ABA) A voluntary professional association of U.S. lawyers founded in 1878. The ABA's activities and mission include providing law school accreditation, continuing legal education classes, information about the law, programs to assist lawyers and judges in their work, and initiatives to improve the legal system for the public.

Americans with Disabilities Act (ADA) A federal law that prohibits discrimination against people with physical or mental disabilities in employment, public services, and places of public accommodation, such as restaurants, hotels, and theaters. The law also requires employers to make reasonable accommodations to allow employees with disabilities to do their jobs.

amicus See: amicus curiae

amicus curiae Latin for "friend of the court," a person or organization that is not a party to a lawsuit but that has a strong interest in the case and wants to participate, usually by filing a brief in support of one party's position. Amicus curiae must be invited by the court or obtain permission from the court before participating.

amnesty A pardon extended to a group or class of individuals by the government, usually before any trial or conviction. Amnesties often follow wars—for example, the amnesty granted to Confederate officials and soldiers after the Civil War or to those who violated the Selective Service Act by evading the draft during the Vietnam War.

amortization 1) A periodic payment plan to pay a debt (such as a mortgage or car loan) by a certain date, in which interest and a portion of the principal is included in each payment. Payments are usually calculated in equal monthly installments. Since the largest portion of the early payments is interest (based on the amount owed), the principal doesn't decline significantly until the latter stages of the loan term. 2) A tax method of recovering costs of certain assets by taking deductions evenly over time. This is similar to straight-line depreciation and unlike an accelerated depreciation method. For example, when someone buys a company, the Internal Revenue Code directs that business goodwill costs must be amortized over 15 years by the buyer.

AMT See: alternative minimum tax

ancillary administration A probate court proceeding conducted in a different state from the one the deceased person resided in at the time of death. Usually, ancillary probate is necessary if the deceased person owned real estate in another state. For example, if Tatiana dies in Montana, where she had been living, and leaves a parcel in Columbus, Ohio, then there must be ancillary administration in Ohio probate court to transfer the property.

ancillary jurisdiction A term used in federal courts for when the court takes control of matters not normally under federal jurisdiction so that it can give a judgment on the entire controversy, part of which is a federal matter that it is authorized by law to determine. (See also: pendent jurisdiction)

ancillary probate See: ancillary administration

angel investor An affluent individual who invests in small, private companies, usually in exchange for company stock or promissory notes that are convertible into shares of company stock. Angel investors often work closely with the company's management to help with introductions or other advice to make the company more successful.

annual exclusion amount The amount that anyone can give to any recipient, free of federal gift tax, in any calendar year. The amount is indexed for inflation and is adjusted by the IRS each year, in $1,000 increments.

annual exclusion gift A gift that is not subject to federal gift tax because it does not exceed the annual exclusion amount.

annual meeting A term commonly used to refer to annual meetings of share-holders or directors of a corporation. Shareholders normally meet to elect directors or to consider major structural changes to the corporation, such as amending the articles of incorporation or merging or dissolving the corporation. Directors meet to consider or ratify important business decisions, such as borrowing money, buying real property, or hiring key employees.

annual percentage rate A yearly interest rate that includes up-front fees and costs paid to acquire the loan, calculated by taking the average compound interest rate over the term of the loan. Mortgage lenders are required to disclose the APR so that borrowers can more accurately compare the actual cost of different loans with different fees.

annuitant The beneficiary of an annuity.

annuity A purchased policy that pays a fixed amount of benefits every year—although most annuities actually pay monthly—for the life of the person who is entitled to those benefits. In a simple life annuity, when the person receiving the annuity dies, the benefits stop; there is no final lump sum payment and no provision to pay benefits to a spouse or other survivor. A continuous annuity pays monthly installments for the life of the retired worker, and also provides a smaller continuing annuity for the worker's spouse or other survivor after the worker's death. A joint and survivor annuity pays monthly benefits as long as the retired worker is alive, and then continues to pay the worker's spouse for life.

annulment A court procedure that dissolves a marriage and treats it as if it never happened. The most common reason for a person to want an annulment instead of a divorce is for religious purposes. Annulments are rare since the advent of no-fault divorce but may be obtained in most states for one of the following reasons: misrepresentation, concealment (for example, of an addiction or criminal record), misunderstanding, and refusal to consummate the marriage.

answer A defendant's written response to a plaintiff's initial court filing (called a complaint or petition). An answer normally denies some or all of the facts asserted by the complaint, and sometimes seeks to turn the tables on the plaintiff by making allegations or charges against the plaintiff (called counterclaims) or providing justification for the defendant's behavior (called affirmative defenses). Normally a defendant has 30 days in which to file an answer after being served with the plaintiff's complaint. In some courts, an answer is called a "response."

antenuptial agreement See: prenuptial agreement

anticipation A situation in which an invention is too similar to an earlier invention to be considered new (or novel). Because novelty is a requirement for patentability, anticipated inventions are not patentable. An invention is usually anticipated by 1) prior publications (a news article, trade journal article, academic thesis, or prior patent), 2) prior inventions (if all significant elements of the later invention are found in an earlier one prior to the date of invention or the application's filing date), 3) placing the invention on sale more than one year prior to an application's being filed, or 4) public use or display of the invention more than a year prior to filing the patent application. (See also: one-year rule, prior art)

anticipatory breach When a party to a contract declares that he or she will not be performing his or her contractual obligations, either by word (for example, "I won't deliver the rest of the goods") or by action (for example, not showing up with goods or stopping payment). The result is that the other party to the contract is excused from having to complete his or her obligations under the agreement. Anticipatory breach is often a defense to a lawsuit for payment or performance on a contract. One cannot repudiate one's obligations and demand that the other person perform.

anticontest clause See: no-contest clause

antilapse statute A statute that passes a bequest in a will to the heirs of the beneficiary, if the beneficiary of the will dies before the testator.

antitransfer laws Laws that penalize people who, in order to become eligible for means-tested benefits such as SSI and Medicaid, have transferred their assets to others for less than fair market value.

antitrust laws Federal and state laws created to regulate trade and commerce by preventing unlawful restraints, price-fixing, and monopolies. The laws are intended to promote healthy market competition and encourage the production of quality goods and services at the lowest prices. The primary federal antitrust laws are the Sherman Act and the Clayton Act.

"All are equal before the law and are entitled without any discrimination to equal protection of the law."

—Article 7, International Declaration of Human Rights

APN See: assessor's parcel number

apparent authority The condition that arises if a third party believes that an agent has the authority to act for another person or company (called the principal) when that authority has not in reality been granted. If an agent acts with apparent authority, the agent's acts legally bind the principal. For example, a customer may believe that an employee who presents a contract on company stationery is authorized to sign that contract on behalf of the company. Even if the employee does not have the authority to enter into contracts, the company will be legally bound by the signed agreement.

appeal A written petition to a higher court to modify or reverse a decision of a lower court (either a trial court or intermediate level appellate court). An appeal begins when the loser at trial (called the appellant) files a notice of appeal within strict time limits (often 30 days from the date of judgment). The appellant and the appellee (the winner at trial) submit written arguments and often make oral arguments explaining why the lower court's decision should be upheld or overturned.

appear To come to court.

appearance Officially coming into court as a party, a lawyer representing a party, or an interested person.

appellant A party to a lawsuit who appeals to a higher court in an effort to have a losing decision modified or reversed.

appellate court A higher court that reviews the decision of a lower court when a losing party files an appeal.

appellate jurisdiction The power of a court to review and revise a lower court's decision. (Compare: original jurisdiction)

appellee A party to a lawsuit who wins in the trial court—or sometimes on a first appeal—only to have the other party (called the appellant) file for an appeal. An appellee files a written brief responding to the appeal, and often makes an oral argument before the appellate court, asking that the lower court's judgment be upheld. In some courts, an appellee is called a respondent.

applicable exclusion amount The amount that a person can leave to any person or entity without paying federal estate tax. In addition, any property left to a qualifying charity or a spouse who is a U.S. citizen passes free of estate tax. (See also: marital deduction)

appraisal A determination of the value of something, such as a house, jewelry, or stock. A professional appraiser—a qualified, disinterested expert—makes an estimate by examining the property, and looking at the initial purchase price and comparing it with recent sales of similar property or items. Courts commonly order appraisals in probate, bankruptcy, or foreclosure proceedings in order to determine the fair market value of property. Banks and real estate companies use appraisals to ascertain the worth of real estate for lending purposes. And insurance companies require appraisals to determine the amount of damage done to covered property before settling insurance claims.

appraise To professionally evaluate the value of property, such as real estate, jewelry, antique furniture, or securities; typically done in order to determine the value of assets for insurance coverage, divide partnership or beneficiary assets, set a house sales price, determine taxes, or make insurance claims.

appraiser A professional who is hired to determine the current value of real estate or other property. Some appraisers specialize in residential houses for the purpose of setting a sales price or securing a mortgage. Other appraisers specialize in particular assets, such as jewelry.

appreciate See: appreciation

appreciation An increase in the value or worth of an asset or piece of property that's caused by external economic factors occurring over time, rather than by the owner having made improvements or additions. For example, increased market demand or inflation can cause property to appreciate. The term is commonly used in the context of real estate.

approach The term lawyers use when they would like to have a conversation with opposing counsel and the judge, out of the earshot of the jury, as in, "Your honor, may I approach the bench?" Judges who initiate the conversation will ask, "Will counsel approach?"

approach the witness A request by an attorney to the judge for permission to go up to a witness on the witness stand to show the witness a document or exhibit. "May I approach the witness?" is the typical request, and it is almost always granted.

appurtenant In real property law, this describes any right or restriction which goes with that property, such as an easement to gain access across the neighbor's parcel or a covenant (agreement) against blocking the neighbor's view. Any subsequent owner has the same right or restriction.

APR See: annual percentage rate

a priori assumption (ay pree-**or**-ee) From Latin, an assumption that is knowable without further need to prove or experience it.

arbiter A person or entity that has the legal authority to decide disputes.

arbitrary Based on individual discretion, not supported by fair or substantial cause or reason, such as discriminating against someone simply because they have a beard or other personal characteristic; often used in reference to a judge's ruling in a court case.

arbitration An out-of-court procedure for resolving disputes in which one or more people—the arbitrator(s)— hear evidence and make a decision.

Arbitration is like a trial in some ways, but typically proceeds much more quickly and with less formality.

arbitrator See: arbitration

arguendo Latin for "for the sake of argument" used by lawyers in the context of "assuming arguendo" that the facts were as the other party contends, but the law prevents the other side from prevailing. For example, a lawyer might say at trial, "even assuming, arguendo, that the court finds our client, the defendant, was negligent, the other party was also so negligent that he cannot recover damages." In short, the lawyer is not admitting anything and wants only to make a legal argument.

argument A persuasive presentation summarizing the law and facts regarding an issue.

ARM See: adjustable rate mortgage

arm's length The description of an agreement made by two parties freely and independently of each other, and without some special relationship, such as being a relative, having another deal on the side, or one party having complete control of the other. It is relevant for determining whether an agreement was freely entered into, and the price, terms, and other conditions were fair. For example, if a man sells property to his son the price paid

may not be the true value since it may not have been an "arm's length" transaction.

arraignment A court appearance in which the defendant is formally charged with a crime and asked to respond by entering a plea. Other matters often handled at arraignment are arranging for the appointment of a lawyer to represent the defendant and the setting of bail. (See also: plea)

True Believer. (1989) A lawyer who has shed his radical ideals for a high-paying career takes on the appeal of a convict at the urging of a young law clerk. James Woods, Robert Downey, Jr., Yuji Okumoto, Margaret Colin.

---

arrearages Overdue alimony or child support payments. Child support arrearages can't be discharged in bankruptcy, and courts usually will not retroactively cancel them. A spouse or parent who falls on tough times and is unable to make payments should request a temporary modification of the payments before the arrearages build up.

arrears Money that a party fails to pay when due. Often the sum of multiple unpaid amounts, such as rent, installments on an account or promissory note, or monthly child support. A person who has failed to make payments is "in arrears" for the amount due.

arrest Being detained by the police in a manner that, to any reasonable person, makes it clear he or she is not free to leave. A person can be "under arrest" even though the police have not announced it; nor are handcuffs or physical restraint necessary. Questioning an arrested person about involvement in or knowledge of a crime must be preceded by *Miranda* warnings.

arrest warrant A document issued by a judge or magistrate that authorizes the police to arrest someone. Warrants are issued when law enforcement personnel present evidence to judges or magistrates that convince them that it is reasonably likely that a crime has taken place and that the person to be named in the warrant is criminally responsible for that crime.

arson The crime of intentionally setting fire to any structure. A death that results from arson is murder.

ART See alternative reproductive technology.

article A paragraph or section of any writing, such as a portion of a corporate charter (called articles of incorporation), a will, or different sections of a statute.

articles of impeachment The formal document filed to impeach a public official. The articles of impeachment state the charges against the official and the reasons why the official should be removed from office. Article of impeachment must be brought by the appropriate legislative body, such as a senate, state legislature, or city council.

articles of incorporation A document filed with state authorities (usually the Secretary of State or Division of Corporations, depending on the state) to form a corporation. As required by the general incorporation law of the state, the articles normally include the purpose of the corporation, its principal place of business, the names of the initial directors who will control it, and the amounts and types of stock it is authorized to issue.

articles of organization A document filed with state authorities (usually the Secretary of State or Division of Corporations, depending on the state) to form a limited liability company (LLC). As required by the general LLC law of the state, the articles normally include the purpose of the LLC, its principal place of business, and the names of its initial members or managers.

as is A term in a sales contract providing that the buyer agrees to take property, such as a house, horse, auto, or appliance in its present condition, without the right to complain if it is faulty. However, the buyer must have had the right to reasonable inspection of the property, so that he or she has a chance to find any obvious deficiency before purchase.

> "Lawyer: One who is willing to go to court and spend your last cent to prove he's right."
>
> —Evan Esar, *Esar's Comic Dictionary*

assault A crime that occurs when one person tries to physically harm another in a way that makes the person under attack feel immediately threatened. Actual physical contact is not necessary; threatening gestures that would alarm any reasonable person can constitute an assault. Assault is often charged with battery, which requires intended physical contact. (See also: battery)

assault and battery The combination of two crimes, of threat (assault) and actual beating (battery). Victims can also sue in a civil suit for the damages suffered as a result of the attack.

assess 1) To determine or evaluate the worth of a piece of property (real or personal), often for the purpose of calculating taxes. The assessed value is multiplied by the tax rate to determine the annual property tax bill. 2) The IRS process of recording a tax liability in the account of a taxpayer.

assessor The government agency that sets a value on real estate parcels for the purpose of local real estate taxes.

assessor's parcel number The designation of property on the local property tax rolls. Some states or counties require the APN to be on a real estate deed before it can be recorded.

asset Generally, any property that has value, whether monetary or sentimental. As used by the IRS, the term means any property with a value and useful life of at least one year that is used in a trade or business—for example, machinery, buildings, vehicles, equipment, patents, and money held by or owed to a business. (See also: capital asset, hidden asset, depreciable asset, fixed asset, liquid asset)

assign To transfer to another person (the assignee) all or some of the rights and responsibilities that another person (the assignor) holds under a contract. For example, a tenant may assign his lease to another person, who then has the right to live in the rental and the obligation to honor all terms of the lease. Also, to assert or point out, as in, "The appellant assigned as errors three of the judge's rulings."

assigned risk A driver with a poor record who would normally be denied coverage by insurance companies, and who is assigned to a state operated or designated insurance program.

assignee A person to whom a property right is transferred. For example, an assignee may take over a lease from a tenant who wants to permanently move out before the lease expires. The assignee takes control of the property and assumes all the legal rights and responsibilities of the tenant, including payment of rent. However, the original tenant remains legally responsible if the assignee fails to pay the rent.

assignment 1) A transfer of property rights or ownership rights from one person to another, called the "assignee." For example, a lease may be assigned from one tenant to another. Or, ownership rights for a patent, copyright, trademark, or trade secret may be transferred by assignment. 2) The property or rights that are transferred.

assignment for benefit of creditors A voluntary transfer of a debtor's property into a trust to be used to pay creditors. The trustee collects any income owed the debtor, liquidates the debtor's property that has been transferred to the trust, and uses the money to pay the debtor's creditors. The debtor receives any money left over once all debts are paid.

assisted suicide Suicide of a terminally ill or otherwise incapable person with help (such as painless drugs) from a physician, family member, or other individual. A form of euthanasia, assisted suicide is illegal in almost all states.

associate In a professional organization, a junior professional; for example, in a law firm, a lawyer with less experience than a partner.

Associate Justice Any U.S. Supreme Court Justice, other than the Chief Justice.

association A group of people who have joined together for a common purpose. Unlike a corporation, an association is not a legal entity. To make this distinction the term "unincorporated association" is often used, although technically redundant.

assume 1) To take over another person's rights and/or obligations. For example, one person might assume another's car lease, residential lease, or debt. 2) In bankruptcy, for the bankruptcy trustee to take over an unexpired lease or executory contract. The bankruptcy trustee has the right to assume or reject these agreements. If the trustee assumes a lease or contract, he or she can either allow the agreement to continue in force or assign that agreement, if the trustee believes doing so could raise money for the debtor's creditors.

assumption See: assume, assumption of risk

assumption of risk 1) An affirmative defense in a negligence case, in which the defendant claims that the situation (taking a ski-lift, climbing a steep cliff) was so inherently or obviously hazardous that the injured plaintiff must have known of the risk, but took the chance of being injured. 2) The act of contracting to take over a risk, such as buying the right to a shipment and accepting the danger that it could be damaged or prove unprofitable.

assured The person or entity that is insured, often found in insurance contracts.

asylum Also sometimes called "political asylum." This is a legal status granted to someone who has fled to the United States and submitted an application proving that he or she fears persecution if forced to return to his or her home country. (The grounds are the same as for refugee status, but the application process is different—refugees apply while they're still outside the United States.) Asylees can apply for a green card one year after their asylum approval.

at issue memorandum A document that states that all parties to a case have been served, that the parties disagree (or are "at issue") over one or more points that need to be resolved at trial, and how much time the parties estimate will be required for trial.

attached 1) In real estate, when equipment, shelving, or furniture is solidly incorporated into a structure, such as bolted to the floor or wired to the ceiling (and not capable of being removed without damage to the structure). If an item is so attached it probably has become a part of the real estate and is called a fixture. 2) In creditor lawsuits, refers to money or property that is seized by court order, based on evidence that the owner of the money or property may soon depart to avoid payment of the debt.

attachment The seizing of a person's property to secure a judgment or to be sold to satisfy a judgment. This is usually performed by a sheriff, based on a writ of attachment issued by a judge.

attempt Starting but not completing an intended criminal act. Attempts involve more than just thinking about doing a criminal act or planning it without at least some concrete steps. Attempted crimes can include attempted murder, attempted robbery, attempted rape, attempted forgery, attempted arson, and a host of other crimes. Attempts are often punished less severely than completed crimes.

attest To state and confirm that something is true or genuine. For example, witnesses to a will attest that the will maker signed the document and declared it to be his or her will.

To Kill a Mockingbird. (1962) Small-town southern lawyer defends a black man accused of rape during the Depression, fighting racism and an unfair judicial system while trying to prove his client's innocence. Adapted from Harper Lee's novel, the screenplay won an Academy Award as did star Gregory Peck. With Mary Badham, Philip Alford, Brock Peters, Robert Duvall.

---

attestation The act of watching someone sign a legal document, such as a will or power of attorney, and then signing your own name as a witness. When you witness a document in this way, you are attesting—that is, stating and confirming—that the person whom you watched sign the document in fact did so. Attesting to a document does not mean that you are vouching for its accuracy or truthfulness. You are only acknowledging that you watched it being signed by the person whose name is on the signature line.

attestation clause A provision at the end of a will or other legal document that sets out the legal requirements of the document and states that those requirements have been met. By signing the attestation clause, a person is stating and confirming that everything within the clause is true.

attorney 1) An agent or someone authorized to act for another. 2) A person authorized to practice law by a state following a bar examination and the meeting of other qualifying requirements.

attorney at law (or attorney-at-law) See: attorney

attorney-client privilege A rule that keeps communications between an attorney and client confidential and protects everything said between attorney and client from being discovered by the opposing party during pretrial investigation, or used as evidence in a trial. The same type of privilege exists between physician and patient, clergy and parishioner, and spouses.

attorney fees See: attorney's fee

Attorney General Head of the United States Department of Justice and chief law officer of the federal government. The Attorney General represents the

United States in legal matters, oversees federal prosecutors, and provides legal advice to the president and to heads of executive governmental departments. Each state also has an attorney general, responsible for advising the governor and state agencies and departments about legal issues, and overseeing state prosecuting attorneys.

attorney-in-fact A person named in a written power of attorney document to act on behalf of the person who signs the document, called the principal. The attorney-in-fact's power and responsibilities depend on the specific powers granted in the power of attorney document. An attorney-in-fact is an agent of the principal.

attorney of record The attorney who has appeared in court or signed pleadings or other forms on behalf of a client. This attorney will remain the attorney of record on a case until the client dismisses the attorney, the court allows the attorney to withdraw, or the case is closed.

attorney's fee The payment made to a lawyer for legal services. These fees may take several forms: hourly, per job or service—for example, $350 to draft a will, contingency (the lawyer collects a percentage of any money she wins for her client and nothing if there is no recovery), or retainer (usually a down payment as part of an hourly or per job fee agreement). Attorney fees must usually be paid by the client who hires a lawyer, though occasionally a law or contract will require the losing party of a lawsuit to pay the winner's court costs and attorney fees. For example, a contract might contain a provision that says the loser of any lawsuit between the parties to the contract will pay the winner's attorney fees. Many laws designed to protect consumers also provide for attorney fees—for example, most state laws that require landlords to provide habitable housing also specify that a tenant who sues and wins using that law may collect attorney fees. And in family law cases—divorce, custody and child support—judges often have the power to order the more affluent spouse to pay the other spouse's attorney fees, even where there is no clear victor.

attorney work product Written materials, charts, notes of conversations and investigations, and other materials related to a the preparation of a case or other legal representation. Their importance is that they cannot be required to be introduced in court or otherwise revealed to the other side.

attorney work product privilege A rule that protects materials prepared by a lawyer in preparation for trial from being seen and used by the adversary during discovery or trial.

attractive nuisance Something on a piece of property that attracts children but also endangers their safety. For example, unfenced swimming pools, open pits, farm equipment, and abandoned refrigerators have all qualified as attractive nuisances. Landowners have a duty to keep their property free of attractive nuisances.

attractive nuisance doctrine A legal doctrine that makes a property owner responsible for harm caused by leaving a piece of equipment or other condition on the property that would be both attractive and dangerous to curious children. Examples of attractive nuisances are tools and construction equipment, unguarded swimming pools, open pits, and abandoned refrigerators.

at-will employment An employment arrangement in which the employee may quit at any time, and the employer may fire the employee for any reason that is not illegal. For example, an employer may fire an at-will employee for poor performance, to cut costs, or because the employer simply doesn't like the employee, but may not fire an at-will employee for discriminatory reasons, to retaliate against the employee for reporting harassment, or because the employee exercised a legal right.

audit An examination of the financial records of a person, business, or organization, typically done to correct careless or improper bookkeeping or to verify that proper records are being kept. Businesses and nonprofits often undergo an annual audit by an independent accounting firm. The IRS also conducts audits, mainly to assess taxes owed.

auditor A person authorized to conduct an audit to verify the accuracy of the financial records and accounting practices of a business or government. Many counties have an appointed or elected Auditor to make independent audits of all governmental agencies in the county government. The term "auditor" is often misused as meaning any accountant.

augmented estate Generally, property owned by both a deceased person and the surviving spouse, plus any property the deceased spouse gave away shortly before death. The concept of an augmented estate is used only in some states. Its value is calculated only if a surviving spouse declines to take what was left by will and instead claims a share of the deceased spouse's estate. (This is called taking against the will.) The amount of the surviving spouse's "statutory share" or "elective share" depends on state law.

authenticate To offer testimony that tells the judge what an item of evidence is and its connection to the case. The purpose of authentication is usually to establish that the evidence can be admitted for purposes of making a decision in the case.

author Under copyright law, the person who creates the work, or the person or business that pays another to create the work under a work for hire arrangement.

authority 1) A power to act or to order others to act. Often one person or entity gives another the authority to act, as an employer to an employee, a principal to an agent, a corporation to its officers, or a government to an agency. 2) A court decision used to make a point or support an argument.

authorize To officially empower someone to act. (See also: authority)

automatic stay An injunction that goes into effect automatically when a debtor files for bankruptcy. The automatic stay prohibits most creditor collection activities, such as filing or continuing lawsuits, making written requests for payment, or notifying credit reporting agencies of an unpaid debt.

autopsy A physician's examination of the body of a deceased person to determine the cause of death.

avails Any amount available to the owner of an insurance policy other than the actual proceeds of the policy. Avails include dividend payments, interest, cash or surrender value (the money you would get if you sold your policy back to the insurance company) and loan value (the amount of cash you can borrow against the policy).

avowal A direct statement or declaration. Often refers to a sworn statement a witness makes after the judge rules that his or her testimony will not be admitted at trial. The avowal creates a record of what the witness would have said, which may be considered by a higher court if a party appeals the judge's refusal to allow the testimony.

avulsion Change in the border of two properties due to a sudden change in the natural course of a stream or river, such as a flood, when the border is defined by the channel of the waterway. A famous American case is the Mississippi River's change which put Vicksburg on the other side of the river.

award 1) The written decision of an arbitrator or commissioner (or any nonjudicial arbiter) setting out the arbitrator's award. 2) The amount awarded in a money judgment to a party to a lawsuit, arbitration, or administrative claim. Example: "Plaintiff is awarded $27,000."

B

Bachelor of Laws A degree in law from a law school, abbreviated to LL.B (for "Legum Baccalaureus"), which means that recipient has successfully completed three years of law studies. Most accredited law schools now grant a Juris Doctor (J.D.) degree instead. Law schools that made the switch allowed their LL.B. holders to claim a J.D. retroactively.

back-to-back life sentences Slang for consecutive life terms imposed by a judge when the defendant was convicted of more than one crime, each of which carries a life sentence. Making the sentences consecutive and not concurrent (served at the same time) lessens the chance of parole: Unless specified "without possibility of parole," a life sentence really means 20 or more years in prison before parole is possible. A convict serving concurrent life sentences could conceivably receive parole on all of them after serving the minimum term, but someone with consecutive sentences would have to begin serving the second sentence upon being paroled for the first.

bad debt A debt that can't be collected. A business that is owed a bad debt may deduct it from ordinary income. A lender who made a personal loan that has become a bad debt may deduct it as a short-term capital loss. In some cases, the debtor must claim the amount of the debt as income—and pay tax on it—in the year when the business or lender writes off the debt as uncollectable.

bad faith The intentional refusal to fulfill a legal or contractual obligation, misleading another, or entering into an agreement without intending to or having the means to complete it. Most contracts come with an implied promise to act in good faith.

badgering the witness When, instead of being questioned, a witness is subjected to derisive comments ("You expect the jury to believe that?"), legal arguments posed as questions ("With all the evidence against you, how can you deny that you stole the watch?"), or questions that assume facts not in evidence ("There were ten people blocking your view, yet you can identify the security guard?").

bail The money paid to the court, usually at arraignment or shortly thereafter, to ensure that an arrested person who is released from jail will show up at all required court appearances. The amount of bail is determined by the local bail schedule, which is based on the seriousness of the offense. The judge can increase the bail if the prosecutor convinces him that the defendant is likely to flee (for example, if he has failed to show up in court in the past), or can decrease it if the defense attorney shows that the defendant is unlikely to run (for example, he has strong ties to the community by way of a steady job and a family).

bail bond A bond that a court accepts in exchange for allowing the defendant to remain at liberty until the end of the case. The defendant pays a certain portion of the bail to a bondsman, usually 10%, and may also have to pledge collateral, such as an interest in real property. The bondsman offers the bond to the court. If the defendant appears at all court dates, the bail will be exonerated, or ended, but the bondsman will keep the 10%. If the defendant fails to appear for a court hearing, the judge can issue a warrant for his arrest and demand the entire bail. Usually, the bondsman will look for the defendant and bring him back, forcibly if necessary, in order to avoid having to pay the entire bail or selling the collateral to satisfy the bail.

bail bondsman A professional agent for an insurance company who specializes in providing bail bonds for people charged with crimes and who do not have the money necessary to post the entire bail with the court. Bail bondsmen usually charge a fee of 10% of the amount of the bond. The offices of a bail bondsman are usually close to the local courthouse and jail, and some make "house calls" to the jail or hand out cards in court. (See also: bail)

 "Injustice anywhere is a threat to justice everywhere."

—Martin Luther King, Jr.

---

bailee (custodian) A person with whom some article is left, usually pursuant to a contract, who is responsible for the safe return of the article to the owner when the contract is fulfilled. Examples include banks holding bonds, storage companies where furniture or files are deposited, a parking garage, or a kennel or horse ranch where an animal is boarded.

bailiff 1) A court official, usually a peace officer or deputy sheriff, who keeps order in the courtroom and handles errands for the judge and clerk. 2) In some jurisdictions, a person appointed by the court to handle the affairs of an incompetent person or to be a keeper of goods or money pending further order of the court.

bailment A legal relationship in which one party (bailor) leaves personal property in the possession, and under the temporary control, of another (bailee). Common examples include leaving a car in a parking garage, lodging a pet at a kennel, or storing household goods in a storage center. While most bailments are considered "bailments for hire" (in which the bailee is paid), there is also "constructive bailment" when the circumstances create an obligation upon the bailee to protect the goods, and "gratuitous bailment" in which there is no payment, but the bailee is still responsible, such as when a finder of a lost diamond ring places it with a custodian pending finding the owner.

bailor Someone who delivers an item of personal property to another person for a specific purpose. For example, a person who leaves a broken computer with a repairman in order to get it fixed is a bailor.

bailout When a government, individual, or business provides emergency financial assistance to a failing business or governmental entity to keep it afloat and avoid the consequences of its collapse.

bait and switch A dishonest sales practice in which a business advertises a bargain price for an item in order to draw customers in and then tells the prospective buyer that the advertised item is of poor quality or no longer available and attempts to switch the customer to a more expensive product. In most states this practice is a crime and can also be the basis for a personal lawsuit if damages can be proved.

***Baker v. Carr* (1962)** A U.S. Supreme Court case in which the Court held that federal courts could decide cases questioning whether state voting districts were properly delineated. (These questions were previously left in the hands of state legislatures.) The case initiated a long series of federal court cases dealing with apportionment issues. (See also: *Reynolds v. Sims*)

balance due The amount of a debt owed on an account, a mortgage, or a promissory note. The balance due is not necessarily the sum of installments due (because the installments may include amortized interest), but may be the principal due without further interest.

balance sheet A financial statement listing a business's assets (what it owns), liabilities (what it owes), and net worth (the difference between the assets and liabilities) at a particular point in time. It is usually prepared each month, quarter of a year, annually, or upon sale of the business. It is intended to show the overall condition of the business.

balloon mortgage A mortgage that is not fully paid off over the loan term (such as five, seven, or ten years), leaving a balance at the end. The borrower must either pay off the remaining mortgage or refinance the loan.

balloon payment A large final payment due at the end of a loan, typically a home or car loan, to pay off the amount the monthly payments didn't cover. Many states prohibit balloon payments in loans for goods or services that are primarily for personal, family, or household use, or require the lender to let the borrower refinance the balloon payment before forcing collection.

ballot 1) A method or process of casting a vote. 2) The actual paper, card, or machine that indicates a voter's choices in an election. 3) The total number of votes cast in an election. 4) A list of candidates running for office.

bank An officially chartered institution empowered to receive deposits, make loans, and provide checking and savings account services. In the United States, banks are organized under federal or state regulations. Banks receive funds for loans from the Federal Reserve System provided they meet established requirements. Most banks

are "commercial" banks with broad powers. Savings and loan associations perform some banking services but are not full-service commercial banks and lack strict regulation. (Compare: credit union)

bankruptcy A federal legal process for debtors seeking to eliminate or repay their debts. There are two types of bankruptcies for consumers: Chapter 7, which allows debtors to wipe out many debts in exchange for giving up nonexempt property to be sold to repay creditors, and Chapter 13, which allows debtors to keep all of their property and repay all or a portion of their debts over three to five years. Business can file for Chapter 7 or Chapter 11 bankruptcy. Chapter 11 lets companies reorganize their debt to stay in business.

bankruptcy court A specialized federal court that hears only bankruptcy cases. Bankruptcy courts are established in districts in every state, and petitioners file for bankruptcy in the district where the petitioner lives or does business.

bankruptcy discharge An order issued by the bankruptcy court at the end of a bankruptcy case, wiping out all of the debtor's dischargeable debts.

bankruptcy estate Everything a debtor owns when filing for bankruptcy, except certain pensions and educational trusts.

bankruptcy petition preparer A nonlawyer who helps debtors complete their bankruptcy paperwork for a fee. Bankruptcy petition preparers may not give legal advice or represent people in court; instead, they act as a typing service, completing the required bankruptcy forms as directed by the debtor who hires them.

bankruptcy proceedings The way a bankruptcy case wends its way through the court system, from the time the bankruptcy petition is filed until the debtor receives a bankruptcy discharge.

bankruptcy trustee A person appointed by the court to oversee a bankruptcy case. In a Chapter 7 case, the trustee's role is to gather the debtor's nonexempt property, sell it, and distribute the proceeds to creditors. In a Chapter 13 case, the trustee's role is to receive the debtor's monthly payments and distribute them to creditors.

bar Collectively, all lawyers qualified to practice in a given court or jurisdiction.

bar association An organization of lawyers. Membership in a state bar association (also called an "integrated" or "unified" bar association) is often mandatory before a lawyer can practice in that state. There are also many voluntary bar associations organized by city, county, or other community.

bar examination An examination for individuals who want a license to practice law. Typically, bar exams are multiday tests of endurance and knowledge, covering a wide range of legal topics. Once licensed in a particular state, an attorney can practice law in that state and in federal courts in that state. Some states require a special bar examination for attorneys who have already passed the bar in other states, while others recognize out-of-state attorneys if they have established local residence. Lawyers from one state may occasionally practice in another with the consent of the court alone.

My Cousin Vinny. (1992) A comedy in which two New Yorkers are wrongly accused of a murder in rural Alabama. They enlist a cousin, inexperienced lawyer Vinny Gambini, to defend them.

bargain A mutual agreement between two parties that is voluntary and involves the exchange of consideration (money, goods, services, or a promise to do something). If the agreement involves an illegal transaction or the consideration is insufficient or illegal, a bargain does not constitute a contract.

barratry Creating legal business by stirring up disputes and quarrels, generally for the benefit of the lawyer who sees fees in the matter. Barratry is illegal in all states and subject to criminal punishment or discipline by the state bar.

barrister In Great Britain, a lawyer who may argue cases in superior courts. (Compare: litigator)

basis For income and capital gains tax purposes, the value that is used to determine profit or loss when property is sold. Often the basis is what you paid for the property, adjusted to reflect improvements made or damage incurred while you own the property. (See also: adjusted basis, carryover basis, stepped-up basis)

basis point A basis point is a unit of measure used in describing interest rates. One basis point is equivalent to 1/100th of a percent, or 0.01%. For example, if the prime rate increases by 50 basis points, it means that the rate has risen 0.5%.

battery A crime consisting of physical contact that is intended to harm someone. Unintentional harmful contact is not battery, no mater how careless the behavior or how severe the injury. A fist fight is a common battery; being hit by a wild pitch in a baseball game is not.

beach bum trust provision A clause in a trust that requires the trust beneficiary to earn his or her own money in order to receive trust funds. This provision is intended to encourage the beneficiary to work, and not just lie around the beach and live off the trust.

bearer A person holding a negotiable instrument, such as a check, promissory note, bank draft, or bond. This becomes important when the document states it is "payable to bearer," which means whoever holds this paper it can receive the funds due on it.

bearer paper A negotiable instrument payable to whoever has possession of it, rather than being payable to a specific person.

belief Convinced of the truth of a statement or allegation. In the phrase "upon information and belief," the so-called belief is based only on unconfirmed information, so the person declaring the belief is hedging his or her bet as to whether the belief is correct.

bench The desk and seat (usually a chair rather than an actual bench) where a judge sits in the courtroom. Sometimes the word "bench" is used in place of the word "judge"—for example, a party to a lawsuit might ask for a bench trial, meaning a trial by a judge without a jury. And lawyers in a trial sometimes "approach the bench," meaning they step up to speak to the judge.

bench trial A trial decided by a judge (sitting on the "bench"), without a jury.

bench warrant An arrest warrant issued by a judge while sitting on the bench, holding court. A bench warrant is used when a defendant on bail fails to show up, or when a witness under subpoena fails to appear. The judge will usually set bail at the same time. Bench warrants for lesser matters (such as failing to appear to answer to a traffic ticket) may simply be noted on the defendant's record. If the defendant is stopped later by the police for any reason, the police will have the ability to act on the warrant and arrest the person.

beneficial interest The right of a party to some profit, distribution, or benefit from a contract or trust. A beneficial interest is distinguished from the rights of someone like a trustee or official who has responsibility to manage the assets, but does not share in the benefits.

beneficial ownership Ownership of the benefits related to property, rather than in the property itself. For example, the beneficiary of trust income has beneficial ownership of that trust. Also, a person may have beneficial ownership of securities, such as voting rights or investment rights, without actually having his or her name on the title of the stocks.

beneficial use The right to enjoy the pleasant qualities of something such as light, air, view, access, or water in a stream even though the title to the property in which the use exists is held by another.

beneficiary A person or organization legally entitled to receive benefits through a legal device, such as a will, trust, or life insurance policy.

beneficiary deed See: transfer-on-death deed

benefit 1) Profit, advantage, or privilege. 2) A perquisite by an employer to an employee, beyond wages, such as vacation time, health insurance coverage, or a pension. 3) A payment from an insurance policy or government program, such as Social Security benefits, workers compensation benefits, or unemployment benefits.

benefit of counsel Advice from an attorney. Typically used in the negative ("without benefit of counsel") to describe a situation in which a person was not advised by an attorney and therefore didn't appreciate the full import of his or her actions.

benevolent society benefits See: fraternal benefit society benefits

bequeath To leave personal property through a will. (Compare: devise)

bequest Personal property (anything but real estate) left under the terms of a will.

Berne Convention An international treaty that standardizes basic copyright protection among all of the signatory countries. A member country will afford the same treatment to a copyright owner from another country as it does to owners in its own country.

best evidence rule A rule of evidence that demands that the original of any document, photograph, or recording be used as evidence at trial, rather than a copy. A copy will be allowed into evidence only if the original is unavailable.

bestiality Copulation by a human with an animal, which is a crime in all states as a "crime against nature."

"True law is right reason in agreement with nature; it is of universal application, unchanging and everlasting; it summons to duty by its commands, and averts from wrongdoing by its prohibitions."

—Cicero

---

best interests (of the child) The test that courts use when making decisions that affect a child. For example, an adoption is allowed when a court declares it to be in the best interests of the child. And in disputes over child custody, the judge will make a decision based on the child's best interests. Factors considered by the court in deciding the best interests of a child include: the child's age, sex, and mental and physical health; age, lifestyle, and mental and physical health of the parents; emotional ties between the parents and the child; ability of the parents to provide the child with food, shelter, clothing, and medical care; potential negative affect of changing the status quo; and the child's preference.

beyond a reasonable doubt See: reasonable doubt

BFOQ See: bona fide occupational qualification

BFP Slang for bona fide purchaser.

bias An actual or potential decision maker's predisposition for or against a party to a lawsuit or a particular group of people. Bias may result from things like discriminatory attitudes, personal opinions, financial dealings, or personal knowledge of one of the parties or witnesses.

bid An offer to pay or charge a specific price, under set terms, for an item or service. People make bids at auctions, at which the highest offer wins. The term is also used to refer to a contractor's offer to build a project or sell goods or services at a given price and other terms, with often the lowest bidder getting the job.

bifurcate See: bifurcated trial

bifurcated trial A trial that is divided into stages: one stage to establish guilt or liability, and the other stage to establish damages or punishment.

bigamy The condition of having two spouses at the same time. A marriage in which one of the parties is already legally married is bigamous and usually therefore void. In most states, if the bigamy was intentional, it is also a crime.

bilateral contract A contract in which both parties exchange promises to perform. (Compare: unilateral contract)

bill 1) A statement of what is owed. 2) A legislative proposal for enactment of a law. 3) An old-fashioned term for various documents filed in lawsuits or criminal prosecutions.

bill of attainder A legislative act that declares a named person guilty of a crime, particularly treason. Such bills are prohibited by Article I, Section 9 of the United States Constitution.

bill of exchange An unconditional written order from one person (the maker or drawer) to another person (the payor) to pay a specified sum of money to a designated person (the payee). It is the same as a draft. A bill of exchange drawn on a bank account is a "check."

bill of lading A document of title for goods being shipped that demonstrates the holder has a right to transport the goods. It also acts as a receipt to the shipper of goods from the carrier (trucking company, railroad, ship, or air freighter) as well as a contract providing the terms of transport.

bill of particulars A document, written by a plaintiff or prosecutor at the request of a defendant in a civil or criminal action, that sets out detailed information about the claims or charges being brought against the defendant. Knowing these particulars, the defendant is able to mount a defense.

Bill of Rights The first ten amendments to the federal constitution, adopted in 1791. The Bill of Rights includes many cornerstones of our democracy: freedom of speech, religion, and assembly; prohibitions against unreasonable search and seizure, cruel and unusual punishment, and compelled self-incrimination; and the rights to due process and a speedy trial if accused of a crime.

bill of sale A written statement attesting to the transfer (sale) of goods, possessions, or a business to a buyer. It is useful to show that the buyer now has ownership and to detail what was actually purchased. A bill of sale may accompany an agreement that states the agreed-upon terms of sale, including the date of transfer, the price, timing of payment, and other provisions.

binder A temporary insurance contract that provides insurance coverage while the permanent policy is being prepared.

binding precedent See: precedent

bird-nesting A custody arrangement in which the children of divorcing parents stay in the family home and the parents take turns living there with them, usually sharing time equally. The parents each have their own place to live when not in the family home with the children (or, occasionally, alternate living in a second home).

blackletter law Legal rules that are so well settled that they require little or no legal discourse. Also called hornbook law.

blackmail An unjustified demand, threatening to reveal embarrassing, disgraceful, or damaging facts (or rumors) about a person to the public, family, spouse, or associates unless paid off to not carry out the threat. Blackmail is charged under the crime of extortion.

blank endorsement An endorsement that passes title to a negotiable instrument without naming the person to whom it should be paid. (Compare: qualified endorsement)

blanket search warrant An unconstitutionally broad authorization from a judge that allows the police to search multiple areas for evidence without specifying exactly what they are looking for.

blind pig See: blind tiger

blind tiger A place where liquor is illegally sold; a speakeasy. This term was commonly used during prohibition and derives from the practice of exhibiting animal curiosities in these establishments.

blind trust A trust in which a trustee manages investments for someone who has no knowledge of the trust's specific assets or the actions taken by the trustee to manage them. Blind trusts are often used by high-ranking elected or appointed officials to avoid conflicts of interest.

blog Short for "Web log," an online journal to which regular entries are posted. Some blogs cover a specific topic, and feature commentaries, videos, and/or other material on that subject; others function more as a personal diary.

Many blogs are interactive, allowing readers to comment on posts.

Bluebook A reference guide considered by legal professionals to be the authority on legal citation. The book's complete title is *The Bluebook: A Uniform System of Citation*. The *Bluebook* is published by the Harvard Law Review Association in collaboration with the editors of the *Yale Law Journal*, the *Columbia Law Review*, and the *University of Pennsylvania Law Review*.

The Pelican Brief. (1993) Based on the John Grisham legal thriller, this film involves the murder of two Supreme Court justices. Included in the big-name cast are Julia Roberts, Denzel Washington, Hume Cronyn, and Robert Culp.

---

blue flu An organized protest by law enforcement officers who call in sick. Police officers may stage these "sick-outs" because they are not legally allowed to go on strike.

blue law A statute or ordinance that forbids or regulates an activity, such as the sale of liquor on Sundays.

blue ribbon jury A jury consisting of persons with special qualities, such as advanced education or special training, sometimes used in complicated civil cases (with the parties' consent) and to investigate suspected governmental corruption. Specialists in a technical field are called a "blue-blue ribbon jury." Blue ribbon juries are not allowed in criminal cases, because doing so would violate a defendant's right to be tried by a jury of his peers.

blue sky laws The laws that aim to protect people from investing in sham companies that consist of nothing but "blue sky." Blue sky laws require that companies seeking to sell stock to the public submit information to and obtain the approval of a state or federal official who oversees corporate activity.

board of directors The policy managers of a corporation or organization elected by the shareholders or members. (See also: director)

boilerplate Slang for standard provisions in a contract, form, or legal pleading that are routine and often preprinted. Boilerplate provisions are meant to be used in many contracts, but some may not apply to every situation.

boiler room A telephone bank operation in which fast-talking telemarketers or campaigners attempt to sell stock, services, goods, or candidates. Such operations, especially securities sales, are often fraudulent and illegal.

bona fide Latin for "good faith," it signifies the "real thing" and the lack of deceit. In the case of a party claiming title as bona fide purchaser or holder, it indicates lack of knowledge of any defect in title.

bona fide occupational qualification (BFOQ) An employer's job requirement that discriminates against a protected class but is not considered illegal because it is reasonably necessary to the operation of a business.

bona fide purchaser Someone who purchased something with no reason to believe that the property belonged to someone else or that the property was subject to another party's claim. The purchaser must have paid a full and fair price for the property and have received the item in the normal course of business. (See also: holder in due course)

bond 1) A written agreement purchased from a bonding company that guarantees a person will properly carry out a specific act, such as managing funds, showing up in court, providing good title to a piece of real estate, or completing a construction project. If the person who purchased the bond fails at his or her task, the bonding company will pay the aggrieved party an amount up to the value of the bond. The bonding company often requires collateral (by placing a lien on the purchaser's real estate), and if it has to pay out on the bond, it will sell the collateral to cover its loss. 2) An interest-bearing document issued by a government or company as evidence of a debt. A bond provides predetermined payments at a set date to the bond holder. Bonds may be "registered" bonds, which provide payment to the bond holder whose name is recorded with the issuer and appears on the bond certificate, or "bearer" bonds, which provide payments to whomever holds the bond in-hand.

bondsman 1) Someone who sells bail bonds. 2) A surety (a guarantor or insurance company) who provides bonds that guarantee another's performance on a contract.

book account An account of a customer kept in a business ledger of debits and credits (charges and payments), containing all the financial transactions with that party during the period. It provides a clear statement of the amount due from or to that party at any time.

booking A quaint phrase that refers to the recording of an arrested person's name, age, address, and reason for arrest when that person is brought to jail and placed behind bars. Nowadays, the book is likely to be a computer. Usually, a mug shot and fingerprints are taken, and the arrestee's clothing and personal effects are inventoried and stored.

bookkeeper A person who records financial data in the financial records of a business. (Compare: accountant)

books The collection of financial records of business activity kept on paper or in a computer file.

book value A method of valuing a corporation's stock or a company's worth by adding up the stated value of assets as shown on the books (records) of the company and deducting all the liabilities (debts) of the company. Because it does not include factors such as earnings potential or the goodwill (reputation) of the company, book value is a conservative method of valuation.

boot In a 1031 exchange, any property, liabilities, or money received that does not qualify for the exchange and is taxed. For example, if a taxpayer sells a relinquished property with a $100,000 gain and buys a replacement property for $10,000 less than the sales price of the relinquished property, he has $10,000 boot.

border patrol See: Customs and Border Protection (CBP)

bottomry A contract, similar to a mortgage, in which a ship and/or its freight is pledged as security for a loan to finance repairs, equipment, or the cost of a journey. The contract is generally called a "bottomry bond." If the loan is not paid back, the lender can sell the ship and/or its freight.

bounty hunter Someone who who chases down defendants who have skipped bail, and turns them in.

boycott An organized effort to damage a business by refusing to patronize it. The goal is attract attention to and influence the business's policies. Labor unions and their sympathizers have boycotted lettuce and grapes not picked by union farm workers, and civil rights activists have boycotted stores and restaurants that had "white only" hiring policies. The term is named for Captain Charles C. Boycott, a notorious land agent, whose neighbors ostracized him during Ireland's Land League rent wars in the 1880s. Boycotts are not illegal in themselves, unless there are threats or violence involved. (See also: secondary boycott)

Brady material Evidence known to the prosecution that is favorable to the defense. Under the U.S. Supreme Court case of *Brady v. Maryland*, the prosecution's failure to hand over this exculpatory evidence is a violation of a defendant's due-process rights, but if the defendant is convicted, this error won't necessarily result in a reversal of the conviction.

breach A failure or violation of a legal obligation—for example, a failure to perform a contract (breaching its terms), failure to do one's duty (breach of duty, or breach of trust), causing a disturbance, threatening, or other violent acts which break public tranquility (breach of peace), or illegally entering property (breach of close).

breach of contract A legal claim that one party failed to perform as required under a valid agreement (written or oral) with the other party. For example you might say, "The roofer breached our contract by using substandard supplies when he repaired my roof."

breach of promise A broken promise, usually to marry. No longer a valid claim, historically breach of promise was used to seek money damages when a fiancee—usually the intended groom—called off the wedding.

breach of the peace The crime of disorderly conduct or creating a public disturbance, usually involving unnecessary or distracting noise. Merely insulting another, or causing annoyance, is not a breach of the peace.

breach of trust An act of a trustee that violates the trustee's duties or the terms of a trust. A breach of trust need not be intentional or malicious; it can be due to carelessness or negligence.

breach of warranty Violation of an agreement between a seller and a buyer as to the condition, quality, or title of the item sold. It can apply to title of real property or goods, or to an assurance about quality of an item sold. The warranty need not be expressed, but may be implied from the circumstances at the time of sale. The party making the warranty is liable to the party to whom the guarantee was made.

breaking and entering Entering any building through the slightest amount of force (even pushing open a door), without authorization. When someone enters in order to commit a crime, this is burglary. If there is no such intent, the breaking and entering alone may be illegal trespass, which is a misdemeanor crime.

bribery The crime of giving or taking money or some other valuable item in order to influence a public official (any governmental employee) in the performance of his or her duties. Bribery can also involve corrupt dealing with the employees of a business competitor in order to secure an advantage.

brief A document used to submit a legal contention or argument to a court. A brief typically sets out the facts of the case and a party's legal arguments. These arguments must be supported by legal authority and precedent, such as statutes, regulations, and previous court decisions. Don't be fooled by the name—briefs are usually anything but brief, as pointed out by writer Franz Kafka, who defined a lawyer as "a person who writes a 10,000-word decision and calls it a brief."

broker A person or entity that arranges contracts (for real estate, insurance, stocks, and the like) between a buyer and seller for a commission. Brokers in many fields are regulated and licensed by each state and have a fiduciary duty to act in the best interests of their customers or clients.

Brown v. Board of Education of Topeka (**1954**) A U.S. Supreme Court case in which Chief Justice Earl Warren ruled for a unanimous Court that separate educational facilities for blacks and whites are inherently unequal and equal conditions for all races must be provided with all deliberate speed, overturning *Plessy v. Ferguson.*

bucket shop An unofficial and usually illegal betting operation in which the prices of stocks and commodities are posted and the customers bet on the rise and fall of prices without actually buying stock, commodities, or commodity futures. Bucket shops are seldom seen today since there are many opportunities to gamble legally on the stock and commodities markets.

building and loan association Another name for a savings and loan association. As the name implies, these institutions were originally meant to provide loans for building a house after the depositor had saved enough for a down payment.

bulk sale The sale of all or most of a business's inventory, merchandise, or equipment. (See also: bulk sales law)

bulk sales law A law that regulates the transfer of business assets so that business owners cannot dispose of assets in order to avoid creditors. If a business owner wants to conduct a bulk sale of business assets—that is, get rid of all or most of its inventory, merchandise, or equipment—the business owner must give written notice to creditors and, in some states, publish and record a notice of the sale. Only a few states still have a bulk sales law, and in most it applies only to companies that manufacture or sell inventory from stock. The Uniform Commercial Code and most states have repealed their bulk sales law since remedies are provided by the Fraudulent Transfer Act.

bulk transfer See: bulk sale

burden A duty or obligation, or anything that restricts an activity or use. This can be intangible—for example, a burden on land such as a zoning restriction or the right of a neighbor to pass over the property to reach his home (easement).

burden of proof A party's job of convincing the decision maker in a trial that the party's version of the facts is true. In a civil trial, it means that the plaintiff must convince the judge or jury by a preponderance of the evidence that the plaintiff's version is true—that is, over 50% of the believable evidence is in the plaintiff's favor. (That said, the burden of proof may shift to the defendant if the defendant raises a factual issue in defense to the plaintiff's claims.) In a criminal case, because a person's liberty is at stake, the government has a harder job, and must convince the judge or jury beyond a reasonable doubt that the defendant is guilty.

"Death and taxes are inevitable, but death does not get worse every time Congress meets."

—Anonymous

---

burglary The crime of entering a building with the intent to commit a crime. Old definitions required that the entering be accompanied by a "breaking," by forcing one's way in or by any physical act that allows entry; and that the crime intended be a felony. Modern statutes are less restrictive. For instance, someone would be guilty of burglary if he entered a house through an unlocked door in order to commit a murder (a felony) or to steal a bicycle (probably a misdemeanor). (See also: felony, misdemeanor)

burial insurance Insurance that covers the cost of disposing of a person's remains.

burial policy An insurance policy that covers the cost of disposing of a person's remains.

***Bush v. Gore* (2000)** The U.S. Supreme Court case that played a pivotal role in the 2000 presidential election. The Court reversed the decision of the Florida Supreme Court that had granted a hand recount of ballots requested by the campaign of Vice President Gore in three Florida counties. The Court held that the Florida Supreme Court's method for recounting ballots was a violation of the Equal Protection Clause of the Fourteenth Amendment. The Court also ruled that no alternative method could be established within the time limits set by the State of Florida, effectively resolving the election in favor of George W. Bush.

business Any activity carried on with the intent to make a profit or any enterprise engaged in such activity. A business does not have to have a formal organization; it can be a corporation, partnership, sole proprietorship, or any other type of entity, ranging from a street peddler to General Motors.

business equity The net worth of a business, equal to its assets minus its liabilities.

business invitee A person who enters commercial premises for the purpose of doing business. A business is liable to a business invitee for injury caused by dangerous conditions of the premises, such as wet floors.

business license A permit issued by a local or state governmental agency for a business to operate. Also called a tax registration certificate.

business records exception An exception to the evidence rule prohibiting hearsay. The business records exception allows a business document to be admitted into evidence if a proper foundation is laid to show the document is reliable.

but-for test One of several tests to determine a defendant's responsibility for the subject of a lawsuit or criminal proceeding. For example, the prosecutor may need to argue that: "But for the defendant's speeding, the car would not have gone out of control, and therefore the defendant is responsible." This is shorthand for whether the action was the "proximate cause" of the damage.

buyout agreement An agreement between two parties to a contract, often a landlord and tenant, that releases one party from the obligations of the contract or lease in exchange for a financial payment to the other party.

buy-sell agreement A binding contract between co-owners that controls the purchase of a withdrawing owner's ownership interest and includes transfer restrictions that control when owners can sell their interest, who can buy an owner's interest, and what price will be paid. These agreements often cover what happens when an owner retires, goes bankrupt, becomes disabled, gets divorced, or dies.

bylaws The rules that govern the internal affairs or actions of a corporation. Bylaws are adopted by the shareholders or the board of directors of a corporation. They generally include procedures for holding meetings and electing the board of directors and officers. The bylaws also set out the duties and powers of the corporation's board of directors and officers.

bypass trust A trust for couples designed to save on federal estate tax at the death of the second spouse. When the first spouse dies, the trust is split into two, one of which is called the bypass trust because the property it holds bypasses taxation when the second spouse dies. (See also: AB trust, credit shelter trust)

C

cafeteria plan A benefit program in which employees choose from a menu of options, such as health coverage, life insurance, disability insurance, and so on.

calendar 1) The list of cases to be called for trial before a particular court. 2) To set and give a date and time for a case, petition, or motion to be heard by a court.

calendar call A hearing at which cases are scheduled for trial or hearing. In general, numerous cases will be set for a calendar call at the same time, and the judge overseeing the hearing schedules each of them based on the status of the specific case.

calendar year accounting period A 12-month period for tax purposes that ends on December 31.

call 1) The demand for payment of money. 2) A request to assemble. (See also: call option)

call option An option to buy a particular commodity or security at a fixed price for a certain amount of time. Sometimes simply called a "call." (Compare: put option)

calumny (**cal**-um-nee) Maliciously misrepresenting another's words or acts, causing injury to that person's reputation; or falsely charging another with a crime.

cancel To cross out or destroy a document by tearing it up, writing on its face that it is cancelled or void, or otherwise defacing it.

cancellation See: cancel

cancellation of removal An immigration benefit allowing an immigrant in removal proceedings to ask the immigration judge to grant permanent residence. The judge's decision will be a matter of discretion. In the case of undocumented immigrants, the applicant must prove 1) having lived continuously in the United States for at least ten years; 2) good moral character during those years; 3) that he or she isn't statutorily barred from entry based on having violated certain U.S. security or criminal laws; and 4) that his or her U.S. citizen or permanent resident spouse, parent, or children would face "extraordinary and exceptionally unusual hardship" if the applicant were forced to leave the United States. In the case of immigrants who already have U.S. permanent residence, but are in removal proceedings because of having committed a crime, the applicant must prove that he or she has 1) been a lawful permanent resident for at least five years; 2) lived in the U.S. for at least seven years in any status; and 3) not been convicted of an aggravated felony.

caning A punishment for crimes used in various countries (currently not including the United States), in which the convicted defendant is lashed with a cane or rod.

"In a democracy the law says that it is just for the poor to have no more advantage than the rich; and that neither should be masters, but both equal."

—Aristotle, *Politics*

---

canon law The laws of a church or religion, especially those of the Roman Catholic Church, that govern the powers of the clergy, administration of the church, and church ceremonies. Roman Catholic laws, which are drawn from ancient church documents, councils of bishops' decisions, and papal rulings, are collected in the Code of Canon Law. In medieval Europe, ecclesiastical courts used canon law to decide cases involving crimes and matters that today would be heard in civil courts.

cap Slang for maximum, as the most interest that can be charged on an adjustable rate promissory note.

capital The basic assets of a business or the investment in a business by its owners.

capital account The record that lists the amount of funds and assets invested in a business by the owners or stockholders, including retained earnings. It states the net worth of the business at a given time.

capital asset Any type of property owned by a business that has a useful life of more than one year, such as a computer or truck.

capital case A prosecution for murder in which the prosecutor asks the jury to decide if the defendant is guilty and, if he is, whether he should be put to death. When prosecutors bring a capital case (also called a death penalty case), they must charge one or more "special circumstances" that the jury must find to be true in order to sentence the defendant to death. Each state (and the federal government) has its own list of special circumstances, but common ones include multiple murders, use of a bomb, or a finding that the murder was especially heinous, atrocious, or cruel.

capital expenditure Payment by a business to acquire a capital asset or make improvements to an asset which increases its value or adds to its useful life. It includes payments by a business for property, fixtures, machinery, or other capital assets but not for day-to-day operations such as payroll, inventory, maintenance, and advertising.

capital gains Profit on the sale of a capital asset, such as stock or real estate. If a person sells a primary residence, current tax law lets the seller exclude $250,000 in profit from capital gains tax. A couple can exclude $500,000.

capital investment See: capital expenditure

capitalization 1) The writing off of a capital expenditure proportionately over future years when the benefit from the expenditure is not confined to the period under consideration. 2) The sum of a corporation's long-term debt, stock, and retained earnings.

capitalized expenditure An expenditure for a capital asset that must be deducted from business income over more than one year, as opposed to an ordinary expense.

capitalized interest 1) Interest on a loan that is added to the principal balance. For example, interest may accrue on a student loan while the debtor is in school, which is then added to the principal on the loan. This results in the debtor having to pay interest on interest. 2) In accounting, interest that is not immediately expensed, but is instead considered an asset and amortized over time.

capitalized value The current value of an asset, based on the total income expected to be realized over its economic life span. The anticipated earnings are discounted (given a lower value) so they take into account the time value of money.

capital offense A criminal charge that is punishable by the death penalty. Crimes punishable by death vary from state to state. These offenses may include first degree (premeditated) murder, murder with special circumstances, rape with additional bodily harm, and the federal crime of treason. (See also: special circumstances)

capital punishment A sentence of death.

capital stock The original amount paid by investors into a corporation for its issued stock. Capital stock bears no direct relationship to the present value of stock, which can fluctuate after the initial issue or first stock offering. Capital stock also does not reflect the value of corporate assets, which can go up or down based on profits, losses, or purchases of equipment.

capricious Unpredictable and subject to whim, often used to refer to judicial decisions which appear arbitrary.

caption A heading required on all pleadings (court documents), listing the name and contact information of the lawyer or self-represented party, identifying the court in which the case is filed, and stating the names of the parties, the case number, and the title of the document.

care Attention, prudence, having responsibility for. Care is the opposite of negligence and a person exercising reasonable care cannot be liable for injuries that occur as a result of that person's actions.

careless 1) Negligent. 2) The opposite of careful. A careless act can result in the careless person being responsible for damages caused to others by the carelessness.

cargo insurance Insurance that pays the beneficiary of the policy if freight covered by the policy is damaged or lost during transit.

carnal knowledge Sexual intercourse between a male and female in which there is at least some slight penetration of the woman's vagina by the man's penis. Carnal knowledge is a necessary legal part of many sexual crimes.

carrier Any business that transports property or people by any means of conveyance (truck, auto, taxi, bus, airplane, railroad, ship) for a charge. There are two types of carriers: common carrier (in the regular business of providing transport) and a private carrier (a party not in the business, but agrees to make a delivery or carry a passenger in a specific instance).

carryback A method for receiving a refund of back taxes by applying a deduction or credit from a current year to a prior year. (See also: carryover)

carrying for hire The act of transporting goods or individuals for a fee.

carrying on business A routine and continuous involvement in an activity undertaken for the purpose of making profit. This can be accomplished with or without a physical or visible business entity.

carryover A method by which deductions and credits for one tax year that could not be used to reduce tax liability in that year are applied against tax liability in subsequent years. (See also: carryback)

carryover basis The tax basis of someone who receives a gift. The recipient's basis is the same as the giver's; it simply "carries over" when the gift is made.

cartel A group of independent corporations or other entities that join together to fix prices, control distribution, or reduce competition. For example, OPEC (Organization of Petroleum Exporting Countries) is an intergovernmental organization that represents 13 oil producing countries. Many private (nongovernmental) cartels operate behind a veil of secrecy, particularly because they are illegal under United States antitrust laws (the Sherman and Clayton Acts).

case 1) A cause of action, lawsuit, or the right to sue (as in, "Do I have a case?"). 2) A written decision of a court that is reported in official "reporters" and can be cited as precedent for other cases.

case law The law based on judicial opinions (including decisions that interpret statutes), as opposed to law based on statutes, regulations, or other sources. Also refers to the collection of reported judicial decisions within a particular jurisdiction dealing with a specific issue or topic.

case of first impression A court case that presents a new question or issue for legal interpretation (or at least new within that court's jurisdiction). For example, the question may concern recently passed or rarely used legislation. In making its decision, the court may consider—but is not bound by—decisions from other state or federal courts or commentaries by legal scholars, as well as the arguments and briefs submitted by lawyers in the case.

case system The method of studying law used in most American law schools, in which students read and outline (brief) appellate opinions (cases), then hear lectures about them and discuss them. Each case stands for a particular rule of law and is printed in "casebooks" on particular topics (such as contracts, torts, criminal law, and constitutional law). The case system is reinforced by textbooks and outlines on the subject matter, which were formerly the principal sources of learning. The method was introduced at Harvard in 1869 by professor Christopher C. Langdell and soon became standard.

cashier's check A check issued by a bank on its own account, not on a depositor's account. The bank receives money from the purchaser in the amount of the cashier's check, then issues the check and guarantees its payment.

cash method of accounting A method of accounting in which income is accounted for when actually received (not, for instance, when an order is taken) and expenses are reported when actually paid (not when liability for paying them is incurred, such as making an order). (Compare: accrual method of accounting)

cash surrender value The amount of cash available upon voluntary termination of an insurance policy before the insurance benefits become payable.

casual labor Sometimes used to refer to work that does not further the business of the employer, typically on a one-time or very sporadic basis. For example, someone who was hired for one day to clean the windows of a car showroom or a group that was hired for a few hours to unload new office furniture might be referred to as casual labor. Casual labor is not a legally recognized category, however: Workers performing casual labor are either independent contractors or employees, and the hiring company's legal and tax obligations to workers performing casual labor are the same as for other workers.

casualty 1) An accident or event which could not have been foreseen or avoided, such as a shipwreck, fire, or earthquake. 2) The liability or loss resulting from such an accident or event. (See also: casualty loss)

casualty loss Financial loss or loss of property arising from a sudden, unexpected, or unusual event such as a storm, flood, fire, shipwreck, or earthquake. Casualty loss qualifies for a tax deduction benefit. (See also: casualty)

causa mortis See: contemplation of death

cause 1) To make something happen. 2) The reason something happens. In order to hold someone responsible for harm to another person, the one must have caused the injury to the other.

In the Name of the Father. (1993) A determined attorney wins exoneration for a young Irishman and his family framed for a terrorist bombing. Oscar nominations went to Emma Thompson, Daniel Day-Lewis, and Pete Poslethwaite.

---

cause of action A specific legal claim—such as for negligence, breach of contract, or medical malpractice—for which a plaintiff seeks compensation. Each cause of action is divided into discrete elements, all of which must be proved to present a winning case. A complaint often states multiple causes of action, and each cause of action is made up of certain required elements—for example, a cause of action for breach of contract must show offer, acceptance, transfer of something of value, and breach of the agreement.

caveat (**kav**-ee-aht) 1) Latin for "let him beware"; a warning or caution. 2) A formal notification by an interested party to a court, judge, or ministerial officer not to do an act till the party giving the notice has the opportunity to be heard.

caveat emptor Latin for "let the buyer beware." The basic premise is that you are buying a product or property at your own risk and should personally examine and test for obvious defects and imperfections. Caveat emptor still applies even if the purchase is "as is" or when a defect is obvious upon reasonable inspection before purchase. Since implied warranties and consumer protections regarding product liability have come upon the legal landscape, the seller is held to a higher standard of disclosure than "buyer beware" and has responsibility for defects which a buyer cannot note by casual inspection.

CC&Rs See: covenants, conditions, and restrictions

CCCS See: Consumer Credit Counseling Service

C corporation Common business slang to distinguish a regular corporation, whose profits are taxed separate from its owners under subchapter C of the Internal Revenue Code, from an S corporation, whose profits are passed through to the shareholders and taxed on their personal income tax returns under subchapter S of the Internal Revenue Code.

cease and desist letter A letter from an intellectual property owner that requests that alleged illegal activity, such as copyright infringement, be stopped immediately.

cease and desist order An order of a court or government agency to a person, business, or organization to stop doing something. In order to obtain such an order, the plaintiff needs to make a strong showing that the activity is harmful to the plaintiff or contrary to law. Likely subjects a cease and desist order might, for example, include the felling of timber contrary to regulation or the selling of stock shares without a proper permit. The order may be permanent or hold until a final judicial determination is made.

census An official count of the number of people living in a certain area, such as a district, city, county, state, or nation. The U.S. Constitution requires the federal government to perform a national census every ten years. The census includes information about the respondents' sex, age, family, and social and economic status. Its results are publicly available.

certificate of citizenship An identity document that USCIS will provide to people who have derived or acquired U.S. citizenship and would like to prove their U.S. citizenship status. (See also:

acquisition of citizenship, derivation of citizenship.)

certificate of deposit (CD) A document issued by a bank in return for a deposit of money. Interest rates on CDs are fixed, and usually higher than on savings accounts, because banking institutions require a commitment to leave the money on deposit for a fixed period of time. Often there is a financial penalty (fee) for cashing in a CD before the pledged time has run out.

certificate of formation A document filed with state authorities (usually the Secretary of State or Division of Corporations, depending on the state) to form a limited liability company (LLC). As required by the general LLC law of the state, the certificate normally includes the purpose of the LLC, its principal place of business, and the names of its initial members or managers. Most states refer to this document as the articles of organization.

certificate of incorporation A document filed with state authorities (usually the Secretary of State or Division of Corporations, depending on the state) to form a corporation. As required by the general incorporation law of the state, the certificate normally includes the purpose of the corporation, its principal place of business, the names of the initial directors who will control

it, and the amounts and types of stock it is authorized to issue. In most states, this document is called the articles of incorporation.

certificate of organization A document filed with state authorities (usually the Secretary of State or Division of Corporations, depending on the state) to form a limited liability company (LLC). As required by the general LLC law of the state, the certificate normally includes the purpose of the LLC, its principal place of business, and the names of its initial members or managers. Most states refer to this document as the articles of organization.

certificate of title Generally, the title document for a motor vehicle issued by the state in which it is registered, describing the vehicle by type and engine number, as well the name and address of the registered owner and any lienholder (financial institution that loaned money to finance purchase of the car). In some states this document is pink and is commonly called a "pink slip."

certificate of trust See: certification of trust

certification of trust A condensed version of a declaration of trust, which leaves out details of what property is held in the trust and the identity of the beneficiaries. You can show a certification of trust to a financial organization or other institution to prove that you have established a valid trust, without revealing specifics that you want to keep private. In some states, this document is called a certificate or abstract of trust.

certification mark A name, symbol, or other device used by an organization that certifies origin, material, mode of manufacture, quality, accuracy, or other characteristics—for example, the "UL" symbol certifying quality standards for electrical appliances.

certified check A check issued and guaranteed by a bank, certifying that the maker of the check has enough money in his or her account to cover the amount to be paid. The bank sets aside the funds so that the check will remain good even if other checks are written on the particular account.

certified copy A copy of a document issued by a court or government agency guaranteed to be a true and exact copy of the original. Many agencies and institutions require certified copies of legal documents before permitting certain transactions. For example, a certified copy of a death certificate is required before a bank will release the funds in a deceased person's payable-on-death account to the person who has inherited them.

certified public accountant (CPA) The most highly qualified of accounting professionals, a CPA has passed a state's Uniform Certified Public Accountant Examination and has met additional state education and experience requirements.

President Franklin D. Roosevelt never graduated from law school, because he failed courses at Columbia in his final semester and did not bother to make them up. He satisfied the courts by oral examination that he was qualified.

certiorari (sersh-oh-**rar**-ee) Latin for "to be fully informed." In cases in which there is no appeal as a matter of right, certiorari is a writ (order) by the appeals court to a lower court to send all the documents in a case so that the appeals court can review the decision. Certiorari is most commonly used by the United States Supreme Court, which grants certiorari when at least four Justices believe that the case involves a sufficiently significant federal issue.

chain of title The line of owners of real estate, stretching from the current owner back in time to the original grant from some government. The chain of title is shown by deeds, judgments in lawsuits over title, affidavits, and other documents showing ownership changes and recorded in the county land records office. An error in this chain of title is what title searches are supposed to find and what title insurance protects purchasers against.

challenge When selecting a jury, the right of each party to request that a potential juror be excused. There may be a "challenge for cause" on the basis the juror had admitted prejudice or shows some obvious conflict of interest (for example, the juror used to work for the defendant) which the judge must resolve. More common is the "peremptory challenge," which is a request that a juror be excused without stating a reason. Each side is normally allowed a limited number of peremptory challenges.

challenge for cause A party's request that the judge dismiss a potential juror from serving on a jury by providing a valid legal reason why he shouldn't serve. Potential bias is a common reason potential jurors are challenged for cause—for example, the potential juror is a relative of a party or one of the lawyers, or admits to a prejudice against one party's race or religion. Judges can also dismiss a potential juror for cause.

chambers A fancy word for a judge's office. It's usually close to the courtroom so that the judge can enter the court from behind the bench and not encounter people on the way. Trial court judges often schedule pretrial settlement conferences and other informal or sensitive meetings in chambers.

champerty An agreement between the party suing in a lawsuit (the plaintiff) and another person, who agrees to finance and carry the lawsuit in return for a percentage of the recovery. In some states, champerty is illegal. However, it is also the basis for the legal and commonly accepted practice of contingency fee arrangements with attorneys, who represent their clients and are paid from any award or settlement the plaintiff receives in the suit.

chancellor From the old English legal system, a chancellor is a judge who sits in what is called a chancery (equity) court. The chancellor has the power to order that something be done, as distinguished from ordering the defendant to pay damages. Almost all U.S. states' courts now combine chancery (equity) functions and law.

chancery A court of equity, in which a judge can order acts performed, such as that a contract be modified or an activity stopped. The chancery court's functions are distinct from those of common law courts, which can order money damages to be paid, and where jury trials are available. The division between chancery and equity courts is partly based on the old English legal system. However, the original reason for the division between courts, which was so that law courts could follow statutory rules and equity courts could rule on issues of fairness, has been mostly lost. Chancery courts still exist in a few U.S. states today (check with the individual court for an exact list of what types of cases it hears). In other states, chancery court functions have been merged into the regular law courts' activities.

change of circumstances A reason for a court to modify an existing order for the payment of alimony and/or child support. In most cases, in order to seek a change in the support amount, the person seeking the change must show that circumstances (such as the employment, health, or income of the payor) have changed from when the order was made.

Chapter 7 bankruptcy A consumer liquidation bankruptcy proceeding in which the trustee sells any nonexempt property the debtor owns and distributes the proceeds to the debtor's creditors. At the end of a Chapter 7 case, many or all of the debtor's debts are discharged.

Chapter 9 bankruptcy A type of bankruptcy available only to municipalities, including towns, cities, villages, counties, and school districts.

Chapter 11 bankruptcy A type of bankruptcy that allows businesses to reorganize their debt load in order to remain in business.

Chapter 12 bankruptcy A type of bankruptcy that allows small farmers to reorganize their debts.

Chapter 13 bankruptcy A type of consumer bankruptcy designed to help debtors reorganize their debts and pay all or a portion of them over three to five years. In Chapter 13 bankruptcy, debtors keep their property and use their income to repay creditors according to a monthly repayment plan. At the end of the three-to-five-year period, the balance of what the debtor owes on many types of debts is erased.

Chapter 13 plan A document the debtor must file in a Chapter 13 bankruptcy, showing the debtor's proposal for repaying debts. Typically, a Chapter 13 plan requires the debtor to make set payments once or twice a month, which the bankruptcy trustee uses to pay creditors. The plan must last for three to five years, and the debtor must devote all disposable income to the plan.

character witness A person who testifies in court on behalf of another as to that person's positive character traits and the person's reputation in the community. Such testimony is often offered when the person's honesty or morality is an issue, as in some criminal cases and in civil cases involving accusations of fraud.

"I would pray, O Lord, never to diminish my passion for a client's cause, for from it springs the flame which leaps across the jury box and sets fire to the conviction of the jurors."

—Louis Nizer,
A Lawyer's Prayer

charge A formal accusation of criminal activity. The prosecuting attorney decides on the charges, after reviewing police reports, witness statements, and any other evidence of wrongdoing. Formal charges are announced at an arrested person's arraignment.

charitable contribution Cash or cash equivalent (goods or property) donated to a charitable organization. If made to a qualified recipient (one officially created for charitable, religious, educational, scientific, artistic, literary, or other good works), then charitable contributions are tax deductible.

charitable gift annuity A contract with a charity under which someone transfers assets to the charity in return for a promise to receive fixed payments for life (or, commonly, for the life of the donor and the donor's spouse). The donor can take an income tax deduction for part of the value of the assets given to the charity. Payments are based on how much is donated and the age of the recipients (called annuitants or beneficiaries). These annuities provide a way to make a gift to a charity, often a university, and receive income for life.

charitable lead trust A kind of charitable trust. The person (grantor) who sets up the trust transfers assets to it, and income from the trust property then goes to the charity for a set period of time. Then the trust property goes back to the person who set up the trust (or another beneficiary that person named, usually the grantor's children or grandchildren). Typically, the charity serves as trustee of the charitable trust. (Compare: charitable remainder trust)

charitable organization A nonprofit organization created and operated for purposes that benefit the public interest, such as educational, scientific, religious and artistic purposes. Charitable organizations that meet the requirements of Internal Revenue Code 501(c)(3) are exempt from federal income tax and are eligible to receive tax deductible charitable contributions.

charitable remainder annuity trust A kind of charitable remainder trust in which the income beneficiary is paid a fixed amount by the trustee each year.

charitable remainder trust A kind of charitable trust in which someone places substantial assets into an irrevocable trust. The trust is set up so that the donor (or other beneficiaries named in the trust) receives trust income for a number of years or for life, after which the assets go to a tax-exempt charity. The IRS allows a large deduction in the year the assets are donated to the trust. The tax savings are sometimes used to buy an insurance policy on the life of the donor payable to children or grandchildren at the donor's death. This way the donor can make the gift to charity, receive income from the trust, and still make a large gift at death to family members. There are several kinds of charitable remainder trusts, including charitable remainder unitrusts and charitable remainder annuity trusts. (Compare: charitable lead trust)

charitable remainder unitrust A kind of charitable remainder trust in which the trustee pays the income beneficiary an amount equal to a percentage of the trust assets each year.

charitable trust A trust designed to make a substantial gift to a charity and also achieve income and estate tax savings for the person who creates the trust (the grantor). These trusts are usually set up during the grantor's lifetime and are irrevocable. (See also: charitable lead trust, charitable remainder trust)

charity See: charitable organization

charter 1) A document that establishes an organization, such as a governmental entity (for example, a city charter) or a company (for example, a corporation's Articles of Incorporation). 2) To hire or rent for temporary use, such as chartering a boat.

chart of accounts A complete list of a business's expense and income accounts in a ledger. The list is arranged either by category (asset, liability, revenue, expense) or in the order of the appearance in the financial statements.

chattel An item of personal property that can be moved from place to place.

chattel mortgage An old term for an arrangement under which an item of personal property (chattel) serves as security (collateral) for a loan taken out to buy the item. Like a mortgage on a house, this was essentially a mortgage on something other than real estate. These agreements are now generally referred to as security agreements and are governed by the Uniform Commercial Code.

check A draft upon a particular account in a bank, in which the drawer or maker (the person who has the account and signs the check) directs the bank to pay a certain amount to the payee. (See also: negotiable instrument)

chief justice A judge who presides over any state supreme court or over the U.S. Supreme Court.

child 1) A person's offspring of any age, which can include biological offspring, unborn children, adopted children, stepchildren, foster children, and children born outside of marriage. 2) A person under an age specified by law, often 14 or 16. For example, state law may require a person to be over the age of 14 to make a valid will, or may define the crime of statutory rape as sex with a person under the age of 16. In this sense, a child can be distinguished from a minor, who is a person under the age of legal majority (18 in most states).

child custody See: custody (of a child)

child's trust A trust created for a minor or young adult. The trustee controls the trust property until the young person reaches the age stated in the trust. At that time, trust funds are transferred to the beneficiary.

child support Financial and other support for children provided by the parents who are legally responsible for them. Most commonly, child support is ordered when parents divorce or separate and one parent is required to pay the other an amount of child support that is determined by state guidelines, based on the parents' incomes and the amount of time each parent spends with the child(ren). Support may also include paying for insurance benefits, school tuition, and other expenses. Child support is not deductible or taxable.

churn See: churning

churning To make a client's account excessively active by the unethical and usually illegal frequent buying and selling of the client's shares of stock, primarily in order to generate commissions.

CID See: common interest development

CIF An acronym for Cost, Insurance, and Freight. CIF is an international commercial term used to describe who will pay these fees when goods are transported by sea (and it's sometimes used to describe air freight as well). These trade terms are often identical in form to domestic terms (such as the American Uniform Commercial Code), but have different meanings. You should consult an international trade lawyer before using this or similar terms.

circuit court 1) The name used for the principal trial court in many states. 2) In the federal system, the term may refer to courts within the 13 circuits. Eleven of these circuits cover different geographic areas of the country—for example, the United States Court of Appeal for the Ninth Circuit covers Alaska, Arizona, California, Hawaii, Idaho, Montana, Nevada, Oregon, and Washington. The remaining circuits are the District of Columbia, and the Federal Circuit, (which hears patent, customs, and other specialized cases based on subject matter). The term derives from an age before mechanized transit, when judges and lawyers rode the circuit of their territory to hold court in various places.

circumstantial evidence Evidence that proves a fact by means of an inference. For example, from the evidence that a person was seen running away from the scene of a crime, a judge or jury may infer that the person committed the crime. Usually, many pieces of circumstantial evidence are needed before a judge or jury will find that they add up to proof beyond a reasonable doubt. Compare: direct evidence

citation A police-issued order to appear in court to defend against a charge. Failure to appear can result in a warrant for the citee's arrest, but often a person may consent to the penalty in writing and forgo an appearance in court. 2) A court-issued writ that commands a person to appear in court to do something demanded in the writ or to show cause for not doing so. 3) A reference to a legal authority, such as a case or statute.

cite 1) To make reference to a legal authority, such as a statute or the decision in another case, to make a legal point in argument. 2) To give notice of being charged with a minor crime and a date for appearance in court to answer the charge rather than being arrested (usually given by a police officer).

citizen A person who, by place of birth, nationality of one or both parents, or having successfully completed any applicable requirements, is granted full rights and responsibilities as a member of a nation or political community. Some countries allow dual citizenship (maintaining citizenship in more than one country).

citizen's arrest An arrest made by a private citizen, in contrast to the typical arrest made by a police officer. Citizen's arrests are lawful in certain limited situations, such as when a private citizen personally witnesses a violent crime and then detains the perpetrator.

civil Noncriminal. (See also: civil case)

civil action See: civil case

civil case A noncriminal lawsuit, usually involving private property rights. For example, lawsuits involving breach of contract, probate, divorce, negligence, and copyright violations are just a few of the many hundreds of varieties of civil lawsuits.

A Civil Action. (1988) Based on John Harr's best-seller about an actual event, John Travolta plays an idealistic attorney challenging a polluter suspected of poisoning a Massachusetts river, causing cancer in the surrounding neighborhoods. This courtroom drama also stars Robert Duvall.

---

civil code In many states, the name for the collection of statutes and laws that deal with business and negligence lawsuits and practices.

civil law 1) A generic term for all non-criminal law, usually relating to settling disputes between private citizens. 2) A body of laws and legal concepts derived from Roman law as opposed to English common law, which is the framework of most state legal systems. In the United States only Louisiana, relying on the French Napoleonic Code, has a legal structure based on civil law.

civil liability A legal obligation that arises to a private party, usually for payment of damages or other court-enforcement of a lawsuit.

civil liberties Rights granted to the people under the Constitution (and derived primarily from the First Amendment), to speak freely, think, assemble, organize, worship, or petition without government interference or restraints. (Compare: civil rights)

civil penalties (**civil fines**) Fines or other financial payments imposed by a state or federal agency for violation of laws or regulations. Examples include fines for late payment of taxes, or penalties for failing to obtain a building permit.

civil procedure The rules set out in both state (usually Code of Civil Procedure) and federal (Federal Code of Procedure) laws that establish the format under which civil lawsuits are filed, pursued, and tried. Civil procedure refers only to form and procedure, and not to the substantive law that gives people the right to sue or defend a lawsuit.

civil rights Rights guaranteed by the Bill of Rights, the 13th and 14th, 15th and 19th Amendments to the Constitution. Civil rights include civil liberties (such as the freedom of speech, press, assembly, and religion), as well as due process, the right to vote, equal and fair treatment by law enforcement and the courts, and the opportunity to enjoy the benefits of a democratic society, such as equal access to public schools, recreation, transportation, public facilities, and housing.

Civil Rights Act of 1964 A federal law that prohibits discrimination on the basis of race, color, national origin, sex (including pregnancy), and religion in employment, education, and access to public facilities and public accommodations, such as restaurants and hotels. The employment provisions of the law are often referred to as "Title VII," based on their location in the U.S. Code.

civil union A relationship available in New Hampshire, New Jersey, and Vermont that provides all of the rights and responsibilities of marriage for same-sex couples who register as civil union partners.

civil union partners Parties to a civil union relationship in New Hampshire, New Jersey, or Vermont, under which the partners have the same rights and responsibilities as married spouses under state law.

claim in bankruptcy See: creditor's claim

claims See: patent claims

class A group that shares common attributes. In legal terms, this might be a group of people with the same level of rights (such as heirs who are equally related to the deceased), or who've

suffered from the same discrimination or other injury. Whether a person is part of a class is often crucial in determining who can sue on the person's behalf or collect a share of a class action judgment.

class action A lawsuit in which a large number of people with similar legal claims join together in a group (the class) to sue someone, usually a company or organization. Common class actions involve cases in which a product has injured many people, or a group of people has suffered discrimination at the hands of an organization.

Clayton Antitrust Act A federal antitrust law, enacted in 1914, that amended and expanded upon the Sherman Act (enacted in 1890), which prohibits direct or indirect interference with interstate trade.

clean hands doctrine The principle that a party who has acted unethically or in bad faith in relation to a lawsuit will not win the suit or be granted equitable relief by the court. For example, if a contractor is suing a homeowner to recover the price of work he did on the home, his failure to perform the work as specified would leave him with unclean hands.

cleaning fee A nonrefundable fee charged by a landlord when a tenant moves in.

The fee covers the cost of cleaning the rented premises after the tenant moves out, even if the tenant leaves the place spotless. Cleaning fees are illegal in some states and specifically allowed in others, but most state laws are silent on the issue. Landlords in every state are allowed to use the security deposit to clean a unit that is truly dirty.

clean room A method of developing proprietary material in which an isolated development team is monitored. The purpose is to provide evidence that similarities to others' works or products are due to legitimate constraints and not copying.

clear and convincing evidence The burden of proof placed on a party in certain types of civil cases, such as cases involving fraud. Clear and convincing is a higher standard than "preponderance of the evidence," the standard typical in most civil cases, but not as high as "beyond a reasonable doubt," the burden placed on the prosecution in criminal cases. (See also: beyond a reasonable doubt, preponderance of the evidence)

clear and present danger Although the U.S. Constitution's First Amendment protects freedom of speech, any speech that poses a "clear and present danger" to the public or government loses this protection. The classic example is that shouting "Fire!" in a crowded theater is not protected speech.

clearly erroneous A standard of review in civil appellate proceedings. Under this standard, an appeals court must accept the lower court's findings of fact unless the appellate court is definitely and firmly convinced that a mistake has been made. In other words, it is not enough that the appellate court may have weighed the evidence and reached a different conclusion; the lower court's decision will only be reversed if it is implausible in light of all the evidence.

clear title Ownership of property that is free of claims or disputes about ownership. Clear title is necessary before property can be sold. (See also: cloud on title, title search)

clerk 1) An official or employee who handles the business of a court or a system of courts, maintains files of each case, and issues routine documents. Almost every county has a clerk of the courts or county clerk who fulfills those functions, and most courtrooms have a clerk to keep records and assist the judge in the management of the court. 2) A young lawyer who helps a judge or a senior attorney research and draft documents.

Clinton v. City of New York (1998) A U.S. Supreme Court case in which the Court declared the line item veto unconstitutional because it gave the executive a legislative function.

Clinton v. Jones **(1997)** A U.S. Supreme Court case in which the Court unanimously ruled that presidential immunity did not protect a sitting president from a civil lawsuit.

 "Wrong must not win by technicalities."
—Aeschylus, *Eumenides*

---

close corporation A corporation owned and operated by a few individuals, often members of the same family, rather than by public shareholders. Close corporations are regulated by state close corporation statutes, which usually limit the number of shareholders to 30 or 35 shareholders and require special language in the articles of corporation. In exchange for following these requirements, state law usually permits close corporations to function more informally than regular corporations. For example, shareholders can make decisions without holding meetings of the board of directors and can fill vacancies on the board without a formal vote of the shareholders. (Compare: closely held corporation)

closed-end loan A loan that must be paid off within a certain period of time. (Compare: open-ended loan)

closed shop A business that hires only union members either by choice or by agreement with the unions, although the Labor-Management Relations Act made closed shops illegal. (Compare: union shop)

closely held corporation Refers to any corporation where the stock is not publicly traded on a stock exchange. Closely held corporations usually have a small number of shareholders. (Compare: close corporation)

closing The final step in the sale and purchase of real estate in which the seller's deed of title is exchanged for the buyer's payment. Some of the final documents, including the deed and mortgage or deed of trust, are then recorded in the county recorder's office. Depending on local practice, the closing is handled by a title company, escrow officer, or attorney. Also called settlement.

closing argument A speech made at trial after all the evidence has been presented by each party. The closing argument reviews and summarizes the evidence, and forcefully explains why the verdict should be granted in favor of the arguing party. In trials before a judge (without a jury), it is common for both parties to waive closing argument on the theory that the judge has almost surely already arrived at a decision.

cloud on title A claim or dispute about the ownership of or an encumbrance on property. For example, a tax lien on a piece of real estate or a possible claim by the heir of a former owner might create a cloud on the title. Or a past mortgage might have been paid off, but the property documents were never recorded (filed in the public land records). These kinds of potential problems are usually turned up in a title search. (See also: clear title)

code A systematic collection of written laws gathered together, often grouped by subject matter. A state may have separate codes such as a civil code, corporations code, evidence code, penal code, and so forth.

codefendant One of two or more defendants charged with the same crime or sued in the same claim. Also called joint defendant.

Code of Federal Regulations (C.F.R.) A set of publications containing regulations issued by federal agencies and organized by subject.

Code of Professional Responsibility A set of rules governing the ethical conduct of attorneys in the practice of the law. It covers such topics as conflicts of interest, honesty with clients, confidentiality, and conduct toward other attorneys and the courts. First developed and pushed by the American Bar Association (ABA), the code has been replaced in most states by the Model Rules of Professional Conduct.

codicil A supplement or addition to a will. A codicil may explain, modify, add to, subtract from, qualify, alter, or revoke existing provisions in a will. Because a codicil changes a will, it must be signed in front of witnesses, just like a will.

codify The process of arranging and labeling a system of laws.

cohabitation Living together in the same residence, either as spouses or unmarried partners. Cohabitation is often a reason for termination of alimony, on the assumption that a person cohabiting with another no longer needs the support of a former spouse.

***Cohan* rule** A federal court decision which allows taxpayers in certain situations to approximate expenses for tax deduction purposes when their records are missing. It cannot be used for travel and entertainment business expenses.

cohousing A type of collaborative living in which residents share in the design of their community. Generally, cohousing means that each resident or family has a private space, and the cohousing community also shares common space and facilities such as a playground for children, laundry facilities, and a common kitchen where members can share meals.

coinsurance 1) A form of insurance in which a person insures property for less than its full value and agrees to be responsible for the difference. Essentially the owner and the insurance company share the risk. 2) Insurance held jointly by two or more insurers.

collaborative divorce A method of resolving a divorce case in which both spouses hire attorneys who practice collaborative law, and the parties and attorneys sign an agreement that requires them to negotiate the divorce through a series of four-way meetings, often with the assistance of professionals such as custody evaluators, appraisers, or accountants. If the divorce cannot be settled through these meetings and one party seeks a court trial, both lawyers must withdraw and the parties must hire new lawyers. This provides a financial incentive for settling.

collaborative law An alternative way to settle disputes in which both parties hire specially trained attorneys who work to help them respectfully resolve the conflict. Every participant in a collaborative case agrees to work together to seek a "win-win" solution to the needs of both parties. A collaborative

law case is not permitted to go to court. If the dispute does end up in court—or if one of the parties threatens to go to court—the collaborative law process ends and neither lawyer can continue to work on the case.

collateral Property that someone promises or gives to a creditor to guarantee payment of a debt—thus creating what's called a secured debt. If the borrower defaults on the loan, the creditor may seize the property and sell it to cover the debt.

collateral attack A legal action in one case challenging another case or another court's ruling. For example, a father ordered to pay child support in a divorce case in Minnesota, collaterally attacks the order in a Maine court claiming that the Minnesota court did not have jurisdiction over him.

collateral consanguinity The relationship between blood relatives who do not descend from one another—for example, cousins. (See also: consanguinity)

collateral descendant A relative descended from a brother or sister of an ancestor—for example, a cousin, niece, nephew, aunt, or uncle.

collateral estoppel A legal doctrine that says that a judgment in one case prevents (estops) a party to that suit from trying to litigate the same issue in another legal action. Also called issue preclusion.

collection agency A company hired by a creditor to collect a debt. Creditors typically hire a collection agency only after having tried—and failed—to collect the debt on their own.

collective mark A name, symbol, or other device used by members of an organization to: 1) identify goods or services it provides; or 2) indicate membership in the organization. For example, the letters ILGWU may be used on a shirt label to signify that the shirt was made by a member of the International Ladies' Garment Workers' Union, or may be used on a button worn by an ILGWU member. (Compare: certification mark)

collective work Under copyright law, a work, such as a periodical, anthology, or encyclopedia, in which a number of separate and independent works are assembled into one work. To create a collective work, permission must be obtained from the copyright owners of the separate parts (assuming such parts are not already in the public domain). Although the author of the collective compilation may not own the copyright to any of the individual parts, the creativity involved in selecting and organizing the constituent materials is often protected by copyright. (See also: compilation)

collision damage waiver Rental car insurance that makes the rental car company responsible for damage to or theft of a rental car. Also known as CDW, damage waiver, and loss damage waiver, this insurance often duplicates coverage provided in a consumer's existing auto insurance policy.

Famous trial attorney Clarence Darrow planted a spy on the staff of the District Attorney, from whom he learned that the prosecution had absolute proof that his clients, the McNamara brothers, were guilty of setting off the bomb at the *Los Angeles Times* in 1911 that killed 20 people.

collision insurance coverage A component of car insurance that pays for damages to the insured vehicle that result from a collision with another vehicle or object. Collision insurance generally covers the amount of damage over and above an amount the insured person must pay, called the deductible amount.

collusion Secret cooperation between two people or entities in order to fool, defraud, or gain an unfair advantage over another. Price fixing by companies supposed to be competitors is one example of collusion.

collusive action A lawsuit brought by parties pretending to be adversaries in order to obtain an answer to a legal question or a precedent-setting decision from the court. The action will be dismissed if a judge determines it does not involve a true controversy.

color of law Conduct based upon what appears to be a legal right or enforcement of statute, but in reality is a violation of law, such as issuing phony traffic tickets in order to raise revenue or extort payoffs.

color of title The appearance of ownership of property, evidenced by possession or a document that purports to show ownership, when there is actually a defect in the title.

comaker One of two or more people who sign the same check or promissory note. Each comaker is liable for the entire amount to be paid. (See also: maker)

comfort care Medical care intended to provide relief from pain and discomfort, such as pain control drugs. (See also: palliative care)

comity (**kom**-i-tee) The principle that one jurisdiction will recognize the executive, legislative, and judicial acts of another jurisdiction and will give effect to the other's laws.

comity of nations Courtesy between nations that obligates their mutual recognition of each other's laws.

commencement of action The formal procedure by which a legal proceeding is initiated. Civil law suits commence when the party suing files a written complaint or petition with the court. Criminal proceedings are typically commenced by a prosecutor filing a petition with the court or seeking an indictment from a grand jury.

comment A statement made by a judge or attorney during a trial that's based on an alleged but as-yet unproven fact. The lawyer for the other side may object, and the judge may remind the jury (if a jury is present) that such comments should not be taken as evidence. (However, as they say, "A bell once rung, cannot be unrung.")

commerce 1) the sale or exchange of commodities, property, or services, typically involving transportation from place to place. 2) As defined by the Lanham Act, trade that the federal government is authorized to regulate, typically trade across interstate lines. To qualify for federal trademark protection and registration, a mark must have first been used in commerce.

commercial frustration An unforeseen and uncontrollable event that excuses a party to a contract from performing his or her duties under that contract. For example, a landlord can break a lease if the property she agreed to rent accidentally burns down before the tenants move in.

commercial law The law that applies to the rights, relations, and conduct of persons and businesses engaged in commerce, merchandising, trade, and sales. In recent years this body of law has been codified in the Uniform Commercial Code (UCC), which has been almost universally adopted by the U.S. states.

commingling The act of mixing the funds belonging to one party with those of another party. Usually, spouses or business partners may commingle assets without a problem. However, in community property states, a spouse may run the risk of turning separate property into community property (transmutation). Business partners may have to account to each other. Trustees, guardians, agents, and other fiduciaries must be careful not to commingle the funds that they are caring for with those of their own, since commingling is generally prohibited as a conflict of interest.

commission 1) A fee paid to an agent or employee for performing a specific service, as distinguished from regular payments of wages or salary. 2) A group appointed by law to conduct certain government business, especially regulation. Examples include a local planning or zoning commission, the Securities and Exchange Commission (SEC), and the Federal Trade Commission (FTC).

commitment A judge's order sending someone to jail or prison, upon conviction or before trial (for diagnostic purposes), or directing that a mentally unstable person be confined to a mental institution. Technically, the judge orders law enforcement personnel to take the prisoner or patient to such places.

common area 1) Facilities and space, such as recreation facilities, parking, laundry rooms, or a courtyard in condominiums, apartment buildings, and some cooperative housing projects. In rental properties, landlords are responsible for maintaining common areas in a safe condition. Common areas in condominiums are not individually owned by the residents, but shared by percentage interest or owned by the management organization. 2) The area in a shopping center or mall outside of the individual stores, for which each business pays a share of maintenance based on percentage of total store space occupied.

common carrier An individual, a company, or a public utility (like municipal buses) that is in the regular business of transporting people or freight, and must do so as long as the approved charge or fare is paid.

common interest development A type of housing, composed of individually owned units, such as condominiums, townhouses, or single-family homes, that share ownership of common areas, such as swimming pools, landscaping, and parking. Common interest developments (also known as community interest developments or CIDs) are managed by homeowners' associations.

common law The body of law that developed over many years in England based on court decisions and custom, as compared to written statutes (codifications of the law). Colonists imported England's common law to what became the United States, and it survives today, greatly expanded and changed by the published decisions of American courts. Many common law principles, however, have been codified in state statutes. Only Louisiana does not take as its basic law the English common law; instead, that state's law is based on France's Napoleonic Code.

common law marriage In some states, a type of marriage in which couples can become legally married by living together for a long period of time, representing themselves as a married couple, and intending to be married. Contrary to popular belief, the couple must intend to be married and act as though they are for a common law

marriage to take effect—merely living together for a long time won't do it.

common property Property owned by two or more parties.

common stock A class of stock for which dividends (payouts) are calculated on a pro rata basis (according to the number of shares a shareholder owns). Holders of common stock have rights to vote on corporate matters and to receive a share of the assets if the corporation is liquidated. (Compare: preferred stock)

"A man's home is his castle."
—Sir Edward Coke,
Comments on Littleton

community interest development See: common interest development

community property A method of defining the ownership of property acquired during marriage, in which all earnings during marriage and all property acquired with those earnings are owned in common and all debts incurred during marriage are the responsibility of both spouses. Typically, community property consists of all property and profits acquired during marriage, except property received by inheritance, gift, or as the profits from property owned before marriage. Community property laws exist in Arizona, California, Idaho, Nevada, New Mexico, Texas, Washington, and Wisconsin. In Alaska, couples can create community property by written agreement. (See also: separate property, equitable distribution)

community property with right of survivorship A way for married couples to hold title to property, available in some community property states. It allows one spouse's half-interest in community property to pass to the surviving spouse without probate.

community service Unpaid work that benefits the community and that may be required of a convicted defendant as an alternative to a jail sentence.

community trust See: pooled trust

commutation Reducing a sentence resulting from a criminal conviction, which can be done by the governor of a state (state convictions) or the president of the United States (federal convictions). A commutation is distinguished from a pardon, which wipes out the conviction and can even stop the actual or potential charge (as when President Gerald R. Ford pardoned ex-President Richard M. Nixon even without charges having been officially made—a rare instance of the use of the presidential pardon power). Commutation implies the penalty was excessive or there is evidence of rehabilitation, reform, community service, or other indications of good conduct.

commute a sentence See: commutation

company Any formal business entity for profit which may be a corporation, a partnership, association, or individual proprietorship. Often people think the term "company" means the business is incorporated, but that is not true. In fact, a corporation usually must use some term in its name such as "corporation," "incorporated," "corp." or "inc." to show it is a corporation.

comparable rectitude An anachronistic doctrine that grants the spouse who is least at fault a divorce when both spouses have shown fault grounds for divorce. It is a response to an old common law rule that prevented a divorce when both spouses were at fault.

comparative negligence A rule of law applied in negligence cases in which responsibility and damages are based on the proportional fault of every party directly involved. Compare: contributory negligence

compensation Payment for work performed or damages suffered (for example, in the form of workers' compensation benefits).

compensatory damages Money damages recovered as compensation for economic loss, such as lost wages.

competence 1) The state of being able or qualified to do something—for example, make a will or testify in court. 2) Authority, authenticity, or admissibility, as in "the competence of the evidence."

competent 1) Able to act in the circumstances, including the ability to perform a job or occupation, or to reason or make decisions. 2) In wills, trusts, and contracts, sufficiently mentally able to understand and execute a document. 3) In criminal law, sufficiently mentally able to stand trial or testify. 4) In evidence, relevant and legally admissible.

competent evidence Legally admissible evidence. Competent evidence tends to prove the matter in dispute. In a murder trial, for example, competent evidence might include the murder weapon with the defendant's fingerprints on it.

competent witness A person who is legally qualified to testify as a witness. Legal qualification may depend on the witness's age, mental capacity, and relationship to the matter at issue.

compilation A work formed by selecting, collecting, and assembling preexisting materials or data. Examples of compila-

tions are databases, anthologies, and collective works. The creative aspects of a compilation—such as the novel way it is organized and the selection of the materials to be included—are entitled to copyright protection whether or not the individual parts are in the public domain or are subject to another owners copyright. (See also: database, collective work)

complainant A person or entity that begins a lawsuit by filing a complaint. Usually called the plaintiff or petitioner.

complaint Papers filed in court by an injured party to begin a lawsuit by setting out facts and legal claims (usually called causes of action). The person filing the complaint is called the plaintiff and the other party is called the defendant. In some states and in some types of legal actions, such as divorce, complaints are called petitions and the person filing is called the petitioner. The plaintiff's complaint must be served on the defendant, who then has the opportunity to respond by filing an answer. A complaint filing must be accompanied by a filing fee payable to the court clerk, unless the party asks a judge to waive the fee based on inability to pay.

compos mentis (**cahm**-puhs **men**-tis) Latin for having a sound mind.

compound interest Interest paid at least in part on accumulated interest. For example, if interest on a savings account is compounded monthly, the depositor is paid interest on the amount deposited after the first month. After the second month, the depositor receives interest on the total amount in the account: the amount deposited plus the interest paid in the first month.

"The law was not made for a righteous man, but for the lawless and disobedient."

—The Bible, St. Paul in Timothy 1:9

---

compound question A single question that actually asks more than one thing. In a trial or deposition, the opposing party can object to such a question. If the objection is sustained, the question must be withdrawn and asked in a series of separate questions.

compounding a felony The decision by a victim of a crime to not prosecute the crime (by refusing to cooperate with the police or prosecuting attorney) or to hamper the prosecution, in exchange for money payment or other recompense. Compounding is a crime.

comprehensive insurance coverage An element of car insurance that pays for damages to your vehicle caused by anything other than a collision, including vandalism, theft, and natural disasters. Like collision insurance, comprehensive coverage usually only pays up to the fair market value of your car (minus any deductible).

compromise An agreement between opposing parties to settle a dispute or reach a settlement in which each gives some ground rather than continue the dispute or go to trial.

compromise verdict A jury verdict that occurs when some jurors compromise their opinions in order to avoid deadlock.

compulsory joinder See: mandatory joinder

compulsory license A statutory arrangement under which permission is not required before using someone else's intellectual property, provided that a fee is paid.

concealed weapon A weapon, particularly a handgun, which is kept hidden on one's person or under one's control (in a glove compartment or under a car seat). Carrying a concealed weapon is a crime unless the person with the weapon is a law enforcement officer or has a permit to carry a concealed weapon. Permits are usually issued by local law enforcement under guidelines that require the applicant to show the need for such a weapon, and require that the appli-cant have a record free of convictions, arrests, or improper activity.

concealment Failure to reveal inform-ation that one knows should be disclosed in good faith. Such conceal-ment can be a cause for rescission (cancellation) of a contract by the misled party or a civil lawsuit for fraud.

conclusion 1) In a trial, the end of all evidence being introduced and final arguments made, so nothing more can be presented. 2) In a trial or court hearing, a final determination of the facts by the jury or judge or a judge's decision on the law. (See also: conclusion of fact, conclusion of law)

conclusion of fact In a trial, the final result of an analysis of the facts presented in evidence, made by the trier of fact (a jury or judge). When a judge is the trier of fact, he or she will present orally in open court or in a written judgment the conclusions of fact supporting the decision.

conclusion of law A judge's final decision on a question of law which has been raised in a trial or a court hearing, particularly those issues which are vital to reaching a judgment. These may be presented orally by the judge in open court, but are often contained in a written judgment, such as an award of damages or denial of a petition.

concurrent condition Under an agree-ment, a situation in which one party must fulfill a condition at the same time that the other party fulfills a mutual condition. (See also: condition)

concurrent sentence When a criminal defendant is convicted of two or more crimes, a judge sentences the defendant to a certain period of time for each crime. Sentences that may all be served at the same time, with the longest period controlling, are concurrent sentences. Judges may sentence concur-rently out of compassion, plea bargain-ing, or the fact that the several crimes are interrelated. When the sentences run one after the other, they are con-secutive sentences.

condemn 1) When a public agency determines that a building is unsafe or unfit for habitation and must be torn down or rebuilt to meet building and health code requirements. 2) When a governmental agency takes private property for public use under the right of eminent domain, but constitutionally the property owner must receive just compensation. If an agreement cannot be reached then the owner is entitled to a court determination of value in a condemnation action (lawsuit), but the public body can take the property immediately upon deposit of the esti-mated value. 3) To sentence a convicted defendant to death. 4) Send to prison.

condemnation See: eminent domain

condemnation action A lawsuit brought by a public agency to acquire private property for public purposes (schools, highways, parks, hospitals, redevelopment, civic buildings, for example), or even for private development that has a public benefit (rare). While the government has the right to acquire the private property (eminent domain), the owner is entitled under the Constitution to receive just compensation for the loss of his land, which will be determined by a court if necessary.

condition A term or requirement stated in a contract whose occurrence or non-occurrence determines the rights and duties of the parties to the contract. (See also: concurrent condition, condition precedent, condition subsequent)

conditional bequest In a will, a gift that will occur only if a stated condition is met. For example, a will clause that says "I give my house to my daughter Sarah if she is married."

conditional ownership Ownership in which the owner does not have full right to the property, but could acquire full ownership if specific conditions are fulfilled—the ownership is conditional on those conditions. For example, George is the alternate remainder beneficiary of his mother's life estate. Joan, his sister, is the primary remainder beneficiary. George only has conditional ownership of the estate because his ownership depends on Joan being dead when their mother dies. Also called contingent ownership.

conditional resident A foreign-born person who, instead of being granted permanent resident status (a green card), is granted U.S. residence on a conditional, two-year basis. Near the end of the two years, the person must petition for the removal of the conditions—in other words, prove continuing eligibility for the same status, with a request to convert to permanent resident status. Under current law, people who apply for green cards as the spouse of a U.S. citizen where the marriage is less than two years old at the time they're approved for U.S. residence, as well as all immigrant investors, are the only two groups who are required to spend time as conditional residents.

conditional sale A sale of property or goods which will be completed only if certain conditions are met by one or both parties to the transaction. Example: Hotrod agrees to buy Tappit's 1939 LaSalle for $1,000 cash if Tappit can get the car running by September 1.

conditional SSI payments Temporary SSI payments made on the condition that the recipient get rid of certain assets in an appropriate manner. They are made if an applicant for SSI has too many assets to qualify for that program.

condition precedent An event or state of affairs that must occur before something else will be required to occur. In a contract, a condition precedent is an event that must take place before the parties must perform the agreement. (Compare: condition subsequent)

conditions of carriage The terms of the contract with an airline after purchasing a ticket. Conditions of carriage cover everything from baggage limitations to the amount of compensation the passenger can recover if injured on the flight. These provisions vary from airline to airline. To read the conditions of carriage for an airline, either check its website or look in the fine print on the back of the ticket (if there's a print version—even if there is, it may not have room for the full contract). If none of that works, the airline is legally obligated to provide a copy.

condition subsequent An event or state of affairs that, if it happens, defeats or modifies an existing arrangement or discharges an existing duty. In a contract, a condition subsequent can often terminate the duty of one party to perform under the agreement. (Compare: condition precedent)

condominium A type of real property ownership in which each owner holds title to his or her individual unit and shares ownership jointly of common areas such as driveways, parking, elevators, outside hallways, and recreation and landscaped areas. A homeowners' association typically manages the common areas and oversees the covenants, conditions, and restrictions (CC&Rs) that apply to the property. Condominiums are often referred to as a common interest development.

 "Government can exist without law, but law cannot exist without government."

—John Locke

---

condonation One person's approval of another's activities, constituting a defense to a fault divorce. For example, if a wife did not object to her husband's adultery even though she was aware of it, and she later tries to use it as grounds for a divorce or the basis for a settlement in her favor, he could counter these efforts by arguing that she had condoned his behavior.

condone To forgive, support, or overlook another person's wrong or illegal action, so that it appears the action is acceptable to the person or entity condoning it.

confess In criminal law, to voluntarily state that one is guilty of a criminal offense. A confession must be truly voluntary (not forced by threat, torture, or trickery) and generally cannot be admitted in trial if it is not. If the confession results from custodial questioning, it generally cannot be used at trial unless the defendant was given and waived the so-called *Miranda* warnings prior to questioning. (See also: *Miranda* warnings)

confession Voluntary statement by an accused, orally or in writing, in which the accused admits guilt of a particular crime or crimes

confession and avoidance A plea, or answer, to a complaint in a civil case, in which the defendant admits the allegations in the lawsuit but alleges other facts that, if found to be true by the trier of fact, will negate the negative effect of the plaintiff's claims. For example, in a few states, a plaintiff who sues over injuries allegedly caused by the defendant's negligence will not recover any damages if the defendant can prove that the plaintiff was in part also negligent (contributory negligence). When a defendant admits having acted negligently, but alleges that the plaintiff was also careless, the defendant has entered a plea of confession and avoidance.

confession of judgment Usually, a clause within a promissory note, allowing the creditor to, upon nonpayment by the borrower, get a court judgment for the amount owed and in some cases collect from the borrower's assets, all without giving the borrower advance notice.

confidence game A swindle in which the perpetrator obtains money by gaining the victim's trust.

confidential communication Information exchanged between two people who 1) have a relationship in which private communications are protected by law, and 2) intend that the information be kept in confidence. The law recognizes certain parties whose communications will be considered confidential and protected, including spouses, doctor and patient, attorney and client, and priest and confessor. Communications between these individuals cannot be disclosed in court unless the protected party waives that protection. The intention that the communication be confidential is critical. For example, if an attorney and his client are discussing a matter in the presence of an unnecessary third party—for example, in an elevator with other people present—the discussion will not be considered confidential and may be admitted at trial. Also known as privileged communication.

confidential relation A relationship of intimacy and trust, especially one in which one person is in a position of greater knowledge or power. (See also: fiduciary)

confine See: imprison

confirmation hearing A federal bankruptcy court hearing at which the judge decides whether or not a debtor's proposed Chapter 13 plan (for repayment of debts over several years) is feasible and meets legal requirements.

confiscate To take private property for public use without reasonable compensation, such as when the government confiscates an automobile used to transport contraband.

conflict of interest 1) A real or apparent conflict between one's professional or official duties and one's private interests. 2) A situation where one duty conflicts with another—for example, if an attorney were to represent both parties in a divorce proceeding.

conflict of laws A conflict of the laws of two jurisdictions (such as two countries, two different states, or state and federal law) when both are applicable to a legal dispute. (Compare: preemption)

conformed copy An exact copy of a document filed with a court. To conform a copy, the court clerk will stamp the document with the filing date and add any handwritten notations to the document that exist on the original, including dates and the judge's signature. A conformed copy may or may not be certified—this is, guaranteed by a court or government agency to be a true and exact copy of the original.

conforming loan A mortgage loan small enough to be bought by Fannie Mae or guaranteed by the Federal Housing Administration. The dollar limit on conforming loans is adjusted periodically and is higher in areas with a high cost of living. (Compare: jumbo loan)

confrontation The right of a criminal defendant, from the Sixth Amendment to the Constitution, to object to the witness and to cross-examine that witness.

confusingly similar In trademark law, when a trademark, logo, or business name is so close to that of an already existing trademark, logo, or name that the public might misidentify the new mark with the older one. Such confusion may not be found if the products or businesses are clearly not in the actual or potential product markets or geographic area of the other.

conjugal rights The intimate rights of marriage, including comfort, companionship, affection, and sexual relations.

Some states allow prisoners to have "conjugal visits," including sexual intercourse, with their spouse or partner.

connivance 1) Ignoring another person's wrongdoing, for example, by indirectly condoning an illegal act by another person. 2) In family law, a (somewhat archaic) defense that says that a person making claims against a spouse connived in the spouse's bad behavior. For example, a husband who invites his wife's lover along on vacation may have connived in her adultery, and if he tried to gain an advantage in the divorce as a result, she could assert his connivance as a defense.

consanguinity An old-fashioned term referring to the relationship of "blood relatives"—people who have a common ancestor. Consanguinity exists, for example, between brothers and sisters but not between husbands and wives.

conscientious objector A person who refuses to serve in the military due to religious or strong philosophical views against war or killing. Refusing to answer a draft call is a federal felony, but when a person's religious beliefs are long-standing and consistent (as with the Quakers) then the objection to service is excused. Conscientious objectors may be required to perform some nonviolent work like driving an ambulance. Those who do not agree with these objectors sometimes call them "draft dodgers."

conscious parallelism Price-fixing between competitors that occurs without an actual agreement between the parties. For instance, one company raises its price for a service and other competitors do the same. Can also be used to describe imitative activity over terms other than price. For example, one airline starts to require double miles for domestic trips and other airlines follow suit.

The oldest Supreme Court justice was Olivier Wendell Holmes, who was 90 when he retired in 1932.

---

consecutive sentence Two or more sentences of jail time to be served one after another. For example, if a convicted felon was sentenced to two consecutive ten-year terms, the total sentence would be 20 years. (Compare: concurrent sentence)

consent Voluntary agreement by a competent person to another person's proposition.

consent decree A court order to which all parties have agreed. It is often done after a settlement between the parties that is subject to approval by the court.

consent judgment See: consent decree

consent order See: consent decree

consequential damages Damage or injury that does not directly and immediately result from a wrongful act, but is a consequence of the initial act. To be awarded consequential damages in a lawsuit, the damages must be a foreseeable result of the initial act.

conservatee A person who requires a court-appointed conservator to handle personal and/or financial affairs. (Compare: ward)

conservator Someone appointed by a judge to oversee the affairs of an incapacitated person. A conservator who manages financial affairs is often called a "conservator of the estate." One who takes care of personal matters, such as health care and living arrangements, is known as a "conservator of the person." Sometimes, one conservator is appointed to handle all these tasks. Depending on where you live, a conservator may also be called a guardian, committee, or curator.

conservatorship A legal arrangement that gives an adult the court-ordered authority and responsibility to manage another adult's financial affairs.

consideration A benefit or right for which the parties to a contract must bargain. In order to be valid, a contract must be founded on an exchange of one form of consideration for another. Consideration may be a promise to perform a certain act—for example, a promise to fix a leaky roof in return for a payment of $1,000—or a promise not to do something, such as build a second story on a house that will block the neighbor's view (in return for money or something else). Whatever its particulars, consideration must be something of value to the people who are making the contract, even if the value is very low. Acts which are illegal or so immoral that they are against established public policy cannot serve as consideration. Examples include prostitution, gambling where it's outlawed, hiring someone to break a skater's knee, or paying someone to breach another agreement (back out of a promise).

consign 1) To give goods to another to sell; profits from the sale are generally divided between the seller and the original owner. 2) To give goods to a carrier for delivery. 3) To give over to the custody or care of another. 4) To be destined for, as in "consigned to oblivion" or "consigned to a life of drudgery."

consignee A person or business to whom something is consigned, typically goods for sale or delivery.

consignment The act of entrusting goods to a person or business who will sell them for you (charging a fee or commission for doing so), and return the goods if unsold.

Consolidated Omnibus Budget Reconciliation Act (COBRA) A federal law that enables employees and their families to continue health care coverage under an employer's group health plan even after they experience an event—such as a layoff, termination, cut in hours, or divorce—that would otherwise end their coverage. Employees and their families must pay the full premium, but they get to pay the employer-negotiated group rate, which is often less expensive than an individual rate. This continued coverage lasts for 18 to 36 months, depending on the event that made the employee eligible.

consortium 1) A group of separate individuals or companies that come together to undertake an enterprise or transaction that is beyond the means of any one member. For example, a group of local businesses might form a consortium to fund and construct a new office complex. 2) The duties and rights associated with marriage. Consortium includes all the tangible and intangible benefits that one spouse derives from the other, including material support, companionship, affection, guidance, and sexual relations. The term may arise in a lawsuit if a spouse brings a claim against a third party for "loss of consortium" after the other spouse is injured or killed.

conspiracy An agreement by two or more people to commit an illegal act or to commit a legal act using illegal means. Proving conspiracy requires evidence that the parties agreed to the plan before taking action. Proving criminal conspiracy usually requires evidence that some overt action occurred in furtherance of the plan. Some conspiracies may give rise to both criminal and civil charges. For example, a scheme by a group of salesmen to sell used automobiles as new, could be the basis for two actions: criminal prosecution for fraud and conspiracy; and a civil action by victims of the scheme for damages for the fraud and conspiracy.

conspirator A person that is a party to a conspiracy—that is, someone that enters into an agreement to commit illegal acts, or to commit legal acts using illegal means.

constable A peace officer for a particular geographic area—most often a rural county—who commonly has the power to serve legal papers, arrest lawbreakers, and keep the peace. Depending on the state, a constable may be similar to a marshal or sheriff.

constitution The fundamental, underlying document which establishes the government of a nation or state. The United States Constitution, originally adopted in convention on September 17, 1787, ratified by the states in 1788, and thereafter amended 27 times, is the prime example of such a document; however, states also have constitutions.

constitutional rights Rights given or reserved to the people by the U.S. Constitution, and in particular, the Bill of Rights.

constitutional tort A violation of one's constitutional rights by a government servant.

construction The act of interpreting and giving meaning to a statute, law, contract, or will when there is some ambiguity or question about its meaning. Strict, or narrow, construction means considering only the literal words, whereas broad, or liberal, construction, means taking into account societal and situational meanings to the language.

constructive a legal fiction for treating a situation as if it were actually so. (See also: constructive fraud, constructive eviction, constructive notice, constructive possession)

constructive discharge When an employee quits a job because working conditions are so intolerable that a reasonable person in the same situation would quit. For purposes of a discrimination or harassment lawsuit, a constructive discharge is like any other tangible employment action.

"The Constitution is either a superior paramount law, unchangeable by ordinary means, or it is on a level with ordinary legislative acts."

—Chief Justice John Marshall, in *Marbury v. Madison*

---

constructive eviction When a landlord provides housing that is so substandard that a landlord has legally evicted the tenant without following state eviction rules and procedures. For example, if the landlord refuses to provide heat or water or refuses to clean up an environmental health hazard, the tenant has the right to move out and stop paying rent, without incurring legal liability for breaking the lease.

constructive fraud When the circumstances show that someone's actions give that person an unfair advantage over someone else by unfair means (lying or not telling a buyer about defects in a product, for example), the court may decide to treat the situation as if there was actual fraud even if all the technical elements of fraud have not been proven.

constructive notice The fiction that someone got notice even though actual notice was not personally delivered to that person. The law may provide that a public notice put on the courthouse bulletin board is a substitute for actual notice. Or the court may authorize service by publication when a spouse has left the state to avoid service in a divorce action. The legal advertisement of the summons in an approved newspaper is treated as constructive notice, just as if the summons and petition had been served personally.

constructive possession When someone does not have actual possession, but has the power to control an asset, that person has constructive possession. Having the key to a safe deposit box, for example, gives one constructive possession.

constructive receipt of income Income not physically received but treated by the tax code as if it had been received because it is accessible to the recipient. For instance, when a business receives a check from a client, it is considered constructive income since the check can be cashed.

constructive trust A relationship that arises when someone has wrongfully obtained title to or possession of assets and has a legal duty to deliver them to the rightful owner. Unlike other common trusts, a constructive trust is a temporary measure ordered by a court to correct a wrong.

construe To determine the meaning of a written document, statute, or legal decision, based upon rules of legal interpretation.

consulate U.S. consulates are branch offices of U.S. embassies, located all over the world. Most consulates accept and process nonimmigrant and immigrant (green card) visa applications.

Consumer Credit Counseling Service (CCCS) A nonprofit agency with offices in a number of states. It offers free or low-cost debt and credit counseling.

Consumer Leasing Act A federal law that requires written lease agreements for personal property for more than four months (for personal, family, or household use), to include certain terms, including a statement of the number of lease payments and their dollar amounts, penalties for not paying on time, and whether a lump sum payment is due at the end of the agreement.

consumer protection laws Federal and state laws established to protect retail purchasers of goods and services from inferior, adulterated, hazardous, and deceptively advertised products, and deceptive or fraudulent sales practices; these laws cover everything from food to cosmetics, from banking to fair housing. Most states have established agencies to actively protect the consumer.

consumer report Written or oral information provided by a consumer reporting agency that relates to a person's creditworthiness, credit standing, credit capacity, character, personal characteristics, or lifestyle, to be used in employment decisions, to decide whether to grant the person credit, to decide whether to rent to the person, or for other legitimate business purposes. Examples of consumer reports include criminal background checks and credit reports. To request a consumer report about someone, the requester must follow the procedures in the Fair Credit Reporting Act.

consummation The actualization of a marriage. Sexual intercourse is required to "consummate" a marriage. Failure to do so is grounds for divorce or annulment.

contemplation of death When anticipation of death due to age, illness, injury, or mortal danger causes a person to make a gift, transfer property, or take some other dramatic action. Also called causa mortis. (See also: gift in contemplation of death)

contempt See: contempt of court

contempt of court Behavior in or out of court that violates a court order, or otherwise disrupts or shows disregard for the court. Refusing to answer a proper question, to file court papers on time, to pay court-ordered child support, or to follow local court rules can expose witnesses, lawyers, and litigants to contempt findings. Contempt of court is punishable by fine or imprisonment.

contest To oppose, dispute, or challenge through formal or legal procedures. For example, the defendant in a lawsuit almost always contests the case made by the plaintiff. Or, a disgruntled relative may formally contest the provisions of a will.

contiguous Connected or "next to"; usually referring to adjoining pieces of real estate.

contingency A provision in a contract stating that some or all of the terms of the contract will be altered or voided by the occurrence of a specific event. For example, a contingency in a contract for the purchase of a house might state that if the buyer does not approve the inspection report of the physical condition of the property, the buyer does not have to complete the purchase.

contingency fee See: contingent fee

contingent Uncertain or dependent on something else. (See also: contingent beneficiary, contingent interest, contingent fee)

contingent annuity An annuity whose amount of payment (or the payee) is not certain and depends on a specific future event.

And Justice for All. (1979) Al Pacino fights corruption in the legal system, with a climactic explosion at a crooked judge. Jack Warden, John Forsythe, Lee Strasberg, Christine Lahti, Craig T. Nelson.

contingent beneficiary 1) An alternate beneficiary named in a will, trust, or other document. 2) Any person entitled to property under a will if one or more prior conditions are satisfied. For example, if Fred is entitled to take property under a will only if he's married at the time of the will maker's death, Fred is a contingent beneficiary.

contingent fee A method of paying a lawyer for legal representation by which, instead of an hourly or per job fee, the lawyer receives a percentage of the money her client obtains after settling or winning the case. Often contingency fee agreements—which are most commonly used in personal injury cases—award the successful lawyer between 20% and 50% of the amount recovered. Lawyers representing defendants charged with crimes may not charge contingency fees. In most states, contingency fee agreements must be in writing.

contingent interest An interest that a party will receive only if specific conditions occur. For example, Bill leaves his "interest in The Centerville Cafe to Sarah, if she is still living in Centerville." If Sarah is not living in Centerville when Bill dies, she will not receive his interest in the cafe.

contingent ownership See: conditional ownership

contingent remainder A future interest in property that will pass only if certain circumstances occur, or that will pass to an unknown person or entity. For example, John makes a will that leaves his farm to Frank for life and then, if Scotty has gone to college by the time Frank dies, to Scotty.

contingent trust A trust that is not currently operational, but will become operational under specific conditions.

contingent will A will that only takes effect if specific conditions occur.

continuance The postponement of a hearing, trial, or other scheduled court proceeding, at the request of one or both parties, or by the judge without consulting them. Unhappiness with long trial court delays has resulted in the adoption by most states of "fast track" rules that sharply limit the ability of judges to grant continuances.

continuing objection An objection to certain questions or testimony during a trial which has been overruled by the judge, but the attorney who made the objection announces that he or she is continuing the objection to all other questions on the same topic or with the same legal impropriety in the opinion of the attorney. Thus there is no need for an objection every time the same question or same subject is introduced.

continuing trespass A repeated or on-going (not one-time) trespass (unlawful entry or possession), especially onto real property. For example, building a road or structure that extends onto a neighbor's property, or piling up rocks or garbage there, would be a continuing trespass.

contra Latin for against or opposite to. This usage is usually found in legal writing in statements like: "The decision in the case of *Hammerhead v. Nail* is contra to the rule stated in *Keeler v. Beach*."

contraband Property that is illegal to possess, produce, distribute, or transport.

contract A legally binding agreement involving two or more people or businesses (called parties) that sets forth what the parties will or will not do. Most contracts that can be carried out within one year can be either oral or written. Major exceptions include contracts involving the ownership of real estate and commercial contracts for goods worth $500 or more, which must be in writing to be enforceable. (See: statute of frauds) A contract is formed when competent parties—usually adults of sound mind or business entities—mutually agree to provide each other some benefit (called consideration), such as a promise to pay money in exchange for a promise to deliver specified goods or services or the actual delivery of those goods and services. A contract normally requires one party to make a reasonably detailed offer to do something—including, typically, the price, time for performance, and other essential terms and conditions—and the other to accept without significant change. For example, if I offer to sell you ten roses for $10 to be delivered next Thursday and you say "It's a deal," we've made a valid contract. On the other hand, if one party fails to offer something of benefit to the other, there is no contract. For example, if Maria promises to fix Josh's car, there is no contract unless Josh promises something in return for Maria's services. (See: bilateral contract, unilateral contract)

contract for deed A contract used for seller financing where the seller will keep title to the property until the buyer pays off the loan. After the buyer pays off the entire loan, the seller signs a deed transferring title to the buyer.

contract of adhesion See: adhesion contract

contractor 1) A person or entity that enters into a contract. 2) A person or entity that agrees to construct a building or to provide or install specialized portions of a construction project. The party responsible for the overall job is the general contractor, and those hired to construct or install certain parts (electrical, plumbing, roofing) are subcontractors, who are responsible to the general contractor and not to the property owner.

contribution 1) The sharing of a loss or discharging of a debt by several persons who may be jointly responsible. Under partnership law, for example, if one partner pays a judgment made against the partnership, that partner may seek contributions from the other partners. 2) A donation to a charitable organization for which no consideration is sought in return.

contributory negligence A doctrine of common law that if a person's own negligence contributes to causing an accident in which that person is injured, the injured party can't collect any damages (money) from another party who caused the accident. Because this doctrine often ended in unfair results (where a person only slightly negligent was prohibited from recovering damages from a person who was much more so), most states now use a comparative negligence test instead, in which the relative percentages of negligence by each person are used to determine how much the injured person recovers.

control The power to direct, regulate, manage, oversee, or restrict the affairs, business, or assets of a person or entity.

controlled substance A drug that has been declared by federal or state law to be illegal for sale or use, but may be dispensed by prescription. The basis for control and regulation may be the danger of addiction, physical or mental harm, the potential for trafficking by illegal means, or dangers posed by those who have used the substances.

controlling law The laws of the state which will be relied upon in interpreting or judging disputes involving a contract, trust, or other documents. Quite often an agreement will state as one of its provisions that the controlling law will be that of a particular state.

controversy A disagreement, argument, or quarrel. See also: actual controversy

contumacy The refusal to follow a court order; contempt of court.

contutor (kahn-**too**-tuhr) A joint guardian of a ward.

conversion The civil wrong (tort) of wrongfully using another's personal property as if it were one's own, holding onto another's property that accidentally comes into one's hands, or purposely giving the impression that the assets of another belong to oneself. The true owner has the right to sue for the property or the value and loss of use of it. The converter can be guilty of the crime of theft.

 "For where no law is, there is no transgression."
—The Bible, Romans 4:15

---

convey To transfer ownership (title) of property to another through a written document such as a deed.

conveyance A document, such as a deed or will, that transfers property from one party to another.

conveyee A person or entity to which property is conveyed.

conveyor A person or entity that transfers or delivers ownership of property to another.

convict 1) To find or prove someone guilty of a crime or offense after a court trial. 2) A person who has been convicted of a crime and is serving a sentence.

conviction A finding by a judge or jury that the defendant who has been on trial is guilty of the crime with which he or she was charged.

cookie Information that a website places and stores on a visitor's hard drive so that the website can retrieve the information when the visitor returns to the site. For example, a website may use a cookie to retrieve a visitor's name and address so the visitor doesn't have to enter that information again. A website can legally use cookies to personalize a visitor's experience, to track a visitor's movements on a site, or to target a visitor for specific advertisements.

cooling-off rule A rule that allows you to cancel a contract within a specified time period (typically three days) after signing it. Federal cooling-off rules apply this three-day grace period to sales made anywhere other than a seller's normal place of business.

Various states have cooling-off rules that sometimes apply even longer cancellation periods to specific types of sales, such as dancing lessons and timeshares.

cooperative An association of individuals, businesses, farmers, ranchers, or manufacturers who cooperate in marketing, shipping, and related activities (sometimes under a single brand name) to sell their products efficiently, and then share the profits based on the production, capital, or effort of each. Cooperatives are democratically owned and operated.

cooperative housing An arrangement in which an association or corporation owns a group of housing units and the common areas for the use of all the residents. The individual participants own a share in the cooperative which entitles them to a proprietary lease to occupy a certain part of the property, to have equal access to the common areas, and to vote for members of the Board of Directors which manages the cooperative. (Compare: condominium)

cop a plea Slang for a plea bargain in which an accused defendant in a criminal case agrees to plead guilty or "no contest" to a crime. In return, the prosecutor promises to recommend a lenient sentence, or may agree to drop some of the charges. Often the judge agrees to the recommendation before the plea is entered (becomes final).

coparcenary 1) Joint ownership. 2) An estate that is jointly inherited, in equal shares, from a single ancestor.

copartner A partner (owner) of a partnership. The prefix "co" is a redundancy, since a partner is a member of partnership. The same is true of the term "copartnership."

copy For copyright purposes, the physical form in which creative expression is reproduced and retained over time, no matter how brief. Copies include such things as books, magazines, photocopies, computer disks, and tape recordings. The exclusive right to prepare copies of an original work is one of the primary rights protected by a copyright.

copyright A bundle of exclusive rights granted to the author of a creative work such as book, movie, song, painting, photograph, design, computer software, or architecture. These rights include the right to make copies, authorize others to make copies, make derivative works, sell and market the work, and perform the work. Any one of these rights can be sold or licensed separately through transfers of copyright ownership. Copyright rights are acquired automatically once the work is fixed in a tangible medium of expression. Registration of the work with the

Copyright Office offers additional benefits to the copyright owner. (See also: fixed in a tangible medium of expression)

copyright notice The formal notice consisting of the copyright symbol (or word, copyright), plus the date of publication and the owner's name, placed on published copies of a copyrighted work. For works published in the U.S. after March 1, 1989, copyright notice is not required. A notice is still useful to remind others that the work is copyrighted, to steer a would-be user in the right direction to obtain permission, and to preclude a defense of "I didn't know it was copyrighted" if someone uses the copyrighted material without permission. (See also: published work)

Copyright Office The branch of the Library of Congress that oversees the implementation of the federal copyright laws. The Copyright Office issues regulations, processes applications for registration of copyrights, and accepts and (for some types of works) stores deposits made in connection with registration. The Copyright Office also issues opinions on whether certain types of items are subject to copyright protection.

copyright owner The person or entity who retains legal control over all (or some) of the rights granted under copyright law, usually the author of the work. (See also: author)

copyright registration The status of a work that meets the requirements of the U.S. Copyright Office. Registration is not required for copyright protection but it is required before a court action may be brought to stop infringement. Registration also confers strategic benefits in an infringement action, including a presumption that the registered owner is the rightful owner, as well as the ability to collect statutory damages and attorney fees.

Judge Priest. (1934) Will Rogers plays a folksy Southern judge in a comedy based on Irvin S. Cobb stories. The film has often been called out for its blatant depiction of racial stereotypes. With Tom Brown, Anita Louise, Stepin Fetchit.

coroner A county official who determines the cause of death of anyone who dies violently (by attack or accident), suddenly, or suspiciously.

corporate charter A document filed with state authorities (usually the Secretary of State or Division of Corporations, depending on the state) to form a corporation. As required by the general incorporation law of the state, the charter normally includes the purpose of the corporation, its principal place of business, the names of the initial directors who will control it, and the amounts and types of stock it is authorized to issue. In most states, this document is called the articles of incorporation.

corporate opportunity A business opportunity that becomes known to a director or officer of a corporation or LLC due to his or her position within the company. The director or officer owes a duty of loyalty to the company not to use the opportunity or knowledge for his or her own benefit unless the company gives its permission.

corporate resolution A written document that describes an action taken and approved by the board of directors of a corporation. For example, when a corporation issues a stock dividend, the declaration of the dividend is a corporate resolution. A board might also pass a resolution to take out a loan, buy or sell real estate, amend the corporate bylaws, or issue more stock. Resolutions are recorded with the corporate minutes.

corporate trustee A bank or other financial institution that provides trustee services for various types of trusts.

corporation A legal structure authorized by state law that allows a business to organize as a separate legal entity from its owners. A corporation is often referred to as an "artificial legal person," meaning that, like an individual, it can enter into contracts, sue and be sued, and do the many other things necessary to carry on a business. One advantage of incorporating is that a corporation's owners (shareholders) are legally shielded from personal liability for the corporation's liabilities and debts (unpaid taxes are often an exception). (See also: nonprofit corporation, C corporation, S corporation)

corporeal A thing that has a physical existence, as opposed to something incorporeal, like a right, which does not. Also called tangible.

corporeal ownership The ownership of actual things, such as land, money, or a business. (Compare: incorporeal ownership)

corpus From the Latin for body, a term used to refer to the principal of a trust, as distinguished from interest earned on that principal.

corpus delicti (**core**-pus dee-**lick**-tie) Latin for the "body of the crime." Used to describe physical evidence that a crime has been committed, such as the corpse of a murder victim or the charred frame of a torched building. It's used to refer to the underlying principle that, without evidence of a crime having been committed, it would be unjust to convict someone.

corpus juris (**kor**-pes jur-es) Latin for "the body of law," meaning a compendium of all laws. There are several encyclopedias of the law which fit this definition, the most famous of which is *Corpus Juris Secundum*. Several states have such series of books covering explanations of the law of that state.

corroborate To confirm and sometimes add substantiating (reinforcing) testimony to that of another witness or a party, particularly in a trial.

corroborating evidence Evidence that strengthens, adds to, authenticates, or confirms already existing evidence.

corroborating witness A witness whose testimony supports or confirms testimony already given.

cosign To sign a document—such as a promissory note or lease—along with another person in order to share responsibility for the obligation.

cosigner A person who signs his or her name to a loan agreement, lease, or credit application. If the primary debtor does not pay, the cosigner is fully responsible for the loan or debt. Many people use cosigners to qualify for a loan or credit card. Landlords may require a cosigner when renting to a student or someone with a poor credit history.

cost basis See: basis

cost bill A list of claimed court costs submitted by the prevailing (winning) party in a lawsuit after the judge issues a judgment. Statutes limit what can be included in these costs.

cost of completion The amount of money damages that will be awarded when a contract has been breached by the failure to perform; the cost will reflect the amount of money required to finish the job. For example, when a general contractor breaches a contract by not completing a house, the cost of completion is the actual cost of bringing in a new builder to complete the construction.

cotenancy The situation when more than one person has an interest in real property (such as by signing a rental agreement to share an apartment) at the same time. (See also: tenancy in common, joint tenancy, tenancy by the entirety)

cotenants Two or more tenants who rent the same property under the same lease or rental agreement. Each cotenant is 100% responsible (also known as joint and severally liable) for carrying out the rental agreement, which includes paying the entire rent if the other tenant skips town and paying for damage caused by the other tenant. In addition, if one cotenant violates the lease or rental agreement, the landlord may evict all of them.

cotrustee One of two or more trustees serving at the same time. Depending on the language of the trust document, the cotrustees may be required to act together, or each may be allowed to act independently.

"[The legal profession is] ever illustrating the obvious, explaining the evident, expatiating the commonplace."

—Prime Minister Benjamin Disraeli

---

counsel 1) The lawyer or lawyers representing a client. For example, on the advice of counsel, the defendant did not take the stand. 2) Used as a verb, to give legal advice.

counselor See: attorney

count In a civil case, each separate statement in the complaint that, standing alone, would support a lawsuit. For example, a complaint might begin with a "first count" for negligence, with detailed factual allegations; a second count for breach of contract, a third count for debt, and so forth. Also known as a "cause of action." In a

criminal case, each count is a statement of a different alleged crime.

countable resource Property that the SSI and Medicaid programs consider available to an applicant or recipient when determining that person's eligibility for benefits.

counterclaim A defendant's court papers that seek to reverse the thrust of the lawsuit by claiming that, despite the plaintiff having brought the lawsuit in the first place, the plaintiff is actually wholly or partly at fault concerning the same set of circumstances. The counterclaim goes on to allege that the plaintiff thus owes the defendant money damages or other relief. A counterclaim is commonly but not always based on the same events that form the basis of the plaintiff's complaint. For example, a defendant in an auto accident lawsuit might file a counterclaim alleging that it was really the plaintiff who caused the accident— or could claim that, as long as they're in court, the plaintiff should pay for having chopped down the defendant's tree the previous week.

counterfeit To fraudulently make money, a document, art, or other item which is forged or created to look real, and intended to pass for real.

counteroffer The rejection of an offer to enter into a contract that simultaneously makes a different offer, changing the terms of the original offer in some way. For example, if a buyer offers $5,000 for a used car, and the seller replies that he wants $5,500, the seller has rejected the buyer's offer of $5,000 and has made a counteroffer to sell at $5,500. The legal significance of a counteroffer is that it completely voids the original offer.

counterpart In the law of contracts, a written paper that is one of several documents that constitute a contract, such as a written offer and a written acceptance. If the parties are in different localities, often a contract is executed in several counterparts that are the same, but each counterpart is signed by a different party.

counter wills See: mutual wills

county attorney A lawyer who represents a county in civil matters and litigates violations of county ordinances.

course of employment The hours and circumstances of an employee's job. An employer is generally responsible for actions an employee takes within the course of employment. An employee who is injured in the course of employment is generally entitled to workers' compensation.

court Any official tribunal presided over by a judge or judges in which legal issues and claims are heard and determined. In the United States, there are essentially two systems: federal courts and state courts. The basic federal court system has jurisdiction over cases involving federal statutes, constitutional questions, actions between citizens of different states, and certain other types of cases. There are also special federal courts such as bankruptcy and tax courts. Each state has local trial courts, which include courts for misdemeanors, smaller demand civil actions (called municipal, city, justice, or some other designation), and then superior or district courts to hear felonies, estates, divorces, and major lawsuits. Some states have speciality courts such as family, surrogate, and domestic relations. Small claims courts are an adjunct of the lowest courts handling lesser disputes.

court calendar A list of the cases and hearings that will be held by a court on a particular day, week, or month. Because the length of time it will take to conduct a particular hearing or trial is at best a guess and many courts have a number of judges, accurately scheduling cases is difficult, with the result that court calendars are often revised and cases are often heard later than initially planned. A court calendar is sometimes called a docket, trial schedule, or trial list.

court costs The fees charged for the use of a court, including the initial filing fee, fees for serving the summons, complaint, and other court papers, fees to pay a court reporter to transcribe depositions (pretrial interviews of witnesses) and in-court testimony, and, if a jury is involved, to pay the daily stipend of jurors. Often costs to photocopy court papers and exhibits are also included. Court costs must be paid by both the plaintiff and the defendant as the case progresses. In many types of cases, however, the losing party is held responsible for both parties' costs.

court docket See: docket

court-martial 1) A military court for trying offenses of the Uniform Code of Military Justice by members of the armed services. 2) To charge a member of the military with an offense against military law.

court of appeal(s) 1) Any court (state or federal) that hears appeals from trial courts or lower appeals courts. 2) The intermediate courts in most jurisdictions—that is the courts positioned between trial courts and the courts of last appeal (usually the supreme court).

Court of Claims A U.S. federal court established in 1855 to hear monetary claims against the United States government, based on contracts, express or implied, or claims referred by Congress. It sits in Washington, DC, and is composed of five judges. Some states also have a court of claims.

Court of Customs and Patent Appeals The court that previously handled appeals from determinations by the U.S. Patent and Trademark Office. Appeals are now heard by the Court of Appeals for the Federal Circuit (CAFC). (See also: Court of Appeals for the Federal Circuit (CAFC))

court of equity Courts that handle lawsuits requesting remedies other than monetary damages, such as writs, injunctions, and specific performance. Such courts existed, separate from courts of law, under English common law and in several states. Federal bankruptcy courts are an example of courts that continue to operate as courts of equity. Compare: court of law

Court of International Trade A U.S. federal court that provides judicial review of civil actions arising out of import transactions and federal laws concerning international trade matters. Formerly called the U.S. Customs Court.

court of law Any tribunal within a judicial system. Under English common law and in some states, it was a court that heard only lawsuits in which money damages were sought, as distinguished from a court of equity, which could grant specific remedies. That distinction has dissolved and today every court (with the exception of federal bankruptcy courts) is a court of law. (Compare: court of equity)

court order See: order

court reporter The person who records every word that is said during official court proceedings (hearings and trials) and depositions, and who prepares a written transcript of those proceedings upon the request of the judge or a party.

court trial A trial in which the judge decides factual as well as legal questions, and makes the final judgment. (Compare: jury trial)

court witness A witness called by the court. For example, a judge may call an expert witness to clarify an issue for the court.

covenant An agreement, contract, or written promise between two parties that constitutes a pledge to do or refrain from doing something. In the case of real property, covenants are found in deeds or in documents that bind everyone who owns land in a particular development. (See also: covenants, conditions, and restrictions)

covenant marriage A type of marriage available only in Arizona, Arkansas, and Louisiana, in which the spouses promise that they'll participate in marriage counseling before filing for divorce and agree to a longer waiting period before the divorce can be final. The filing spouse also must allege fault grounds for the divorce. (See also: fault divorce, no-fault divorce)

"A lawyer has no business with the justice or injustice of the cause which he undertakes, unless his client asks his opinion, and then he is bound to give it honestly. The justice or injustice of the cause is to be decided by the judge."

—Samuel Johnson

---

covenant not to compete See: noncompetition agreement

covenant of quiet enjoyment See: quiet enjoyment

covenants, conditions, and restrictions A set of rules, commonly called "CC&Rs," that governs the use of real estate, usually enforced by a homeowners' association. For example, CC&Rs may tell you how big your house can be, how you must landscape your yard, or whether you can have pets. CC&Rs "run with the land," meaning any subsequent owner must also abide by them. Most state laws require that a copy of the CC&Rs

be recorded with the county land records office and be provided to any prospective purchaser.

covenant that runs with the land A formal agreement or promise that passes with land from owner to owner so that the land cannot be conveyed to a new owner without the covenant.

cramdown In Chapter 13 bankruptcy, a reduction in the amount of a secured debt the debtor must repay to the replacement value of the collateral securing the debt. For example, if a debtor owes $5,000 on a car that's worth only $3,500, a cramdown would reduce the amount of the debt that had to be repaid in Chapter 13 to $3,500.

credibility The quality making testimony worthy of belief.

credible witness A witness whose testimony is believable based on his or her experience, knowledge, training, and appearance of honesty and forthrightness.

credit See: tax credit

credit bureau See: credit reporting agency

credit counseling Counseling that explores the possibility of repaying debts outside of bankruptcy and educates the debtor about credit, budgeting, and financial management. Under the 2005

bankruptcy law, a debtor must undergo credit counseling with an approved provider before filing for bankruptcy.

credit file See: credit report

credit insurance An insurance policy a lender requires a borrower to purchase to cover a loan. If the borrower dies or becomes disabled before paying off the loan, the policy will pay off the remaining balance.

creditor A person or entity (such as a bank or credit card company) to whom a debt is owed.

creditor's claim 1) A written claim filed in federal bankruptcy court by a person or entity owed money by a debtor who has filed for bankruptcy. 2) A written claim filed in probate court by a person or entity owed money by a person who has died. State law sets a deadline, usually a few months, for filing a claim in probate court. If the executor or administrator in charge of the probate denies the claim, the creditor can request a court hearing.

creditor's rights The legal procedures and rights available to creditors for collecting debts and judgments.

credit report A written account of a consumer's credit history prepared by a credit reporting agency. Credit reports generally include information on loans, credit cards, and other bills and accounts, as well as a record of the consumer's addresses and employers. To get and use a consumer's credit report, a business must follow the procedures laid out in the Fair Credit Reporting Act.

credit reporting agency A private company that collects and sells information about a person's credit history. Clients, such as banks, mortgage lenders, credit card companies, landlords, and potential employers, use the information to screen applicants. There are three major credit reporting agencies, Equifax, Experian, and TransUnion, and they are regulated by the federal Fair Credit Reporting Act.

credit score Numerical calculation that creditors use to evaluate the creditworthiness of someone applying for credit, such as a mortgage or credit card. High credit scores (over 700) indicate less risk that you will default on payments, and low scores (under 400) indicate potential problems. Credit scores are based on information in your credit report, such as bill-paying history and outstanding debt. The biggest credit scoring company is Fair Isaac Corporation (FICO).

credit shelter trust See: bypass trust

credit union A cooperative financial institution owned and controlled by its members and operated for the purpose of promoting savings with fair interest rates and offering loans at reasonable rates. The National Credit Union Administration (NCUA) charters and supervises federal credit unions.

crime A type of behavior that is has been defined by the state as deserving of punishment, which usually includes imprisonment in the county jail or state or federal prison. Crimes and their punishments are defined by Congress and state legislatures.

crime against nature An archaic term used to describe sexual practices deemed deviant or not natural by a legislature or a court. Examples range from bestiality (intercourse between a human and an animal) to necrophilia (intercourse with a dead body). Few states have "crime against nature" statutes on the books, and any that still include consensual sexual acts, such as sodomy, between adults are unconstitutional under a 2003 United States Supreme Court decision, *Lawrence v. Texas.*

crime of passion A crime committed while in the throes of passion, with no opportunity to reflect on what is happening and what the person is about to do. For example, a husband who discovers his wife in bed with a lover and who attacks and kills the lover in a blind rage has committed a crime of passion. Because the husband has been overcome with emotion, he lacks the specific intent to kill, which is necessary for a conviction of murder. If a jury believes that he acted in the heat of passion, they will convict him only of manslaughter, which does not require an intent to kill. (See also: manslaughter, specific intent)

criminal 1) A popular term for anyone who has committed a crime, whether convicted of the offense or not. More properly, it applies only to those actually convicted of a crime. Repeat offenders are sometimes called habitual criminals. 2) Certain acts or people involved in or relating to a crime. Examples include "criminal taking," "criminal conspiracy," a "criminal gang."

criminal attorney A popular term for an attorney who specializes in representing people charged with crimes, at the trial or appellate level. Many lawyers handle criminal defense and also have other clients. In some states, the licensing agency that regulates the practice of law certifies lawyers as "criminal law specialists" based on experience and extra training in that field.

criminal calendar The list of criminal cases to be called in court on a particular day. The parties charged and their attorneys are given a written notice of the time and place to appear. The criminal calendar may include arraignments, bail settings, cases continued (put off) awaiting a plea, changes of pleas, setting hearing or trial dates, motions brought by attorneys, sentencing hearings, hearings to review reports from probation officers, appointing public defenders or other attorneys, and other business concerning criminal cases.

Compulsion. (1959) Based on the 1920s Loeb-Leopold thrill killing by spoiled rich young men, the highlight is Orson Welles's encapsulated version of Clarence Darrow's argument against the death penalty. With Dean Stockwell, Diane Varsi, E.G. Marshall.

criminal case A lawsuit brought by a prosecutor employed by the federal, state, or local government that charges a person with the commission of a crime.

criminal complaint See: information

criminal insanity A mental defect or disease that, as understood in most states, makes it impossible for a person to know what he or she is doing; or if he or she does know, to know that what they are doing is wrong. Some states define as insane those defendants who acted under an irresistible impulse, even if they knew their actions were wrong.

Defendants who are criminally insane cannot be convicted of a crime, because criminal conduct involves the conscious intent to do wrong—a choice that the criminally insane cannot meaningfully make. (See also: irresistible impulse test, *McNaghten* Rule)

criminal justice A generic term for the procedure by which criminal conduct is investigated, arrests made, evidence gathered, charges brought, defenses raised, trials conducted, sentences rendered, and punishment carried out.

criminal law Laws written by Congress and state legislators that make certain behavior illegal and punishable by fines and/or imprisonment. Criminal law also includes decisions by appellate courts that define crimes and regulate criminal procedure in the absence of clear legislated rules. By contrast, civil laws are not punishable by imprisonment. In order to be found guilty of a criminal law, the prosecution must show that the defendant intended to act as he did; in civil law, you may sometimes be responsible for your actions even though you did not intend the consequences. For example, civil law makes you financially responsible for a car accident you caused but didn't intend.

criminal procedure The legal rules dealing with investigating, prosecuting, adjudicating, and punishing individuals for violating criminal laws. The rules, whether federal or state, may cover procedural issues such as criminal arraignment, bail, pretrial release, preliminary hearings, plea bargaining, criminal trials, and criminal discovery. (Compare: civil procedure)

cross-claim See: cross-complaint

cross-complaint Sometimes called a cross-claim, legal paperwork that a defendant files to initiate his or her own lawsuit against the original plaintiff, a codefendant, or someone who is not yet a party to the lawsuit. A cross-complaint must concern the same events that gave rise to the original lawsuit. For example, a defendant accused of causing an injury when she failed to stop at a red light might cross-complain against the mechanic who recently repaired her car, claiming that his negligence resulted in the brakes failing and that, therefore, the accident was his fault. In some states where the defendant wishes to make a legal claim against the original plaintiff and no third party is claimed to be involved, a counterclaim, not a cross-complaint, should be used.

cross-examination At trial, the opportunity to question any witness who testifies on behalf of any other party to the lawsuit (in civil cases) or for the prosecution or other codefendants (in criminal cases). The opportunity to cross-examine usually occurs as soon as a witness completes his or her initial testimony, called direct testimony. Cross-examiners attempt to get the witness to say something helpful to their side, or to cast doubt on the witness's testimony by eliciting something that reduces the witness's credibility—for example, that the witness's eyesight is so poor that she may not have seen an event clearly. When a witness's direct testimony ends up being hostile to the party that called the witness, sometimes that party's lawyer is allowed to cross-examine his own witness.

cross-licensing The sharing of patent rights through licensing agreements so that businesses can use each other's technology and not fear infringement lawsuits.

cruel and unusual punishment Punishment that is extremely excessive in relation to the crime, shocking to ordinary sensibilities, or equivalent to torture. It is prohibited, but not defined, by the Eighth Amendment to the U.S. Constitution. The definition of cruel and unusual punishment changes over the years, as the courts respond to "evolving standards of decency." The U.S. Supreme Court has ruled that the death penalty, if it could be meted

out by juries with wide discretion and little guidance or applied to insane or mentally retarded defendants, is cruel and unusual punishment. There is still much debate about whether certain methods of carrying out the death penalty, including lethal injection, violate the Eighth Amendment's ban on cruel and unusual punishment.

cruelty Any act of inflicting unnecessary emotional or physical pain. Cruelty or mental cruelty is the most frequently used fault ground for divorce because as a practical matter, courts will accept minor wrongs or disagreements as sufficient evidence of cruelty to justify the divorce. Now that every state has some version of no-fault divorce, cruelty is rarely used as a ground for divorce.

cruelty to animals A crime that is defined differently in different states and municipalities, but usually involves the willful infliction of pain, suffering, or death on an animal, or the intentional or malicious neglect of an animal.

CSI effect A phenomenon reported by prosecutors who claim that television shows based on scientific crime solving have made actual jurors reluctant to vote to convict when, as is typically true, forensic evidence is neither necessary nor available.

culpability See: culpable

culpable Sufficiently responsible for criminal acts or negligence to be at fault and liable for the conduct.

Cumis counsel An attorney employed by a defendant in a lawsuit when there is an insurance policy supposedly covering the claim, but there is a conflict of interest between the insurance company and the insured defendant. Such a conflict might arise if the insurance company is denying full or partial coverage. In California, the defendant can demand that the insurance company pay the attorney fees of a selected attorney rather than use an insurance company lawyer. The term is derived from the name of a 1984 California case.

cum testamento annexo See: administrator with will annexed.

cumulative sentence See: consecutive sentence

cumulative voting In corporations, a system of voting by shareholders for directors in which the shareholder can multiply his or her voting shares by the number of candidates and vote them all for one person for director. This is intended to give minority shareholders a chance to elect at least one director. For example, there are five directors to be elected and 10,000 shares issued. A shareholder with 1,000 shares could vote 5,000 for his or her candidate rather than being limited to 1,000 for each of five candidates and always being outvoted by shareholders with 1,001 or more shares.

curator See: conservator

cure To eliminate or correct a violation or defect. For example, a landlord's cure or quit notice gives the tenant a set amount of time to correct, or cure, a lease violation or face an eviction lawsuit.

cure or quit The type of written notice given to a tenant by a landlord, telling the tenant that he or she must cease a certain behavior within a certain number of days, or move out. If the tenant does neither, the landlord may proceed with an eviction lawsuit in most situations. Common reasons for a cure or quit notice are having a pet in violation of a no-pets lease clause, causing a nuisance or disturbance, and having an unauthorized occupant in the rental.

current monthly income As defined by the 2005 amendments to the bankruptcy law, a debtor's average monthly gross (before tax) income over the six months before the debtor files for bankruptcy. If the debtor's income has recently declined—for example, because the debtor lost a job in the last few months—then his or her current monthly income calculated according to this formula could be much more than the debtor is actually earning each month when he or she files for bankruptcy. The debtor's current monthly income is used to determine whether the debtor can file for Chapter 7 bankruptcy, among other things.

curtesy See: dower and curtesy

custodial interference The taking of a child from a parent with the intent to interfere with that parent's physical custody of the child. This is a crime in most states, even if the taker also has custody rights.

custodial parent A parent who has sole custody or primary custody of a child following divorce. (Compare: noncustodial parent)

custodian A term used by the Uniform Transfers to Minors Act (UTMA) and Uniform Gifts to Minors Act (UGMA) for the person named to manage property left or given to a child under the terms of either of those Acts. The custodian manages the property until the child reaches the age specified by state law—21, in most states. Then the child receives the property outright, and the custodian has no further role in its management.

custody 1) In family law, the right to make decisions about or physically live with a child. 2) Holding property

under one's control. 3) Holding an accused or convicted person in the control of the state, beginning with the arrest of the person.

"The Constitution is either a superior paramount law, unchangeable by ordinary means, or it is on a level with ordinary legislative acts."

—Chief Justice John Marshall,
in *Marbury v. Madison*

---

custody (of a child) The legal authority to make decisions affecting a child's interests (legal custody) and the responsibility of taking care of the child (physical custody). When parents separate or divorce, they may share legal and physical custody, or one parent may have physical custody with the other parent having visitation. (See also: joint custody, sole custody, physical custody, legal custody)

Customs and Border Protection (CBP) Formerly referred to as the Border Patrol, this is now an agency within the Department of Homeland Security (DHS). One of its responsibilities is to keep the U.S. borders secure from people crossing illegally. Another one is to meet travelers and returning residents arriving at U.S. airports and border posts, and to check their visas or other admission documents in order to decide whether they should be allowed into the United States. If not, CBP has the power to order them to return home immediately.

Customs Court See: Court of International Trade

cybersquatting The practice of acquiring a business name, trademark, or celebrity name as a domain name, hoping to later profit by reselling the domain name back to the company or person who has been disadvantaged. The Anticybersquatting Consumer Protection Act of 1999 authorizes a cybersquatting victim to file a federal lawsuit to regain a domain name or sue for financial compensation.

Victims of cybersquatting can also use the provisions of the Uniform Domain Name Dispute Resolution Policy adopted by ICANN, an international tribunal administering domain names.

cy pres doctrine (see-**pray**-doctrine) A doctrine used to give a gift to a similar beneficiary when the true beneficiary no longer exists or is not available. The cy pres doctrine is most often used with charitable gifts when the charity named in an estate planning document no longer exists. In that case, the trustee or court may use the cy pres doctrine to give the gift to a similar charity to match the donor's intention as closely as possible.

D

D.A. See: District Attorney

damages 1) In a lawsuit, the harm caused to a party who is injured. 2) In a lawsuit, the money awarded to one party based on injury or loss caused by the other. For either definition, there are many different types or categories of damages. (See also: compensatory damages, actual damages, special damages, general damages, exemplary damages, punitive damages, statutory damages, nominal damages)

dangerous weapon Any object, such as a gun, knife, sword, crossbow, or slingshot, that is intrinsically capable of causing serious bodily harm to another person. The definition becomes important in cases where criminal laws attach particular consequences to crimes performed with a dangerous weapon. (See also: deadly weapon)

Darby v. United States (1941) A U.S. Supreme Court case in which the Court, in a decision by Justice Harlan Stone, sustained the portion of the 1938 Fair Labor Standards Act prohibiting child labor and regulating wages and hours, on the basis that the federal government's power to regulate interstate commerce included the authority to promote commerce as well as prohibit it, a position argued in a dissent by Oliver Wendell Holmes in 1916.

database A collection of information arranged in a way to facilitate updating and retrieval. Computer databases commonly consist both of materials protected by copyright and materials that are said to be in the public domain, either because their copyright has run out or because they consist of ideas and facts that themselves do not receive copyright protection. Despite the fact that the database owner may not own any copyright interest in any of the material in the database, the structure and organization of the database itself can qualify as an original work of authorship and thus be subject to copyright protection as a compilation. (See also: compilation)

date rape Forcible sexual intercourse by a male acquaintance of a woman, during a voluntary social engagement in which the woman did not intend to submit to the sexual advances and resisted the acts by verbal refusals, denials, pleas to stop, and/or fighting back. The fact that the parties knew each other or that the woman willingly accompanied the man are not legal defenses to a charge of rape.

d.b.a. (also known as DBA) See: doing business as

deadhand control An attempt to keep property in the hands of chosen family members or organizations through ownership interests that vest far into the future. In the law of wills and estates, deadhand control is restricted to lives in being at the time the will is executed plus 21 years. (This is known as the rule against perpetuities.)

deadly weapon A gun or other instrument, substance, or device, which is used or intended to be used in a way that is likely to cause death. A prosecutor who charges a defendant with "assault with a deadly weapon" must prove not only that the defendant assaulted the victim, but did so with a device that was capable of causing death. Some laws list "deadly weapons per se," which are weapons that by themselves are likely to cause death, such as a gun, regardless of the user's intent.

dead man's statute In the law of evidence, a rule that prevents a person making a claim against an estate from testifying about statements, actions, or promises made by the deceased person.

dealer Anyone who buys goods or property for the purpose of selling as a business. It is important to distinguish a dealer from someone who occasionally buys and occasionally sells, since dealers may need to obtain business licenses, register with the sales tax authorities, and may not defer capital gains taxes by buying other property.

death benefit Insurance or pension money payable to a deceased person's designated beneficiary.

death penalty The sentence of execution for murder and some other capital crimes. (See also: capital punishment)

death row The portion of a prison that houses prisoners who are under death sentences and are awaiting appeals or execution.

death taxes Taxes levied at death, based on the value of property left behind. There are two main types of death taxes in the United States: estate taxes and inheritance taxes. The federal government and some state governments impose estate taxes on decedent's estates. And some states levy inheritance taxes on people who inherit property.

debenture A type of bond (an interest-bearing document that serves as evidence of an investment or debt) that does not require security in the form of a mortgage or lien on a specific piece of property. Repayment of a debenture is guaranteed only by the general credit of the issuer. For example, a corporation may issue a secured bond that gives the bondholder a lien on the corporation's factory. But if it issues a debenture, the loan is not secured by any property at all. When a corporation issues debentures, the holders are considered creditors of the corporation and are entitled to payment before shareholders if the business folds.

Boomerang! (1947) Dramatic tale of legal ethics in which a D.A. realizes the defendant is not guilty, based on an actual trial case tried by future Attorney General Homer Cummings. Dana Andrews, Lee J. Cobb, Arthur Kennedy, Ed Begley, Sr., Karl Malden.

debit card A card issued by a bank that combines the functions of an ATM card and a check. A debit card can be used to withdraw cash at a bank, like an ATM card. It can also be used like a check at stores, to pay for goods and services. A debit card is linked to the user's bank account, from which money is automatically withdrawn when the card is used.

debt 1) An amount owed by one person or entity to another. 2) A cause of action in a lawsuit to recover a set amount owed by another person or entity. 3) The total of everything a person or entity owes to all creditors. For example, everything the United States government owes is collectively called "the national debt," and that amount is made up of a number of debts.

debt collector Someone who works in the in-house collections department of an original creditor or for a collection agency to track down debtors and get them to pay what they owe. (See also: Fair Debt Collection Practices Act)

debtor A person or entity (such as a business) who owes money.

debtor in possession A business that has filed for Chapter 11 bankruptcy and is allowed to continue operating during the bankruptcy process.

debt relief agency Any person or company—including lawyers and bankruptcy petition preparers, but excluding banks, nonprofits, and government agencies—that provides advice, information, counsel, document preparation, or other services to a person who is contemplating, or filing for, bankruptcy. Under the bankruptcy law passed in 2005, debt relief agencies are subject to certain legal requirements and must provide debtors with a prescribed notice about their services.

debt-to-income ratio The percentage of a person's monthly gross income that is spent on paying debts, such as housing and credit card payments. Banks and lenders use this ratio to decide how much money (and on what terms) they will lend someone for a mortgage, car, or other loan. Traditionally, lenders have said that your housing costs (mortgage principal and interest, homeowner's insurance, and property taxes, also known as PITI) shouldn't exceed 28% of your gross income, and that your overall debt (PITI plus car and other loan payments) shouldn't exceed 36%.

deceased See: decedent

decedent A person who has died, also called the deceased.

deceit A deliberate misrepresentation made by someone who knew it was false and with the intent to deceive someone who justifiably relies on the falsehood. Deceit is a civil wrong (tort). (See also: fraud)

deception See: deceit

decide To reach a determination of who is right and wrong in a legal matter, after looking at the facts and the law. Judges, hearing officers, magistrates, and arbitrators all may decide the outcome of cases that come before

them. By contrast, mediators help disputing parties reach a mutually agreeable resolution, but do not decide matters themselves.

decision The outcome of a proceeding before a judge, arbitrator, government agency, or other legal tribunal. Decision is a general term often used interchangeably with the terms judgment or opinion. But to be precise, a judgment is the written form of the court's decision in the clerk's minutes or notes, and an opinion is a document setting out the reasons for reaching the decision.

declarant A person who signs a statement or declaration alleging that the information contained in the statement is true. (Compare: affiant)

declaration Any statement made, particularly in writing, including a formal statement made under penalty of perjury and signed by the declarant.

declaration against interest When a nonparty witness in a lawsuit is not available to testify, a statement made by the witness that is against his or her own interest may be admitted in court as evidence as an exception to the hearsay rule. (Compare: admission)

declaration of mailing A legal form stating that a particular document has been mailed to someone involved in a legal action (such as opposing attorneys or the clerk of the court), to prove compliance with court requirements. The declaration must be signed by its sender, usually under penalty of perjury.

declaration of trust The document that creates a trust. It names a trustee and beneficiaries, sets out how trust assets are to be managed and distributed, and may list the assets that are to be held in trust. It is signed by the person creating the trust, who is usually called the grantor, settlor, or trustor. A trust declaration is also called a trust instrument.

declaration under penalty of perjury A signed statement, sworn to be true by the signer, that will make the signer guilty of the crime of perjury if the statement is shown to be materially false—that is, the lie is relevant and significant to the case.

declaratory judgment A court decision in a civil case that tells the parties what their rights and responsibilities are, without awarding damages or ordering them to do anything. Courts are usually reluctant to hear declaratory judgment cases, preferring to wait until there has been a measurable loss. But especially in cases involving important constitutional rights, courts will step in to clarify the legal landscape. For example, many cities regulate the right to assemble by requiring permits to hold a parade. A disappointed applicant who thinks the decision-making process is unconstitutional might hold his parade anyway and challenge the ordinance after he was cited; or he might ask a court beforehand to rule on the constitutionality of the law. By going to court, the applicant may avoid a messy confrontation with the city—and perhaps a citation, as well.

declaratory relief See: declaratory judgment

decree An order by a judge, resolving issues in a court case. Similar to the term "judgment," but preferred in certain types of cases, like probate matters. (See also: judgment)

decree of distribution The final court order distributing a probate estate.

decriminalization The repeal or amendment of statutes which made certain acts criminal, so that those acts no longer are crimes or subject to prosecution.

dedication The giving of land by a private person or entity to the government, typically for a street, park, or school site, as part of and a condition of a real estate development. The local county or city (or other public body) must accept the dedication before it is complete.

dedimus potestatum An outdated legal procedure that permitted a party to take and record the testimony of a witness before trial, but only when that testimony might otherwise be lost. For example, a party to a lawsuit might use the procedure to obtain the testimony of a witness who was terminally ill and might not be able to testify at the trial. Nowadays, the Federal Rules of Civil Procedure routinely permit the taking of testimony before trial if that testimony might otherwise be lost.

 "Delay works always for the man with the longest purse."

—William Howard Taft

---

deductible Something that is taken away or subtracted. Under an insurance policy, for example, the deductible is the maximum amount that an insured person must pay toward his own losses before he can recover from the insurer. For example, Julie's car insurance policy has a $500 deductible. One day she forgets to set her parking brake and the car rolls backwards into a telephone pole, sustaining $2,500 in damage. Julie's insurance company deducts $500 from the total amount and issues a check to the auto body shop for $2,000.

deductible business expense An expenditure that is ordinary and necessary for running a business and deductible from the business's gross receipts so that it is not counted toward taxable income.

deduction In tax law, an amount that an individual or business can subtract from its gross income (total income) to determine its taxable income (the total income on which it owes tax). Examples of federal income tax deductions include mortgage interest, charitable contributions, and certain state taxes.

deed A document that transfers ownership of real estate and is recorded in the local public land records. (See also: deed of trust, quitclaim deed, transfer-on-death deed, warranty deed)

deed in lieu of foreclosure A means of escaping an overly burdensome mortgage. If a homeowner can't make the mortgage payments and can't find a buyer for the house, many lenders will accept ownership of the property in place of the money owed on the mortgage. Even if the lender won't agree to accept the property, the homeowner can prepare a quitclaim deed that unilaterally transfers the homeowner's property rights to the lender.

deed of trust See: trust deed

deep link A link from one website to another that bypasses the second website's home page and takes the user directly to an internal page on the site. For example, a deep link from Yahoo! might take the user directly to a news article on a news site instead of linking to the home page of the site. (Compare: link)

de facto Latin for "in fact." A recognition of authority even when legal or formal requirements have not been met. (See also: de facto corporation, de jure)

de facto corporation A business that has not completed all of the legal steps to become a corporation will be treated as a corporation by the court to shield the directors, officers, and shareholders who in good faith thought they were operating the business as a duly formed corporation. (Compare: de jure corporation)

defalcation The failure to turn over or account for funds entrusted to one's care. Defalcation may be, but is not necessarily, criminal or fraudulent.

defamation A false statement that harms a person's reputation. If the statement is published, it is libel; if spoken, it is slander. Most states have retraction statutes under which a defamed person who fails to seek a retraction from the publisher, or who seeks and obtains a retraction, is limited to compensation equal to the actual (or special) damages. Public figures, including officeholders and candidates, can only prevail in defamation lawsuits if they can show that the defamation was made with knowledge that it was false or with reckless disregard for the truth. (See also: libel per se)

default 1) Failure to file an answer or other response to a summons or complaint in a lawsuit. After a certain period has passed, the plaintiff may ask the court for a default judgment, which means the defendant who failed to respond loses the case. A defendant who has a legally sufficient reason for failing to respond (for example, the defendant never received the summons) may file a motion asking the court to overturn the default judgment and allow the defendant to defend the lawsuit. 2) Failure to pay a debt or meet other obligations of a loan agreement. For example, a debtor may default on a car loan by failing to make required monthly payments or by failing to carry adequate insurance as required by the loan agreement.

default divorce A divorce in which one party obtains a judgment of divorce based on the other party's failure to file a response to the divorce petition. A default divorce can be obtained when one spouse truly can't find the other or when the second spouse refuses to participate in the divorce action, or when the parties agree to enter a default as part of an uncontested divorce proceeding. (See also: uncontested divorce)

default judgment At trial, a decision awarded to the plaintiff when a defendant fails to contest the case or comply with required procedural steps. For instance, the defendant may fail to respond to the plaintiff's complaint within the required time, or simply neglect to show up in court. To appeal a default judgment, a defendant must first file a motion in the court that issued it, asking to have the default vacated (set aside).

defeasance The act of rendering something null and void, or a clause in a deed, lease, will, or other legal document that completely or partially negates the document if a certain condition occurs or fails to occur. For example, a will may provide that a gift of property is defeasable—that is, void—if the beneficiary fails to marry before a certain time.

defeasible remainder A vested remainder that can be destroyed if a specific condition occurs. For example, "To Jorge, unless he gets divorced." Jorge has a vested remainder, but it's also a defeasible remainder because it can be taken away from him if he gets divorced.

defect An imperfection in a product, machinery, process, or written docu-ment that makes the item unusable or harmful, such as faulty brakes in a car, or invalid, such as a deed signed by someone who does not have title to the property. A defect may also be minor, such as scratches on a car door, that lessens value or use of the item, but does not make it dangerous or useless.

defective Incapable of fulfilling its function, due to an error or flaw.

defective title Property ownership that is subject to claims by someone else, making it impossible to sell the property. (See also: clear title, title search)

defendant The person against whom a lawsuit is filed. In some types of cases (such as divorce) a defendant may be called a respondent.

defense 1) A general term for the effort of an attorney representing a defendant during trial and in pretrial maneuvers to defeat the party suing or the prosecution in a criminal case. 2) A response to a complaint, called an affirmative defense, to counter, defeat, or remove all or a part of the contentions of the plaintiff.

defense attorney The attorney represent-ing the defendant in a lawsuit or crimi-nal prosecution. Attorneys who regularly represent clients in civil lawsuits are often called "plaintiffs' attorneys."

Defense of Marriage Act (DOMA) So-called Defense of Marriage laws define marriage as a relationship between one man and one woman, for the purpose of excluding same-sex couples from the institution of marriage. The federal DOMA prohibits the federal government from recognizing same-sex legal relationships entered into in one of the states that recognize same-sex unions. Individual states' DOMA laws provide that those states do not allow same-sex marriage and, often, do not recognize same-sex unions from other states.

deferred compensation An arrangement in which a portion of an employee's income is paid at a later date than the date when it is earned. In most cases, the primary benefit is the tax deferral on the deferred income.

deficiency 1) In tax, a difference found by the IRS between a taxpayer's reported tax liability and the amount of tax the IRS says that the taxpayer should have reported. 2) In lending, the remaining balance of the debt after the security for the loan has been sold following repossession or foreclosure.

deficiency judgment A judgment for the amount a homeowner owes the lender after a house or other asset is foreclosed upon and sold by the creditor for less than the actual debt (mortgage or car loan, for example) that is secured by the asset. In most states, the lender can file a separate lawsuit to recover a deficiency owed by the borrower. Some states restrict deficiency judgments after a home foreclosure.

deficit In a budget, an excess of expenditures or liabilities over revenues or assets.

The Trial. (1963) A French adaptation of Kafka's novel about a clerk who is arrested and tried without knowing what crime he's been accused of, directed by Orson Welles. Anthony Perkins plays the accused, with Jeanne Moreau, Romy Schneider, Elsa Martinelli, and Welles himself.

---

defined benefit plan A type of pension plan that promises a specific benefit upon retirement. The benefit may be a set amount (such as $1,000 per month) or may be calculated according to a formula based on, for example, years of service and average salary. (Compare: defined contribution plan)

defined contribution plan A type of retirement plan that creates an individual account for each employee funded by contributions by the employer, the employee, or both. The amount contributed is set, either as a dollar amount or by formula (for example, a certain percentage of the employee's earnings). Unlike a defined benefit plan, which guarantees that the employee will be paid a certain amount on retirement, a defined contribution plan guarantees the employee only the value of his or her account upon retirement: amounts contributed to the plan plus or minus investment gains or losses. A 401(k) plan is a type of defined contribution plan.

defraud To use deceit, falsehoods, or trickery to obtain money, an object, rights, or anything of value belonging to another.

degree of kinship The level of the relationship between two persons related by blood—for example parent to child, one sibling to another, grandparent to grandchild, uncle to nephew, and so on. This may become important when determining the heirs of an estate when there is no will because most states disburse intestate estates to the relatives with the closest degree of kinship to the decedent.

de jure (deh **jur**-ay) Latin for according to the law. (Compare: de facto)

de jure corporation A corporation formed in compliance with all applicable laws. (Compare: de facto corporation)

delayed exchange An exchange of property to put off capital gain taxes, in which the funds are placed in a binding trust for up to 180 days while the seller acquires an "exchanged" (another similar) property, pursuant to Internal Revenue Code Section 1031.

delegate 1) To assign authority to another. 2) A person chosen to attend a convention, conference, or meeting on behalf of an organization, constituency, interest group, or business.

deliberate 1) (duh-**lib**-er-et) Done with care, intention, or premeditation. 2) (duh-**lib**-er-ate) Consideration and discussion of facts, laws, and other matters, particularly by members of a jury, a panel of judges, or by any group including a legislature.

delinquent 1) A payment that is past due or not paid in full. 2) A person who disobeys rules or breaks the law such as a juvenile delinquent.

delivery The transfer of an object, money, or document to another. To be effective, real estate deeds must be delivered, but delivery does not necessarily require that the new owner be given physical possession of the deed. If a deed is acknowledged and recorded, the law generally presumes that delivery was made.

demand A claim or an assertion of a legal right or a right to compensation. (See also: demand letter)

demand letter Correspondence from one party to a dispute to the other, stating the drafting party's version of the facts of the dispute and making a claim for compensation or other action to resolve it. Often drafted by an attorney, a demand letter is generally an opening gambit in an effort to settle a legal claim.

demand note A promissory note that's payable any time the holder of the note makes a request. This is different from a note due at a specific time, upon occurrence of an event, or by installments.

de minimis (dee **minn**-uh-miss) Trifling or of little importance. Usually refers to something so small, whether in dollar terms, importance, or severity, that the law will not consider it.

demise Transfer of real estate by a lease or will. Traditionally, the transfer was limited to term of years but the expression has come to refer to outright gifts as well.

demonstrative evidence Objects, pictures, models, and other devices used in a trial or hearing to demonstrate or explain facts that the party is trying to prove.

demur Presenting a demurrer to a court.

demurrer (dee-**mur**-ur) A written response to a complaint filed in a lawsuit that asks the court to dismiss the lawsuit on the grounds that even if the facts alleged in the complaint were true, there is no legal basis for the suit. A hearing before a judge will then be held to determine the validity of the demurrer. Some parts of a lawsuit may be defeated by a demurrer while others may survive. Some demurrers contend that the complaint is unclear or omits an essential element of fact. If the judge finds these errors, the judge will usually sustain the demurrer (state it is valid), but "with leave to amend" in order to correct the original complaint. If after amendment the complaint is still not legally good, a demurrer will be granted. In rare occasions, a demurrer can be used to attack an answer to a complaint. Some states have substituted a motion to dismiss for failure to state a cause of action for the demurrer.

denial A statement by a defendant that an allegation (claim of fact) is not true. When a defendant in a civil lawsuit files an answer to a plaintiff's complaint, the defendant is limited to three choices: admitting, denying, or denying the allegations on the basis that he or she has no information to affirm or deny them. If a defendant denies all of the allegations, it is called a general denial. The defendant's answer may also include affirmative defenses.

de novo (day **noh**-voh) Latin for "anew," meaning to do something over again as if for the first time. (See also: trial de novo)

Department of Homeland Security
(**DHS**) A government agency created in 2003 to handle immigration and other security-related matters. Within DHS's immigration responsibilities, it oversees U.S. Citizenship and Immigration Services (USCIS, which replaced the former Immigration and Naturalization Service or INS); as well as Immigration and Customs Enforcement (ICE) and Customs and Border Protection (CBP).

When future president John Adams came to court in Boston to be sworn in as an attorney he forgot to bring his lawyer sponsor to attest to his skill and honesty. Another attorney stepped forward and swore to Adams's talent, saving the young man further embarrassment.

Department of Labor (**DOL**) A federal government agency that interprets and enforces a number of labor and employment laws, including the Occupational Safety and Health Act, the Family and Medical Leave Act, the federal minimum wage and overtime laws, and laws that govern child labor.

Department of State (**DOS**) A U.S. department that handles foreign relations under the leadership of the Secretary of State. Among its many functions, DOS operates U.S. embassies and consulates in other countries. Generally, the DOS determines who is entitled to a visa or green card when an application is filed outside the United States. U.S. Citizenship and Immigration Services (USCIS), under the Department of Homeland Security, regulates immigration processing inside the United States.

dependent 1) A person receiving support from another person (such as a parent), which may qualify the party supporting the dependent for an exemption to reduce income taxes. 2) Requiring an event to occur, as the fulfillment of a contract for delivery of goods is dependent on the goods being available.

dependent care plan A fringe benefit that eligible employees of a business can be given tax-free to care for their dependents. This expense is generally deductible to the business.

dependents benefits A type of Social Security benefit available to spouses and minor or disabled children of retired or disabled workers who qualify for either retirement or disability benefits under the program's rigorous qualification guidelines.

deponent Someone whose deposition is being taken.

deportation See: removal

depose To question a witness or a party to a lawsuit at a deposition (testimony under oath taken outside of the courtroom before trial).

deposition The taking and recording of the testimony of a party or witness under oath before a court reporter, in a place away from the courtroom, before trial. A deposition is part of pretrial discovery. The testimony is recorded by the court reporter, who will prepare a transcript that can be used for pretrial preparation or in trial to contradict or refresh the memory of the witness, or be read into the record if the witness is not available.

depreciable asset Property with a useful life of at least one year that gradually loses its value over time. A business deducts the cost of a depreciable asset over a period of time.

depreciate In accounting, to reduce the value of an asset each year on the basis that the asset (such as equipment, a vehicle, or a structure) will eventually become obsolete, worn out, and of little value.

depreciation The actual or theoretical gradual loss of value of an asset (particularly business equipment or buildings) through increasing age, natural wear and tear, or deterioration, even though the item may retain or even increase its replacement value due to inflation. Depreciation may be used as a business deduction for income tax reduction, spread out over the expected useful life of the asset (straight line) or at a higher rate in the early years of use (accelerated).

depreciation reserve A business fund in which the probable replacement cost of equipment is accumulated each year over the life of the asset, so it can be replaced readily when it becomes obsolete and totally depreciated.

derelict Something or someone who is abandoned, such as a ship left to drift at sea or a homeless person ignored by family and society.

dereliction 1) Abandoning possession, which is sometimes used in the phrase "dereliction of duty." It includes abandoning a ship, which then becomes a derelict which salvagers can board. 2) Increase of land due to gradual lowering of a tide line (which means the land is building up).

derivation of citizenship An immigration law concept allowing children who already have U.S. green cards to obtain U.S. citizenship automatically, in most cases when one or both parents become naturalized U.S. citizens. The exact requirements depend on what laws were in effect during certain key events, in most cases the year in which the parent naturalized.

derivative A financial instrument whose value is based on the value of an underlying security, such as a commodity, currency, or bond. The most common derivatives are futures, options, and swaps. They are used to manage risk and fluctuations in the value of the underlying security but are often risky and complicated investments.

derivative action A lawsuit brought by a shareholder against the corporation's directors, other shareholders of the corporation, or a third party for failure of management or fraud. The suing shareholder sues on behalf of the corporation (usually because the directors are failing to exercise their authority for the benefit of the company), and any proceeds of a successful action are awarded to the corporation and not to the suing shareholder.

derivative work In copyright, a new creative work based upon an existing work. To be separately protected under copyright law, a derivative must include sufficient original creative work. Examples of derivative works include a translation of a book, a toy based on a cartoon character, or a movie script based on a novel.

descent The passing of estate property through inheritance, either by law or through estate planning—as opposed to acquisition of property through other means, such as purchase.

descent and distribution The rules by which an estate is distributed after the owner's death. This may occur according to the decedent's estate plan or according to intestate laws if the decedent died without an estate plan.

descriptive mark A trademark or service mark that describes some characteristic of the product or service with which it is associated. For instance, "Jiffy Lube" describes a purportedly fast lube service. Descriptive trademarks are harder to protect, at least until the owner can demonstrate that consumers associate the mark with the source of the goods or services (a status referred to as a secondary meaning). (See also: secondary meaning, Supplemental Register)

desert To intentionally abandon a person or thing.

desertion The voluntary abandonment of one spouse by the other, without the abandoned spouse's consent. Commonly, desertion occurs when a spouse leaves the marital home for a specified length of time. Desertion is grounds for divorce in states with fault divorce. Desertion can also be the basis for a court to grant an adoption where a parent has deserted a child for a specified period of time. (See also: abandonment)

design patent A patent granted for a new design that is not obvious to those in the field of design, and that is used for ornamental reasons—that is, the design does not affect the functioning of the underlying device. Design patents last for 14 years from the date the patent is issued. (Compare: utility patent)

 "Defiance of the law is the surest road to tyranny."

—John F. Kennedy

---

detain See: imprison

determinable 1) Capable of being determined by a court. 2) Capable of being terminated on the occurrence of a particular event, usually used to describe an interest in real estate.

determinate sentence A jail or prison sentence that is definite and not subject to review by a parole board or other agency. For example, a sentence of six months in the county jail is determinate, because the prisoner will spend no more than six months (minus time off for good behavior, in some situations). By contrast, an

indeterminate sentence (such as 20 years to life) has a minimum term but the release date, if any, will be chosen by a parole board as it periodically reviews the case. (Compare: indeterminate sentence)

deuce A slang term originating in California for a drunk driving violation.

devise An old legal term that is generally used to refer to real estate left to someone under the terms of a will, or to the act of leaving such real estate. In some states, devise now applies to any kind of property left by will, making it identical to the term bequest. (Compare: bequest, legacy)

devisee A person or entity who inherits real estate under the terms of a will. (Compare: legatee)

devisor Someone who leaves real estate by will. (See also: testator)

devolution The transfer of rights, powers, or an office (public or private) from one person or government to another.

devolve When property is automatically transferred from one party to another by operation of law, without any act required of either past or present owner. The most common example is passing of title to the natural heir of a person upon his death.

dicta The plural of dictum.

dictum A remark, statement, or observation of a judge that is not a necessary part of the legal reasoning needed to reach the decision in a case. Although dictum may be cited in a legal argument, it is not binding as legal precedent, meaning that other courts are not required to accept it. Dictum is an abbreviation of the Latin phrase "obiter dictum," which means a remark by the way, or an aside.

Digital Millennium Copyright Act A federal statute that addresses a number of copyright issues created by the use of new technology and the Internet including digital rights management (methods for stopping infringement), and certain rights and privileges (safe harbors) that protect Internet Service Providers.

digital signature See: electronic signature

diligence Reasonable care or attention to a matter.

dilution When a famous trademark or service mark is used in a context in which the mark's reputation for quality is tarnished or its distinction is blurred. For example, the use of the word Candyland for a pornographic site on the Internet diluted the reputation of the Candyland mark for the well-known children's game, even though

the traditional basis for trademark infringement (probable customer confusion) wasn't an issue.

diminished capacity An impaired mental condition, caused by disease, trauma, or intoxication but short of insanity, that can reduce the criminal responsibility of a defendant. Not all states allow defendants to offer this plea in response to criminal charges.

diminution in value A way of assessing damages after a breach of a contract, which measures the difference between the value of the property as it was contractually promised and the value of the property as it currently exists or was constructed.

direct and proximate cause The immediate reason that something happened that caused harm to another person. The words are often used together, as in "The defendant's negligent act in running the red light was the direct and proximate cause of the plaintiff's injuries." (See also: legal cause)

directed trust A trust in which certain assets are managed by someone other than the trustee. For example, someone might set up a trust and name a bank's trust department as trustee, but specify in the trust document that a business held in trust be managed by someone else. The outside manager goes by different names in different states: a cotrustee, special trustee, trust protector, or adviser. Directed trusts are authorized by law in about 30 states. Most hold at least $1 million in assets, and often much more.

directed verdict A ruling by a judge, typically made after the plaintiff has presented all of its evidence but before the defendant puts on its case, that awards judgment to the defendant. A directed verdict is usually made because the judge concludes the plaintiff has failed to offer the minimum amount of evidence to prove the case even if there were no opposition. In other words, the judge is saying that, as a matter of law, no reasonable jury could decide in the plaintiff's favor. In a criminal case, a directed verdict is a judgment of acquittal for the defendant.

direct evidence Real, tangible, or clear evidence of a fact, happening, or thing that requires no thinking or consideration to prove its existence, as compared to circumstantial evidence.

direct examination At trial, the initial questioning of a party or witness by the side that called him or her to testify. The major purpose of direct examination is to explain your version of events to the judge or jury and to undercut your opponent's version. Good direct examination seeks to prove all facts necessary to satisfy the plaintiff's legal claims or causes of action—for example, that the defendant breached a valid contract and, as a result, the plaintiff suffered a loss.

direct inheritance Property left outright to a person, rather than put into a trust or account. For those who qualify for SSI or Medicaid, direct inheritance may cause a reduction or elimination of those benefits because the inheritance is counted as income in the month received and as a resource in the following months. Property left to a special needs trust is not counted as direct inheritance.

directive to physicians See: living will

director A member of the governing board of a corporation, typically elected at an annual meeting of the shareholders. As a group, the directors are responsible for making important business decisions—especially those that legally bind the corporation—leaving day-to-day management to the corporation's officers and employees. For example, a decision to borrow money, lease an office, or buy real property would normally be authorized by the board of directors.

disability 1) For purposes of antidiscrimination law, a physical or mental impairment that substantially limits one or more major life activities. 2) A legal impediment to taking a certain action, such as being a minor who cannot legally enter into a contract.

disability benefits Money available from Social Security to benefit those younger than 65 who qualify because of their work and earning record and who meet the program's medical guidelines defining disability. The benefits are roughly equal to those available in Social Security retirement benefits.

"You cannot change people's hearts merely by laws. Laws presumably express the conscience of a nation and its determination or will to do something."

—Dwight D. Eisenhower

---

disallowance A finding by the IRS after an audit that a business or individual taxpayer was not entitled to a deduction or other tax benefit claimed on a tax return.

disbar The removal of an attorney's license to practice law. This penalty is usually invoked by the state bar association where the attorney is licensed to practice and will prohibit the attorney from practicing law before the courts in that state or from giving advice for a fee to clients. Causes of disbarment include: a felony involving "moral turpitude," forgery, fraud, a

history of dishonesty, consistent lack of attention to clients, alcoholism or drug abuse which affect the attorney's ability to practice, theft of funds, or any pattern of violation of the professional code of ethics.

disbarment See: disbar

discharge 1) To perform one's legal duties or meet one's obligations. 2) To fire someone from a job. 3) In bankruptcy, an order of the court that wipes out all dischargeable debts.

discharge (of debts) In bankruptcy, the bankruptcy court's action, at the end of the case, to wipe out the debts of the person or business that filed for bankruptcy. Once a debt is discharged, the debtor no longer owes it, and the creditor may no longer take action to collect it.

discharge (of personal representative) A court order releasing the personal representative (administrator or executor) from any further duties connected with the probate of an estate. This typically occurs when the duties have been completed but may happen sooner if the executor or administrator wishes to withdraw or is dismissed.

dischargeable debts Debts that can be wiped out in bankruptcy, such as credit card debts, medical bills, and back rent. (Compare: nondischargeable debts)

discharge in bankruptcy See: bankruptcy discharge

disclaim 1) To refuse or give away a claim or a right to something. For example, if your aunt leaves you a white elephant in her will and you don't want it, you can refuse the gift by disclaiming your ownership rights. 2) To deny responsibility for a claim or act. For example, a merchant that sells goods secondhand may disclaim responsibility for a product's defects by selling it as is.

disclaimer 1) A contractual provision in which one party renounces or refuses a right or a responsibility. 2) A formal statement by a patent or trademark owner that it does not claim certain intellectual property rights. 3) An irrevocable refusal to accept property that has been left by will, trust, or other method, sometimes used in estate planning to reduce overall taxes paid by a family. (See also: intellectual property)

disclaimer trust A kind of bypass trust that gives the surviving spouse the option of not splitting the trust after the first spouse's death if it's not necessary to save on estate tax. A surviving spouse may disclaim (decline to accept) some trust property; that property goes into the bypass trust.

disclosure The making known of a fact that had previously been hidden; a revelation. For example, in many states you must disclose major physical defects in a house you are selling, such as a leaky roof or potential flooding problem; and in all states, you must disclose the presence of lead-based paint hazards in buildings constructed before 1978.

discount Payment of less than the full or regular amount of the price for goods or services or less than the amount due on a promissory note.

discovery A formal investigation—governed by court rules—that is conducted before trial by both parties. Discovery allows each party to question the other parties, and sometimes witnesses. The most common types of discovery are interrogatories, consisting of written questions the other party must answer under penalty of perjury; depositions, at which one party to a lawsuit has the opportunity to ask oral questions of the other party or witnesses under oath while a written transcript is made by a court reporter; and requests to produce documents, by which one party can force the other to produce physical evidence. Parties may also ask each other to admit or deny key facts in the case. Discovery allows parties to assess the strength or weakness of an opponent's case, in order to support settlement talks and also to be sure that the parties have as much knowledge as possible for trial. Discovery is also present in criminal cases, in which by law the prosecutor must turn over to the defense any witness statements and any evidence that might tend to exonerate the defendant. Depending on the rules of the court, the defendant may also be obliged to share evidence with the prosecutor.

discretion The power of a judge, public official, or private party to make decisions based on his or her opinion within general legal guidelines. Discretion is often granted under a contract, trust, or will. Examples: 1) A judge may have discretion as to the amount of a fine or whether to grant a continuance of a trial. 2) A trustee or executor of an estate may have discretion to divide assets among the beneficiaries. 3) A district attorney may have discretion to charge a crime as a misdemeanor or felony. 4) A governor may have discretion to grant a pardon. 5) A planning commission may use its discretion when deciding whether or not to grant a variance to a zoning ordinance.

discretionary trust A common type of trust that grants the trustee broad power to decide when and how much income or property to distribute to a beneficiary.

discrimination To treat similarly situated people differently on the basis of a protected characteristic, such as race, gender, or disability.

dishonor To refuse to pay the face amount of a check or the amount due on a promissory note.

disinherit To deliberately prevent someone from inheriting something. This is usually done by a provision in a will stating that someone who would ordinarily inherit property—a close family member, for example—should not receive it. In most states, you cannot completely disinherit your spouse; a surviving spouse has the right to claim a portion (usually one-third to one-half) of the deceased spouse's estate. With a few exceptions, however, you can expressly disinherit children.

disinheritance The act by which one refuses to leave property to a would-be heir.

disinterested witness A witness who has no personal interest in the case.

disjunctive allegations Claims by someone who files a lawsuit that that one thing *or* another occurred, and in criminal case that the accused committed one crime or another. Such allegations are not allowed because the defendant is entitled to know what allegations to defend against.

dismiss 1) In a court setting, a judge may dismiss or throw out all or a portion of a plaintiff's lawsuit without further evidence or testimony upon being persuaded that the plaintiff has not and cannot prove the case. This judgment may be made before or at anytime during the trial. The judge may independently decide to dismiss or may do so in response to a motion by the defendant. Also, the plaintiff may voluntarily dismiss an action before or during trial if the case is settled, if it is not provable, or if trial strategy dictates getting rid of a weak claim. A defendant may also be dismissed from a lawsuit, meaning the suit is dropped against that party. 2) To discharge or let an employee go.

dismissal See: dismiss

dismissal without prejudice When a case is dismissed without prejudice, it leaves the plaintiff free to bring another suit based on the same grounds, for example if the defendant doesn't follow through on the terms of a settlement. (Compare: dismissal with prejudice)

dismissal with prejudice When a lawsuit is dismissed with prejudice, the court is saying that it has made a final determination on the merits of the case, and that the plaintiff is therefore forbidden from filing another lawsuit based on the same grounds. (Compare: dismissal without prejudice)

disorderly conduct Behavior that disturbs others, including minor criminal offenses such as public drunkenness, loitering, and breach of the peace.

disorderly house A place of illegal gambling or a house of prostitution.

disparate impact When a facially neutral policy disproportionately affects one group, this can be the basis of a discrimination lawsuit if the group affected is protected by discrimination laws (such as race, sex, or age). For example, an employer's policy requiring all employees have the ability to lift 50 pounds could disproportionately affect women. Unless the employer had a good reason for such a policy, it could be discriminatory, even though it doesn't explicitly exclude women.

disparate treatment When two individuals are treated different based on their status or membership in a protected class.

disposable income In bankruptcy, the difference between a debtor's current monthly income and allowable expenses. The law assumes the debtor could pay this amount into a Chapter 13 repayment plan each month. (See also: current monthly income)

disposing mind and memory See: sound mind and memory

disposition 1) The court's final determination of a lawsuit or criminal charge. 2) The act of transferring care, possession, or ownership to another, such as by deed or will.

dispossess To eject someone from real property, either legally or by self help.

dispute The assertion of conflicting claims or rights between parties involved in a legal proceeding, such as a lawsuit, mediation, or arbitration.

dispute resolution See: alternative dispute resolution

disregarding the corporate entity See: piercing the veil

dissent A stated disagreement with prevailing thought. Also, the opinion of a judge of a court of appeals, including the U.S. Supreme Court, that disagrees with the majority opinion.

dissenting opinion The opinion of a judge who does not agree with the majority opinion. (See also: dissent)

dissolution The process of dissolving (ending) a marriage or a business. (See also: divorce, dissolution of corporation)

dissolution of corporation Termination of a corporation with the Secretary of State or state corporations division by filing documents to withdraw the corporation as a business entity. Dissolution can either be started voluntarily, by resolution of the shareholders, or involuntarily, for not paying corporate taxes or some other action of the government.

dissolution of marriage Another term for a divorce, used in many states.

Kramer v. Kramer. (1979) This award winner focused on a heart-wrenching child custody battle. Academy Awards for Best Picture, plus Best Actor, Director, Supporting Actress, and Screenplay. Dustin Hoffman, Meryl Streep, Jane Alexander, Justin Henry.

---

distinctive trademark A standard of trademark protection. Trademarks and service marks are judged on a spectrum of distinctiveness. The most unusual (in the context of their use) are considered the most memorable. Distinctive marks typically consist of terms that are fanciful or coined (Maalox or Xerox), arbitrary (Penguin for books, Arrow for shirts), or suggestive (Accuride tires). Distinctive marks receive maximum judicial protection under state and federal laws. Trademarks that describe some aspect of the goods or services are not considered distinctive and cannot acquire federal registration absent proof that consumers associate the goods or services with the mark (known as secondary meaning). (See also: secondary meaning)

distinguish To differentiate the ruling in one case from another even though both may have similarities of fact.

distress The seizure of another's property in order to obtain payment for money owed.

distribute To give assets, usually from an estate or trust, to the people who are entitled to receive them under the terms of a will, trust document, state law, or beneficiary designation.

distributee Someone who receives something. Usually, the term refers to someone who inherits property from a deceased person (a distribution from the deceased person's estate) or receives distributions from a trust. Also called a beneficiary.

distribution Transferring at least some assets of an estate or trust to beneficiaries or paying out profits or assets of a corporation or other business to its owners.

distribution of profits The withdrawal of profits from a partnership or LLC by a partner or LLC member.

District Attorney (DA) A lawyer who is elected or chosen by local government officials to represent the state government in criminal cases brought in a designated county or judicial district. A DA's duties typically include reviewing police arrest reports, deciding whether to bring criminal charges against arrested people, and prosecuting criminal cases in court. The DA may also supervise other attorneys, called Deputy District Attorneys or Assistant District Attorneys. In some states, a District Attorney may be called a Prosecuting Attorney, County Attorney, or State's Attorney. In the federal system, the equivalent to the DA is a United States Attorney. The country has many U.S. Attorneys, each appointed by the president, who supervise regional offices staffed with prosecutors called Assistant United States Attorneys.

State's Attorney. (1931) John Barrymore stars as a flashy district attorney defending a mobster who was his childhood friend. With Helen Twelvetrees, William Boyd, Ralph Ince.

---

district court 1) in the federal court system, a trial court for federal cases in a court district, which is all or a portion of a state. Thus, if you file suit in federal court, your case will normally be heard in federal district court. 2) A local court in some states. States may also group their appellate courts into districts—for example, The First District Court of Appeal.

disturbance of the peace See: breach of the peace

disturbing the peace See: breach of the peace

diversion In a criminal case, an alternative procedure in which the case is handled outside of the court, instead as part of the normal criminal justice system. A defendant who agrees to be diverted will escape the criminal charges altogether if he successfully completes the rehabilitation program and stays out of trouble for a specified time. Only very minor offenses, typically drug possession cases, are eligible for diversion; and defendants must show that they are good candidates for rehabilitation before being diverted.

diversity jurisdiction The power of the federal courts to decide civil disputes between citizens of different states, provided the amount the plaintiff seeks in damages exceeds an amount set by Congress (currently $75,000). The so-called citizens may include companies incorporated or doing business in different states or a citizen of a foreign country. However, note that the federal courts traditionally refuse to exercise their diversity jurisdiction over cases involving domestic relations and probate.

diversity of citizenship A basis for taking a lawsuit to federal court, in which the opposing parties are citizens of different states (including corporations incorporated or doing business in different states) or one is a citizen of a foreign country. It's also required that the amount in controversy exceed a statutory amount.

Diversity Visa Program (the Lottery) Every year, the U.S. Department of State allows people from certain countries who have sent the fewest immigrants to the U.S. in recent years, and who meet specified educational and financial criteria, to enter a lottery program. The "winners," who are randomly selected, may then apply for a U.S. green card (permanent residence).

divestiture The disposition or sale of an asset by a company or government entity. It may be voluntary or ordered by a court.

divestment The disposal or reduction of an investment or business interest, for financial, legal, or ethical reasons.

dividend A portion of profits distributed by a corporation to its shareholders based on the type of stock and number of shares owned. Dividends are usually paid in cash, though they may also be paid in the form of additional shares of stock or other property. The amount of a dividend is established by the corporation's board of directors; however, state laws often restrict a corporation's ability to declare dividends by requiring a minimum level of profits or assets before the dividend can be approved.

divorce The legal termination of a marriage. All states require a spouse to identify a legal reason for requesting a divorce when that spouse files the divorce papers with the court. These reasons are referred to as grounds for a divorce. (See also: dissolution, no-fault divorce, fault divorce)

divorce agreement An agreement made by a divorcing couple regarding the division of property, custody and visitation of the children, child support, and alimony. The agreement must be put in writing, signed by the parties, and accepted by the court. (See also: marital settlement agreement)

DNA Deoxyribonucleic acid, a double chain of chromosomes in the nucleus of each living cell, whose combination determines each individual's hereditary characteristics. Because each person's DNA is different and is found in each living cell, testing the DNA of a person and comparing that to the DNA found on a drop of blood, hair, or other body substance, can be used to help identify the perpetrator of a criminal act. DNA tests performed on physical evidence years after a trial have repeatedly

proved that convicted people on death row did not commit the crimes for which they were sentenced.

docket See: court calendar

doctor-patient privilege See: physician-patient privilege

doctrine of equivalents A form of patent infringement that occurs when an invention performs substantially the same function in substantially the same manner and obtains the same result as a patented invention. As a result of a Supreme Court decision, the doctrine of equivalents must be applied on an element-by-element basis to the patent claims. (See also: patent claims)

document Usually, a paper with writing on it. Technically, a document could be any item with a message imprinted on it, such as a piece of wood on which someone scratched out a will.

documentary evidence A document—for example, a contract, deed, or will—that is offered as evidence at a trial or hearing. Before being admitted as evidence, it must be proved that the document is genuine. This is called "laying a foundation."

documentation The act of providing documents or supporting records or evidence. For example, any tangible proof that substantiates an item on a tax return, such as a canceled check for an expense claimed as a deduction.

dog-bite statute A state law that makes dog owners liable for injuries caused by their dogs, even if an owner didn't know that the dog was likely to cause that kind of injury. More than half the states now have such dog-bite statutes. (Compare: one-bite rule)

doing business Carrying on business activities, especially a company doing business in a foreign state. Whether an out-of-state company will be subject to another state's laws will depend on whether it does business within that state. (See also: long-arm statute)

doing business as (**DBA**) A situation in which a business owner operates a company under a name different from its legal name. The owner must file a fictitious name statement, dba statement, or an assumed name statement with the appropriate agency—for example, the county clerk or Secretary of State—that records the names of the business's owners. This enables consumers to discover the names of the business owner(s), which is important if a consumer needs to sue the business.

DOMA See: Defense of Marriage Act

domain name A combination of letters and numbers that identifies a specific computer or website on the Internet. A domain name usually consists of three parts: a generic "top-level" domain such as ".com" or ".gov" that identifies the type of organization; a second level domain such as nolo or yahoo, which identifies the organization, site, or individual; and a third level domain such as "www," which is used to identify a particular host server. Domain names have various functions. They can serve as an address (whitehouse.com), as a trademark (amazon.com), or as an expression of free speech (generalmotorssucks. com). Trademark owners can, under some circumstances, stop others from using a domain name if it conflicts with their existing trademark. (See also: uniform resource locator)

> "In respect of civil rights, common to all citizens, the Constitution of the United States does not, I think, permit any public authority to know the race of those entitled to be protected in the enjoyment of such rights."
>
> —Justice John M. Harlan, dissent in *Plessy v. Ferguson*

domestic partner adoption An adoption by one registered domestic partner, usually of a child born to the other partner, in one of the states that allows domestic partner registration (California, the District of Columbia, Maine, Oregon, and Washington).

domestic partners 1) Couples registered under domestic partnership laws in California, the District of Columbia, Maine, Oregon, and Washington State. In California, Maine, and Oregon, these couples have all the same rights and responsibilities as spouses under state law. 2) Unmarried couples of the same or opposite sex living together in committed relationships, who may be entitled to some of the same benefits as married partners under employer policies or city or county rules.

domestic relations The field of law that includes divorce, child custody, child support, and alimony.

domestic violence Behavior used by one person in a relationship to hurt or dominate the other. Domestic violence can include physical violence and sexual assault (which are crimes that can be prosecuted), intimidation, emotional abuse, and isolating the victim from others. Applies to partners whether they are married or unmarried, straight or gay, living together or simply dating.

domicile The state in which a person has or intends to maintain permanent residence, or the state in which a business locates its headquarters. Domicile governs such matters as the state in which a deceased person's estate is probated, where a party can begin divorce proceedings, and whether there

is "diversity of citizenship" between two parties that may give federal courts jurisdiction over a lawsuit. A person may have many residences but only one legal domicile.

dominant estate See: dominant tenement

dominant tenement Property that carries a right to use a portion of a neighboring property (called an easement). For example, property that benefits from a beach access trail across another property is the dominant tenement.

donation A gift of property. The IRS allows you to take an income tax deduction for the value of donations made to charitable organizations that are recognized as such by the IRS.

donative intent The conscious desire to make a gift, as distinguished from giving something as a gift by mistake or under pressure.

donee Someone who receives a gift.

donor Someone who gives a gift.

dooced Fired for what one writes in a personal blog. The term comes from the name of a website (www.dooce.com) kept by Heather Armstrong, who was fired after she wrote about annoying habits of her coworkers and managers and what she was actually doing when she was supposed to be working at home, among other things.

double-entry accounting A system of accounting that records each business transaction twice (once as a debit and once as a credit). For example, if you pay your monthly rent of $1,000, you you make a debit of $1,000 to the rent expense account and a credit of $1,000 to cash. Used for tracking inventory, loans, assets, and liabilities. (Compare: single-entry accounting)

double jeopardy A rule from the Fifth Amendment to the U.S. Constitution that prohibits a criminal defendant from being twice made to stand trial for the same offense. A defendant is put "in jeopardy" once the jury is sworn. If the prosecutor moves to dismiss the case after that, the defendant cannot be retried. When a judge dismisses a case, however, a retrial is generally possible unless the dismissal was engineered by the prosecutor's misconduct, or there was no overriding necessity to dismiss the case. Double jeopardy protects defendants only for retrials brought within the original jurisdiction, which is why a defendant can be tried in federal court after being tried in state court. Double jeopardy does not prevent trial in a civil court on underlying facts that previously formed the basis of a criminal trial.

double taxation 1) Taxation of corporate dividends twice: once to the corporation as corporate income and then once to the shareholders, if corporate profits are distributed as dividends. 2) Taxation of the same property for the same purpose twice in one year.

double wills See: mutual wills

doubling A married couple's right to double the amount of certain property exemptions when filing for bankruptcy together. For example, if a state allows doubling and provides an exemption for equity in a motor vehicle up to $4,000, a married couple filing for bankruptcy together could exempt up to $8,000 in equity.

dower See: dower and curtesy

dower and curtesy A surviving spouse's right to receive a set portion of the deceased spouse's estate—usually one-third to one-half. Dower (not to be confused with a "dowry") refers to the portion to which a surviving wife is entitled, while curtesy refers to what a man may claim. Until recently, these amounts differed in a number of states. However, because discrimination on the basis of sex is now illegal in most cases, most states have abolished dower and curtesy and generally provide the same benefits regardless of sex—and this amount is often known simply as the statutory share. Under certain circumstances, a living spouse may not be able to sell or convey property that is subject to the other spouse's dower and curtesy or statutory share rights.

down payment A lump sum cash payment paid by a buyer when he or she purchases a major piece of property, such as a car or house. The buyer typically takes out a loan for the balance remaining, and pays it off in monthly installments over time.

dowry The money and personal property a bride brings to her new husband to support and maintain the marriage. (Compare: dower)

After World War II many states waived the bar examination for servicemen who had been in their final year of law school or had graduated without taking the state examination when they went into the armed forces.

---

draft 1) A written order for the payment of money, such as a check. The person who writes the draft is called the drawer, the person who holds the money—for example, the bank—is called the drawee, and the person who ultimately receives the money is called the payee. After receiving the draft, the payee can demand payment at any time unless the draft specifies a particular time for payment. Also called a bill of exchange. 2) A preliminary version of a written document, such as a law or a legal brief, that is ready for revision or correction. 3) To select for some purpose, such as military service.

dram shop rule A law that makes a business that sells alcoholic drinks or a host who serves liquor to an obviously intoxicated person strictly liable to anyone injured by the drunken patron or guest.

draw 1) The withdrawal of profits from a partnership or LLC by a partner or LLC member. 2) To prepare any legal document. 3) To prepare and sign a bill of exchange or check.

drawee The party who is to be paid on a bill of exchange or check.

drawer The party who signs a bill of exchange directing that it be paid; for example, a person who signs a check.

Dredd Scott v. Sanford (**1857**) A U.S. Supreme Court case in which the Court ruled that a slave taken to a free state was still a slave. This decision helped to trigger the Civil War.

driving under the influence (**DUI**) The crime of operating a motor vehicle while under the influence of alcohol or drugs, including prescription drugs. State laws specify the level of blood alcohol content at which a person is presumed to be under the influence.

Also called driving while intoxicated (DWI and drunk driving).

driving while Black Slang for police profiling of drivers who deviate from the ethnic standards of a community—for example, regularly stopping African American drivers in a Caucasian neighborhood, or stopping Mexican American drivers near U.S. borders.

driving while intoxicated See: driving under the influence

driving while intoxicated (DWI) See: driving under the influence

drop dead date A provision in a contract or a court order that sets the last date that an event can take place (such as payment), or otherwise certain consequences will automatically follow, such as cancelling a contract, taking property, or entering a judgment.

drunk driving See: driving under the influence

due 1) Owed as of a specific date. 2) Immediately enforceable—for example, payment is due at time of service. 3) Proper, just, or reasonable—for example, due care.

due and owing See: due

due care See: reasonable care

due diligence Care or attention to a matter that is sufficient enough to avoid a claim of negligence, though not necessarily exhaustive.

due-on-sale clause A provision in a mortgage or deed of trust that allows the lender to demand immediate payment of the balance of the mortgage upon sale or transfer of ownership of the property used to secure the mortgage. (See also: acceleration clause)

due, owing, and unpaid See: due

due process of law A fundamental principle of fairness in all legal matters, both civil and criminal, especially in the courts. All legal procedures set by statute and court practice, including notice of rights, must be followed for each individual so that no prejudicial or unequal treatment will result. While somewhat indefinite, the term can be gauged by its aim to safeguard both private and public rights against unfairness.

DUI See: driving under the influence

dump-buyback A plan by which the owners of a failing business form a new legal entity which then purchases some or all of the assets of the first business for their liquidation value. This can be done informally with the consent of the failing business's creditors, who will use the proceeds to recoup a portion of the money owed to them, or it can be accomplished via a public auction or an assignment for benefit of creditors proceeding. Occasionally "dump-buyback" is also used to describe a business bankruptcy where the owners of the bankrupt business form a new business entity and submit a formal bid to purchase their former assets, usually for a fraction of what was originally owed.

durable power of attorney A power of attorney that remains in effect if the person who made the document—called the principal—becomes incapacitated. If a power of attorney is not specifically made durable, it automatically expires if the principal becomes incapacitated. (See also: durable power of attorney for finances, durable power of attorney for health care)

durable power of attorney for finances A legal document that gives someone authority to manage your financial affairs if you become incapacitated. The person you name to represent you is usually called your agent or attorney-in-fact.

durable power of attorney for health care A legal document that you can use to give someone permission to make medical decisions for you if you are unable to make those decisions yourself. The person you name to represent you may be called your agent, attorney-in-fact, health care proxy, patient advocate, or something similar, depending on where you live.

duress The use of force, false imprisonment, coercion, threats, or psychological pressure to compel someone to act contrary to his or her wishes or interests. If, for example, duress is used to make a person sign an agreement or execute a will, a court may find the document null and void. A defendant in a criminal prosecution may raise the defense that others used duress to force him or her to take part in a crime.

duty 1) A legal relationship, created by law or contract, in which a person or business owes something to another. The breach of this obligation can result in liability. 2) A tax on imported goods.

duty of care The duty of a person or business to act toward others and the public with vigilance, caution, and prudence. Someone whose actions breach the duty of care is considered negligent, and may be sued for resulting damages. (See also: standard of care)

DWI 1) Short for driving while intoxicated. 2) Abbreviation for dying without issue (children). (See also: driving under the influence)

dying declaration A statement by someone who believes he or she is about to die, relating to the cause or circumstances of that condition. A dying declaration is an exception to the hearsay rule under the Federal Rules of Evidence. In a trial for murder, for example, a witness may be allowed to testify that the victim said, "Frank shot me" while bleeding to death in the street.

dynamite charge A judge's admonition to a deadlocked jury to go back and try harder to reach a verdict. The judge might remind jurors to respectfully consider the opinions of others and will often assure them that if the case has to be tried again, another jury won't necessarily do a better job than they're doing. Because of its coercive nature, some states prohibit the use of a dynamite charge as a violation of the state constitution, but the practice passed federal constitutional muster in the case of *Allen v. Gainer.* The instruction is also known as a dynamite instruction, shotgun instruction, *Allen* charge, or third-degree instruction.

dynasty trust A trust designed to pass down family wealth for many generations while avoiding transfer taxes (estate tax and generation-skipping tax) to the greatest extent possible.

EA See: enrolled agent

earned income Compensation for services rendered, such as wages, commissions, and tips.

earned surplus See: retained earnings

earnest payment A partial payment (deposit) demonstrating commitment in a contractual relationship, and commonly made in real estate transactions. The remainder of the payment is due on a particular date or after a particular event has occurred. The seller keeps the earnest money if the buyer fails to make timely payment in full (or if there is a similar breach of the agreement).

earnings record The record of a person's earnings over his or her lifetime that is maintained by the Social Security Administration for purposes of calculating the amount of benefits to which one may be entitled—including retirement benefits, disability benefits, or dependents or survivors benefits. Ask the Social Security Administration for a copy of your Social Security Statement to make sure your earnings record is accurate.

earwitness Someone who heard something but didn't actually see it, and can so testify in court. (Compare: eyewitness)

easement A right to use another person's real estate for a specific purpose. The most common type of easement is the right to travel over another person's land, known as a right of way. In addition, property owners commonly grant easements for the placement of utility poles, utility trenches, water lines, or sewer lines. An easement may be for an identified path or for use at any reasonable place.

easement by prescription See: prescriptive easement.

eavesdropping Listening to conversations or observing conduct that is meant to be private. The term comes from the common law offense of listening to private conversations by crouching under the windows or eaves of a house. Generally, the term is used when the activity is not legally authorized by a search warrant or court order. (Compare: surveillance)

EEOC See: Equal Employment Opportunity Commission

effective assistance of counsel The right of a criminal defendant or appellant to have competent legal representation, whether the lawyer was appointed by the court or retained by the defendant. In general, competent legal representation is without errors that would result in the denial of a fair trial. This means that most attorney errors do not amount to ineffective assistance.

effective date The date at which a contract or statutory obligation commences. The effective date may be different than the date a contract is signed or a statute is enacted. For example, the effective date for the Copyright Act of 1976 is January 1, 1978.

effluxion of time The normal expiration of a lease due to the passage of time, rather than due to a specific event that might cause the lease to end, such as destruction of the building.

e.g. An abbreviation of the Latin words *exempli gratia*, meaning "for example." (Compare: i.e.)

***Egelhoff v. Egelhoff* (2001)** U.S. Supreme Court decision in which the Court ruled that a woman who was named as the beneficiary of her former husband's 401(k) plan was entitled to inherit the money in the plan, even though state

law said that the divorce had automatically revoked her right to inherit. Because a 401(k) plan is ruled by federal law (ERISA), it overruled the state law.

"In hearing cases I am like everyone else. The important thing, however, is to see to it that there are no cases."

—Confucius

eggshell skull A legal rule that a person who causes injury is at fault for all the consequences whether foreseen or not. It is derived from a situation in which a light blow to the head killed an individual, even though it could not have been predicted that such a blow would cause death.

egress An exit, or the act of exiting. The most famous use of this word was by P.T. Barnum, who put up a large sign in his circus tent saying "This Way to the Egress." Thinking an egress was some type of exotic bird, people eagerly went though the passage and found themselves outside the tent. (Compare: ingress)

EIR See: environmental impact report

ejectment A lawsuit brought to remove a party who is occupying real property. This is not the same as an unlawful detainer (eviction) suit, because it is against someone who has wrongfully tried to claim title to the property, not a tenant who only has a right of possession. Example: George lives on a ranch which he claims he has inherited from his great uncle, but Betty sues for ejectment on the basis that, in fact, she was entitled to the property through her parents.

ejusdem generis (**ee-joose**-dem **gen**-ris) Latin for "of the same kind." Used to interpret statutes when a law lists classes of persons or things. For example, if a law refers to automobiles, trucks, tractors, motorcycles, and other motor-powered vehicles, a court might use *ejusdem generis* to hold that such vehicles would not include airplanes, because the list included only land-based transportation.

elder law An area of law that addresses the legal needs of elderly people, including retirement benefits, estate planning, health care, and other issues.

electioneering Campaigning near a polling place. Electioneering is prohibited within a certain distance from a polling place, typically 100 feet.

election of remedies An outmoded requirement that if a party files a claim based on two inconsistent legal theories, the party must choose one theory to pursue, usually just before the trial begins. Because it's unfair to force the party to choose before all of the evidence is presented, courts now generally won't require the party to make a choice.

election under the will See: taking against the will

elective share The portion of a deceased person's estate that the surviving spouse is entitled to claim under state law. In many states, the elective share (also called the statutory share) is about one-third of the deceased spouse's property. In some states, however, the amount the surviving spouse can claim depends on whether or not the couple has young children and, in a few states, on how long the couple was married. In most states, if the deceased spouse left a will, the surviving spouse must choose either what the will provides or the elective share. (See also: dower and curtesy)

Electronic Funds Transfer Act A federal law that gives consumers the right to correct errors in ATM or bank statements relating to electronic funds transfers (such as ATM use, point-of-sale purchases, and preauthorized withdrawals from a bank account) and limits a consumer's liability for losses in the event of a stolen or lost ATM card.

electronic signature A paperless method of entering into an electronic contract. Under the Electronic Signatures Act, enacted in 2000, electronic contracts (with a few exceptions) are as enforceable as those executed on paper. The law does not specify an approved method of signing electronic agreements and various methods have been improvised including clicking an "I Accept" button, typing "Yes," typing in a name, or using a "key" to encrypt (scramble) information that uniquely identifies the signer.

electronic surveillance An advanced form of eavesdropping. Electronic surveillance employs sophisticated electronic equipment to intercept private conversations or observe conduct that is meant to be private. It includes the use of small radio transmitters or "bugs" to listen in on telephone or in-person conversations, the use of lasers to intercept conversations inside a room from the slight vibrations of the window glass, and the use of thermal imaging scopes for observing conduct inside a structure. Many of these sophisticated forms of surveillance require a search warrant because they violate a person's reasonable expectation of privacy. This area of law is in a constant state of flux as courts interpret the use of new technologies.

eleemosynary (eh-luh-**moss**-uh-nary) Charitable, as applied to a purpose or institution.

element 1) An essential requirement necessary to make a claim or defense in court. For example, one element of assault is the intention to cause apprehension of harmful or offensive contact. If there is no evidence that the defendant intended to cause apprehension, there is no assault. 2) An essential requirement of a General Plan (a government's long-range land-use policy).

elements (of a case) The component parts of a legal claim or cause of action. To win a lawsuit, a plaintiff must prove every element of a legal claim. For example, here are the elements of a breach of contract claim: There was a valid contract. The plaintiff performed as specified by the contract. The defendant failed to perform as specified by the contract. The plaintiff suffered an economic loss as a result of the defendant's breach of contract.

elements (of a crime) The component parts of crimes. For example, "robbery" is defined as the taking and carrying away of property of another by force or fear with the intent to permanently deprive the owner of the property. Each of those four parts is an element that the prosecution must prove beyond a reasonable doubt.

emancipated minor A minor who has been released from the custody and control of his or her parents.

emancipation 1) The act of setting free or liberating from a restraint or bondage (as in slavery). 2) To release a minor child from the care and control of the minor's parents. Rules for emancipation vary from state to state.

embassy U.S. embassies represent the U.S. government in other countries, and are where the U.S. ambassador works. The United States has embassies located in many countries around the world, usually in their capital city. The U.S. may also operate smaller versions of the embassy called "consulates" in other cities within the same country, presided over by a U.S. consul. Most U.S. embassies and consulates accept and process applications for both non-immigrant and immigrant visas.

The Paradine Case. (1948) An Alfred Hitchcock mystery with Gregory Peck as a lawyer defending a beautiful woman (Alida Valli) on a charge that she murdered her wealthy husband. With Ann Todd, Charles Laughton, Charles Coburn, Ethel Barrymore.

embezzlement The crime of stealing the funds or property of an employer, company, or government or misappropriating money or assets held in trust.

embezzler A person who commits the crime of embezzlement by fraudulently taking funds or property of an employer or trust.

emblements Annual crops to which a tenant who cultivated the land is entitled. If the tenant dies before harvest, the right to harvest the crops will pass to his or her heirs.

emergency A sudden, unforeseen happening requiring action to protect lives or property.

emergency doctrine A doctrine that excuses a person from having to act with reasonable care if that person acted with a sudden and urgent need for aid in an emergency.

emergency protective order Any court-issued order intended to protect a person from harm or harassment. An emergency protective order is issued by the police, when court is out of session, to prevent domestic violence. Most emergency protective orders are stopgap measures that last only for a weekend or holiday, after which the abused person is expected to seek a temporary restraining order (TRO) from a court.

eminent domain The power of the federal or state government to take private property for a public purpose, even if the property owner objects. The Fifth Amendment to the United States Constitution allows the government to take private property if the taking is for a public use and the owner is "justly compensated" (usually, paid fair market value) for his or her loss. A public use is virtually anything that is sanctioned by a federal or state legislative body, but such uses may include roads, parks, reservoirs, schools, hospitals, or other public buildings. Sometimes called condemnation, taking, or expropriation.

emolument Payment, profit, or gain as a result of employment or holding an office.

emotional distress Suffering in response to an experience caused by the negligence or intentional acts of another; a basis for a claim of damages in a lawsuit brought for such an injury. Originally damages for emotional distress were awardable only in conjunction with damages for actual physical harm, but recently some courts have recognized a right to an award of money damages for emotional distress without physical injury or contact. In sexual harassment and defamation claims, emotional distress can sometimes be the only harmful result. Professional testimony by a therapist or psychiatrist may be required to validate the existence and depth of the distress and place a dollar value upon it.

employee A person who is hired to work for another person or business (the employer) for compensation and is subject to the employer's direction as to the details of how to perform the job. Employees are subject to payroll tax code rules. (Compare: independent contractor)

Employee Retirement Income Security Act (ERISA) A federal law that sets minimum standards for pension plans and health benefit plans, to protect the employees covered by these plans. ERISA requires plans to provide certain information to plan participants, imposes responsibilities on those who manage and control the plans, and requires plans to establish procedures for participants to get benefits from their plans, including an appeals process.

employer The person or entity that hires someone (an employee) to do work for compensation and has the right to control how the employee does the job.

employer identification number (EIN) A number assigned to a business by the IRS after the business submits an application that is used for tracking payments made to employees and taxes paid by the business.

employment 1) The hiring of a person for compensation, in which the employer has the right to control how the employee does the job. 2) The job for which an employee is hired.

Employment Authorization Document (EAD) More commonly called a work permit, this is a photo identification card that certain nonimmigrants (foreign-born persons with a temporary right to be in the United States) may apply for in order to show employers evidence of their right or approval to work.

employment taxes See: payroll taxes

enabling clause A provision in a new law that empowers a particular public official—such as governor or state treasurer—to put it into effect, including making expenditures.

en banc French for "on the bench," used to indicate that all of the judges on an appeals court panel are participating in a case. Courts generally hear cases *en banc* when a significant issue is at stake or at the request of the parties.

enclosure (inclosure) The act of creating a boundary around land that limits access to it, for example by a fence, wall, hedge, ditch, or other physical barrier.

encroach To build a structure in whole or in part on another's real property. This may occur due to incorrect surveys, guesses or miscalculations by builders and or owners when erecting a building, or by deliberate choice. The solutions vary from giving the encroaching party an easement or lease (for a price, usually), or if the structure is small, actually moving it onto the owner's property.

encroachment The building of a structure entirely or partly on a neighbor's property. Encroachment may occur due to faulty surveying or by the builder's deliberate decision. Solutions range from paying the rightful property owner for the use of the property to the court-ordered removal of the structure.

encumber To place a lien, mortgage, or other encumbrance on real estate.

encumbrance Any claim or lien on real estate. Examples include mortgages, deeds of trust, tax liens, mechanic's liens, easements, and water or timber rights. Documents showing encumbrances are usually recorded in the local land records office (commonly called the county recorder or registry of deeds). Also called incumbrance.

endorsement (indorsement) The placing of a signature on the back of a check, bill of exchange, or other negotiable instrument so as to make it cashable or transferable.

endowment Money or property given to an institution for a specific purpose. Most often, an endowment is a gift of money and the principal isn't spent—instead, the income from the principal is used for the benefit of the institution or its members.

endowment insurance Provides that an insured person who lives for the specified endowment period receives the face value of the insurance policy—that is, the amount paid at death. If the policyholder dies sooner, the beneficiary named in the policy receives the proceeds.

Engel v. Vitale **(1962)** A U.S. Supreme Court case based on the doctrine of separation of church and state, in which, organized prayer in public schools was declared unconstitutional.

English-only rule A workplace requirement that prohibits employees from speaking any language other than English. An English-only rule is valid only if it is justified by business necessity and limited in scope to serve those business needs. For example, if an employer adopted an English-only policy for workers on a factory line for safety purposes, that would be justified by business necessity. If the same employer prohibited employees from speaking any other language while eating lunch or smoking in the company parking lot, that would probably be too broad.

enjoin A court order that someone do a specific act, cease a course of conduct, or be prohibited from committing a certain act. To obtain such an order, called an injunction, a private party or public agency has to convince a judge that speedy action is needed in order to prevent irreparable harm or injury. The court will hold a hearing to consider evidence from both sides. If the court grants the writ, the injunction can be preliminary (the court will consider more evidence later, at trial) or permanent (but despite its name, a permanent injunction might not last forever).

"In colonial America Esq. seems to have been confined to justices of the peace, who acquired thereby the informal title of Squire, but inasmuch as every lawyer of any dignity became a justice almost automatically, it was eventually applied to most members of the bar."

—H.L. Mencken

---

enjoyment 1) To exercise a right. 2) The use of funds or occupancy of property. (See also: quiet enjoyment)

enrolled agent **(EA)** A type of tax professional who is permitted to practice before the IRS and can represent taxpayers in audits, collections, and appeals.

enter a judgment To officially record a judgment on the "judgment roll" after the judge has approved and signed it. This task is the responsibility of the court clerk.

entity An organization, institution, or being that has its own existence for legal or tax purposes. An entity is often an organization with an existence separate from its individual members—for example, a corporation, partnership, trust, estate, or government agency. The entity is treated like a person; it can function legally, be sued, and make decisions through agents.

entrapment An act by the police or their agents, such as informants, to induce a person to commit a crime for the purpose of prosecuting that person for that induced crime. If the judge or jury believes that the person was predisposed to commit the crime anyway, even when the government agent suggested the crime or even helped with its commission, they are unlikely to accept an entrapment defense. Entrapment defenses are difficult to mount for defendants with prior convictions.

entry A transaction recorded in the bookkeeping records of a business.

entry of judgment Placement of a judgment on the official roll of judgments.

environmental impact report (EIR) A detailed, written analysis of all the effects that a land development or construction project would have on the local environment, such as on the air quality, noise levels, population, traffic patterns, fire danger, endangered species, archeological artifacts, and community beauty. Many states require submission of such reports to local governments, with a process for public comment, before a development or project can be approved.

environmental law A body of state, federal, and international statutes and court decisions intended to protect the environment (natural resources, wildlife, landscape, and amenities) from pollution, misuse, overuse, and other damage. Environmental laws both regulate activities and give individuals and groups the right to bring legal actions to enforce its protections or remedy environmental harms.

Equal Employment Opportunity Commission (EEOC) The federal agency responsible for interpreting and enforcing laws that prohibit employment discrimination, such as Title VII of the Civil Rights Act of 1964, the Age Discrimination in Employment Act, and the Americans with Disabilities Act.

equal-opportunity employer An employer that does not discriminate on the basis of race, color, national origin, gender, religion, age, or disability. Employers typically claim to be equal-opportunity employers in job advertisements or postings (sometimes using the abbreviation EOE) to make themselves more attractive to job candidates.

Equal Pay Act A federal law that prohibits sex-based wage discrimination between men and women in the same establishment who are performing under similar working conditions.

equal protection The right, guaranteed by the Fourteenth Amendment to the U.S. Constitution, to be treated the same, legally, as others in the same situation. If a law discriminates between one group of people and another, the government must have a rational basis for doing so. A law that discriminates on the basis of a suspect classification—that is, it makes a distinction based on race, gender, or another trait that has historically resulted in discriminatory treatment—is constitutional only if there is a very compelling reason for the distinction.

equitable Fair; based on principles of justice. (See also: equitable relief)

equitable distribution A legal principle followed by most states, under which assets and earnings acquired during marriage are divided equitably (fairly) at divorce. Some states start with the presumption that equitable means

equal, but the court is not required to divide assets equally. In some states, a spouse who is guilty of "fault" actions like adultery may receive less than an equal share, and other factors may contribute to an unequal distribution that is still considered equitable and fair. (Compare: community property)

equitable estoppel See: estoppel

equitable lien A lien on property, imposed by a court to achieve a fair result. For example, if someone has embezzled money from a business, the business might sue an ask the court for an equitable lien on the embezzler's property. (See also: constructive trust)

equitable ownership See: beneficial ownership

equitable relief When a court awards a nonmonetary judgment, such as an order to do something (mandamus or specific performance) or refrain from doing something (injunction), when monetary damages are not sufficient to repair the injury.

equity 1) The net value of real estate, determined by subtracting the amount of unpaid debts secured by the property from its market value. 2) A set of legal principles that operates in addition to statutes and common law and is intended to give judges flexibility to achieve a just result. If traditional legal remedies (which usually involve compensation with money) wouldn't be fair in a particular case, a judge can use an equitable remedy. A court might issue an order (injunction) directing someone to do something or stop doing something. For example, if someone has built a garage that extends over the neighbor's property, a court might order the garage owner to tear it down. By contrast, the legal remedy would be for the owner to compensate the neighbor for the loss in property value. The rules of equity arose in England when the strict limitations of common law would not solve all problems, so the crown set up courts of chancery (equity) to provide remedies through the royal power. Most eastern states had courts of equity or chancery separate from courts of law, but now most states combine law and equity.

"Now, as always, the conflict over technicalities, mostly procedural, between judge and lawyers, takes more time than is occupied by the actual evidence."

—Harold J. Laski

equity of redemption In foreclosure, the homeowner's right, for a certain period of time, to redeem the mortgage and keep the house by refinancing and paying off the original mortgage. State statutes usually spell out the terms under which redemption is available. (See also: redemption)

equivalent Equal in value, force, or meaning.

ergo Latin for therefore.

ERISA See: Employee Retirement Income Security Act

erroneous See: clearly erroneous

error 1) A legal mistake. 2) A mistake of law or fact by a judge or court.

errors and omissions Shorthand for malpractice insurance, which gives physicians, attorneys, architects, accountants, and other professionals coverage for claims by patients and clients for alleged professional errors and omissions that amount to negligence.

escalator clause Provision in a lease or other agreement which provides for an increase (in rent, installment payments, alimony, or some other financial payment) when the cost of living index (or a similar gauge) goes up. Often there is a maximum amount or cap on the increase.

escape clause A provision in a contract that allows one of the parties to be excused from an obligation if a certain event occurs.

escheat The forfeit of all property to the state when a person dies without heirs, descendants, or named beneficiaries. (Compare: intestate)

escrow The holding of funds or documents by a neutral third party prior to closing a sale. For example, buyers and sellers of real estate commonly hire an escrow agent to facilitate the transfer. Business sales also sometimes involve escrow arrangements.

escrow agent A person (often an attorney) or a company that handles escrow arrangements. Also sometimes called a title agent.

escrow instructions Written instructions, signed by a buyer and seller, telling an escrow agent what needs to happen before the deal (usually a real estate sale) closes.

espionage The act of spying on or monitoring the activities of a government or company in order to gather secret information.

espousal 1) A promise between two people that they will marry each other. 2) Taking up an idea or cause.

esquire A form of address showing that someone is an attorney, usually written Albert Pettifog, Esquire, or simply Esq.

essential job functions The fundamental duties of a position—those things that the person holding the job absolutely must be able to do. An employee with a disability must be able to perform the essential job functions, with or without a reasonable accommodation, to be protected by the Americans with Disabilities Act.

estate Generally, all the property a person owns at death.

estate by entirety See: tenancy by the entirety

estate planning The art of continuing to prosper when you're alive, and passing your property to your loved ones with a minimum of fuss and expense after you die. Planning your estate may involve making gifts, buying insurance, and creating a will, living trust, health care directives, durable power of attorney for finances, or other documents.

estate tax A tax imposed by the federal government, and by some states, on property transferred at someone's death. All property, however owned and whether or not it goes through probate court before being given to inheritors, is subject to estate tax. In practice, however, very few estates—fewer than 1%—actually owe federal estate tax. That's because the first $3.5 million of property is exempt from the tax, and you can leave an unlimited amount tax-free to a surviving spouse or charity. The federal estate tax is scheduled to be repealed entirely in 2010 and then come back with a $1 million exemption in 2011, but it's more likely that Congress will make the $3.5 million exemption permanent before 2010. (Compare: inheritance tax)

estate tax threshold The dollar amount of an estate at which estate tax might be due. For example, if you die in a year where the federal estate tax exception is $3.5 million, then your estate may owe estate taxes if your estate is larger $3.5 million at that time.

estimated taxes Quarterly tax payments made by self-employed individuals to the IRS and state tax agencies for their anticipated income tax liability for the year, in lieu of withholding from a paycheck. Estimated tax payments are used to pay both income and self-employment taxes.

estop To halt, bar, or prevent. (See also: estoppel)

estoppel A legal principle that prevents a person from asserting or denying something in court that contradicts what has already been established as the truth. (See also: equitable estoppel, promissory estoppel, collateral estoppel, estoppel by deed, estoppel in pais)

estoppel by deed A legal principle that prevents a person from asserting or denying the truth of anything that

he or she stated in a deed, especially regarding who has valid ownership of property.

estoppel by silence A type of estoppel that prevents someone from asserting something when that person had both the duty and the opportunity to speak up earlier, and his or her silence put another person at a disadvantage.

estoppel in pais See: equitable estoppel

et al. (et **ahl**) Abbreviation for the Latin phrase "et alia," meaning "and others." This is commonly used in shortening the name of a court case, so that instead of listing all the plaintiffs or defendants, one of them will be listed followed by the term "et al."

ethical will A document or materials in which a person expresses the beliefs and experiences that have mattered most in his or her life. An ethical will has no legal significance; it is intended to convey the maker's core values to loved ones.

et seq. (et **sek**) Abbreviation for the Latin phrase "et sequentes," meaning "and the following." It is commonly used by lawyers to include numbered lists, pages, or sections after the first number is stated, as in "the rules of the road are found in Vehicle Code Section 1204, et seq."

et ux. See: et uxor

et uxor (et-**ux**-or) Latin for "and wife." Often appears in its abbreviated form, et ux. In older deeds and documents, the phrase was used to indicate that a property was owned by a couple, consisting of a named man and his unidentified wife (for example, John Smith et ux.). In the present day, both parties are usually identified by name.

euthanasia Bringing about the death of a person who is terminally ill and, usually, suffering. Sometimes called mercy killing.

evaluation agreement A contract in which one party promises to submit an idea and the other party promises to evaluate it. After the evaluation, the evaluator will either enter into an agreement to exploit the idea or promise not to use or disclose the idea.

evasion of tax The intentional attempt to avoid paying taxes through fraudulent means, as distinguished from errors, late payment, or using legal "loopholes."

eviction Removal of a tenant from rental property by a law enforcement officer. First, the landlord must file and win an eviction lawsuit, also known as an "unlawful detainer."

evidence The many types of information presented to a judge or jury designed to convince them of the truth or falsity of key facts. Evidence typically includes testimony of witnesses, documents, photographs, items of damaged property, government records, videos, and laboratory reports. Strict rules limit what can be properly admitted as evidence, but dozens of exceptions often mean that creative lawyers find a way to introduce such testimony or other items into evidence. (See also: admissible evidence, inadmissible evidence)

evidentiary 1) Constituting evidence or having the quality of evidence. For example, someone's statement at the scene of a car wreck that one of the drivers was speeding has evidentiary value because it says something about how the accident happened. 2) Something that relates to the evidence in a particular case. For example, if a judge holds a hearing to decide whether or not a particular piece of evidence can be admitted at trial, that hearing might be called an evidentiary hearing.

examination 1) The questioning of a witness by an attorney (or other party if the other party is self-represented). Direct examination is interrogation by the attorney who called the witness, and cross-examination is questioning by the opposing attorney. 2) In bankruptcy, the questions asked of a debtor by the judge, trustee in bankruptcy, attorneys, or creditors, to determine the state of the debtor's affairs. 3) In criminal law, a preliminary examination is a hearing to determine whether a defendant charged with a felony should be held for trial.

examination report The report issued by an IRS auditor after an audit is concluded with its findings.

exception 1) A flowery way a lawyer might tell a judge that the lawyer disagrees with the judge's ruling, often said after the judge rules against a lawyer who has objected to the admission of evidence. In modern practice, it is not necessary "to take exception" to a judge's adverse ruling, because it is assumed that the attorney against whom the ruling is made objects. 2) In contracts, statutes, and deeds, a statement that something is not included, as in "Landlord rents to Tenant the first floor, with the exception of the storage room."

exception in deed A statement in a deed transferring real estate, reserving certain rights—for example, mineral rights or a life estate—to the transferor.

excessive bail An amount of bail that's more than necessary or usual to assure that the defendant will appear for subsequent court appearances. A defendant can claim excessive bail and make a motion to have it reduced.

exchange 1) To trade or barter property, goods, or services for other property, goods, or services. 2) The act of making

a trade or barter. 3) Short for "Starker" exchange, an exchange of investment real estate to defer capital gains tax.

excise A federal or state tax imposed on the manufacture, sale, or use of goods or on an occupation or activity (such as a business license). Sometimes called an excise tax.

excited utterance An exception to the hearsay rule that finds an out-of-court statement to be inherently reliable if it is made about a startling event while the person making the statement is experiencing that event.

exclusionary rule A rule of evidence that disallows the use of illegally obtained evidence in criminal trials. For example, the exclusionary rule would prevent a prosecutor from introducing at trial evidence seized during an illegal search.

exclusive license A written contract in which the owner of a patent, copyright, trademark, or trade secret authorizes, for a limited time, someone (the licensee) to exclusively exercise one or more of the rights. For example, the copyright owner of a comic book may exclusively license the video game rights to a game company. Once a license terminates, the owner regains the rights. (Compare: assignment)

exculpatory A description of evidence in a criminal trial that serves to justify, excuse, or introduce a reasonable doubt about the defendant's alleged actions or intentions. Exculpatory evidence may ultimately show that the defendant is not guilty. No wonder police and prosecutors must, to uphold the defendant's constitutional right to due process, tell the defense about any exculpatory evidence they've discovered.

exculpatory clause A provision in a lease that absolves the landlord in advance from responsibility for all damages, injuries, or losses occurring on the property, including those caused by the landlord's actions. Most states have laws that void exculpatory clauses in rental agreements, which means that a court will not enforce them.

exculpatory evidence Evidence that points toward a defendant's innocence. Prosecutors are required to automatically hand over such evidence to the defense, even if the defense doesn't request it, and a showing that this rule was violated can sometimes result in a conviction being reversed.

excusable neglect A legitimate excuse for the failure of a party or his or her lawyer to take required action on time (like filing an answer to a complaint). This is usually claimed to set aside a default judgment for failure to answer or otherwise respond

within the required time period. Illness, press of business by the lawyer (but not necessarily the defendant), or an understandable oversight by the lawyer's staff ("just blame the secretary") are common excuses which the courts will often accept.

"A government of laws and not of men"
—Constitution of the Commonwealth of Massachusetts, written by John Adams

---

ex delicto (ex dee-**lick**-toe) Latin phrase referring to something that arises out of a fault or wrong (tort), but not out of a contract.

execute 1) To finish, carry out, or perform as required, as in fulfilling one's obligations under a contract, plan, or court order. 2) To complete and otherwise make valid a document, such as a will, deed, or contract, for example by signing it and having it notarized. 3) To put someone to death pursuant to a court-rendered sentence (capital punishment). 4) To murder or assassinate.

executed remainder See: vested remainder

execution The act of executing a task or carrying out a murder or death sentence. (See also: execute)

executive clemency The power of a president or governor to pardon a person convicted of a crime or commute (shorten) the sentence to be served.

executive order A declaration by the president or a governor which has the force of law, usually based on existing statutory powers, and requiring no action by the Congress or state legislature.

executive privilege The privilege that allows the president and other high officials of the executive branch to keep certain communications private if disclosing those communications would disrupt the functions or decision-making processes of the executive branch. As demonstrated by the Watergate hearings, this privilege does not extend to information germane to a criminal investigation.

executor The person named in a will to handle the property of someone who has died. The executor collects the property, pays debts and taxes, and then distributes what's left, as specified in the will. The executor also handles any probate court proceedings and notifies people and organizations of the death. Also called personal representative. (Compare: administrator)

executory Not yet performed or done. For example, an executory contract is one in which all or part of the required performance has not been done, and an executory bequest is a gift in a will

that has not yet been distributed to the beneficiary.

executory interest An interest in property (particularly real estate) that will pass to another only if certain events occur.

executory remainder See: contingent remainder

executrix An old-fashioned term for a female executor—the person named in a will to handle the distribution of the deceased person's property. Now, whether male or female, this person is called the executor or personal representative.

exemplary damages Damages awarded over and above special and general damages to punish a losing party's willful or malicious misconduct. Sometimes called punitive damages.

exempt employee An employee who is not entitled to extra pay for overtime hours worked under the Fair Labor Standards Act (FLSA).

exemption 1) In tax law, an amount taxpayers are allowed to deduct from their taxable income based on a circumstance or their status. Each year, taxpayers get an exemption for themselves, each dependent, blindness or other disability, and for being over age 65. 2) In debt and bankruptcy, protection for certain types and amounts of assets from being taken by creditors or by the trustee in bankruptcy court to pay off debts. (See also: homestead exemption)

exemption trust A bypass trust funded with an amount no larger than the personal federal estate tax exemption for the year of death. If the trust grantor leaves property worth more than that amount, it usually goes to the surviving spouse. The trust property passes free from estate tax because of the personal exemption, and the rest is shielded from tax under the surviving spouse's marital deduction.

exempt property Property that may not be seized by creditors and does not have to be forfeited in Chapter 7 bankruptcy. Each state has its own list of exempt property; in some states, debtors may choose between the state's list and a federal list. Typically, states exempt clothing, household furnishings, tools of the debtor's trade, personal belongings, and other basic possessions. Many states also exempt a certain amount of the debtor's equity in a home and a vehicle.

exhaustion A principle in patent law that a patent owner cannot later sue a customer who purchased an authorized copy of a patented product. In other words, the patent owner's rights are exhausted after the sale.

exhibit 1) A document or object (including a photograph) introduced as evidence during a trial. 2) a copy of a paper attached to a pleading (any legal paper filed in a lawsuit), declaration, affidavit, or other document, which is referred to and incorporated into the main document.

ex officio (ex oh-**fish**-ee-oh) Latin for "from the office." Used when someone holds one position because of the authority he or she has from another position (such as being on a committee simply because one is president of the corporation).

ex parte Latin meaning "for one party," referring to motions, hearings, or orders granted on the request of and for the benefit of one party only. This is an exception to the basic rule of court procedure that both parties must be present at any argument before a judge, and to the otherwise strict rule that an attorney may not notify a judge without previously notifying the opposition. Ex parte matters are usually temporary orders (like a restraining order or temporary custody) pending a formal hearing, or an emergency request for a continuance.

expectancy The possibility of future enjoyment of something one counts on receiving, usually referring to real property or the estate of a deceased person, such as a remainder, reversion, or distribution after the death of someone who has use for life.

expense In business accounting and business taxation, any current cost of operation, such as rent, utilities, and payroll, as distinguished from a capital expenditure for long-term property and equipment.

The so-called Field Codes, used as the model for basic laws in California and several other western states, were written by attorney David Dudley Field for New York, but were never fully adopted by that state. However, his brother, Stephen Field, came to California in the Gold Rush, became a member of the California state legislature and had the codes adopted there. Soon they were copied by several other states. Stephen Field was later appointed to the U.S. Supreme Court. Other Field brothers were Cyrus, who laid the Atlantic Cable, and Henry, a noted writer and theologian.

expenses of administration The costs of wrapping up a deceased person's estate and distributing property. They may include attorney fees, appraisal, costs, and probate court fees.

expert testimony An opinion stated during a trial or deposition (testimony under oath before trial) by an expert witness on a subject relevant to a lawsuit or a criminal case.

expert witness A person who is a specialist in a subject who is asked present his or her expert opinion in a trial or deposition without having been a witness to any occurrence relating to the lawsuit or criminal case. Expert witnesses are paid for their services.

ex post facto Latin for "after the fact." Refers to laws adopted after an act is committed, making it illegal retroactively. Or, it can refer to laws that increase the penalty for a crime after it is committed. Such laws are specifically prohibited by the U.S. Constitution, Article I, Section 9.

express Directly and unambiguously stated or communicated, particularly in a contract.

express contract A contract in which all of the essential terms are explicitly stated. (Compare: implied contract)

express notice See: actual notice

express warranty 1) In consumer or commercial transactions, a guarantee about the quality of goods or services made by a seller, such as, "This item is guaranteed against defects in construction for one year." Most express warranties come directly from the manufacturer or are included in the sales contract. 2) An assurance or promise made by a contracting party.

expropriation Taking of property or rights by governmental authority, most commonly by eminent domain.

expunge To intentionally destroy, obliterate, or strike out records or information in files, computers, and other depositories. For example, state law may allow the criminal records of a juvenile offender to be expunged when he reaches the age of majority, to allow him to begin his adult life with a clean record. Or, a company or government agency may routinely expunge out-of-date records to save storage space.

ex rel. Abbreviation for Latin ex relatione, meaning "upon being related" or, more loosely, "on behalf of." The phrase is typically used in the title of a legal proceeding filed by the government, to indicate the name of an interested private party who pushed for the instigation of the suit. For example, a case caption might read: *The State of Tennessee ex rel. Archie Johnson v. Hardy Products.* Such suits usually happen when the private party's interests happen to coincide with those of the government or the public.

extended warranty contracts Warranty coverage on an item that kicks in after the warranty coverage provided by the manufacturer or seller expires.

Many consumers are encouraged to buy extended warranties (also called service contracts) when they buy cars or appliances. In the case of appliances and electronic equipment, extended warranties are all profit for the seller and not much benefit to the buyer because only a small percentage of these goods ever break down during an extended warranty period. An extended warranty may make sense, however, if you are buying a brand new model in the first few months after it has been manufactured.

extension The granting of a specific amount of extra time to make a payment, file a legal document after the date due, or continue a lease after the original expiration of the term.

extenuating circumstances Surrounding or mitigating factors that reduce a party's level of responsibility or guilt, whether in a civil or criminal trial. Successfully showing extenuating circumstances might result in a lower damage award, a more lenient punishment, or a lesser charge.

extinguishment The cancellation or destruction of a right or interest, quite often because the time for enforcement has passed.

extortion The crime of obtaining money or property by threat to a victim's property or loved ones, intimidation, or false claim of a right (such as pretending to be an IRS agent). A direct threat to harm the victim is usually treated as the crime of robbery, however. Extortion is a felony in all states. Blackmail is a form of extortion in which the threat is to expose embarrassing and damaging information to family, friends, or the public.

extradite To surrender someone who has been charged with a crime to another state or country, or to obtain the surrender of someone from another jurisdiction.

extradition When a state or country surrenders a person charged with a crime to the state or country that made the charge (literally, sends the person back). The rules and procedures for extradition are governed by international treaties, the U.S. Constitution, and U.S. federal and state laws. Occasionally a leader will refuse to extradite a person if satisfied that the prosecution is not warranted.

extrajudicial Actions outside the judicial (court) system, such as an extralegal confession, which, if brought in as evidence, may be recognized by the judge during a trial.

extraordinary compensation See: extraordinary fees

extraordinary fees Attorneys fees claimed in the administration of a dead person's estate for work beyond normal estate administration, including filing collection suits, preparing tax returns, or requiring unusual effort beneficial to the estate. This claim is in addition to the usual statutory or court-approved legal fees. An attorney claiming extraordinary fees must submit proof of time, effort, and benefit to justify the claim, and the final determination is at the judge's discretion.

 "Laws grind the poor, and rich men rule the law."

—Oliver Goldsmith

extreme cruelty A ground for divorce based on the infliction of physical or mental harm on one spouse by the other. Although all states now have "no-fault divorce," some states still recognize fault as a ground for divorce, and in other states evidence of cruelty may result in division of property that favoring who was the victim of extreme cruelty.

extrinsic evidence Evidence relating to a contract but not contained in the written document, such as circumstances surrounding the agreement or statements made by the parties. This evidence may be admitted if the document's meaning is ambiguous. (See also: parol evidence rule)

extrinsic fraud Fraudulent acts which keep a person from obtaining information about his or her rights to enforce a contract or getting evidence to defend against a lawsuit. This could include destroying evidence or misleading an ignorant person about the right to sue.

eyewitness A person who has actually seen or observed an event and can so testify in court. (Compare: earwitness)

F

face amount The original amount due on a promissory note or insurance policy as stated in the document, without calculating interest. (See also: par value)

face value See: face amount

fact An actual thing or happening, which must be proved at trial by presentation of evidence and which is evaluated by the finder of fact (a jury in a jury trial, or by the judge if he or she sits without a jury).

fact finder In a trial of a lawsuit or criminal prosecution, the jury or judge (if there is no jury) who decides if facts have been proven. Occasionally a judge may appoint a "special master" to investigate and report on the existence of certain facts.

factor A person who buys or sells in his or her own name on behalf of others, taking a commission for services. Also, a person or company that buys or sells accounts receivable at a discount or as security for short-term loans.

failure of consideration The refusal or inability of a contracting party to perform its side of a bargain.

failure of issue A situation in which a person dies without children or other direct descendants who could have inherited property.

fair comment A statement of opinion (no matter how ludicrous) based on facts which are correctly stated, and which does not allege dishonorable motives on the part of the target of the comment. The U.S. Supreme Court has ruled that to protect free speech, statements made about a public person (politician, officeholder, movie star, author, etc.), even though untrue and harmful, are fair comment unless the victim can prove the opinions were stated maliciously—with hate, dislike, intent, or desire to harm. Fair comment is a crucial defense used by members of the media against libel suits.

Fair Credit Billing Act (FCBA) An amendment to the Truth in Lending Act that gives consumers the right to challenge errors on their credit card statements. Once notified of an error, the company must either correct it or explain why it believes the statement is correct within set time limits.

Fair Credit Reporting Act (FCRA) A federal law that regulates the use and content of credit reports to protect consumer privacy and ensure the accuracy of the information they contain. The FCRA restricts the information that may be included in a credit report, limits who may request a credit report and how the report may be used, and requires credit reporting agencies and those who use credit reports (such as employers and landlords) to follow specified procedures in dealing with consumers.

Fair Debt Collection Practices Act (FDCPA) A federal law that prohibits certain debt collection practices, including harassing, abusing, or lying to debtors, contacting third parties about a debt (except in limited circumstances), and contacting debtors at work or at inconvenient hours. The FDCPA applies only to debt collectors who work for collection agencies, not those who work for the original creditor.

Fair Housing Act & Fair Housing Amendments Act Federal laws that prohibit housing discrimination on the basis of race or color, national origin, religion, sex, familial status, or disability. The federal Acts apply to all aspects of the landlord/tenant relationship, from refusing to rent to members of certain groups to providing different services during the tenancy. They also apply to the buying and selling of real estate.

Fair Labor Standards Act (FLSA) A federal law that guarantees a worker's right to be paid fairly. The FLSA sets out the federal minimum wage, states requirements for overtime, and places restrictions on child labor.

fair market value The amount for which property would sell on the open market. This is distinguished from "replacement value," which is the cost of duplicating the property.

 "Woe unto you, lawyers, for ye have taken away the key of knowledge."
—The Bible, Luke 11:52

---

fair trade laws State laws that permitted manufacturers or producers to set minimum rates for the resale of the product. They have been repealed in most states.

fair use A copyright principle that excuses unauthorized uses of a work when used for a transformative purpose such as research, scholarship, parody, criticism, or journalism. When determining whether an infringement should be excused on the basis of fair use, a court will use several factors including the purpose and character of the use, amount and substantiality of the portion borrowed, and effect of the use on the market for the copyrighted material. Fair use is a defense rather than an affirmative right—that is, a particular use only gets established as a fair use if the copyright owner decides to file a lawsuit and the court upholds the fair use defense.

false arrest See: false imprisonment

false imprisonment A crime in which the perpetrator intentionally restrains another person without having the legal right to do so. This can literally mean physical restraint, such as locking someone in a car or tying the person to a chair. However, it's not necessary that physical force be used; threats or a show of apparent authority are sufficient. False imprisonment is a misdemeanor and a tort (a civil violation). If the perpetrator confines the victim for a substantial period of time (or moves the victim a significant distance) in order to commit a felony, the false imprisonment may become a kidnapping. People who are arrested and get the charges dropped, or are later acquitted, often think that they can sue the arresting officer for false imprisonment (also known as false arrest). These lawsuits rarely succeed: As long as the officer had probable cause to arrest the person, the officer will

not be liable for a false arrest, even if it turns out later that the information the officer relied upon was incorrect.

false pretenses The crime of knowingly making untrue statements for the purpose of obtaining money or property fraudulently. It is one form of theft. False pretenses include claiming zircons are diamonds, turning back the odometer on a car, or falsely stating that a mine has been producing gold when it has not.

family A group of people related by consanguinity or affinity.

family allowance A certain amount of a deceased person's money to which immediate family members are entitled at the beginning of the probate process. The allowance is meant to help support the surviving spouse and children during the time it takes to probate the estate. The amount is determined by state law and varies greatly from state to state.

Family and Medical Leave Act (FMLA) A federal law that requires qualifying employers to provide eligible employees with 12 weeks of unpaid leave during a 12-month period to bond with a new child, care for a family member with a serious medical condition, or recover from a serious medical condition. At the end of the leave, the employer must allow the employee to return to the same or an equivalent position to that held before taking the leave.

family court A separate court or a separate division of the regular state trial court, that considers only cases involving family-related issues, which could include divorce, child custody and support, guardianship, adoption, and the issuance of restraining orders in domestic violence cases.

family limited partnership A type of partnership comprising only related family members, usually created by parents in order to pass on a family business or investments to their children. It provides significant federal gift and estate tax benefits because members of a family limited partnership (sometimes referred to as a FLP—pronounced "flip") own shares in the partnership which can be transferred between generations at lower tax rates.

family pot trust See: pot trust

family purpose doctrine The doctrine that the registered owner of a vehicle is liable for any damage caused by any member of the owner's family while operating the vehicle.

FAPE See: free appropriate public education

fault divorce A tradition that required one spouse to prove that the other spouse was legally at fault, to obtain a divorce. The "innocent" spouse was then granted the divorce from the "guilty" spouse. The traditional fault grounds for divorce are adultery, cruelty, desertion, confinement in prison, physical incapacity, and incurable insanity. Today, all states offer no-fault divorce, but quite a few states also still allow a spouse to allege fault in obtaining a divorce, and some states also allow the court to consider fault in dividing property or awarding custody or visitation.

FCBA See: Fair Credit Billing Act

FCRA See: Fair Credit Reporting Act

FDCPA See: Fair Debt Collection Practices Act

FDIC See: Federal Deposit Insurance Corporation

federal benefit rate The share of the SSI grant paid by the federal government. Many states add a supplementary grant to the federal benefit rate.

federal court A branch of the United States government with power derived directly from the U.S. Constitution. Federal courts decide cases involving the U.S. Constitution, federal law—for example, patents, labor law, federal taxes, and federal crimes, such as robbing a federally chartered bank. Federal courts may also decide cases where the parties are from different states and are involved in a dispute for $75,000 or more.

federal courts See: federal court

Federal Deposit Insurance Corporation (FDIC) A federal agency that promotes public confidence in the U.S. financial system by insuring deposits in banks and by limiting the effect on the economy when a bank fails.

federal question A basis for filing a lawsuit in federal district court— namely, that it is based on subjects enumerated in the U.S. Constitution or a federal statute is involved. Existence of a federal question gives the federal court jurisdiction.

federal tax deposits (FTD) The biweekly or monthly deposit an employer is required make in a federal depository (bank) to submit payroll taxes withheld from employees, as well as employer contributions for Social Security and Medicare taxes, to the IRS.

Federal Tort Claims Act A statute that allows recovery for damages caused by a federal employee if the injury occurred in the scope of the employee's job. It also establishes regulations and procedures for making such claims in federal courts.

Federal Trade Commission (FTC) A federal government agency established to regulate business practices and enforce antitrust laws. The FTC often shows up in the news when big businesses attempt to merge, but it also plays a role in protecting consumers from unfair business practices, including actions by collection agencies and credit bureaus. While the FTC generally does not have authority to intervene in specific consumer disputes, it can take action against a company about which it has received numerous consumer complaints.

Federal Unemployment Tax Act (FUTA) Legislation which requires employers to contribute to a fund that pays unemployment insurance benefits.

fee 1) Absolute title in land. It often appears in deeds which transfer title as "Mary Jo Stone grants to Howard Takitall in fee …." The word "fee" can be modified to show that the title was "conditional" on some occurrence or could be terminated ("determinable") upon a future event. 2) A charge for services.

fee simple An old term meaning complete ownership of real estate. Owners with fee simple have no legal restrictions on their freedom sell the property, give it away, or leave it at death. it is sometimes used in real estate deeds, as in "Harry Hernandez grants to Roberta Irving title in fee simple …." (Compare: fee tail)

fee tail A form of real estate ownership, now abolished, that required property to be passed only to the descendants of a certain person. This kept land in the family indefinitely.

felon A person who has been convicted of a felony, which is a serious crime punishable by imprisonment or in for the most serious felonies, death.

felonious 1) Refers to an act done with criminal intent. The term is used to distinguish between a wrong that was not malicious and an intentional crime, as in "felonious assault," which is an attack meant to do real harm. 2) Relating to a felony.

felony A serious crime (contrasted with less serious crimes such as misdemeanors and infractions), usually punishable by a prison term of more than one year or, in some cases, by death. For example, murder, extortion, and kidnapping are felonies; a minor fist fight is usually charged as a misdemeanor, and a speeding ticket is generally an infraction. In some states, certain crimes (known as wobblers) may be charged as both a misdemeanor and a felony, and the eventual designation depends on the defendant's ability to fulfill the conditions of his sentence. (See also: wobbler)

felony murder doctrine A rule that allows a killing that occurs in the course of a dangerous felony, even an accidental death, to be charged against the felon as first-degree murder. A felon can be guilty of murder during the course of the dangerous felony even if the felon is not the killer, as might happen when a robber kills a clerk—the driver of the getaway car, as well as the robber, may be charged with first-degree murder. The rule extends to unusual circumstances, such as the killing of one of two bank robbers by a bank security officer (the surviving robber may be charged with murder).

Feres doctrine A legal doctrine that prevents people who are injured as a result of military service from successfully suing the federal government under the Federal Tort Claims Act. The doctrine comes from the U.S. Supreme Court case *Feres v. United States*, in which servicemen who picked up highly radioactive weapons fragments from a crashed airplane were not permitted to recover damages from the government. Also known as the *Feres-Stencel* doctrine or the *Feres* rule.

fertile-octogenarian rule An unrealistic legal fiction that any living person (male or female) is capable of having a child. In estate planning, this rule could defeat the intentions of a person leaving property to others. For example, if property could not pass to one's child as long as he or she might acquire a sibling, then the child would have to wait until both parents died, unnecessarily tying up the property. Most states have passed laws to cure this anomaly.

A Few Good Men. (1992) Tom Cruise, assisted by Demi Moore, defends young marines charged with murder. With Jack Nicholson.

FICA tax Short for Federal Insurance Contributions Act tax, it is a payroll tax that incorporates the Social Security tax and Medicare tax. The FICA tax is 15.3% of an individual's earned income up to a certain limit (called the Social Security Wage Base) that increases each year, and then 2.9% of wages without limit.

FICO Abbreviation for Fair Isaac Corporation, the biggest credit scoring company. (See also: credit score)

fictitious business name See: fictitious name

fictitious defendants When a party suing (plaintiff) is not sure whether there are unknown persons involved in the suit, they are given fictitious names, usually designated Doe I, Doe II, and so forth, with an allegation in the complaint that if and when the true names are discovered they will be inserted in the complaint by amendment. Fictitious

defendants are not permitted in federal cases.

fictitious name Fictitious names are often used in conducting a business. They may also be used when filing a lawsuit against a party whose real name is unknown or when it is appropriate to conceal the true name of the party. (See also: doing business as)

fiduciary A person or company that has the power and obligation to act for another under circumstances which require total trust, good faith, and honesty. Fiduciaries can include trustees, business advisers, attorneys, guardians, administrators of estates, real estate agents, bankers, stock brokers, title companies, or anyone who undertakes to assist someone who places complete confidence and trust in that person or company.

fiduciary relationship A relationship in which an individual places complete confidence, trust, and reliance in someone who has a fiduciary duty to act for the individual's benefit. A fiduciary relationship need not be formally or legally established; it may be assumed where the fiduciary has superior knowledge and training compared to the person whose affairs the fiduciary is handling.

field sobriety test A preliminary test used by law enforcement officers to evaluate whether a driver is intoxicated. The test is performed on the side of the road where the driver was pulled over, and is designed to test the driver's ability to perform the type of mental and physical multitasking that is required to operate an automobile. The driver is often asked to stand on one foot and then the other, walk in a straight line, touch his or her nose with the forefinger of each hand, say the alphabet backward, and so on.

fieri facias (**fee**-air-ee **fay**-shee-es) Latin for "that you cause to be done." This is a court document that instructs a sheriff to seize and sell a defendant's property in order to satisfy a monetary judgment against the defendant.

fighting words Inflammatory words that are either injurious by themselves or might cause the hearer to immediately retaliate or breach the peace. Use of such words is not necessarily protected "free speech" under the First Amendment. If the hearer is prosecuted for assault, claiming fighting words may establish mitigating circumstances.

file A term commonly used to describe both the process of submitting a document to a court—for example, "I filed my small claims case today"—and to describe the physical location where these papers are kept. Traditionally, a court's case files were kept indefinitely

in one or more cardboard folders. Today most files—especially those for inactive cases—are stored electronically.

filing fee A fee charged by a public official to accept a document for processing. For example, you must usually pay a filing fee to submit pleadings to the court in a civil matter, or to put a deed on file in the public record.

final beneficiary The person or institution designated to receive trust property upon the death of a life beneficiary. For example, Jim creates a trust through which his wife Jane receives income for the duration of her life. Their daughter, the final beneficiary, receives the trust principal after Jane's death.

final decree A final judgment in a court case.

final judgment The final determination of a court case, put in writing by the judge who presided over the case. (See also: final decree)

final settlement An agreement reached by the parties to a lawsuit, usually in writing or read into the record in court, settling all issues. Usually there are elements of compromise, waiver of any right to reopen or appeal the matter even if there is information found later which would change matters (such as recurrence of a problem with an injury), mutual release of any further claim by each party, a statement that neither side is admitting fault, and some action or payment by one or both sides. In short, the case is over, provided the parties do what they are supposed to do according to the final settlement's terms.

financial guardian See: guardian of the estate

finder's fee A fee charged by real estate brokers and apartment-finding services in exchange for locating a rental property. These fees are permitted by law. Some landlords, however, charge finder's fees merely for renting a place. This type of charge is not legitimate and, in some areas, is specifically declared illegal.

finding The determination by the trier of fact (judge or jury) of a factual question submitted to it for decision. Often referred to as a finding of fact. A finding of fact is distinguished from a conclusion of law, which is determined by the judge as the sole legal expert.

finding of fact See: finding

fire insurance An insurance policy that pays the beneficiary of the policy if property covered by the policy is damaged by fire. Fire insurance often covers damage caused other events as well, such as wind or rain damage.

firm offer An offer (usually in writing) which states it may not be withdrawn, revoked, or amended for a specific period of time. If the offer is accepted without a change during that period, there is a firm, enforceable contract.

first degree murder The intentional killing of another person by someone who has acted willfully, deliberately, or with planning. All murder that is committed with poison or by lying in wait is first degree murder.

first impression See: case of first impression

fiscal year accounting period A 12-month period ending on the last day of any month except December. Many businesses are required to use a calendar year as their tax year, but if you can prove that your business has a natural business year that is different from the calendar year, you might be able to adopt a fiscal tax year.

fishing expedition Legal grasping at straws; the use of pretrial investigation discovery or witness questioning in an unfocused attempt to uncover damaging evidence to be used against an adversary.

fitness The ability of a prospective adoptive parent to provide for the best interests of a child the parent wishes to adopt. A court may consider many aspects of the prospective parents' lives in evaluating their fitness to adopt a child, including financial stability, marital stability, career obligations, other children, physical and mental health, and criminal history.

fixed annuity An annuity that provides payments of a set amount for the recipient's life or some other specified term. (Compare: variable annuity)

fixed asset Long-term tangible property used in the operation of a business that is not readily converted into cash or consumed in the ordinary course of business. Examples include machinery, buildings, fixtures, and equipment. Also referred to as a capital asset.

fixed in a tangible medium of expression A requirement for copyright protection. A work must be recorded in some physical medium, whether on paper, canvas, disk, or computer hard drive. This means that spontaneous speech or musicianship that is not recorded, (a jazz solo at a live performance, for instance) is not protected by copyright.

fixed rate mortgage A mortgage loan that has an interest rate that remains constant throughout the life of the loan, usually 15 or 30 years.

fixed trust See: nondiscretionary trust

fixture Anything that has been attached to real estate in such a way as to become part of the premises. Unless the owner of the fixture and the owner of the real estate agree otherwise, the fixture becomes the property of the landowner once it is attached. When a tenant has installed a heater, window box, or other item that is bolted, nailed, screwed, or wired into the wall, ceiling, or floor, it becomes the property of the landlord. A trade fixture is an item needed by a business, such as machinery or other equipment, and despite its name, these usually do not become part of the building (commercial leases typically include a clause allowing tenants to remove these fixtures when the lease is up).

"Laws are made for men of common understanding, and should therefore be construed by the ordinary rules of common sense."

—Thomas Jefferson

flexible savings account (FSA) An account into which employees may set aside pretax income for medical expenses not paid by health insurance (such as co-payments, premiums, and expenses that are outside of the employer's plan) or for dependent care expenses.

flight Running away or hiding to avoiding arrest or prosecution.

flipping A popular real estate investment strategy in hot markets where someone buys a property for investment and resells it a short time later for a profit (often after making improvements to the property).

floating easement An easement (a right to use another's property for a particular purpose) which allows access but does not spell out the exact dimensions and location of the easement.

FMLA See: Family and Medical Leave Act

FOB See: free on board

forbearance Voluntarily refraining from doing something, such as asserting a legal right. For example, a creditor may forbear on its right to collect a debt by temporarily postponing or reducing the borrower's payments.

forced sale The sale of goods by a creditor of their owner, authorized by court order. For example, forced sales may occur when someone files for bankruptcy or goes through foreclosure.

forced share See: elective share

force majeure A contract provision that excuses performance if it's rendered impractical by a supervening event (sometimes known as an "Act of God")—for example, a fire. French for "a greater force."

forcible entry The crime of taking possession of a house, other structure, or land by the use of physical force or serious threats against the occupants. This can include breaking windows, doors, or using terror to gain entry, as well as forcing the occupants out by threat or violence after having come in peacefully.

foreclosure The legal process by which a creditor with a claim (lien) on real estate forces a sale of the property in order to collect on the lien. Foreclosure typically begins when a homeowner falls behind on mortgage payments for several months. (See also: judicial foreclosure, nonjudicial foreclosure)

foreclosure sale The forced sale of real estate, usually at public auction, that has been foreclosed on—that is, that has been seized by the lender after the borrower defaulted on mortgage payments.

foreign corporation A corporation that is incorporated under the laws of a different state or nation. In the U.S., it usually refers to an out-of-state corporation. Out-of-state corporations must file a notice of doing business in any state in which they do business.

foreign divorce A divorce obtained in a different state or country from the place where one spouse resides at the time of the divorce. As a general rule, foreign divorces are recognized as valid if the spouse requesting the divorce became a resident of the state or country granting the divorce, and if both parties consented to the jurisdiction of the foreign court. A foreign divorce obtained by one person without the consent of the other is normally not valid, unless the nonconsenting spouse later acts as if the foreign divorce were valid, for example, by remarrying.

forensic Any material, such as evidence or testimony, suitable for use in court or other legal matters.

forensic animation Computer animation used in court to recreate the events of an accident.

forensic medicine The area of medical science that helps solve a legal question using scientific or technical facts. For example, coroners can often determine cause of death.

forensics Generally, suitable for debate or argument. More specifically, forensics also refers to the use of science or technology to discover evidence for a court of law. For example, the forensics department of a police force may investigate crimes using science and technology.

forensic testimony Testimony given by an expert witness who uses expertise in science or technology to reach conclusions for a lawsuit or prosecution.

foreseeability The ability to reasonably anticipate the potential results of an action, such as the damage or injury that may happen if one is negligent or breaches a contract.

foreseeable risk A likelihood of injury or damage that a reasonable person should be able to anticipate in a given set of circumstances. Foreseeable risk is a common affirmative defense put up by defendants in lawsuits for negligence, essentially claiming that the plaintiff should have thought twice before taking a risky action. Signs that warn "use at your own risk" do not bar lawsuits over injuries or damages from risks that weren't foreseeable.

forfeit To involuntarily lose property or rights as a penalty for violating the law. For example, one may have to forfeit one's driver's license due to multiple traffic violations or drunk driving.

forfeiture The loss of property or a privilege due to breaking a law.

forger Someone who creates or attempts to pass off a false document, signature, or other imitation of an object of value.

forgery A false document, signature, or other imitation of an object of value used with the intention to deceive another into believing it is the real thing. Those who commit forgery are commonly charged with the crime of fraud.

form interrogatories Preprinted sets of questions that one party in a lawsuit asks an opposing party during the discovery process. Form interrogatories cover the issues commonly encountered in the kind of lawsuit at hand. For example, there are form interrogatories designed for contract disputes, landlord-tenant cases, personal injury cases, and others. Form interrogatories are often supplemented by specific questions written by the lawyers about the specific issues in the particular case.

formula AB trust A trust funded with an amount no larger than the personal federal estate tax exemption of the year of death. (See also: AB trust)

fornication Sexual intercourse between a man and woman who are not married to each other. Fornication is still on the books as a misdemeanor crime in some states, but following the Supreme Court decision in *Lawrence v. Texas*, can't be enforced.

for sale by owner Selling your house without a real estate broker. Doing so can save you a commission but requires that you devote time and energy not only to marketing and showing the house but also to learning and following the legal rules controlling sales of real estate in

your area. Commonly referred to as FSBO, pronounced "fizzbo."

forthwith A term found in contracts, court orders, and statutes, meaning as soon as can be reasonably done. It implies immediacy, with no excuses for delay.

 "The common law is nothing else but reason."

—Sir Edward Coke,
Commentary on Littleton

forum Refers to the court in which a lawsuit is filed or in which a hearing or trial is conducted. The appropriate forum depends on which court has personal jurisdiction over the parties and the subject matter of the case.

forum non conveniens Latin for an inconvenient court. The idea that a court may change the venue of a lawsuit if that is more convenient for the parties. However, because strict written rules of jurisdiction and venue are used to decide where a case can and cannot be properly filed, this term has largely lost any real meaning. Also called forum inconveniens.

forum shopping The process by which a plaintiff chooses among two or more courts that have the power— technically, the correct jurisdiction and venue—to consider the plaintiff's case. This decision is based on which court is likely to consider the case most favorably. In some instances, a case can properly be filed in two or more federal district courts as well as in the trial courts of several states—and this makes forum shopping a complicated business. It often involves weighing a number of factors, including proximity to the court, the reputation of the judge in the particular legal area, the likely type of available jurors, and subtle differences in governing law and procedure.

for value received A phrase used in a promissory note, bill of exchange, or other contract to show that some consideration (money or other value) has been given in exchange for whatever the contract requires.

foster care Court-ordered care provided to children who are unable to live in their own homes, usually because their parents have abused or neglected them. Foster parents have a legal responsibility to care for their foster children, but do not have all the rights of a biological parent—for example, they may have limited rights to discipline the children, to raise them according to a certain religion, or to authorize nonemergency medical procedures for them.

foster child A child placed by a government agency or a court in the care of someone other than the child's natural parents. Foster children may be removed from their family home because of parental abuse or neglect. Occasionally, parents voluntarily place their children in foster care.

foster parent An adult who takes over care of a minor child who has been placed in the foster care system because the child's own family cannot take care of the child or have had custody taken away by a court or agency.

four corners of an instrument The principle that a document's meaning should be derived from the document itself, without reference to anything outside of the document (extrinsic evidence), such as the circumstances surrounding its writing or the history of the party signing it.

401(k) plan A deferred compensation retirement savings arrangement in which employers withhold a portion of their employees' pretax wages and invest them in a plan where they may earn income, tax-free, until the employee withdraws the money. Some employers also contribute to their employees' 401(k) plan, often through matching employee contributions, at least up to a certain amount. Because a 401(k) is a retirement plan, employees must pay a penalty for early withdrawals, although some plans allow employees to borrow money from their plans without penalty for certain expenses.

framing The act of displaying another company's Web page within a bordered area of a website—similar to the picture-in-picture feature offered on some televisions. For example, when a user enters a search engine request, the search engine might display the contents of an online store within the search engine's website, framed by the search engine's text and logos. When a Web page is framed within another website, the URL or domain name of the framed Web page is usually not displayed and users are not able to bookmark that site. (See also: URL, domain name)

franchise 1) A right granted by the government to a person or corporation, such as a taxi permit, bus route, an airline's use of a public airport, business license, or corporate existence. 2) To grant (for a periodic fee or share of profits) the right to operate a business or sell goods or services under a brand or chain name. Well-known franchise operations include McDonald's, Holiday Inns, Ace Hardware, Rexall Drug Stores, and Amway Distributors.

franchise agreement The contract that establishes the terms of a franchise relationship.

franchisee An individual or entity that is granted a franchise.

franchiser An individual or entity that grants a franchise; also spelled franchisor.

franchise tax A state tax on corporations or businesses.

frank 1) The privilege of sending mail for free, granted to members of Congress. 2) A mark, stamp, or signature on mail that substitutes for postage. 3) A letter or package that has been franked. 4) The act of franking—for example, to frank a letter.

fraternal benefit society benefits Benefits, often group life insurance, fraternal societies provide to their members. The Elks, Masons, or Knights of Columbus are common fraternal societies that provide benefits. Also called benefit society, benevolent society, or mutual aid association benefits. Under bankruptcy laws, these benefits are virtually always considered exempt property

fraud Intentionally deceiving someone and causing that person to suffer a loss. Fraud includes lies and half-truths, such as selling a car that is a lemon and claiming "she runs like a dream." Or, failing to point out a mistake in a contract, such as a survey that shows ten acres of land being purchased and not 20 as originally understood. Fraud can be the basis of a civil lawsuit for damages and for prosecution as a crime.

fraud in the inducement The use of deceit or trick to cause someone to act to his or her disadvantage, such as signing an agreement or deeding away real property. The heart of this type of fraud is misleading the other party as to the facts upon which that person will base his or her decision to act. Example: "There will be tax advantages to you if you let me take title to your property," or "You don't have to read the rest of the contract—it is just routine legal language" but actually includes a balloon payment.

fraudulent conveyance The transfer (conveyance) of title to real property for the express purpose of putting it beyond the reach of a known creditor. In such a case, the creditor may bring a lawsuit to void the transfer.

fraudulent transfer In a bankruptcy case, a transfer of property to another for less than the property's value for the purpose of hiding the property from the bankruptcy trustee—for instance, when a debtor signs a car over to a relative to keep it out of the bankruptcy estate. Fraudulently transferred property can be recovered and sold by the trustee for the benefit of the creditors.

Fraudulent Transfer Act Act allowing a creditor to sue a debtor who intended to defraud a creditor by transferring property to another person without receiving reasonably equivalent value in return. In other words, if a business does not pay off its debts before selling its assets, the creditors of the business can void the transfer or get a judgment against the new owner of the assets and seize them to pay the debts. Most states have adopted this Act or an older version of it.

free and clear Property ownership that is not subject to a secured debt, such as a mortgage or car loan. For example, if you have paid off the mortgage on your house and no creditor has filed a lien (claim) against it, you own your house free and clear.

Philadelphia. (1993) Academy Award winner Tom Hanks brings an anti-discrimination lawsuit against the law firm that fired him after discovering he had AIDS. The all-star cast includes Denzel Washington, Jason Robards, Mary Steenbergen, Antonio Banderas, and Joanne Woodward.

---

free appropriate public education A requirement of the Individuals with Disabilities Education Act that a child with disabilities is entitled to an educational program (including classroom setting, teaching strategies, and services) that is individually tailored to meet his or her unique needs.

freehold An antiquated term for any interest in real estate that is of indeterminate length. It's distinguished from an interest that has a definite ending date, such as a lease. A life estate is an example of a freehold.

freelancer See: independent contractor

free on board (**FOB**) A reference to the place where purchased goods will be shipped without transportation charge. Free on board at the place of manufacture shows there is a charge for delivery. Example: if an automaker in Detroit sells a car "FOB Detroit," then there will be a shipping charge if delivery is taken anywhere else.

freeze-out Majority shareholders in a company using their power to deprive one or more minority shareholders of their role in governing the company. This is done to force the minority shareholders to sell their stock at a reduced price and exit the company.

fresh pursuit Also known as "hot pursuit," the chase by police of a person whom police have reason to believe has just committed a crime. In this situation, the officer may arrest the suspect without a warrant. Fresh pursuit also enables an officer to enter another jurisdiction (county or state) to pursue a fleeing suspect (normally, officers' abilities to arrest people are limited to their county and state).

friendly suit A lawsuit brought by two parties, not as adversaries, but by agreement in order to resolve a legal question that affects them both. For example, two companies might bring a friendly suit to court in order to clarify the legal interpretation of a contract between them.

friendly witness A witness whom you have called to testify on your behalf, and whom you may not cross-examine. If the witness testifies in a way that hurts your case, you can ask the judge to declare him or her a "hostile witness," which means that you can begin to cross-examine with leading questions.

fringe benefit A benefit given to employees in addition to salary. Examples include health and life insurance, retirement plans, and paid holidays. Fringe benefits usually are not taxable for the employee and are generally tax deductible for the employer.

frisk Quickly patting down the clothes of a suspect to search for a concealed weapon.

frivolous In a legal context, a lawsuit, motion, or appeal that lacks any basis and is intended to harass, delay, or embarrass the opposition. This can result in a successful claim by the other party for the costs of defense, including attorney's fees. Judges are reluctant to find an action frivolous, based on the desire not to discourage people from using the courts to resolve disputes.

"Decency, security and liberty alike demand that government officials shall be subjected to the same rules of conduct that are commands to the citizen."

—Justice Louis D. Brandeis

frolic and detour Employee conduct that is outside the scope of employment and is undertaken purely for the employee's own benefit. Although an employer is generally liable for the acts of its employees, an employer is not liable for damages employees cause while on a frolic and detour. For example, a delivery company could be liable for injuries one of its drivers causes while racing to make a delivery; it probably would not be liable if the same driver shot a guard while robbing a bank on his lunch hour.

fruit of the poisonous tree In criminal law, the doctrine that evidence dis-covered through unconstitutional means (such as a forced confession or illegal search and seizure), may not be used as evidence against a criminal defendant. For example, if a suspect is arrested but is not read the *Miranda* rights, then tells the police the location of stolen property, and the police then find the stolen property as a result of the interrogation, the stolen property is inadmissible because it was acquired through an unconstitutional interrogation.

frustration of purpose See: commercial frustration

FSBO See: for sale by owner

FTC See: Federal Trade Commission

FTCA See: Federal Tort Claims Act

fugitive from justice A person convicted or accused of a crime who hides from law enforcement or flees the jurisdiction (perhaps across state lines) to avoid arrest or punishment.

full disclosure 1) The need in certain situations (such as real estate transactions) for both parties to tell the whole truth about all information relevant to the transaction. 2) Securities and Exchange Commission rule that a publicly traded company must release its financial statements and other important information relating to the company's business.

full faith and credit A Constitutional doctrine contained in Article IV, Section 1 of the U.S. Constitution that requires courts and agencies in one state to recognize, respect, and enforce legal judgments and other actions from other states.

fundamental right In constitutional law, certain rights protected by the due process or equal protection clause that cannot be regulated unless the regulating law passes a rigorous set of criteria (strict scrutiny). Fundamental rights, as defined by the Supreme Court, include various rights of privacy (such as marriage and contraception), the right to interstate travel, and the right to vote.

funding a trust Transferring ownership of property to a trustee, so the property will be held in trust. With the most common kind of revocable living trust, this transfer takes place on paper only, because the person who sets up the trust and owns the property also serves as trustee.

fungible things Sometimes called "fungibles," they are goods which are interchangeable, often sold or delivered in bulk, since any load is as good as another. Grain or gravel are fungibles, as are securities which are identical.

future interest A right to receive property sometime in the future, either on a particular date or upon the occurrence of an event. For example, John's will leaves his house to his sister Marian, but only after the death of his wife, Hillary. Marian has a future interest in the house.

G

gag order A judge's order prohibiting the attorneys and parties in a pending lawsuit or criminal prosecution from talking about the case to the media or the public.

garnish To get a court order requiring a third party that holds funds belonging to a debtor to set some portion of that money aside for the benefit of the creditor. For example, a court might issue an order garnishing the wages of a parent who owes child support; the employer is then required to withhold a certain amount of the parent's paycheck each month and send that money to someone—often, the local sheriff—to be paid to the other parent.

garnishee The person or entity (often a bank or employer) that receives a court order garnishing wages or funds it owes to a debtor. (See also: garnish)

garnishment A court-ordered procedure for taking money or property from someone to satisfy a debt. For example, a debtor's wages might be garnished to pay child support, back taxes, or a lawsuit judgment.

GATT See: General Agreement on Tariffs and Trade

gender bias Prejudice against people of a particular gender, usually women. Gender bias may result in discriminatory treatment or unequal opportunity.

gender identity A person's self-identified gender, versus their anatomical gender at birth. In some states, it is illegal for employers to discriminate based on gender identity.

General Agreement on Tariffs and Trade (GATT) A comprehensive free-trade treaty signed by most developed nations. Among other things, member countries are required to treat all other member countries equally in the application of import and export tariffs, offer basic copyright protection to authors from member countries, consult with each other about trade matters, and attempt to resolve differences in a peaceful manner. GATT created an international regulatory body known as the World Trade Organization (WTO) to enforce compliance with the agreement.

general appearance The first time an attorney appears in court on behalf of a client; after making a general appearance, the attorney is then responsible for all future appearances in court unless officially relieved by court order or substitution of another attorney.

general bequest A bequest of money in a will. (Compare: specific bequest)

general counsel The senior attorney for a corporation.

general damages Monetary recovery in a lawsuit for injuries suffered or breach of contract for which there is no exact dollar value that can be calculated. General damages can include, for example, pain and suffering, compensation for a shortened life expectancy, and loss of the companionship of a loved one.

general denial An answer to a lawsuit or claim, in which the defendant denies everything alleged in the complaint without specifically denying any allegation. (See also: denial)

general journal See: general ledger

general ledger A book or computer file where double-entry accounting entries are recorded for a business.

general partner A person who joins with at least one other to own and operate a business for profit—and who (unlike a corporation's owners) is personally liable for all the business's debts and obligations. A general partner's actions can legally bind the entire business. (See also: partnership, limited partnership)

general plan A term sometimes used to describe a land-use document that lays forth the plan of a city, county, or area, typically establishing zones for different types of development, uses, traffic patterns, and future development. (See also: zoning)

"The right to be left alone—the most comprehensive of rights and the right most valued by civilized men."

—Justice Louis D. Brandeis

---

general power of attorney A broad power of attorney document that gives the named agent power to handle all matters permitted by law on behalf of the person (called "the principal") who executed the document. (Compare: limited power of attorney)

generation-skipping transfer A transfer (during life or at death) made by a grandparent to a grandchild, skipping the middle generation. Very large transfers of this kind are subject to a special federal generation-skipping transfer tax.

generation-skipping transfer tax A federal tax imposed on large amounts of money given or left to a grandchild or great-grandchild. Its purpose is to keep families from avoiding the estate tax that would be due if the oldest generation left property to their children, who then left it to their children (the original giver's grandchildren). Currently, the exempt amount is $3.5 million, so this tax applies only to people wealthy enough to transfer more than that to their grandchildren. It is imposed in addition to any estate tax due.

generation-skipping trust A trust designed to save on estate tax. The trust principal is preserved for the trust maker's grandchildren, with his or her children receiving only income from the trust. Because the children (the middle generation) never legally own the property, it isn't subject to estate tax at their death. (See also: generation-skipping transfer tax)

generic In trademark law, the status of a word or symbol commonly used to describe an entire type of product or service rather than to distinguish one product or service from another. An example is "raisin bran," used by several manufacturers of breakfast cereals to describe their products. Generic terms can never receive trademark protection because they don't serve the basic function of trademarks to distinguish goods and services in the marketplace. (See also: genericide)

genericide A process by which a trade-mark owner loses trademark rights

because the trademark is used widely and indiscriminately to refer to a type of product or service. For example, escalator was originally a protected trademark used to designate the moving stairs manufactured by a specific company. Eventually, the word became synonymous with the very idea of moving stairs and thus lost its trademark protection. Other examples of trademarks that have become generic terms are lite beer, soft soap, and cola. (See also: generic)

Genetic Information Nondiscrimination Act (GINA) A federal law passed in 2008, which prohibits health insurers and employers from discriminating on the basis of an employee's or applicant's genetic information.

Gibbons v. Ogden (**1824**) A U.S. Supreme Court case in which Chief Justice John Marshall's decision struck down state barriers to interstate commerce. The case involved a steamboat operator who was denied a license by one of the states he serviced.

Gideon v. Wainright (**1963**) A U.S. Supreme Court case in which the Court used the due process clause of the Fourteenth Amendment to extend the constitutional right to an attorney in federal criminal cases for those who could not afford representation to indigent defendants in state prosecutions.

The indigent defendant was represented gratis by future Supreme Court Justice Abe Fortas. The ruling greatly increased the use of public defenders. In 2002, the Court ruled the right applied in all cases where jail time is a possible punishment.

gift 1) A voluntary transfer of property without payment or conditions. 2) The thing that is transferred.

gift causa mortis See: gift in contemplation of death

gift in contemplation of death A gift of personal property (not real estate) by a person expecting to die soon. If a gift is made in contemplation of death, it is included in the value of the deceased person's estate for federal tax purposes. In Latin, called a gift causa mortis.

gift tax Federal taxes assessed on any gift, or combination of gifts, from one person to another that exceeds $13,000 in one year. Several kinds of gifts are exempt from this tax: gifts to tax-exempt charities, gifts to your spouse (limited to $133,000 annually if the recipient isn't a U.S. citizen), and gifts made for tuition or medical bills. In addition to the annual gift tax exclusion, there is a $1 million cumulative tax exemption for gifts. In other words, you can give away a total of $1 million during your lifetime—over and above the gifts you give using the annual exclusion—without paying gift taxes.

***Gitlow v. New York* (1925)** A U.S. Supreme Court case in which the Court ruled that the First Amendment right to free speech applied to state laws under the Fourteenth Amendment.

go bail Slang for putting up the bail money to get an accused defendant out of jail after an arrest or pending trial or appeal. (See also: bail)

going out Court slang for going to trial, meaning the trial will start either right away or shortly. For example, a clerk might tell assembled lawyers who are expecting to go to trial that day, "Your case is going out today at 10 a.m. in Department 9."

golden parachute An agreement by a corporation with an executive to provide substantial payments to the executive in the event of a change in ownership or early retirement.

golden rule argument During a jury trial, an attempt to persuade the jurors to put themselves in the place of the victim or the injured person and deliver the verdict that they would wish to receive if they were in that person's position. For example, if the plaintiff in a personal injury case has suffered severe scarring, the plaintiff's lawyer might ask the jury to come back with the verdict they themselves would want to receive had they been disfigured in such a manner. As a rule, judges frown upon this type of argument, because jurors are supposed to consider the facts of a case in an objective manner.

good cause A legally sufficient reason for a ruling or other action by a judge.

In a medieval trial by fire, a suspect was forced to hold a red-hot iron in his hand or to walk blindfolded and barefoot among nine red-hot ploughshares scattered on the ground. If the suspect passed through the ordeal unharmed, he was innocent.

good faith Honest intent to fulfill a promise to act or to act without taking an unfair advantage over another person. Absence of intent to defraud someone.

good faith estimate (GFE) A disclosure that real estate mortgage lenders must, under the Real Estate Settlement Procedures Act (RESPA), give to all mortgage loan applicants within three days of when they apply. The disclosure must estimate all settlement charges the homebuyer will need to pay at closing, such as the lender's fees and other closing costs.

Good Samaritan rule The doctrine that protects a volunteer who comes to the aid of an injured or ill stranger from being sued for contributory negligence, as long as the volunteer aid-giver (the Good Samaritan) acted with reasonable care.

goods Items held for sale in the regular course of business, as in a retail store.

goods and chattels See: personal property

good title See: clear title

goodwill The benefit a business has through its name and good reputation. Goodwill is not a tangible asset like equipment or inventory. In an acquisition, goodwill is valued as the amount paid for the business above the fair market cost of all the business's assets.

governing law A contract provision (also known as a "choice of law") that determines which state's laws should be followed in the event of a dispute.

governmental immunity See: sovereign immunity

grace period A period of time during which a debtor is not required to make payments on a debt or will not be charged a fee. For example, most credit cards offer a grace period of 20 to 30 days before interest is charged on purchases; as long as you pay your bill in full within the grace period, you won't owe any interest. Similarly, many student loans offer a grace period for at least a few months after graduation, so new graduates don't have to start repaying their loans right away.

grandfather clause 1) A provision in a new law that limits its application to individuals or businesses that are new to the system, while those already in the system are exempt from the new regulation. For example, when Washington, DC, raised its drinking age from 18 to 21, people between those ages, who could drink under the old law, were allowed to retain the right to legally consume alcohol under a grandfather clause. 2) A provision of several Southern states' constitutions in the late 1800s designed to to keep blacks from voting; now unconstitutional, these grandfather clauses denied the vote to people who were illiterate or did not own property, unless their descendants had voted before 1867.

grandfathered in See: grandfather clause

grand jury A group of people chosen at random that sits on a regular basis to hear evidence brought by a prosecutor. The prosecutor presents evidence against a person that he or she thinks will justify an indictment (formal charges) and a trial. Grand juries, unlike petit juries, meet in secret, need not reach unanimous decisions, and do not decide on a person's guilt or evidence (they only decide whether the person should stand trial). (See also: petit jury)

grand jury witness A witness who testifies before a grand jury.

grand larceny The crime of theft of another's property over a certain value set by state law (for example, $500). It is distinguished from petty (or petit) larceny, which is the theft of property that is lesser in value. Some states recognize only the crime of larceny, but have both misdemeanor larceny (punishable by imprisonment in a local jail and a fine) and felony larceny (punishable by state prison time).

grand theft See: grand larceny

grant To give, sell, or otherwise transfer something to someone. (See also: grant deed)

grant deed A deed to real estate containing an implied promise that the person transferring the property actually has good title and that the property is not encumbered in any way, except as described in the deed. This is the most commonly used type of deed. (Compare: quitclaim deed, warranty deed)

grantee Someone who receives title to real estate from a seller (grantor) in a document called a grant deed or quitclaim deed.

grantor 1) Someone who transfers ownership of real estate through a grant deed. 2) Someone who creates a trust; also called settlor or trustor.

grantor-grantee index A set of records found in the county land records office, listing current and past owners of all parcels of real estate in the county. You can find information about the ownership of real estate by looking up the name of a grantor (person selling or leaving the property) or grantee (buyer or inheritor). These records, once kept in large bound books, are now generally on microfilm or digital media.

grantor-retained annuity trust See: grantor-retained trust

grantor-retained income trust See: grantor-retained trust

grantor-retained trust An irrevocable trust designed to save on estate tax. There are several kinds; with all of them, you keep income from trust property, or use of that property, for a period of years. When the trust ends, the property goes to the final beneficiaries you've named. These trusts are for people who have enough wealth to feel comfortable giving away a substantial hunk of property. They come in three flavors: grantor-retained annuity trusts (GRATs), grantor-retained unitrusts (GRUTs), and grantor-retained income trusts (GRITs).

grantor-retained unitrust See: grantor-retained trust

gratuitous Voluntary or free.

> "Man is a creature endowed with reason and free will; but when he goes to law as plaintiff, his reason seems to have left him; while, if he stands in the position of defendant, it is generally against his free will."
>
> —Gilbert Abbot A. Beckett, *The Comic Blackstone*

gravamen The essential element of a lawsuit. For example, the gravamen of a lawsuit involving a car accident might be the careless driving (negligence) of the defendant.

green card The well-known term for an Alien Registration Card (ARC). This plastic photo identification card is given to people who are legal permanent residents of the United States. It serves as a U.S. entry document, enabling holders to return to the United States after temporary absences, and it proves their right to work in the United States. The green card expires after a certain number of years and must be renewed—but note that the holder's permanent residence itself doesn't expire, only the ability to prove it using the card.

greenmail A situation in which a person or entity (the greenmailer) buys enough stock in a public company to threaten a hostile takeover. The greenmailer offers to end the threat to the company by selling its stock back at a higher price. The term combines the words greenback and blackmail.

Gregg v. Georgia (**1976**) A U.S. Supreme Court case in which the Court held that the death penalty for murder was not in and of itself a cruel and unusual punishment prohibited by the Eighth Amendment. The Court also ruled that the character of the defendant was to be considered when deciding whether to impose the death penalty.

Griswold v. Connecticut (**1965**) A U.S. Supreme Court case in which the Court struck down, as an invasion of privacy, laws against the sale or use of contraceptives.

gross estate For the purpose of determining whether or not an estate must file a federal estate tax return, the total of all property someone owned at death, without regard to any debts or liens against the property or the costs of probate. Taxes are due only on the value of the property the person actually owned (the net estate) plus the amount of taxable gifts made during the last three years of life. In a few states, the gross estate is used when computing attorney fees for probating estates; the lawyer gets a percentage of the gross estate.

gross income The total income of an individual or business from all sources, before subtracting adjustments, exemptions, or deductions, allowed by tax law.

gross lease A commercial real estate lease in which the tenant pays a fixed amount of rent per month or year, regardless of the landlord's operating costs, such as maintenance, taxes and insurance. A gross lease closely resembles the typical residential lease. The tenant may agree to a "gross lease with stops," meaning that the tenant will pitch in if the landlord's operating costs rise above a certain level. In real estate lingo, the point when the tenant starts to contribute is called the "stop level," because that's where the landlord's share of the costs stops.

gross negligence A lack of care that demonstrates reckless disregard for the safety or lives of others, which is so great it appears to be a conscious violation of other people's rights to safety. It is more than simple inadvertence, and can affect the amount of damages.

grounds for divorce Legal reasons for requesting a divorce. All states require a spouse who files for divorce to state the grounds. Now that no-fault divorce is prevalent, the most common ground for divorce is "irreconcilable differences."

group insurance A single insurance policy, such as life or health insurance, under which individuals in a group— for example, employees (and sometimes their dependents)—are covered, as long as they remain part of the group.

group life insurance Life insurance available through an employer or association that covers participating employees and members under one master insurance policy. Most group life insurance policies are term insurance policies, that terminate when the member or employee reaches a certain age or leaves the organization and do not accumulate any cash surrender value.

guarantee See: guaranty

guaranteed reservation A hotel or rental car reservation secured by a credit card number. In exchange for your card number, the hotel or rental agency promises to have a room or vehicle for you no matter when you show up. If you have a guaranteed reservation with a hotel, it must provide you with a room, either at that hotel or at another comparable establishment. If you have a guaranteed reservation with a car agency, it must provide you with a

vehicle. The downside of a guaranteed reservation is that if you don't show up and haven't cancelled your reservation, you will be billed for one night in the room or one day's use of the vehicle.

guaranteed signature A signature that has been witnessed by a person— commonly, a bank employee—who is qualified to guarantee signatures. Companies often require guaranteed signatures on documents requesting the reregistration of stocks in the name of someone who has inherited them.

guarantor A person or entity that makes a legally binding promise to be responsible for another's debt or performance under a contract, if the other defaults or fails to perform. The guarantor gives a "guaranty," which is an assurance that the debt or other obligation will be fulfilled.

guaranty When used as a verb, to agree to pay another person's debt or perform another person's duty, if that person fails to come through. As a noun, the written document in which this assurance is made. For example, if you cosign a loan, you have made a guaranty and will be legally responsible for the debt if the borrower fails to repay the money as promised. The person who makes a guaranty is called the guarantor. Also known as a guarantee or warranty.

guardian An adult who has been appointed by a court to control and care for a minor or the minor's property. Someone who looks after a child's property is usually called a "guardian of the estate." An adult who has legal authority to make personal decisions for the child, including responsibility for his physical, medical, and educational needs, is often called a "guardian of the person." Sometimes just one person will be named to take care of all these tasks. An individual appointed by a court to look after an incapacitated adult may also be known as a guardian, but is more frequently called a conservator.

guardian ad litem A person, not necessarily a lawyer, who is appointed by a court to represent and protect the interests of a child or an incapacitated adult during a lawsuit. For example, a minor who is a party to a lawsuit must have a guardian ad litem (often a parent) to act in the minor's behalf with regard to decisions like whether or not to take a settlement offer. A guardian ad litem (GAL) may also be appointed to represent a child whose parents are locked in a contentious battle for custody.

guardian of the estate Someone appointed by a court to care for the property and finances of a minor child or an incapacitated adult. A guardian of the estate may also be called a property guardian, financial guardian, or conservator of the estate. (Compare: guardian of the person)

> *"It is not what a lawyer tells me I may do; but what humanity, reason, and justice tell me I ought to do."*
>
> —Edmund Burke

guardian of the person Someone appointed by a court to make personal decisions for a minor child or an incapacitated adult, commonly called a ward. Such decisions usually include day-to-day living arrangements, health care, education, and other matters related to the ward's comfort and well-being. A guardian of the person may also be called a personal guardian or conservator of the person. (Compare: guardian of the estate)

guardianship A legal relationship created by a court between a guardian and a ward—either a minor child or an incapacitated adult (although the latter relationship is more commonly called a conservatorship). The guardian has a legal right and duty to care for the ward. This may involve making personal decisions on the ward's behalf, managing the ward's property, or both.

guest statute A law in only a few states that prevents a nonpaying automobile passenger from suing the driver when the passenger is hurt as a result of the simple negligence of the driver. In general, the social passenger can sue the driver only if the driver's actions constitute gross, or extreme, negligence. Examples might include drunk driving, playing "chicken," driving a car knowing that the brakes are faulty, or continuing to drive recklessly after the passenger has asked the driver to stop or asked to be let out.

guilty In a criminal case, the admission by a defendant that he has committed a charged crime, or the finding by a judge or a jury that the defendant has committed the crime.

H

habeas corpus (**hay**-bee-us **kor**-pus)
Latin for "you have the body." A
prisoner files a petition for writ of
habeas corpus in order to challenge
the authority of the prison or jail
warden to continue to hold him or
her. If the judge orders a hearing after
reading the writ, that becomes the
prisoner's opportunity to argue that
the confinement is illegal. Habeas
corpus is an important protection
against illegal confinement, once
called "the great writ." For example,
it can be used in cases where a person
is being held without charges, or
when due process obviously has been
denied, bail is excessive, parole has
been granted, an accused has been
improperly surrendered by the bail
bondsman, or probation has been
summarily terminated without cause.
A particularly frequent use of habeas
writs is by convicted prisoners arguing
that the trial attorney failed to prepare
the defense and was incompetent.
Prisoners sentenced to death also
file habeas petitions challenging the
constitutionality of the state death
penalty law. Note that habeas writs
are different from and do not replace
appeals, which are arguments for
reversal of a conviction based on claims
that the judge conducted the trial
improperly. Often, convicted prisoners
file both.

habeas corpus ad subjiciendum See:
habeas corpus

habitable A residence that is safe and
fit for human habitation. By law in
every state but Colorado, landlords
must offer habitable premises and
keep them up. Although the definition
of a habitable dwelling varies from
state to state, all agree that basic
services (adequate heat, hot water, and
plumbing) and a sound structure that
does not pose unreasonable safety risks
are required in every rental. Tenants
have various remedies when premises
become substandard. (See also:
implied warranty of habitability, rent
withholding, repair and deduct)

habitual criminal A person who has
been convicted of multiple felonies (or
of numerous misdemeanors), a fact
that may increase punishment for any
further criminal convictions. (See also:
three strikes)

half blood 1) Siblings who share only one
parent. 2) A half brother or half sister.

harass To engage in harassment.

harassment In employment law, offensive, unwelcome conduct based on the victim's protected characteristic, that is so severe or pervasive that it affects the terms and conditions of the victim's employment. Harassment may take the form of words, actions, gestures, demands, or visual displays, such as photographs or cartoons. Sometimes, harassment is used more generally to refer to repeated irritating or bothersome behavior, such as persistent telephone calls from a debt collector. (See also: protected characteristic, sexual harassment)

harmless error An error by a judge in the conduct of a trial that an appellate court finds was not damaging enough to the appealing party's right to a fair trial to justify reversing the judgment. Harmless errors include technical errors that have no bearing on the outcome of the trial, and an error that was corrected (such as mistakenly allowing testimony to be heard, but then ordering it stricken and admonishing the jury to ignore it). In general, the more overwhelming the evidence against the appealing party (appellant), the harder it will be to convince the appellate court that any errors were harmful. In such situations, courts rule that even in the absence of the errors, the appellant could not have won.

hazard insurance A type of insurance, found for example in homeowners' and business policies, that protects against physical damage to the property caused by unexpected and sudden events such as fires, storms, and vandalism.

headnote In a printed legal opinion, the summary appearing above the decision that summarizes the key legal points of the case.

head of family See: head of household

A Few Good Men. (1992) Tom Cruise, assisted by Demi Moore, defends young marines charged with murder. With Jack Nicholson.

---

head of household 1) For purposes of federal income taxes, a filing category for someone who is unmarried or legally separated from a spouse and who provides a home for at least one dependent for more than half of the year. The tax rate for someone filing as head of household is lower than it would be for someone filing as a single person. 2) The primary breadwinner in a family.

health benefits Benefits paid under health insurance plans, such as Blue Cross/Blue Shield, to cover the costs of health care.

health care declaration See: living will

health care directive A legal document that allows you to set out written wishes for your medical care, name a person to make sure those wishes are carried out, or both. (See also: living will, durable power of attorney for health care, advance directive)

health care proxy A person named in a health care directive to make medical decisions for the person who signed the document, called the principal. A health care proxy may go by many other names, including agent, attorney-in-fact, or patient advocate.

health maintenance organization (**HMO**) A group plan for medical insurance in which members prepay a flat fee and are given access to the services of participating doctors, hospitals, and clinics. Members typically make copayments, but do not need to pay deductibles.

hearing Any proceeding before a judge or other qualified hearing officer without a jury, in which evidence and argument is presented to determine some issue of fact or both issues of fact and law. The term usually refers to a brief court session that resolves a specific question before a full trial takes place, or to such specialized proceedings as administrative hearings. In criminal law, a "preliminary hearing" is held before a judge to determine whether the prosecutor has presented sufficient evidence that the accused has committed a crime to hold him/her for trial.

hearsay A rule of evidence that prohibits the use of out-of-court statements that are offered as proof of the subject of the statement. These statements are not admitted as evidence because person who made the statement isn't in court for the other party to cross-examine. For example, if Cathy, an eyewitness to an accident, later tells Betsy that the pickup ran the light, Betsy would not be allowed to recount Cathy's remarks. Out-of-court statements that aren't offered to prove the truth of the statement are admissible, however. Suppose Tom is called to testify, "On January 1, Bob said the Steelers stink." If the party calling Tom wants to prove that Bob was alive on January 1, Tom's testimony would be admitted, because the other side could question Tom about whether the conversation really took place on that date. Whether the Steelers are a poor team is beside the point. Even statements that are hearsay may be admitted if they fall within one of the many exceptions to the rule. In general, hearsay will be admitted if the circumstances of the statement indicate a high probability that the statement is true. For example, a statement uttered spontaneously and under duress—such as a victim's remarks immediately following an accident—could be admitted because the judge might find that the person had little time to plan to say anything other than the truth.

hearsay rule A rule of evidence that prohibits secondhand testimony at a trial. For example, if an eyewitness to an accident later tells another person what she saw, the second person's testimony is hearsay. The reason for this rule is that the opposing party has no ability to confront and cross-examine the person who has firsthand knowledge of the event.

heat of passion A mitigating circumstance that may be raised by an accused criminal, claiming to have been in an uncontrollable rage, terror, or fury at the time of the alleged crime, especially one provoked by the victim.

heir Someone who has a right, under state law, to inherit a deceased person's property (which means the closest family members). The term is often used in a broader sense, to include anyone who receives property from the estate of a deceased person.

heir apparent One who is expected to inherit property from the estate of a family member.

heir at law A person entitled to inherit property under intestate succession laws.

heiress A female heir, usually used to describe a woman who has inherited a large fortune from a relative—for example, a "department store heiress."

heir hunter A business that searches for relatives legally entitled to inherit from the estate or trust of a deceased person, in exchange for a portion of what they inherit. Heir hunters often tell a potential inheritor that there is the possibility of inheritance but won't provide details unless the heir agrees to pay a fee of one-tenth to one-third of the amount that's eventually inherited. Probate courts sometimes review heir-hunter arrangements and may modify their terms or even declare them invalid as against public policy—that is, as so unfair that courts won't enforce them.

heirs of the body Descendants of one's bloodline, such as children or grand-children, until such time as there are no direct descendants. If the bloodline runs out, the property will "revert" to the nearest relative traced back to the original owner.

held Decided or ruled, as in "the court held that the contract was valid."

hereditament An archaic term, still found in some wills and deeds, for any kind of property that can be inherited.

hereditary succession See: intestate succession

hidden asset An item of value that does not show on the books of a business, often excluded for an improper purpose, such as escaping taxation or hiding it from a bankruptcy trustee.

high seas International marine waters not included in the territorial waters of any country.

highway Any public street, road, or turnpike that any member of the public has the right to use.

hiring firm Commonly refers to a business that hires one or more independent contractors. Unlike an employer, a hiring firm does not have to withhold tax, contribute to Social Security and Medicare, or provide workers compensation for an independent contractor, nor does it have to follow a variety of employment laws that prohibit discrimination, impose wage and hour obligations, or require time off.

hit and run statute A law that requires motorists who get in an accident to stay at the scene of the accident to exchange information with the other motorists or to give a report to the police.

hobby loss A loss from a business activity engaged in more for enjoyment than for profit, which can be deducted against annual income only.

holder Anyone in possession of property. Specifically, holder usually refers to someone possessing a promissory note, check, or bond, for which the holder is entitled to receive payment as stated in the document.

"[The legal profession is] ever illustrating the obvious, explaining the evident, expatiating the commonplace."

—Prime Minister Benjamin Disraeli

---

holder in due course Someone who 1) holds a check or promissory note that was received in good faith and in exchange for value and 2) who has no suspicion that there is a claim against it by another party or that it was previously dishonored. Such a holder is entitled to payment by the maker of the check or note. (See also: bona fide purchaser)

hold harmless In a contract, a promise by one party not to hold the other party responsible if the other party carries out the contract in a way that causes damage to the first party. For example, many leases include a hold harmless clause in which the tenant agrees not to sue the landlord if the tenant is injured due to the landlord's failure to maintain the premises. In most states, these clauses are illegal in residential tenancies, but may be upheld in commercial settings.

holding 1) Any ruling or decision of a court. 2) Any real property to which one has title. 3) Investment in a business.

holding cell Courthouse jail cells (also called lockups and sometimes bullpens) where defendants who are in custody and who are to appear in court are forced to wait. After their court appearance, such defendants are taken back to the regular jail where they are being held.

holding company A company, usually a corporation, that owns and controls other companies.

holding over The continued occupancy of a rental past the date that the lease or rental agreement ends. Most of the time, a residential tenant who holds over with the consent of the landlord will become a month to month tenant.

holdover tenant A tenant who continues to occupy a residence after the term of the lease or rental agreement has expired, and without the consent of the landlord. To get rid of a holdover tenant, the landlord must give the tenant a notice to quit (get out). If the tenant does not leave, the landlord must go to court and file an unlawful detainer (eviction) lawsuit.

holographic will A will that is completely handwritten, dated and signed by the person making it. Holographic wills are generally not witnessed and may be in the form of a letter. Although it's legal in many states, making a holographic will is never advised except as a last resort.

home equity The current market value of a house minus how much is owed on it. A home equity loan borrows against this amount.

home office The portion of a taxpayer's home in which he or she carries on a business activity. If the home office meets certain IRS tests, the taxpayer may take a tax deduction for expenses related to the business portion of the home, such as rent paid and utilities.

homeowners' association An organization made up of neighbors concerned with managing the common areas of a subdivision or condominium complex. These associations take on issues such as garden, pool, and fence maintenance; noise abatement; snow removal; parking areas; repairs; and dues. The homeowners' association is also responsible for enforcing any covenants, conditions, and restrictions (CC&Rs) that apply to the property.

home rule The power of a local city or county to act autonomously in, for example, setting up a system of government and enacting local ordinances. Within the U.S. system, such power must ordinarily be granted by the state government.

homestead 1) The house in which a family lives, plus any adjoining land and other buildings on that land. 2) Real estate that is not subject to the claims of creditors as long as it is occupied as a home by the head of the household. (See also: homestead exemption, Homestead Act)

Homestead Act A federal law, passed in 1862, which allowed people to become owners of up to 160 acres of unappropriated public land by filing an application, living on the land and improving it for five years, and paying a filing fee to acquire title.

homestead declaration A form filed with the county recorder's office to put on record your right to a homestead exemption. In most states, the homestead exemption is automatic—that is, a homeowner is not required to record a homestead declaration in order to claim the homestead exemption. A few states do require such a recording, however.

homestead exemption An exemption from liability given to all or a portion of a primary residence. In most states, only a portion of the homeowner's equity, such as $20,000, can be protected from a bankruptcy trustee or creditors who wish to sell the home to pay off debts owed by the homeowner. Other states exempt all of a homeowner's primary residence from repayment of debts, and still other states exempt all of a homeowner's primary residence only if it is under a certain size.

home study An investigation of prospective adoptive parents to make sure they are fit to raise a child, required by all states. Common areas of inquiry include financial stability, marital stability, lifestyles and other social factors, physical and mental health, and criminal history.

hometowned Slang for a lawyer or client suffering discrimination by a judge who favors locals over out-of-towners. Also referred to as a "home advantage," "home field advantage," or "home court advantage."

home warranty A service contract that covers a major housing system—for example, plumbing or electrical wiring—for a set period of time from the date a house is sold. The warranty guarantees repairs to the covered system and is renewable.

homicide The killing of one human being by the act or omission of another. The term applies to all such killings, whether criminal or not. Homicide is noncriminal in a number of situations, including deaths as the result of war and putting someone to death by the valid sentence of a court. Killing may also be legally justified or excused, as it is in cases of self-defense or when someone is killed by another person who is attempting to prevent a violent felony. Criminal homicide occurs when a person purposely, knowingly, recklessly, or with extreme negligence causes the death of another. Murder and manslaughter are examples of criminal homicide.

hornbook law See: blackletter law

hostile possession Occupancy of a piece of real property in contravention of the rights of others, including the holder of recorded title. Hostile possession is often a prerequisite to claiming ownership by adverse possession.

hostile witness A witness who testifies against the party who has called the person to testify. The examiner may ask a hostile witness leading questions, as in cross-examination. Also called an adverse witness.

hostile work environment Working conditions that are created when unwelcome, discriminatory conduct that is so severe or pervasive that it alters the conditions of a victim's employment and creates an abusive working environment. Employers can be liable when their employees are subjected to a hostile work environment—for example, when a female employee is subject to repeated sex-based taunting or slurs by her male co-workers.

hotchpot Putting together or mixing various properties in order to achieve equal division among beneficiaries or heirs. For example, an estate may contain cash, securities, personal belongings, and even real estate which are part of the residue of an estate to be given to "my children, share and share alike." To make such distribution possible, all of the items are put in the hotchpot and then divided.

Inherit the Wind. (1960) The 1920s Scopes Monkey Trial is fought out between Spencer Tracy as Clarence Darrow and Fredric March as William Jennings Bryan, arguing over teaching Darwin's theory of evolution. With Gene Kelly, Florence Eldridge, Dick York, Harry Morgan.

---

hot pursuit An exception to the general rule that police officers need an arrest warrant before they can enter a home to make an arrest. If a felony has just occurred and an officer has chased a suspect to a private house, the officer can forcefully enter the house in order to prevent the suspect from escaping or hiding or destroying evidence.

house closing The final transfer of the ownership of a house from the seller to the buyer, which occurs after both have met all the terms of their contract and the deed has been recorded.

house counsel An attorney who works only for a particular business.

household People living together in one dwelling, who may or may not be related.

householder A person who supports and maintains a household, alone or with other people; more commonly referred to as head of household. In bankruptcy law, a householder may claim a homestead exemption.

housekeeper See: householder

Housing and Urban Development (HUD) The U.S. Department of Housing and Urban Development. This is the agency responsible for managing the Federal Housing Administration and other housing finance programs, and for enforcing the federal Fair Housing Act and Fair Housing Amendments Act.

HUD See: Housing and Urban Development

HUD-1 A standard form that closing agents give to mortgage loan borrowers on the date the real estate purchase closes, detailing all the costs associated with the closing. These costs include not only those arising from the loan itself, but others such as escrow fees, real estate agent commissions, homeowners' insurance, and transfer taxes.

hung jury A jury unable to come to a final decision, resulting in a mistrial. Judges do their best to avoid hung juries, typically sending juries back into deliberations with an assurance (sometimes known as a "dynamite charge") that they will be able to reach a decision if they try harder. If a mistrial is declared, the case is tried again unless the parties settle the case (in a civil case) or the prosecution dismisses the charges or offers a plea bargain (in a criminal case).

hybrid adjustable rate mortgage An adjustable rate mortgage that starts with a fixed interest rate for a set term (such as five, seven, or ten years), after which the rate can adjust.

hyperlink See: link

hypothecate To pledge as security for a loan without giving up possession, as in the case of property the borrower pledges as collateral and keeps.

I

I-94 card A small green or white card given to all nonimmigrants when they enter the United States. The I-94 card serves as evidence that a nonimmigrant has entered legally. It is stamped with a date indicating how long the non-immigrant may stay for that particular trip. (It is this date—and not the expiration date of the visa—that must be followed in determining when the immigrant must leave.) A new I-94 card with a new date is issued each time the nonimmigrant legally enters the United States. Canadian visitors are not normally issued I-94 cards.

i.e. An abbreviation for *id est*—Latin for "that is"—and used to expand or explain a general term. For example, "his children (i.e., Matthew, Mark, Luke, and Joan)." It should not be confused with "e.g." which means "for example."

IEP See: individualized education program

illegal Against or not authorized by the law. Also called illicit or unlawful.

illegal immigrant See: undocumented immigrant

illicit Unlawful or prohibited. For example, the laws may make it a crime to engage in "illicit trade" or possess "illicit drugs." (Compare: licit)

illusory promise A promise that pledges nothing, because it is vague or because the promisor can choose whether or not to honor it. Such promises do not create contracts and are not legally binding.

immaterial 1) In court, a commonly heard objection to introducing evidence in a trial on the ground that it had nothing substantial to do with any issue in the case. 2) In a lawsuit, a matter that has no bearing on the issues in dispute.

immediate relative Although the common meaning of this is a close family relation, it has a more specific meaning in immigration law. Immediate relatives are a category of prospective immigrants who include a U.S. citizen's spouse, minor children (under the age of 21), and parents (so long as the citizen is at least 21 years old). Immediate relatives have an immediate right to apply for U.S. permanent residence (assuming their U.S. family member agrees to start the process on their behalf)—unlike more distant relatives, they aren't subject to yearly limits on the numbers who can apply for permanent residence.

immigrant visa A type of U.S. visa that a U.S. consulate or embassy issues to people who have just qualified for U.S. permanent residence (a "green card"). The immigrant visa enables the holder to enter the United States, take up permanent residence, and receive his or her green card.

Immigration and Customs Enforcement (ICE) This agency of the Department of Homeland Security handles enforcement of the immigration laws within the U.S. borders; for example, by going to workplaces and checking for undocumented workers.

Immigration and Naturalization Service (INS) Formerly, the federal agency in the Department of Justice that administered and enforced immigration and naturalization laws. In 2003, however, the INS officially ceased to exist, and its functions were taken over by various branches of the Department of Homeland Security.

immunity Exemption from penalties, payments, or legal requirements, granted by authorities or statutes. Generally there are four types of immunity at law: 1) a promise not to prosecute for a crime in exchange for information or testimony in a criminal matter, granted by the prosecutors, a judge, a grand jury, or an investigating legislative committee; 2) public officials' protection from liability for their decisions (like a city manager or member of a public hospital board); 3) governmental (or sovereign) immunity, which protects government agencies from lawsuits unless the government agreed to be sued; 4) diplomatic immunity which excuses foreign ambassadors from most U.S. criminal laws.

"There is far too much law for those who can afford it, and far too little for those who cannot."

—Derek Bok,
President of Harvard University

---

impairs an exemption When a lien, in combination with other liens and the amount a debtor may claim as exempt, exceeds the value of property. For example, if a debtor's home is worth $200,000, the debtor is entitled to a $35,000 homestead exemption, and the home is subject to a mortgage of $150,000, a lien that exceeds $15,000 impairs the debtor's homestead exemption: Once the mortgage was paid off, there wouldn't be enough equity left to pay both the exemption and the lien.

impanel To select a jury and assign the jury to decide a court case.

impaneling The act of selecting a jury from a list of potential jurors.

impeach 1) To discredit, for example, to show that a witness is not believable—perhaps because the witness made statements that are inconsistent with present testimony, or has a reputation for not being a truthful person. 2) The process of charging a public official, such as the U.S. president or a federal judge, with a crime or misconduct, which results in a trial by the Senate to determine whether the official should be removed from office.

impeachment See: impeach

impleader A procedure in which one party brings a third party into a lawsuit. Usually a defendant initiates the proceeding to show that the third party is liable to the plaintiff. (Compare: interpleader)

implied Circumstances, conduct, or statements which substitute for explicit language to prove authority to act, warranty, promise, or consent, among other things.

implied consent Consent when surrounding circumstances exist that would lead a reasonable person to believe that this consent had been given, although no direct, express, or explicit words of agreement had been uttered. For example, implied consent to a contract can be inferred when one person has been performing on the contract, and the other person has accepted the first person's performance without objecting or complaining.

implied contract A contract that is found to exist even when its terms are not explicitly stated because 1) the parties assumed a contract existed (implied-in-fact contract), or 2) denying the contract's existence would result in unjust enrichment to one of the parties (implied-in-law contract). (Compare: express contract)

implied covenant of good faith and fair dealing An implied obligation that assumes that the parties to a contract will act in good faith and deal fairly with one another without breaking their word, using shifty means to avoid obligations, or denying what the other party obviously understood.

implied warranty A guarantee that is not written down or explicitly spoken. (See also: implied warranty of merchantability, implied warranty of fitness, implied warranty of habitability)

implied warranty of fitness A warranty implied by law that, if a seller knows or has reason to know a buyer will use property for a specific purpose, the property is suitable for that purpose.

For example, if a buyer tells a seller he wants to purchase a watch suitable for deep sea diving, the seller can violate the implied warranty by selling the buyer a watch that isn't waterproof and depth-tolerant.

implied warranty of habitability A legal doctrine that requires landlords to offer and maintain livable premises for their tenants. If a landlord fails to provide habitable housing, tenants in most states may legally withhold rent or take other measures, including fixing the problem and deducting the cost from the rent, or moving out. (See also: constructive eviction)

implied warranty of merchantability A warranty implied by law that property is fit for the ordinary purpose for which it is used.

impossibility When an act cannot be performed due to physical impediments, nature, or unforeseen events. It can be a legitimate basis to rescind (mutually cancel) a contract.

impotence A man's inability to copulate. Impotence can be grounds for annulment of a marriage if the condition existed at the time of the marriage and is grounds for divorce in some states.

impound In a criminal proceeding, when the court or police take possession of personal property. The property may be returned to the owner at the end of the proceeding or it may be forfeited to the state (for example, in the case of illegal drugs).

imprison To put a person in prison or jail or otherwise confine him or her as punishment for committing a crime.

improvement As applies to real estate, any permanent structure or work (such as planting trees) on real property, which increases its value or extends its useful life. As defined by the IRS, an addition to or alteration of a capital asset, which either increases its value or extends its useful life.

impute 1) To attach or ascribe. 2) To place responsibility or blame on one person for acts of another person because of a particular relationship, such as mother to child, guardian to ward, employer to employee, or business associates. Example: a child's negligence in driving a car without a license may be imputed to the parent. 3) To attribute knowledge to a person because of the person's relationship to the one actually possessing the information. Example: if one partner in a business is informed of something, that knowledge is imputed to other partners. (See also: vicarious liability)

in absentia (in ab-**sen**-shah) Latin for "in absence," or more fully, in one's absence.

inadmissible In immigration law, being ineligible to enter the United States (or obtain any type of visa or green card) because one matches one of the grounds of inadmissibility found at Immigration and Nationality Act Section 212, or 8 U.S. Code Section 1182. Commonly applied grounds of inadmissibility include having a criminal record, a history of certain immigration law violations, being without a source of financial support, or having a communicable disease.

Music Box. (1989) Jessica Lange stars as a lawyer who is the daughter of an accused war criminal. She defends her father, though she is unsure of his innocence. With Armin Mueller-Stahl, Frederic Forrest, Donald Moffat.

---

inadmissible evidence Testimony or other evidence that fails to meet state or federal court rules governing the types of evidence that can be presented to a judge or jury. The main reason evidence is ruled inadmissible is because it falls into a category deemed so unreliable that a court should not consider it as part of a deciding a case—for example, hearsay evidence or an expert's opinion that is not based on facts generally accepted in the field. Evidence will also be declared inadmissible if it suffers from some other defect—for example,

as compared to its value, it will take too long to present or risks inflaming the jury. In addition, in criminal cases, evidence that is gathered using illegal methods is commonly ruled inadmissible.

inalienable Not transferable; impossible to take away.

in camera Latin for "in chambers." A legal proceeding is in camera when a hearing is held before the judge in private chambers or when the public is excluded from the courtroom. Proceedings are often held in camera to protect victims and witnesses from public exposure, especially if the victim or witness is a child.

incapacitated 1) Lacking the physical or mental abilities to manage one's own personal care, property, or finances. 2) Lacking the ability, due to illness or injury, to perform one's job.

incapacity 1) A lack of physical or mental abilities that results in a person's inability to manage his or her own personal care, property, or finances. 2) A lack of ability to understand one's actions when making a will or other legal document. 3) The inability of an injured worker to perform his or her job. This may qualify the worker for disability benefits or workers' compensation. 4) Under the Family Medical Leave Act (FMLA), the inability to work, attend school, or perform other regular daily activities due to a serious health condition, treatment for the condition, or recovery from the condition.

incentive stock option (ISO) An option to purchase stock (usually given to senior employees) which provides favorable tax treatment for the option holder, as long as certain holding period requirements are met. If the holding period requirements are met, the options are not taxable at the time they are granted or exercised, and any profit is taxed at long-term capital gains rate instead of ordinary income rates.

incest Sexual contact between close blood relatives, including brothers and sisters, parents and children, grandparents and grandchildren, or aunts or uncles with nephews or nieces; 18 states also include copulation or cohabitation between first cousins in the definition of incest. Incest is a crime in all states, even if consensual by both parties.

in chambers Discussions or hearings held in the judge's office, called his or her chambers. (See also: in camera)

inchoate Something that has begun but has not been completed, such as a potential crime for which all the elements have not been accomplished, or a contract that has not been formalized.

incidental beneficiary Someone who benefits as the result of a contract or trust but is not a direct, intended beneficiary. For example, a neighbor might benefit from a homeowner's contract with a tree service, and children might benefit if their parent receives distributions from a trust. (Compare: third-party beneficiary)

incidents of ownership Any control over property. If you give away property but keep an incident of ownership—for example, you give away an apartment building but retain the right to receive rent—then legally, no gift has been made. This distinction can be important if you're making large gifts to reduce your eventual estate tax.

income Money, goods, or other economic benefit received. Under income tax laws, income can be active through one's efforts or work, or passive from rentals, stock dividends, investments, and interest on deposits in which there is neither physical effort nor management. For tax purposes, income does not include gifts and inheritances received. Taxes are collected based on income by the federal government and most state governments.

income in respect of decedent Any income a deceased person would have received, had he or she lived.

income statement See: profit and loss statement

income tax A tax on an individual or a corporation's net income after deductions for various expenses and payments, such as charitable gifts or business expenses. There is a federal income tax and most states assess income tax but at a lower rate than the federal government.

incompatibility A conflict in personalities that makes married life together impossible. In a number of states, incompatibility is the accepted reason for a no-fault divorce. (See also: irreconcilable differences)

incompatible Unable to live together as husband and wife due to irreconcilable differences. If one spouse desires to end the marriage, that fact proves incompatibility, and a divorce will be granted even though the other spouse does not want a divorce.

incompetence 1) The inability or lack of qualifications to do something—for example, perform a job duty or testify at a trial. 2) The inability, as determined by a court, to handle one's own personal or financial affairs.

incompetency See: incompetence

incompetent 1) Unable to manage one's affairs due to mental incapacity or sometimes physical disability.

Incompetence can be the basis for the appointment of a guardian or conservator to handle the incapacitated person's affairs. 2) In criminal law, unable to understand the nature of a trial, and therefore not qualified to stand trial or testify. 3) A general reference to evidence that is not admissible at trial.

incompetent evidence Evidence that is inadmissible because it's irrelevant or immaterial to the issues in the lawsuit. See also: inadmissible evidence

incontrovertible evidence Evidence that leaves no doubt as to a particular conclusion. Examples might include a fingerprint showing that someone was present in a room, or a blood test proving who parented a child.

incorporate To create a corporation by submitting articles of incorporation for an organization, which may be a profit-making business or a nonprofit entity that operates for charitable, social, religious, or educational purposes. The process includes having one or more incorporators file articles of incorporation with the Secretary of State or Division of Corporations, appoint a board of directors, hold a first meeting of the board of directors to launch the enterprise, and issue stock according to state laws and regulations of the Securities and Exchange Commission.

incorporate by reference In documents, to include language from another document by referring to it (rather than repeating it). For example: Plaintiff incorporates by reference all of the allegations contained in the First and Second Causes of Action set forth above.

incorporation The act of incorporating an organization. (See also: incorporate)

incorporator Any person who joins in incorporating a company; specifically, a person who files the articles of incorporation or certificate of incorporation for a new corporation.

incorporeal A thing that is not physical, such as a right. Also called intangible. (Compare: corporeal)

incorporeal ownership Not ownership of a thing, but ownership in a right related to a thing. For example, if you own piece of land, that is corporeal ownership. But if you own a right of way on that piece of land, that is incorporeal ownership. (See also: corporeal ownership)

incriminate To suggest, charge, accuse, show, or admit involvement in a crime.

incumber See: encumber

incumbrance See: encumbrance

incurable insanity A legal reason for obtaining a divorce. It is rarely used, however, because of the difficulty of proving both the insanity of the spouse being divorced and that the insanity is incurable.

The Insider. (1999) A former employee of a tobacco company is persecuted for disputing tobacco executives' claims that nicotine is not addictive. Starring Al Pacino, Russell Crowe, and Christopher Plummer.

indecent exposure Revealing one's genitals under circumstances likely to offend others. Exposure is indecent under the law whenever a reasonable person would or should know that his act may be seen by others—for example, in a public place or through an open window—and that it is likely to cause affront or alarm. Indecent exposure is considered a misdemeanor in most states.

indefeasible Incapable of being altered or voided, usually used to describe an absolute interest in real estate that cannot be changed.

indefeasible remainder A vested remainder that cannot be undone. (Compare: defeasible remainder)

indemnify To guarantee against a loss or damage that another might suffer.

indemnity An agreement to compensate another party for loss or damage.

indenture 1) Generally, any written agreement between two parties. 2) A real estate deed in which two parties agree to continuing obligations; for example, one party may agree to maintain the property and the other to make periodic payments. 3) In finance, a written agreement that describes the borrowers' responsibility to the lenders in a bond or debenture issue and states the maturity date and the interest rate; also called a bond indenture.

independent contractor A legal category of worker that is distinct and different from an employee. The key to the definition is that, unlike employees, independent contractors retain control over how they do their work. Employers are not required to withhold and pay federal, state, and Social Security (FICA) taxes on behalf of independent contractors, as they must do for employees.

independent trustee A trustee who is not related to the beneficiary of the trust and does not stand to inherit any property under the trust. Independent trustees are preferred when family members are likely to disagree over management of the trust. However, independent trustee's fees are usually higher than those charged by a family member.

indeterminate sentence A prison sentence that consists of a range of years (such as "five to ten years"). The state parole board holds hearings that determine when, during that range, the convicted person will be eligible for parole. The principle behind indeterminate sentences is the hope that prison will rehabilitate some prisoners; those who show the most progress will be paroled closer to the minimum term than those who do not. (Compare: determinate sentence)

index A market-sensitive interest rate that determines interest-rate changes on adjustable-rate mortgages and other variable rate loans. Common indices include the six-month London Interbank Offered Rate (LIBOR), the Federal Home Loan Bank 11th District Cost of Funds (COFI), and the prime rate as listed in *The Wall Street Journal*.

indicia (in-**dish**-eeh-yah) From Latin for "signs," or "to point out." Indications or marks suggesting that something is probable. Used, for example, in the terms "indicia of title" and "indicia of partnership."

indictable offense A crime that the prosecutor can charge by bringing evidence of it to the grand jury. These are serious crimes that include murder, manslaughter, rape, kidnapping, grand theft, robbery, burglary, arson, conspiracy, and fraud, as well as attempts to commit them.

indictment A grand jury's conclusion that a serious crime has occurred, and that it is reasonably probable that the defendant committed it. Prosecuting attorneys may generally choose how to charge a crime: by indictment or by using a criminal complaint. To proceed by way of indictment, the prosecutor will show the grand jury enough evidence to persuade them that the target of the investigation should be brought to trial. The target does not have a right to be present, and the proceeding is not public. By contrast, a criminal complaint is followed by a preliminary hearing, at which the defendant is present and where the defendant can question opposing witnesses and call witnesses of his own. When prosecutors want to charge someone but reveal as little as possible of their case and evidence, they often choose the indictment option. (See: indictable offense)

indigent Impoverished, or unable to afford the necessities of life. A defendant who is indigent has a constitutional right to court-appointed representation, according to a 1963 Supreme Court decision, *Gideon v. Wainright.*

indispensable party A person or entity (such as a corporation) that must be included in a lawsuit in order for the court to render a final judgment. For example, if a person sues his neighbors to force them to prune a tree that poses a danger to his house, the lawsuit must name all owners of the relevant property.

individual retirement account (**IRA**) A retirement plan established by an individual that allows annual contributions of income and provides some tax advantages.

individualized education program The process provided under the federal Individuals with Disabilities Education Act to evaluate the educational needs of and develop an academic plan for students with disabilities. It refers both to 1) the meetings where the school district determines whether or not a child is eligible for special education services and if so, the plan for the coming year, and 2) the annual detailed written description of the program and services to help children with special needs succeed in school.

indorse See: endorsement

indorsement See: endorsement

ineffective assistance of counsel Representation of a criminal defendant, at trial or on appeal, by a court-appointed lawyer or a retained lawyer, that involved errors that were so serious that they resulted in the denial of a fair trial. Most errors do not rise to the level of ineffective assistance, though some are (such as failing to investigate the defendant's background in a death-penalty case, where the evidence might have led jurors to impose a sentence of life without parole instead of death).

in extremis Facing imminent death.

infancy 1) Very early childhood. 2) The period of a person's life when they have not reached legal majority or adulthood.

inference A conclusion arrived at by logically drawing on known facts—as in, if A and B are true, then C is.

in forma pauperis (in form-ah **paw**-purr-iss) Latin for "in the form of a pauper." A party to a lawsuit who cannot afford the court costs and fees can ask that they be waived (forgiven) in order to proceed "in forma pauperis."

information The name of the document, sometimes called a criminal complaint or petition, in which a prosecutor charges a criminal defendant with a crime, either a felony or a misdemeanor. The information tells the defendant what crime he or she is being charged with, as well as against whom and when the offense allegedly occurred. However, the prosecutor need not go into great detail. A defendant who wants more specifics must ask by way of a discovery request. (Compare: indictment)

Swift justice was meted out to Giuseppe Zangara, who tried to shoot President-elect Franklin D. Roosevelt in Florida on February 15, 1933, but mortally wounded Chicago Mayor Anton Cermak instead. Cermak died March 6. The murder trial began the next day. Zangara was convicted in a brief trial and was electrocuted March 20, just 33 days after the shooting.

information and belief Language used in legal proceedings to qualify a statement and prevent a claim of perjury. A person making a statement based on information and belief often lacks personal knowledge as to the statement but has a belief that the information is correct. In effect, the person is saying, "I am only stating what I have been told, and I believe it."

informed consent An agreement to do something or to allow something to happen, made with complete knowledge of all relevant facts, such as the risks involved or any available alternatives. For example, a patient may give informed consent to medical treatment only after the health care professional has disclosed all possible risks involved in accepting or rejecting the treatment. A health care provider or facility may be held responsible for an injury caused by an undisclosed risk. In another context, a person accused of committing a crime cannot give up his constitutional rights—for example, to remain silent or to talk with an attorney—unless and until he has been informed of those rights, usually via the well-known *Miranda* warnings.

infra Latin for "below," this is legal shorthand to indicate that the details or citation of a case will come later in the document, such as a legal brief.

infraction A minor violation of law commonly punishable by a fine—for example, a traffic or parking ticket. (Compare: misdemeanor)

infringement 1) Violation or breach of a legal right, contract, or statute. 2) Unauthorized use of a patent, copyright, or trademark. (See also: infringement (of copyright), infringement (of patent), infringement of (trademark))

infringement (of copyright) The unauthorized violation of a copyright owner's exclusive rights in a work. Common examples include the illicit distribution of software or music, the adaptation of another's work in one medium (such as a book or play) for use in another medium (such as a movie or CD-ROM), or the unauthorized public performance of a recording or film.

infringement (of trademark) Unauthorized use of a trademark or service mark (or a substantially similar mark) on competing or related goods and services. The success of a lawsuit to stop the infringement turns on whether the defendant's use causes a likelihood of confusion in the average consumer. If a court determines that confusion is likely, the owner of the original mark can prevent the second user's use of the infringing mark and sometimes collect damages. (Compare: dilution)

infringement (of utility patent) The unauthorized manufacture, sale, or use of (a) a literal copy of a patented invention, or (b) an invention that performs substantially the same function in substantially the same manner as a patented invention. (See also: doctrine of equivalents)

ingress An entrance, or the act of entering. (Compare: egress)

in haec verba (in heek **verb**-ah) Latin for "in these words," or verbatim. This is often used when stating the exact language of an agreement within a complaint or other pleading rather than attaching a copy of it.

inherit To receive property from someone who has died. Traditionally, the word "inherit" applied only when one received property from a relative who died without a will. Currently, however, the word is used whenever someone receives property from the estate of a deceased person.

inheritance Property received upon the death of a relative due to the laws of descent and distribution.

inheritance tax A tax some states impose on people or organizations who inherit property from a deceased person. The tax rate depends on the inheritor's relationship to the deceased person; typically, spouses or children pay no tax, but less closely related inheritors do pay inheritance tax. (Compare: estate tax)

inheritors Persons or organizations who receive property from someone who dies.

in-house counsel See: house counsel

injunction A court decision commanding or preventing a specific act, such as an order that an abusive spouse stay away from the other spouse or that a logging company not cut down first-growth trees. Courts grant injunctions to prevent harm—often irreparable harm—as distinguished from most court decisions, which are designed to provide a remedy for harm that has already occurred. Injunctions can be temporary, pending a consideration of the issue later at trial (these are called interlocutory decrees or preliminary injunctions). Judges can also issue permanent injunctions at the end of trials.

injunctive relief A court-ordered act or prohibition against an act that has been requested in a petition to the court for an injunction. Usually injunctive relief is granted only after a hearing at which both sides have an opportunity to present testimony and legal arguments.

injury Harm done to a person by the acts or omissions of another. Injury may be physical or may involve damage to reputation, loss of a legal right, or breach of a contract.

in-kind Refers to payment, distribution, or substitution of goods or services in lieu of money. Used in wills and trusts, it empowers the executor or trustee to distribute property "in kind" to beneficiaries—that is regardless of whether the property is money, goods, or services—as long as property in the correct value is given to each beneficiary.

in-kind income See: in-kind support and maintenance

in-kind support and maintenance (ISM) Shelter or food provided to an SSI recipient. The value of ISM is considered income. An SSI recipient's monthly grant is reduced dollar for dollar by the total value of the ISM received in a month, up to a certain amount. Also called in-kind income.

in lieu Instead of. For example, a "deed in lieu of foreclosure" is a deed to a house offered to the lender by the homeowner so that the lender will not foreclose.

in limine (in **lim**-in-ay) From Latin for "at the threshold," referring to a request made to the judge before a trial begins, such as a request to exclude evidence.

inlining The process of incorporating a graphic file from one website onto another website. For example, inlining occurs if a user at site A can, without leaving site A, view a cartoon-of-the-day featured on site B.

in loco parentis (in loh-coh par-**ent**-iss) Latin for "instead of a parent" or "in place of a parent." People or institutions that stand in loco parentis to a child might be a foster parent, a county custodial agency, or a boarding school.

innocent A term that is often mistakenly equated to a plea of "not guilty." Innocence is not a legal term, but rather a philosophical, moral, or religious expression of nonresponsibility. By contrast, a not guilty plea simply means that the defendant is demanding that the prosecutor prove every part of the charged crime beyond a reasonable doubt. Many defendants who plead (and are found by the jury to be)

not guilty are probably not innocent under any reasonable understanding of that term. Instead, the prosecutor may have simply failed to produce enough compelling evidence, failing to convince the jury beyond a reasonable doubt.

innocent spouse rule An Internal Revenue Service rule that says that a spouse who unknowingly signs a fraudulent joint tax return prepared by the other spouse can be excused from having to pay penalties on that return.

innuendo From Latin innuere, "to nod toward." In law it means an indirect hint. In defamation cases, defendants sometimes use innuendo when making a comment about the person suing. For example, if there is only one living ex-mayor, the statement "the former mayor is a crook" uses innuendo.

in pari delicto (in pah-ree dee-**lick**-toh) Latin for "in equal fault." In a lawsuit, it refers to situations where the parties are equally at fault or guilty of wrongdoing. They may thus be prevented from collecting damages from the others.

in perpetuity Forever—for example, one may have the right to keep the profits from land in perpetuity.

in personam (in-purr-**soh**-nam) Latin for "against a person." In a lawsuit against a specific person, this concept means the defendant must be served with a summons and complaint to give the court jurisdiction to try the case, and the judgment the court applies to that person only. (Compare: in rem)

in pro per See: pro per

in propia persona See: pro per

inquest A coroner or medical examiner's investigation or hearing into a suspicious death. A jury hearing may be held under some circumstances.

in re Latin for "in the matter of." Used in legal documents to refer to a case, particularly a case without an opposing party. For example, "In re Estate of Ruth Bentley" might be used to refer to a probate case about the estate of Ruth Bentley.

in rem Latin for "against or about a thing," referring to a lawsuit or other legal action directed toward property, rather than toward a particular person. Thus, if title to property is the issue, the action is "in rem." The term is important since the location of the property determines which court has jurisdiction, and enforcement of a judgment must be upon the property and does not follow a person.

INS See: Immigration and Naturalization Service

insanity See: criminal insanity

insanity defense The claim of a defendant in a criminal prosecution that he or she was insane when the crime was committed, and therefore should not be held accountable. (See also: diminished capacity, *McNaughten* rule)

insertion The addition of language into an existing typed or written document (generally initialed by all parties to the document).

insider Someone who has a position in a business or stock brokerage, which allows him or her privy to confidential information (such as future changes in management, upcoming profit and loss reports, secret sales figures, and merger negotiations) which will affect the value of stocks or bonds. Use of such confidential information unavailable to the investing public in order to profit through sale or purchase of stocks or bonds is unethical and a crime under the Securities and Exchange Act.

insider trading The use of confidential information about a business gained through employment in a company or a stock brokerage, to buy or sell stocks and bonds based on the private knowledge that the value will go up or down. The victims are the unsuspecting investing public. It is a crime under the Securities and Exchange Act.

insolvency 1) Generally, the state of having more debts than assets or being unable to pay debts as they come due. 2) For tax purposes, when a person who has had a debt cancelled still has more debts than assets. Someone who is insolvent even after a debt is cancelled does not have to pay income tax on the amount of the cancelled debt.

 "Judges must beware of hard constructions and strained inferences, for there is no worse torture than the torture of laws."

—Sir Francis Bacon

---

inspection of documents The process of examining and copying documents in the possession of an opposing party in a lawsuit.

installment agreement An agreement between the IRS and a taxpayer that allows the taxpayer to pay unpaid federal taxes under a monthly payment plan.

installment contract An agreement in which performance is done in installments. For example, where payments of money, delivery of goods, or performance of services are to be made in a series of payments, deliveries, or performances, usually on specific dates or upon certain happenings.

installment sale A sale where the purchaser of an asset or business pays the seller over several years. This allows the capital gain, and thus the capital gains tax, to be spread over several years rather than all be in the year of the sale.

instruction See: jury instruction

instrument A written legal document such as a contract, lease, deed, will, or bond.

insufficient evidence Evidence so inadequate that a court will find that the prosecution or plaintiff has no basis upon which to proceed, and will most likely dismiss the case.

insurance A contract in which the insured pays a fee to the insurance company, and in exchange, the insurance company agrees to pay the beneficiary of the policy a given amount if specific events occur. For example, life insurance pays a beneficiary on the death of the insured, auto insurance pays the beneficiary if the insured gets into an auto accident, and health insurance pays for health care if the insured gets sick. There are many, many kinds of insurance including: life insurance, auto insurance, health insurance, mortgage insurance, unemployment insurance, accident insurance, burial insurance, cargo insurance, fire insurance, title insurance.

insured The person or entity who is covered by an insurance policy.

insurer The person or entity (usually an insurance company) that agrees to pay for losses suffered by the insured. (See also: insurance)

intangible property Personal property that has no physical existence, such as stocks, bonds, bank notes, trade secrets, patents, copyrights, and trademarks. Such "untouchable" items may be represented by a certificate or license that fixes or approximates the value, but others (such as the goodwill or reputation of a business) are not easily valued or embodied in any instrument. (Compare: tangible personal property)

integrated pension plan A pension plan that takes anticipated Social Security benefits into account when determining plan benefits.

integration 1) To combine the full agreement of the parties into a contract, such that any earlier versions or understandings that aren't included in the contract are superseded. (See also: integration clause) 2) Bringing together people of different races into institutions, such as schools, housing, employment, or the military, that have historically been segregated.

integration clause A provision in a contract stating that the contract represents the full and final agreement of the parties and supersedes any other agreements, oral or written, on the same subject. The purpose of an integration clause is to prevent one party from later claiming that what the parties actually agreed to was different from what was written in the contract.

intellectual property Property such as books, inventions, business secrets, and trademarks, that—unlike real or personal property—is created by the human mind. Intellectual property is typically protected by patent, copyright, trademark, and trade secret laws (jointly called intellectual property laws).

intent The mental desire to act in a particular way. Many crimes require that in order to be found guilty, the perpetrator must have intended to do what he did. An act may be one of many possible crimes depending on the intent of the perpetrator. For example, if A shoots and wounds B, the offense could be attempted murder (if A intended to kill B), assault with intent to cause great bodily injury (A was intending to merely wound B), a minor misdemeanor (A shot on purpose but could not have known that B was around), or no crime at all (A fired the gun completely by accident). (See also: specific intent)

intentional tort A deliberate act that causes harm to another, for which the victim may sue the wrongdoer for damages. Acts of domestic violence, such as assault and battery, are intentional torts (as well as crimes).

intent to levy A notice to a delinquent taxpayer that the IRS intends to seize (levy) property to satisfy a tax obligation, though the levy may not be imminent.

intent-to-use application (ITU) An alternative method for seeking federal trademark registration based on the applicant's bona fide intent to use the mark in commerce in the near future. Although an ITU applicant may reserve the mark for a limited time, registration on the Principal Register will not occur until the mark is actually used in commerce.

inter alia (in-tur **ay**-lee-ah) Latin for "among other things." This phrase is often found in legal pleadings and writings, for example: "The judge said, inter alia, that the time to file the action had passed."

interest A fee paid to a bank or other creditor for lending money or extending credit. The interest rate represents the yearly price charged by the lender for the loan and is usually expressed as a percentage of the total amount borrowed. For example, if you have a $100,000 loan with a 5% interest rate, you will have to pay $5,000 in interest each year until the loan is paid back.

interested witness A witness in a trial who has a personal interest in the outcome of the matter at hand.

"The law is the last result of human wisdom acting upon human experience for the benefit of the public."

—Samuel Johnson

interference An administrative proceeding before the U.S. Patent and Trademark Office to determine who gets the patent in situations where two pending applications (or a pending application and a patent issued within one year of the pending application's filing date) both claim the same invention.

interim order A temporary order made by a judge pending a hearing or trial, where a final order will be entered.

interlineation The act of writing between the lines of a document, usually to add something that was omitted or thought of later. Good practice is either to have all parties initial the change at the point of the writing or have the document retyped and then signed.

interlocutory Provisional and not intended to by final. This usually refers to court orders which are temporary. (See also: interlocutory decree)

interlocutory appeal An appeal that occurs before the trial court's final ruling on an entire case.

interlocutory decree A court judgment that is not final until the judge decides other matters in the case or until enough time has passed to see if the interim decision is working. In the past, interlocutory decrees were most often used in divorces. The terms of the divorce were set out in an interlocutory decree, which would become final only after a waiting period.

interlocutory judgment See: interlocutory decree

intermediate scrutiny A legal standard to determine the constitutionality of a statute, when the statute applies to a quasi-suspect classification (such as gender). To determine if a statute passes the test, a court considers whether the statute involves important governmental interests and whether the law is substantially related to the achievement of important government objectives. (See also: strict scrutiny)

intermittent leave Leave taken under the Family and Medical Leave Act (FMLA) in separate blocks of time rather than all at once. For example, an employee with chronic asthma may occasionally need a day or afternoon off when the condition flares up, or an employee receiving chemotherapy may need to take a few hours off every other week for treatment.

Internal Revenue Code (IRC) The federal tax laws of the United States.

Internal Revenue Service (IRS) The branch of the United States Treasury that administers the tax laws and collects taxes.

international law While there is no one, specific body of international law, the term is taken to mean the collection of treaties, customs, and multilateral agreements governing the interaction of nations and multinational businesses or nongovernmental organizations.

Internet service provider (ISP) A business that provides access to the Internet. An ISP may also offer services such as website hosting. An ISP can sometimes be held accountable for copyright violations for material posted by subscribers and users, but is often protected by the Digital Millennium Copyright Act. The Communications Decency Act usually protects ISPs from the posting of obscenities or defamation by subscribers or users.

interpleader A court case between two parties who both claim the right to money from a third party, when the third party agrees the money is owed but doesn't know to whom. The debtor deposits the funds with the court ("interpleads"), asks the court to be dismissed from the lawsuit, and lets the court decide who gets the money. (Compare: impleader)

interrogation Vigorous questioning, usually by the police of a suspect in custody. Other than providing their names and addresses, suspects are not obligated to answer the questions, which must be preceded by *Miranda* warnings. When suspects refuse to answer, their silence generally cannot be used by the prosecution to help prove that they are guilty of a crime. If the suspect has asked for a lawyer, the police must cease questioning. If they continue to question, they usually cannot use the answers against the suspect at trial. (See also: *Miranda* warnings)

interrogatories Written questions sent by one party to another as part of the pretrial investigation process, called "discovery." Interrogatories must be answered in writing under oath or under penalty of perjury within a specified time (such as 30 days). Lawyers can write their own sets of questions, or can use form interrogatories designed for the most common types of lawsuits.

in terrorem clause (in te-**ror**-em) Latin meaning "in fear." This phrase is used to describe provisions in contracts or wills meant to scare a person into complying with the terms of the agreement. For example, a will might state that an heir will forfeit an inheritance if the heir challenges the validity of the will. Of course, if the will is challenged and found to be invalid, then the clause itself is also invalid, and the heir takes whatever he or she would have inherited if there were no will. Also called a terrorem clause or a no-contest clause.

inter se (in-**tur** say) Latin for "among themselves," referring to rights and duties owed among certain parties rather than to others. For instance, shareholders have certain rights and duties to each other.

interstate commerce The buying, selling, or moving of products, services, or money across state borders. The commerce clause of the U.S. Constitution allows the federal government to regulate trade so that the free flow of commerce between states is not obstructed.

intervene To enter into a lawsuit that has already started between other parties, because a claim exists that is related to the existing case. Example: A grocery store sues a dairy producer for providing sub-par butter. A second grocery chain has been buying from the same producer, so the second chain asks to intervene in the lawsuit.

intervening cause An event that occurs after a party's improper or dangerous action and before the damage that could otherwise have been caused by the dangerous act, thereby breaking the chain of causation between the original act and the harm to the injured person. The result is that the person who started the chain of events may no longer be considered responsible for damages to the injured person since the original action is no longer the proximate cause.

intervention The procedure under which a third party may join an ongoing lawsuit, providing the facts and the legal issues apply to the intervenor as much as to one of the existing parties. (See also: intervene)

inter vivos (in-**tur vee**-vohs) Latin for "among the living." Inter vivos usually refers to the transfer of property during life, rather than after death through a will or other estate planning instrument. It may also refer to a trust created while living, rather than a trust that comes into being upon the trust maker's death.

inter vivos trust The Latin name for a living trust. "Inter vivos" is Latin for "between the living."

intestacy The condition of having died without a valid will. In the absence of a will or other valid estate planning documents, the deceased person's property will be distributed according to the state's "intestacy statutes."

intestate The condition of dying without a valid will. The probate court appoints an administrator to distribute the deceased person's property according to state law.

intestate succession The method by which property is distributed when a person dies without a valid will. Each state's law provides that the property be distributed to the closest surviving relatives. In most states, the surviving spouse or registered domestic partner, children, parents, siblings, nieces and nephews, and next of kin inherit, in that order.

in toto Latin for in its entirety or completely. For example, if a judge accepts a lawyer's argument in toto, it means that the judge accepts the whole thing.

intoxication 1) The condition of being under the influence of alcohol or drugs. Intoxication is not criminal until it impairs a person's ability to operate a vehicle with normal caution ("drunk driving") based on specific levels of alcohol in the blood or, in the case of public drunkenness, when the person becomes unable to care for himself, dangerous to himself or others, or the cause of a disturbance. 2) The defense to a criminal charge, in which the defendant claims that intoxication made it impossible for him to form the intent or specific intent to commit the crime. This defense is available only rarely. (See also: intent, specific intent)

Ghosts of Mississippi. (1996) The true story of investigating and trying the killer of civil rights leader Medgar Evers, two decades after a jury had acquitted the accused murderer in a Mississippi state trial. Alec Baldwin, Whoopi Goldberg.

---

intrinsic fraud An intentionally false representation (lie) which is part of the fraud and can be considered in determining general and punitive damages.

inure To take effect, or to benefit someone. In property law, the term means "to vest." For example, Jim buys a beach house that includes the right to travel across the neighbor's property to get to the water. That right of way is said, cryptically, "to inure to the benefit of Jim." Also spelled "enure."

inurement Benefit. For example, a nonprofit organization with tax-exempt status cannot provide employees with private inurement. That is, employees cannot receive benefits greater than he or she provides in return.

invasion of privacy A legal claim that another person or business has illegally used someone's likeness or unjustifiably intruded into that person's personal affairs. Examples of invasion of privacy include using someone's likeness for commercial advantage (for example, falsely claiming that a particular person has endorsed a product), public disclosure of private facts (for example, that a person has a particular disease or has had an affair), putting someone in a false light to the public (for example, publicizing false information that someone was arrested or said something inflammatory), and intrusion into someone's private affairs (for example, secretly eavesdropping on someone's phone conversations).

inventory 1) Property a business owns for resale. 2) In probate, a complete listing of all property owned by a deceased person at the time of death. The inventory is filed with the court during probate. The personal representative (executor or administrator) of the estate is responsible for filing the inventory.

inverse condemnation The taking of a portion of property by a government agency which so greatly damages the use of a parcel of real property that it is the equivalent of condemnation of the entire property. Example: the city of Los Angeles widens a boulevard and thereby takes the entire parking lot of Bennison's Market. The city offers to pay for the lot, but Bennison claims the market has lost all its business since no one can park and wants the value of the entire parcel, including the market building.

invest To contribute money to a business venture, or to buy property or securities, with the intention and expectation of making a profit.

investigative background check See: investigative consumer report

investigative consumer report A consumer report from a consumer reporting agency that includes information on a person's character, general reputation, personal characteristics, or lifestyle that is based at least in part on personal interviews with the person's friends, family members, neighbors, and others who have information about the person. To request an investigative consumer report, the person making the request must follow the procedures laid out in the Fair Credit Reporting Act. (See also: consumer report, consumer reporting agency)

investment Money spent to acquire an asset for the purpose of making a profit, such as the purchase of stock in a corporation. Also refers to the property or business interest purchased in order to make a profit.

investor A person who makes investments. An investor may act either for him or herself or on behalf of others. A stock broker or mutual fund manager, for instance, makes investments for others who have entrusted that person with their money.

invitee A person who comes onto another's property, premises, or business establishment upon invitation. The invitation may be direct and express or "implied," as when a shop is open and the public is expected to enter to do business. Property owners must protect invitees from dangers on the property, and are liable for damages if they fail to do so.

involuntary To act without intent, will, or choice.

IP See: intellectual property

ipse dixit (**ip**-see **dix**-it) Latin for "he himself said it." A statement that, while unsupported and unproven, may carry some weight based solely on the authority or standing of the person or court that issued it.

ipso facto (**ipp**-soh **fact**-oh) Latin for "by the fact itself." This term is used by Latin-addicted lawyers when something is so obvious that it needs no elaboration or further explanation. A simple example: "A blind person, ipso facto, is not entitled to a driver's license."

IRA See: individual retirement account

IRC See: Internal Revenue Code

irreconcilable differences The most common basis for granting a no-fault divorce. As a practical matter, courts seldom, if ever, inquire into what the differences actually are, and routinely grant a divorce as long as the party seeking the divorce says the couple has irreconcilable differences. (Compare: incompatibility, irremediable break-down)

irrelevant Not pertinent, or germane, to the matter at hand or to any issue before the court. This is the most common objection raised by attorneys to questions asked or to answers given during testimony in a trial. For example, if A is charged with hitting B, evidence of A's honest nature would probably be irrelevant, but that evidence would be relevant if A is charged with embezzlement.

irremediable or irretrievable breakdown An accepted ground for a no-fault divorce. As a practical matter, courts seldom, if ever, inquire into whether the marriage has actually broken down, and routinely grant a divorce as long as

the party seeking the divorce says the marriage has fallen apart. (Compare: incompatibility, irreconcilable differences)

Adam's Rib. (1949) Husband and wife lawyers argue, with great wit, two sides of a murder case. Spencer Tracy, Katharine Hepburn.

---

irreparable harm See: irreparable injury

irreparable injury Harm that no measurable monetary compensation can cure or reverse, such as cutting down shade trees, polluting a stream, or not giving a child needed medication. Proving irreparable injury is often required in order to request a judicial injunction, writ, temporary restraining order, or other assistance in immediately blocking the activity (usually pending further court proceedings). Also referred to as irreparable harm.

irresistible impulse test A seldom-used test for criminal insanity that labels the person insane if he could not control his actions when committing the crime, even though he knew his actions were wrong.

irrevocable life insurance trust (ILIT) See: life insurance trust

irrevocable trust A permanent trust. Once it is created, it cannot be revoked, amended, or changed in any way.

IRS See: Internal Revenue Service

IRS expenses A table of national and regional expense estimates published by the IRS. Debtors whose current monthly income is more than their state's median family income must use the IRS expenses to calculate their average net income in a Chapter 7 case, or their disposable income in a Chapter 13 case.

IRS Regulations IRS written interpretations of selected provisions of the Internal Revenue Code.

ISP See: Internet service provider

issue A term generally meaning all of one's children and their children down through the generations, including grandchildren, great-grandchildren, and so on. Also called lineal descendants.

issue preclusion See: collateral estoppel

itemized deductions Expenses allowed by the tax code to be subtracted from income, such as medical expenses, mortgage interest, and charitable expenses.

J

J. Abbreviation for Judge, as in Hon. William B. Boone, J.

JAG See: judge advocate

Jane Doe 1) A fictitious name used for a possible female defendant who is unknown at the time a complaint is filed to start a lawsuit. 2) The temporary fictitious name given to an unidentified hospitalized or dead woman.

jaywalking The act of crossing a street illegally, for example by walking outside marked cross-walks. (The term "jay" once referred to a foolish rural person who cannot navigate city streets.)

J.D. See: Juris Doctor

jeopardy Being put at risk for a criminal conviction. Jeopardy "attaches" once the jury has been sworn. (See also: double jeopardy)

JNOV See: judgment notwithstanding the verdict

jobber Someone who buys products (usually in bulk or lots) and then resells them to various retailers. This middleman generally specializes in specific types of products, such as auto parts, electrical and plumbing materials, or petroleum.

John Doe 1) A fictitious name used for a possible male defendant who is unknown at the time a complaint is filed to start a lawsuit. 2) The temporary fictitious name given to an unidentified hospitalized or dead man.

joinder The joining together of several lawsuits or several parties all in one lawsuit because the legal issues and the factual situation are the same for all plaintiffs and defendants, or because a party is necessary to the resolution of the case. Joinder may be mandatory if a person necessary to a fair result was not included in the original lawsuit, or it may be permissive if joining the cases together is only a matter of convenience or economy.

joinder of issue The point in a lawsuit when the defendant has challenged some or all of the plaintiff's allegations or when it is known which legal questions are in dispute—in other words, the "issue is joined." Usually this point arrives when pretrial discovery is complete.

joint Undivided and shared by two or more persons or entities. It can refer to rights, responsibilities, or ownership. For example, when property is held in joint tenancy, each joint tenant (owner) has the right to the use and enjoyment of the entire property.

> *"The first thing we do, let's kill all the lawyers."*
>
> —William Shakespeare,
> *Henry VI, Part II*

joint adventure When two or more people go together on a trip or some other action, not necessarily for profit, which may make them all liable for an accident or debt arising out of the activity. (See also: joint venture)

joint and several Refers to a debt or a judgment for negligence against two or more defendants, in which each debtor (person who owes) or defendant is responsible for the entire amount of the debt or judgment, regardless of each individual's precise share of responsibility. For example, a promissory note for a debt often states that if there is more than one debtor, the debt is joint and several. This means the creditor can collect the entire amount from any of the signers of the note. Or, if a party injured in an accident sues several parties for causing damages, the court may find that several people were jointly negligent. The entire judgment may then be collected from any of the defendants found responsible, unless the court finds that different amounts of negligence of each defendant contributed to the injury.

joint custody An arrangement by which parents who do not live together share the upbringing of a child. Joint custody can be joint legal custody (in which both parents have a say in decisions affecting the child), joint physical custody (in which the child spends a significant amount of time with both parents), or both.

joint defendant See: codefendant

joint enterprise An activity joined into by two or more people, with common interests and level of control. The enterprise may be for profit, such as a business partnership or joint venture; or it may be a criminal conspiracy or an instance of group negligence.

joint liability When two or more persons are both responsible for a debt, claim, or judgment. It can be important to the person making the claim, as well as to a person who is sued, who can demand that anyone with joint liability for the alleged debt or claim for damages be joined in (brought into) the lawsuit with them. (Compare: several liability)

joint ownership The ownership of property by two or more people, usually with the right of survivorship.

joint powers agreement A contract between a city and a county and a special district in which the city or county agrees to perform services, cooperate with, or lend its powers to, the special district.

joint tax return A single tax return filed by a married couple on which they report their combined income and deductions.

joint tenancy A way for two or more people to share ownership of real estate or other property. In almost all states, the co-owners (called joint tenants) must own equal shares of the property. When one joint tenant dies, the other owners automatically own the deceased owner's share. For example, if spouses own a house as joint tenants and one dies, the survivor automatically becomes full owner. Because of this right of survivorship, the property goes directly to the surviving joint tenants without the delay and costs of probate. (Compare: tenancy by the entirety, tenancy in common)

joint tortfeasors Two or more persons whose collective negligence in a single accident or event causes damages to another person. Joint tortfeasors may be held jointly and severally liable for damages, meaning that any of them can be responsible to pay the entire amount, no matter what proportion of responsibility each has.

joint venture An enterprise entered into by two or more people for profit and for a limited purpose, such as the purchase or improvement of real estate. A joint venture has most of the elements of a partnership, except that it anticipates a defined period of operation after which it terminates.

joint work Under copyright law, a collaboration between two or more authors in which their contributions are joined into a single cohesive work. Each author of a joint work has equal rights to register and enforce the copyright, regardless of how their shares in the work are divided.

Jones Act A federal law which covers injuries to crewmen at sea, gives jurisdiction to the federal courts, and sets up various rules for conduct of these cases under maritime law.

journal See: general journal

joyriding Driving someone else's vehicle without permission, without intending to take it permanently.

judge 1) An official with the authority and responsibility to preside in a court, try lawsuits, and make legal rulings. Judges are almost always attorneys.

In some states, "justices of the peace" may need only pass a test, and federal and state "administrative law judges" are often lawyer or nonlawyer hearing officers specializing in the subject matter upon which they are asked to rule. 2) The word "court" often refers to the judge, as in the phrase "The court found the defendant at fault," or "May it please the court?" when addressing the judge. 3) To make a legal conclusion, as in "The court judged the defense of self-defense to be unpersuasive."

judge advocate A military officer who is part of the Judge Advocate General's Corps. The Corps is the judicial arm of each of the U.S. armed forces. Judge advocates are charged with upholding military law, as contained in the Uniform Code of Military Justice. Officers of the Corps are the chief officers in courts-martial and military courts of inquiry. Judge advocates also provide legal services to service members, and advise commanders on the laws concerning armed combat.

judgment A final court ruling resolving the key questions in a lawsuit and determining the rights and obligations of the parties. For example, after a trial involving a vehicle accident, a court will issue a judgment stating which party was at fault and how much money that party must pay the other. (See also: decree)

judgment by default See: default judgment

judgment creditor A person or entity that wins a lawsuit and receives a judgment for money damages against the other party.

judgment debt A debt that arises out of a judgment in a lawsuit.

judgment debtor A person or entity that loses a lawsuit and owes a judgment for money damages to the judgment creditor.

judgment notwithstanding the verdict (JNOV) Reversal of a jury's verdict by a judge when the judge believes that there were insufficient facts on which to base the jury's verdict, or that the verdict did not correctly apply the law. This procedure is similar to a situation in which a judge orders a jury to arrive at a particular verdict, called a directed verdict.

judgment proof A condition of having little money and/or property that a creditor who wins a lawsuit could take. A person might be judgment proof because he or she has no property and no steady income. Even a person who owns property might be judgment proof if all of the property is exempt and, therefore, can't be taken by creditors.

judicial Referring to a judge, a court, or the court system.

judicial discretion A judge's power to make decisions based on fairness or a weighing of the facts and circumstances, particularly in cases where a party requesting relief or a benefit has no automatic or clearcut legal right to it.

"You [should] recognize in any society that the individual must have rights that are guarded."

—Eleanor Roosevelt

judicial foreclosure A foreclosure in which the foreclosing party files a lawsuit in the county where the real estate is located, seeking a court judgment allowing the property to be sold at a foreclosure sale because the owner has defaulted on mortgage payments. A few states use what are called strict foreclosures, which let the judge order ownership of the property transferred to the foreclosing party without a sale. Judicial foreclosures commonly take much longer than nonjudicial ones. (Compare: nonjudicial foreclosure)

judicial notice The court's authority to accept matters of common knowledge or indisputable fact without anyone having to present evidence on the point. For example, a court might take judicial notice of the fact that ice melts in the sun.

judicial proceeding Any court proceeding undertaken by a judge, such as a trial or hearing.

judicial sale A sale ordered by a court, or under the supervision of a court, often conducted by an official (keeper, trustee, or sheriff) appointed by the court, usually to satisfy a judgment or implement a court order.

jumbo loan A mortgage loan that's too large to be guaranteed by the Federal Housing Administration and which usually comes with a higher interest rate as a result. (Compare: conforming loan)

jump bail A colloquial term for fleeing or failing to appear for a court appearance after depositing (posting) bail. Also called skipping bail. (See also: bail)

jurat (jur-**at**) From the Latin "to swear." A jurat is the portion of an affidavit or deposition in which a person swears that the contents of the written statement are true. It usually includes the date, the name of the person swearing, the name of the authority before whom the oath was made, and sometimes the place where sworn—for example, "Sworn to this 12th day of October, 2008, by Martha J. Milner, before me, a notary public for said state and county. Barbara A. Stenerson, Notary Public." (Compare: acknowledgment)

jurisdiction The authority of a court to hear and decide a case. To make a legally valid decision in a case, a court must have both "subject matter jurisdiction" (power to hear the type of case in question, which is granted by the state legislatures and Congress) and "personal jurisdiction" (power to make a decision affecting the parties involved in the lawsuit, which a court gets as a result of the parties' actions). For example, a state court's subject matter jurisdiction includes the civil and criminal laws passed by its own state, but doesn't include patent disputes or immigration violations, which Congress allows to be heard only in federal courts. And no court can hear or decide a case unless the parties agree to be there or live in the state (or federal district) where the court sits, or have enough contacts with the state or district that it's fair to make them answer to that court. (Doing business in a state, owning property there, or driving on its highways will usually be enough to allow the court to hear your case.) The term "jurisdiction" is also commonly used to define the amount of money a court has the power to award. For example, small claims courts

have jurisdiction only to hear cases up to a relatively low monetary amount—depending on the state, typically in the range of $2,000–$10,000. If a court doesn't have personal jurisdiction over all the parties and the subject matter involved, it "lacks jurisdiction," which means it doesn't have the power to render a decision.

jurisdictional amount The monetary amount that determines whether or not a particular court can hear a case. For example, under the law of a particular state, the jurisdictional amount of a justice, municipal, or city court might be limited to cases involving less than $25,000. Small claims courts have low jurisdictional limits, usually under $15,000 and sometimes as low as $2,500.

Juris Doctor (J.D.) The degree awarded to a law school graduate in the United States. Also called a Doctor of Jurisprudence.

jurisprudence The study and philosophy of law and the legal system.

jurist 1) A judge. 2) Someone who studies the law.

juror A person who serves on a jury. Lists of potential jurors are obtained from sources such as voter registration rolls, telephone directories, and department of motor vehicles' lists. Individuals who are selected to serve on a jury receive from the court a very small fee for their time and sometimes the cost of traveling from home to court.

jury A group of people selected to apply the law, as stated by the judge, to the facts of a case and render a decision, called the verdict. Traditionally, an American jury was made up of 12 people who had to arrive at a unanimous decision. But today, in many states, juries in civil cases may be composed of as few as six members, and non-unanimous verdicts may be permitted. (Almost every state still requires 12-person, unanimous verdicts for criminal trials.) The philosophy behind the jury system is that—especially in a criminal case—an accused's guilt or innocence should be judged by a group of people from the same community ("a jury of peers"), acting impartially and without bias. Recently, some courts have been experimenting with increasing the traditionally rather passive role of the jury by encouraging jurors to take notes and ask questions.

jury box The enclosed area in which the jury sits during a jury trial.

jury duty The obligation to serve on a jury. In most states, employers are prohibited from discriminating against employees who are called for jury duty—that is, they cannot demote or fire an employee for serving. And a few states require that the employer continue to pay the absent employee.

jury fees The rather minimal amount paid each day to jurors for serving in a trial (a flat fee plus mileage from home to court). In criminal trials this amount is paid by the government, while in civil lawsuits it's paid by the parties to the lawsuit, in equal amounts. The winner is usually entitled to reimbursement of the jury fees paid.

jury instruction A direction or explanation that a judge gives to a jury about the law that applies to a case.

jury nullification A decision by the jury to acquit a defendant who has violated a law that the jury believes is unjust or wrong. Jury nullification has always been an option for juries in England and the United States, although judges will prevent a defense lawyer from urging the jury to acquit on this basis. Nullification was evident during the Vietnam War (when selective service protesters were acquitted by juries opposed to the war) and currently appears in criminal cases when the jury disagrees with the punishment—for example, in "three strikes" cases when the jury realizes that conviction of a relatively minor offense will result in lifetime imprisonment.

jury of one's peers The constitutionally guaranteed right of criminal defendants to be tried by their equals, that is, by an impartial group of citizens from the legal jurisdiction where they live. This has been interpreted by courts to mean that the jurors should include a broad representation of the population, particularly with regard to race, national origin, and gender. Notice that this doesn't mean that, for example, women are to be tried by women, Asians by Asians, or African Americans by African Americans. When selecting a jury, the lawyers may not exclude people of a particular race or intentionally narrow the spectrum of possible jurors.

jury panel A list of people who've been summoned to the court for jury duty, from which jurors for a particular trial may be chosen.

jury selection The process by which a jury is chosen for a particular trial. In brief, a panel of potential jurors is called, they're questioned by the judge and attorneys, some may be dismissed for cause (such as bias), others based on peremptory challenges (in which the attorneys don't need to state a cause), and finally the jury is chosen and impaneled. (See also: voir dire)

jury stress The mental and physical tension found to affect juries in long trials due to exhaustion, sequestration, the mountain of evidence, and the desire to do the right thing.

jury tampering The crime of attempting to influence a jury through any means other than presenting evidence and argument in court, such as conversations about the case outside the court, offering bribes, making threats, or asking acquaintances to exert their influence on a juror.

jury trial A trial of a lawsuit or criminal prosecution in which the case is presented to a jury for final determination of the factual questions. (Compare: court trial.)

jus cogens (jes **koh**-jens) Latin for "cogent law." A principle or norm of international law that is based on values taken to be fundamental to the international community that cannot be disregarded.

jus naturale (jus natch-**ray**-lee) Latin for "natural law." This is a system of legal principles ostensibly derived from universal divine truths.

just cause See: good cause

just compensation 1) In general, a fair and reasonable amount of money to be paid for work performed or to make one whole after loss due to damages. 2) The full value to be paid for property taken by the government for public purposes guaranteed by Fifth Amendment to the U.S. Constitution.

justice 1) A concept of fairness and moral rightness. 2) A scheme or system of law. 3) Judges on the U.S. Supreme Court, the federal courts of appeal, and state appellate courts.

justice of the peace (JP) An official who handles minor legal matters such as misdemeanors, small claims actions, marriages, and traffic matters. Dating back to early English Common Law, "JPs" were very common up to the 1950s, but are now primarily found in rural areas from which it is unreasonable for the public to travel to the county seat for minor matters.

justice system A term that describes the courts and other bureaucracies that handle American's criminal legal business, including offices of various state and federal prosecutors, public defenders, and probation offices.

justiciable A matter which is capable of being decided by a court. Usually it is combined in such terms as: "justiciable issue," "justiciable cause of action," or "justiciable case."

justifiable homicide A killing without evil or criminal intent, for which there is no blame. For example, an accidental shooting, a killing in the course of self-defense, or a death that results from the necessary actions of a police officer would all be justifiable homicides. Justifiable deaths are not the same as a crime of passion or a claim of diminished capacity, which refer to defenses aimed at reducing the penalty or degree of crime. (See also: crime of passion, diminished capacity)

juvenile court A court that hears cases involving the morale, health, or welfare of children, usually under the age of 18. Children who are alleged to have committed crimes will normally have their cases heard in juvenile court, but the prosecution may, in extreme cases and where allowed by statute, ask that the case be handled in regular adult court. Children whose parents or guardians have neglected or abused them may also appear in juvenile court, where the case is between the state (which appears on behalf of the child) and the parents.

juvenile delinquent Slang for a minor who has been found to have committed a criminal offense. Minors may not end up with "convictions," (they are often simply adjudged to have committed the crime), and are usually punished by laws that do not apply to adults, such as by confinement in a facility solely for juveniles. Also termed juvenile offender, youthful offender, or delinquent minor.

K

K The shorthand symbol for "contract" used by lawyers and law students.

kangaroo court Slang for a court that operates unjustly or with unfair bias.

Keogh plan A type of retirement plan for self-employed people, allowing part of their earnings to be taken from their income to accumulate tax-deferred in an investment account until withdrawn.

key employee For purposes of the Family and Medical Leave Act (FMLA), a salaried employee who is in the highest-paid 10% of the company's employees working within 75 miles of the employee's work site. An employer does not have to reinstate a key employee after FMLA leave if doing so would cause the company substantial and grievous economic injury.

kidnapping Taking a person away by means of fear, force, or fraud. Kidnapping is a felony. It is also a federal crime, due to the assumption that the victim can be carried across state lines; this gives the FBI jurisdiction to pursue the alleged kidnapper.

kin A blood relative.

kindred Under some state's probate laws, all relatives of a deceased person.

kiting Illegally taking advantage of the time it takes checks or other instruments to clear (the float), by writing bad checks between different accounts. Because a bank doesn't realize that there are insufficient funds in the account, it may honor a bad check. Also called check kiting.

know-how A particular kind of technical knowledge that may not be confidential but that is needed to accomplish a task.

land Real estate that can be transferred by deed. It usually includes permanent structures such as buildings.

L

L3C See: low-profit limited liability company

labor and materials (time and materials) What some builders or repair people contract to provide and be paid for, rather than a fixed price or a percentage of the costs. In many states, if the person performing the work is not a licensed contractor, he or she is limited to labor and materials in any lawsuit for contract payment, and may not receive a profit above that amount.

labor certification A required procedure for many foreign nationals who have a job offer from a U.S. employer and want to use it to apply for U.S. permanent residence (a green card). The employer must prove that there are no qualified U.S. workers available and willing to take the job. To do so, the employer must conduct an advertising and hiring process and then turn to the U.S. Department of Labor for individual approval of a labor certification. The intending immigrant can then continue with the process and apply for a green card. This process is also referred to as "PERM," meaning Program Electronic Review Management.

laches A legal defense to a claim for equitable relief asserting that the plaintiff's long delay in bringing the claim has prejudiced the defendant (as a sort of legal ambush). For example, if a homeowner watches while the neighbor builds a house over their property line, and only then brings a suit to have the house removed, the encroaching neighbor may raise the defense of laches. Don't confuse laches with "statutes of limitations," which set forth specific periods of time within which plaintiffs must file certain types of lawsuits.

land Real estate that can be transferred by deed. It usually includes permanent structures such as buildings.

landlady Female of landlord or owner of real property from whom one rents or leases residential or commercial real estate.

landlocked A parcel of real property that has no access to a public street and cannot be reached except by crossing another's property. (See also: easement)

landlord The owner of real estate, such as a house, apartment building, or land, that is leased or rented to another person or entity, called the tenant.

landlord and tenant The area of law concerning renting and leasing residential or commercial property and the rights of both the owner and the renter or lessee.

landlord's lien The right of a landlord to seize and sell personal property belonging to tenants, to cover unpaid rent or damages to the property. Few states still allow landlord liens, and of those that do, the process is extremely complicated, requiring written notice to the tenant, exclusion of property that is needed for basic living, and a public sale.

land trust An agreement by which a trustee holds ownership of land for the benefit of an individual or entity. Land trusts are often used by nonprofit organizations for conservation purposes, by large corporations to amass significant landholdings, and by individuals to keep their names out of the public records.

Lanham Act The federal statute that governs trademarks, service marks, and unfair competition. The Lanham Act covers matters that include the procedures for federally registering trademarks, when owners of trademarks may be entitled to federal judicial protection against infringement, and other guidelines and remedies for trademark owners.

lapse Under a will, the failure of a gift of property. A gift lapses when the beneficiary dies before the person who made the will, and no alternate has been named. Some states have antilapse statutes, which prevent gifts to relatives of the deceased person from lapsing unless the relative has no heirs of his or her own. A lapsed gift becomes part of the residuary estate.

lapse statute See: antilapse statute

larceny Another term for theft. Although the definition of this term differs from state to state, it typically means taking property belonging to another with the intent to permanently deprive the owner of the property. If the taking is not forceful, it is larceny; if it is accompanied by force directed against a person, it is robbery, a much more serious offense. Many states differentiate between petit larceny (usually a misdemeanor, punishable by time in the county jail) and grand larceny (theft of a large amount, punishable as a felony in state prison).

last antecedent rule A doctrine of interpretation by which a court finds that qualifying words or phrases refer to the language immediately preceding the qualifier, unless common sense shows that it was meant to apply to something more distant or less obvious. For example, in the phrase "the commercial vehicular license shall not apply to boats, tractors, and trucks under three tons," the qualifier "under three tons" applies only to trucks and not to boats or tractors.

last clear chance A rule, most commonly applied to auto accidents, providing that the negligence of a party suing for damages for an accident is irrelevant if the party being sued could have avoided the accident by reasonable care in the final moments before the accident. Example: a driver drifts over the center line, and an oncoming driver notes the drifting but proceeds without taking simple evasive action and crashes into the first driver. The oncoming driver may be liable for the injuries to the first driver who was over the line.

last will and testament An old-fashioned term for what is now usually called just a "will," which is a document in which you state who should inherit your property, direct how to pay debts and taxes, and name a guardian for your minor children in case one is ever needed.

latent ambiguity See: ambiguity

latent defect A hidden flaw, weakness, or imperfection that cannot be discovered by reasonable inspection. It may refer to real property (a hidden defect in the title to land) or personal property (a defect in the steering mechanism of a car). Discovery of a latent defect generally entitles the purchaser to a refund or a nondefective replacement. (Compare: patent defect)

"The law was not made for a righteous man, but for the lawless and disobedient."
—The Bible, St. Paul in Timothy 1:9

lateral support A landowner's right to have his or her land supported by the land that lies next to it, for example, against any slippage, cave-in, or landslide. Example: a developer excavated into a hill to build an apartment building, without putting in a retaining wall. Surrounding buildings caved in, and the developer had to pay the entire value of the destroyed buildings.

law 1) Any system of regulations to govern the conduct of the people of an organization, community, society, or nation. 2) A statute, ordinance, or regulation enacted by the legislative branch of a government.

law and motion calendar A description of the kinds of legal matters a particular judge or courtroom will hear that day, week, or any other block of time. The law and motion calendar consists of pretrial motions (such as a motion to compel the other side in a civil case to answer discovery requests) or other legal requests that are not connected to a trial, and does not include trials themselves.

lawful issue Formerly, statutes governing wills used this phrase to specify children born to married parents, and to exclude those born out of wedlock. Now, the phrase means the same as the words issue and lineal descendant.

lawful permanent resident (LPR) A non-U.S. citizen who has been given permission to make a permanent home (and work) in the United States. Permanent residents are given "green cards" (not really green) to prove their status. U.S. permanent residents may travel as much as they like, but their place of residence must remain in the United States and they must keep that residence on a permanent basis. Otherwise, they'll be said to have abandoned their U.S. residence, and could lose their right to the green card. A permanent resident who leaves the United States and stays away for more than six months risks having the U.S. immigration officials believe that he or she has abandoned residence.

law in books Legal rules found in texts. This term is most often used in a

derogatory way to refer to old rules that no longer reflect the way the law actually works.

law of admiralty See: maritime law

law of the case Once judges have decided a legal question during the conduct of a lawsuit, they are unlikely to change their views and will respond that the ruling is the "law of the case."

law of the land The body of rules, regulations, and laws that govern a country or jurisdiction. The United States Constitution declares itself "the supreme law of the land."

lawsuit 1) A legal action by one person or entity against another person or entity, to be decided in a court of law. 2) The complaint or petition that begins a court case.

lawyer See: attorney

lay a foundation The act of demonstrating to a judge that a piece of evidence a litigant would like to introduce meets evidence rules requirements concerning authenticity and trustworthiness. For example, a medical report cannot be introduced unless the physician who wrote it testifies that he wrote it; and a photograph must be authenticated by the photographer or by testimony that it truly reflects a particular place or event. Even after a proper foundation is laid, however, evidence can still be excluded if, for example, it is not relevant to the point for which it is being offered.

lay witness A witness who is not an expert. Lay witnesses may not offer opinions, unless they are based on firsthand knowledge or help to clarify testimony.

lead hazard A health hazard resulting from the breakdown of lead paint or lead solder, and the creation of lead dust or lead in drinking water. When such lead is ingested, it can cause brain damage and other damage. A 1996 federal law, "Title X," and the ensuing federal regulations set standards for permissible levels of lead hazards.

leading question A question asked of a witness who is under oath, which suggests the answer. An improper leading question would be "Didn't the defendant appear to you to be going too fast in the limited visibility?" The proper question would be: "How fast do you estimate the defendant was going?" followed by "What was the visibility?" and "How far could you see?" Leading questions are not allowed on direct examination (questioning by the side that called the witness), but are allowed on cross-examination (questioning by adverse parties) or when a party's own witness has been

declared a "hostile witness" by the judge. (See also: hostile witness)

lease An oral or written agreement (a contract) between two people concerning the use by one of the property of the other. A lease for more than one year must be in writing. A person can lease real estate (such as an apartment, house, or business property) or personal property (such as a car or a boat). A lease should cover basic issues such as when the lease will begin and end, the rent or other costs, how payments should be made, and any restrictions on the use of the property. The property owner is often called the "lessor," and the person using the property is called the "lessee."

leasehold The tenant's interest in real estate or right to occupy it, as established by a written or oral lease or by implicit permission of the owner.

lease option A provision in a lease (for real property, such as a house) or contract (for personal property, such as a car) that gives the tenant or lessee the right to buy the real or personal property at the end of the lease or contract period, for a price established in advance.

least restrictive environment A requirement of the Individuals with Disabilities Education Act that school districts place disabled children in the classroom setting that best meets their individual needs, rather than automatically assume that a special class or school is the best option. In many cases, the least restrictive environment, or LRE, is a regular classroom with nondisabled children (also known as mainstreaming), with additional services provided to help the disabled child succeed at school.

"The law embodies the story of a nation's development through many centuries, and it cannot be dealt with as if it contained only the axioms and corollaries of a book of numbers."

—Justice Oliver Wendell Holmes, Jr.

leave year Under the Family and Medical Leave Act (FMLA), the 12-month period by which an employer measures an employee's entitlement to FMLA leave. Eligible employees have a right to take up to 12 weeks of leave in each 12-month leave year.

legacy A gift of personal property to a beneficiary of a will. Technically, legacy does not include gifts of real estate, but the term is often used to refer to any gift from the estate of someone who has died. The more common term for legacy is bequest. (See also: devise)

legal In accordance with and not in violation of the law; having any relation to the law.

legal action Any lawsuit, judicial proceeding, or prosecution, brought to protect a right or remedy a legal violation or injustice.

legal advertising 1) Legal notices required by law to be published in court-approved local newspapers. 2) Advertising for the legal services of lawyers and law firms.

legal age The age of legal majority, at which a person becomes responsible for his or her own actions. In almost all states the basic legal age is 18. State laws vary as to legal age for drinking or buying alcoholic beverages, marriage with or without parental consent, driving, prosecution for crimes, the right to choose an abortion, and liability for damages.

legal aid Free or low-cost legal services for consumers with limited financial means; legal aid services are often provided by local bar associations.

legal cause A cause that produces a direct effect, and without which the effect would not have occurred. (See also: direct and proximate cause)

legal custody The right and obligation to make decisions about a child's upbringing, including schooling and medical care. Many states typically have both parents share legal custody of a child. Compare: physical custody.

legal duty See: duty

legalese Slang for the sometimes arcane, convoluted, and specialized jargon of lawyers and legal scholars.

legal fiction A presumption of fact assumed by a court for convenience, consistency, or to achieve justice.

legal malpractice See: malpractice

legal papers Documents containing a statement of legal status, identity, authority, or ownership, or providing evidence of some type of obligation. Such documents may include wills, deeds, leases, titles, birth certificates, and contracts. Legal papers may also refer to documents such as a complaint or summons, prepared in order to pursue a legal or court action.

legal risk placement A type of adoption in which the child is placed with the prospective adoptive parents before the birth parents have legally given up their rights or had their rights terminated. If the termination of rights doesn't occur, then the adopting parents must give the child back. This is a risk for the adopting parents, who may lose a child to whom they've become attached. Legal risk placements are sometimes used in the case of foster children when the expectation is that the parents' rights will be terminated.

legal separation The legal status of living apart while remaining legally married. Parties who legally separate may petition for property division and support rights, and in all ways end their marital relationship while retaining the status, usually for religious reasons or to retain insurance benefits.

legal services The work performed by a lawyer for a client.

legal succession Succession of right and property in a manner defined by the law. For example, intestate succession is legal succession because the law determines who inherits. However, testate succession is not legal succession because the testator decides who gets what.

legal tender Currency that is issued by a government. Checks, credit cards, and other noncash payments are generally not legal tender.

legatee A person or organization who receives a gift under the terms of a will. Historically, a legatee receives only personal property, not real property; however the word now is most often used to refer to a person who takes any kind of property under a will. (Compare: devisee)

legislative immunity A legal doctrine that prevents legislators from being sued for actions performed and decisions made in the course of serving in government. This doctrine does not protect legislators from criminal prosecution, nor does it relieve them from responsibility for actions outside the scope of their office.

legitimate 1) Legal, proper, or real. 2) A child born to parents who are married.

lemon A car that continues to be defective after a reasonable number of attempts at repair, or after the car has been out of commission for a certain period of time. Under most state lemon laws, the owner has the option—often exercised after arbitration or a lawsuit —of getting a refund or a replacement vehicle.

lemon law Statutes adopted in some states to make it easier for a buyer of a new vehicle to sue for damages or replacement if the dealer or manufacturer cannot make it run properly after a reasonable number of attempts to fix the car.

lessee Also known as the tenant, the person who rents real estate from the owner (the lessor).

lesser crime Also known as a lesser-included offense, a crime that is necessarily part of a more complex crime. For example, in most situations murder would include the lesser crime of assault and battery.

lessor The owner of real property, who rents it to the tenant, or lessee.

let To lease or rent real property to another person, as in "Room to Let."

letter of credit A letter from a bank or other financial institution guaranteeing payment of a certain amount on behalf of a customer. The letter of credit substitutes the bank's credit for the customer's credit. Letters of credit are used primarily to facilitate international transactions.

letter of request A document from a court to a foreign court requesting some type of judicial assistance. Often used to ask the foreign court to serve process on, or take evidence from, someone in the foreign jurisdiction. Also known as rogatory letters or letters rogatory.

letters See: letters of administration, letters testamentary

letters of administration The document a probate court issues to the person appointed as administrator (personal representative) of the estate of someone who died without a will. The letters authorize the administrator to settle the deceased person's estate according to the state's intestate succession laws.

Banks, brokerages, and government agencies often require a certified copy of the letters before accepting the administrator's authority to collect the deceased person's assets. (See also: letters testamentary)

letters rogatory See: letter of request

 "The law is a jealous mistress."
—Justice Joseph Story

---

letters testamentary The document a probate court issues to an executor (personal representative) of a deceased person's estate, authorizing the executor to settle the estate according to the terms of the person's will. Banks, brokerages, and government agencies often require a certified copy of the letters before accepting the executor's authority to collect the deceased person's assets. (See also: letters of administration)

leverage 1) The use of borrowed money to purchase real estate or business assets, usually involving borrowed money that equals a high percentage of the value of the purchased property. The dangers of high leverage are overappraisal of the property, a decline in the value of the property, and high carrying costs (interest, insurance, taxes, maintenance). 2) To borrow most of the funds

necessary as a loan against real estate to buy other real estate or business assets.

levy 1) To seize property to satisfy a debt or lawsuit judgment. Sometimes used as a noun to refer to the property seizure. 2) To impose or assess, as a tax.

lewd Any conduct that is considered indecent or offensive. Today the term is often used when referring to pornography, prostitution, and indecent exposure.

lewd and lascivious Conduct that is sexual in nature and deemed by judges to be criminal. Examples include indecent exposure, prostitution, and indecent acts.

lex loci (lecks **loh**-see) Latin for the "law of the place." It means local law.

LGBT An abbreviation for Lesbian, Gay, Bisexual, and Transgender people or groups.

liability 1) In law, the state of being liable—that is, legally accountable for an act or omission. 2) In business, money owed by a business to others, such as payroll taxes, a court judgment, an account payable, or a loan debt.

liability insurance coverage Insurance that provides compensation to third parties who are injured or whose property is damaged due to the fault of the insurance holder. You may have liability insurance for your car or your home, or to cover actions you take in the course of your profession. Liability policies are sometimes called "third-party policies."

liable Legally responsible. For example, a person may be liable for a debt, liable for an accident due to careless behavior, liable for failing do something required by a contract, or liable for the commission of a crime. Someone who is found liable for an act or omission must usually pay money damages or, if the act was a criminal one, face punishment. (See also: liability)

libel An untruthful statement about a person, published in writing or through broadcast media, that injures the person's reputation or standing in the community. Libel is a tort (a type of civil wrong), and the injured person can bring a lawsuit against the person who made the false statement. Libel and slander (an untruthful statement that is spoken, but not published in writing or broadcast through the media), are both considered forms of defamation.

libel per se False statements that are so widely understood to be harmful that they are presumed to be defamatory, such as an accusation that a person has committed a crime, has a dreaded disease, or is unable to perform one's occupation.

liberty Freedom from restraint, slavery, or imprisonment, and the power to follow one's own will within the limits set by the law or society.

license 1) Permission to do something otherwise prohibited under law—for example, a license to practice law or drive a car. 2) A contract giving written permission, for a limited time, to someone to exploit an invention, creative work, or trademark. A license provides a way for an innovator to make money from an invention or creative work without having to manufacture and sell copies, and without having to permanently relinquish ownership. Some licenses are exclusive (limiting the grant to one company) while others are nonexclusive (permitting several companies in an industry to market the product). 3) A private grant of right to use real property for a particular purpose, such as putting on a concert.

licensee A person or entity that obtains a license.

licensor A person or entity that grants a license.

licit Lawful, permitted. (Compare: illicit)

lie detector test The popular name for a polygraph, which tests a person's physiological response (for example, changes in blood pressure and respiration) to questions asked by a testing expert to judge whether the person is telling the truth. The test's reliability is a matter of ongoing controversy, and in most U.S. states polygraph test results are not admissible in court.

lien A creditor's legal claim against particular property owned by a debtor as security for a debt. Liens the debtor agrees to, called security interests, include mortgages, home equity loans, car loans, and personal loans for which the debtor pledges property as collateral. Nonconsensual liens are liens placed on property without the debtor's consent, and include tax liens, judgment liens (liens a creditor obtains by suing and getting a court judgment against the debtor), and mechanics' liens (liens filed by a contractor who worked on the debtor's house but didn't get paid).

lienor A person or entity that holds a lien on the funds or property of another.

life beneficiary Someone who receives benefits, under a trust or by will, only for his or her lifetime (or in rare cases, for someone else's lifetime). For an example, see bypass trust. (See also: life estate)

life estate The right to the use and enjoyment of certain property (usually real estate) for life only. So someone who inherits a life estate in a house may live in the house for his or her life but has no right to sell it or to leave it at death. Life estates aren't as commonly used as they once were, but are still useful in certain situations. For example, a man in his second marriage might leave a life estate in his house to his surviving wife, with the provision that at her death, it is to go to his children from his previous marriage. (See also: remainderman)

life expectancy The length of time a person is expected to live based on age, gender, health, and many other factors. In insurance, and sometimes in court, life expectancy is based on standard tables called actuarial tables.

life insurance A contract in which an insurance company agrees to pay money to a designated beneficiary upon the death of the policyholder. In exchange, the policyholder pays a regularly scheduled fee, known as the insurance premiums. The purpose of life insurance is to provide financial support to those who survive the policyholder, such as family members or business partners. When the policy-holder dies, the insurance proceeds pass to the beneficiaries free of probate, though they are counted for federal estate tax purposes. There are many types of life insurance, including: term life insurance, whole life insurance, and universal life insurance.

life insurance avails See: avails

life insurance trust A trust set up to own a life insurance policy, so that the policy proceeds aren't subject to estate tax when the original policy owner dies. Life insurance trusts are usually irrevocable.

In Illinois, you may be arrested for vagrancy if you do not have at least one dollar bill on your person—and it is illegal to give a dog whiskey.

life tenant Someone who has a life estate in property.

life-prolonging procedure See: life-sustaining treatment

life-sustaining procedure See: life-prolonging procedure

life-sustaining treatment Medical procedures that would only prolong the process of dying or sustain a condition of permanent unconsciousness. A patient who is receiving life-sustaining treatment will die soon, whether or not treatment is administered. Life-sustaining treatment may include a respirator, cardiopulmonary resuscitation (CPR), dialysis, surgery, and other medical procedures.

life without possibility of parole A prison sentence for life, with no parole possible. In a death penalty case, a jury that decides not to sentence the defendant to death may instead sentence to life without parole. In states without the death penalty, this is the most extreme sentence.

like-kind property Property that is similar to property being sold in a 1031 exchange. Property must be like-kind to be eligible for an exchange, but that does not mean it need be similar. Properties must simply be of the same nature or character (meaning both are investment or business properties), but not the same grade or quality.

likelihood of confusion See: confusingly similar

limitation of actions See: statute of limitations

limited equity housing (Also referred to as limited equity housing cooperatives, or LEHCs.) An arrangement designed to encourage low- and moderate-income families to buy their own place to live. The housing is offered for sale, usually by a nonprofit organization, at an extremely favorable price with a low down payment. Typically the housing has been built (or an apartment building has been converted) for multiple families, who then share common areas and some decision making. The catch is that, upon selling, the owner gets none of the profit if the market value of the unit has gone up. Any profit returns to the organization that built the home, which then resells the unit at an affordable price.

limited jurisdiction When a particular court has a narrowly defined authority over certain types of cases, such as bankruptcy, claims against the government, probate, family matters, or immigration.

limited liability A feature of corporations and LLCs where the business owners are legally responsible for paying business debts, claims, and judgments only to the extent of the capital they invested in the business. This means that if the business folds, creditors cannot seize or sell the business owner's home, car, or other personal assets.

limited liability company (LLC) A business ownership structure that shields its owners' personal assets through the doctrine of limited liability (like a corporation) but has pass-through taxation (like a partnership), where profits (or losses) are passed through to the owners and taxed on their personal income tax returns.

limited liability partnership (LLP) A type of partnership recognized in a majority of states that protects a partner from personal liability for negligent acts committed by other partners or by employees not under his

or her direct control. Some states also protect partners from personal liability for contract breaches or intentional torts. Some states restrict this type partnership to professionals, such as lawyers, accountants, architects, and health care providers.

limited partnership A business structure that allows one or more partners (called limited partners) to enjoy limited personal liability for partnership debts while another partner or partners (called general partners) have unlimited personal liability. The key difference between general and limited partners is with management decision making—general partners run the business and limited partners (who are usually passive investors) are not allowed to make day-to-day business decisions. If they do, they risk being treated as general partners with unlimited personal liability.

limited personal liability See: limited liability

limited power of attorney A power of attorney that gives the agent power to handle only a specified matter—for example, to sign papers completing a single business transaction or property transfer. (Compare: general power of attorney)

limiting instructions Jury instructions in which a judge instructs that evidence is admissible for one purpose but not for another. The judge will often instruct jurors to consider the evidence only for the legitimate purpose, and ignore it for any other purpose. (See also: jury instruction)

lineal consanguinity The relationship between blood relatives where one is a direct descendant of the other. For example, a person has consanguinity with her mother, grandmother, and daughter. (See also: consanguinity)

lineal descendant See: issue

lineup A procedure in which the police place a suspect in a line with a group of other people and ask an eyewitness to the crime whether the person he saw at the crime scene is in the lineup. The police are supposed to choose similar-looking people to appear with the suspect. If the suspect alone matches the physical description of the perpetrator, evidence of the identification may be excluded at trial. For example, if the robber is described as a Latino male, and the suspect, a Latino male, is placed in a lineup with ten white males, a witness's identification of him as the robber will be challenged by the defense attorney.

link Any component of a Web page that connects to another Web page or another portion of the same Web page. Clicking on underlined text or a graphic image activates most links. For example, if a user clicks on the words, financial calculator, or an image of a calculator, the user will be transported to a page that contains a calculator. Links are sometimes called hyperlinks. (Compare: deep link)

liquid asset Business or personal property that can be quickly and easily converted into cash, such as stock, bank accounts, and accounts receivable.

liquidate To sell the assets of a business, pay the business's debts, and divide the remainder among shareholders, partners, or other investors.

liquidated damages In a contract, an amount of money agreed upon by both parties that a party who breaches the contract will pay to the other party. Liquidated damages clauses may not be enforced by judges when they appear in consumer contracts, because they are often used to punish the party who breaks the contract, rather than to compensate the other side for its actual damages.

liquidating partner The member of an insolvent or dissolving partnership responsible for paying the debts and settling the accounts of the partnership.

lis pendens (lease **pen**-denz) 1) Latin for "a suit pending." The term may refer to any pending lawsuit. 2) A written notice that a lawsuit has been filed concerning real estate, involving either the title to the property or a claimed ownership interest in it. The notice is usually filed in the county land records office. Recording a lis pendens alerts a potential purchaser or lender that the property's title is in question, which makes the property less attractive to a buyer or lender. After the notice is filed, anyone who nevertheless purchases the land or property described in the notice takes it subject to the ultimate decision of the lawsuit.

listed property Certain types of depreciable assets used in a business for which the IRC requires special record keeping to prorate personal and business use. These assets are prone to being used for personal use, such as cellular phones, home-based computers, boats, airplanes, and vehicles.

literary works One of the broad categories of material protected under the copyright laws. Literary works are expressed in words, numbers, or other verbal or numerical symbols or indicia. Under this broad definition, software—because it is expressed in programming code in numbers and letters—is considered a copyrightable literary work.

litigant Any party to a lawsuit. This might include a plaintiff, defendant, petitioner, respondent, cross-complainant, or cross-defendant, but not a witness or attorney.

litigation The process of bringing and pursuing (litigating) a lawsuit.

 "Avoid litigation."
—Abraham Lincoln

litigator A trial lawyer; an attorney who represents plaintiffs or defendants in court.

litigious Description of a person or company with a disposition toward bringing or prolonging lawsuits, even if the suits are unnecessary, unfounded, or largely retaliatory.

living trust A trust that is set up during a person's life. Living trusts are a common and excellent way to avoid probate at death, and may also reduce federal estate tax. Also called "inter vivos trust." (See also: revocable living trust, testamentary trust)

living will A legal document in which you state your wishes about the types of medical care you do or do not want if you are unable to speak for yourself. This document may go by many other names, including health care directive, advance directive, declaration, or directive to physicians.

LLC See: limited liability company

LLP See: limited liability partnership

loan broker A person or entity that specializes in matching homebuyers with appropriate mortgage lenders. Loan brokers (also known as mortgage brokers) make most of their money by marking up the costs on the loan the wholesale lender is offering. Loan brokers provide an easy and effective way to find the cheapest mortgage rates, given the borrower's financial situation and goals. Many states require loan brokers to be licensed.

loan consolidation Combining a number of loans into a single new loan. Consolidation typically extends the repayment period, lowers the monthly payments, and thereby increases the interest the borrower will have to pay over the life of the consolidated loan.

local rules See: rules of court

locus (**low**-cuss) Latin for "place," or the location where something occurred.

loiter To linger or hang around in a public place with no purpose. Many states and cities have laws that prohibit loitering.

loitering A crime best understood as just hanging out.

long-arm statute A law that gives a court jurisdiction over a nonresident company or individual who has had sufficient contacts with the jurisdiction to warrant being subject to its laws.

long cause A lawsuit in which it is estimated that the trial will take more than one day to complete, and must be fitted into the court calendar accordingly.

loss 1) The value placed on injury or damages due to an accident caused by another's negligence, breach of contract, or other wrongdoing. The amount of monetary damages can be determined in a lawsuit. 2) When expenses are greater than profits, the difference between the amount of money spent and the income.

loss carryover See: carryover

loss damage waiver (LDW) See: collision damage waiver

loss of bargain rule The concept that the amount of damages to be paid to a party in a breach of contract case should be sufficient to put that party in the position that it would have been in if the contract had been fully performed by both parties.

loss of consortium A type of legal claim made by a spouse when the other spouse has been injured to a point of being unable to provide the benefits of a family relationship, including intimacy, affection, company, and sexual relations.

"Justice should remove the bandage from her eyes long enough to distinguish between the vicious and the unfortunate."

—Robert G. Ingersoll

---

loss of use The inability to use an automobile, premises, or some equipment due to damage caused by the negligence or wrongdoing of another. This concept may entitle claimants to damages. For example, during the period of non-occupancy while a burned building is restored, the regular occupant has lost its use and may be entitled to compensation for the days he or she must live or work elsewhere.

lower court 1) Any court of relatively lesser rank, such as municipal or justice court below a superior or county court, a superior or county court below an appeals court, or a federal district court of appeals below the U.S. Supreme Court. 2) A reference in an appeal to the trial court that originally heard the case.

low-profit limited liability company A cross between a nonprofit and for-profit organization, also called an L3C. Low-profit limited liability companies are designed to attract private investors and donors who want to provide social benefits. Unlike a regular LLC, the primary purpose of an L3C is charitable. But the L3C is permitted to distribute after-tax profits to owners or investors.

LRE See: least restrictive environment

L.W.O.P. A life prison sentence, literally "life without parole."

M

MACRS Short for modified accelerated cost recovery system. A method of depreciation, established by the Internal Revenue Code, for rapidly claiming depreciation tax deductions.

magistrate 1) In the U.S., a generic term for a court judge. 2) In a few U.S. states, a justice of the peace or other lower-level officer of the court, with limited power to hear certain types of cases, such as small claims lawsuits or minor crimes, or to conduct particular types of proceedings, such as preliminary hearings. 3) In U.S. federal district courts, a magistrate judge is an official who conducts routine hearings assigned by the federal judges, including preliminary hearings in criminal cases.

Magna Carta An historical document from England that helped establish common law and statutes—in other words, it is a founding document of the law as we know it today. When King John reluctantly signed it in 1215, it was essentially a document for the nobility; however it became the basis of modern individual rights.

mailbox rule In contract law, the acceptance of a contract is effective when a properly prepaid and addressed letter of acceptance is posted, as long as it is sent within the time in which the offer must be accepted (and unless the offer requires acceptance by personal delivery on or before the specified date). The mailbox rule is an exception to the general principle is that a contract is formed when acceptance is actually communicated to the offeror.

Mail or Telephone Order Rule A Federal Trade Commission rule that requires a seller to ship goods ordered by mail, phone, computer, or fax to a customer within the time promised or, if no time was stated, within 30 days. If the seller cannot ship within that period, the seller must send the customer a notice with a new shipping date and give the options of canceling the order and getting a refund or agreeing to the delay.

maim To inflict serious bodily injury, including mutilation, disfigurement, or any harm that limits the victim's ability to function physically. Originally, in English common law it meant to cut off or permanently cripple a part of the body such as an arm, leg, hand, or foot. In criminal law, such serious harm can turn an ordinary assault into an aggravated assault.

mainstreaming See: least restrictive environment

majority 1) More than half of something, such as the votes cast in an election. 2) The age at which a person can exercise the legal rights of an adult, such as entering into contracts or voting. (See also: age of majority)

major life activity Functions such as caring for oneself, performing manual tasks, walking, seeing, hearing, speaking, breathing, learning, and working. Under the Americans with Disabilities Act, an individual is considered to have a disability if he or she has an impairment that substantially limits a major life activity.

make To sign a check, promissory note, agreement, or other document—for example, to make a contract.

make one whole To award an amount of damages sufficient to put the injured party back into the position that party was in before the injury.

maker 1) The person who signs a check or promissory note, which makes that person responsible for payment. 2) A person who endorses a check or note over to another person before it is delivered, making the endorser obligated to pay until it is delivered. (See also: check, promissory note, payor, payee)

malfeasance Intentionally doing something that is illegal. This term is often used when a professional or public official commits an illegal act that interferes with the performance of his or her duties. For example, an elected official who accepts a bribe in exchange for political favors has committed malfeasance. (Compare: misfeasance; nonfeasance)

malice A willful or intentional state of mind, in which the actor intends to bring about an injury or wrongdoing. 1) In criminal law, malice can be evident by the act itself, as when someone purposefully injures someone else. Murder requires proof of malicious intent, and first-degree murder requires "malice aforethought." 2) In a defamation lawsuit (libel or slander), the jury's finding that the defendant acted with malice may increase the plaintiff's damages. In order for a public figure to win a defamation lawsuit, he or she must prove malice on the part of the defendant. (See also: malice aforethought)

malice aforethought The state of mind necessary to prove first-degree murder.

The prosecution must prove that the defendant intended to cause death or great bodily harm, or exhibited extreme and reckless indifference to the value of life. Any intentional killing that does not involve justification, excuse, or mitigation is a killing with malice aforethought.

malicious prosecution Filing a civil or criminal lawsuit for an improper purpose (civil) or without probable cause (criminal). If a wrongful prosecution ends in the defendant's favor, the defendant can sue the plaintiff for the wrong he has suffered.

malpractice The delivery of substandard care or services by a lawyer, doctor, dentist, accountant, or other professional. Generally, malpractice occurs when a professional fails to provide the quality of care that should reasonably be expected in the circumstances, with the result that a patient or client is harmed. Such an error or omission may be through negligence, ignorance (when the professional should have known), or intentional wrongdoing. In the area of legal malpractice, the claimant must prove two things to show harm: first, that the lawyer failed to meet the standard of professional competence; and second, that if the lawyer had handled the work properly, you would have won the original case. (See also: errors and omissions)

malum in se (**mal**-uhm in **say**) Latin for something "wrong in itself," even in the absence of a law making it illegal. In criminal law, it describes acts that have traditionally been considered crimes, whether or not a specific written law made them crimes, because they violate the principles of civilized society. Examples are murder, rape, and theft. By contrast, making a left turn at an intersection where a traffic law prohibits it would not be malum in se, because it is based only on statutory law. (Compare: malum prohibitum)

> "It is far better to have less learning and more moral character in the practice of law than it is to have great learning and no morals."
>
> —Vice President Thomas R. Marshall

malum prohibitum (**mal**-uhm prohibit-uhm) Latin for "wrong due to being prohibited," referring to acts made illegal by statute to benefit public welfare, not because they are inherently evil and obvious violations of society's standards. Generally, they do not involve immediate injury or damage to others. Examples include violations of regulatory acts, insider trading, and tax avoidance. (Compare: malum in se)

mandamus (man-**dame**-us) Latin for "we command." A writ of mandamus is a court order that requires another court, government official, public body, corporation, or individual to perform a certain act. For example, after a hearing, a court might issue a writ of mandamus forcing a public school to admit certain students on the grounds that the school illegally discriminated against them when it denied them admission. A writ of mandamus is the opposite of an order to cease and desist, or stop doing something (an injunction). Also called a "writ of mandate."

mandate 1) Any mandatory order or requirement under statute, regulation, or by a public agency. 2) An order from an appellate court to a lower court (usually the original trial court in the case) directing the lower court to enforce a court order or to comply with the appeallate court's ruling. (See also: mandamus)

mandatory Required, compulsory, or obligatory.

mandatory injunction An injunction that requires a person to carry out a positive act—for example, return stolen computer code. (See also: injunction)

mandatory joinder The required inclusion in a lawsuit of a party whom the court finds is absolutely necessary to a resolution of all issues in the case. (See also: joinder)

manifest 1) Apparent, obvious, or evident. 2) A written list or invoice of cargo.

Mann Act A federal law that makes it a crime to transport women across state lines for prostitution or similar sexual activities. The Mann Act was intended to prevent the movement of prostitutes from one state to another or in and out of the country in the so-called "white slave" trade.

manslaughter The crime of killing someone, but without the malice (evil intent) needed to make the killing murder. 1) Involuntary manslaughter is a death that results from criminal, or extreme, negligence; or during the commission of a crime not included within the felony-murder rule. 2) Voluntary manslaughter is an act of murder that is reduced to manslaughter due to extenuating circumstances, such as when the defendant acts in "the heat of passion" or is subject to diminished capacity. (See also: felony murder doctrine, diminished capacity)

manual accounting system An accounting system maintained by hand, using paper, rather than on a computer.

Mapp v. Ohio (1961) A U.S. Supreme Court case in which the Court ruled that evidence obtained by illegal search and seizure could not be introduced in state or federal trials.

Marbury v. Madison (1803) A U.S. Supreme Court case in which Chief Justice John Marshall used a dispute over judicial appointments to declare a judiciary act unconstitutional, establishing the power of the Supreme Court to decide the constitutionality of statutes.

margin 1) The difference between the net sales price of an item or security and its cost. This is often called a profit margin and is frequently expressed as a percentage. For example, if you pay 50 cents for a pencil and sell it for a dollar, your profit margin is 50%. 2) The difference between the face value of a loan and the market value of the collateral that secures it. 3) An investor's equity in securities purchased on credit through a broker. 4) Cash or collateral that must be deposited with a broker who agrees to finance the purchase of securities.

marginal tax rate See: tax bracket

marital deduction A deduction allowed by the federal estate tax laws for all property passed to a surviving spouse who is a U.S. citizen. This deduction (which really functions as an exemption) allows anyone, even a billionaire, to pass his or her entire estate to a surviving spouse without any estate tax at all. Under current federal law, this deduction is not available to same-sex couples even if they were validly married in a state that allows same-sex marriage.

marital misconduct See: fault divorce

marital privilege In a civil (noncriminal) court case, the right of spouses not to testify about confidential communications between them. In a criminal case, the right not to testify against a spouse.

marital property Property that is considered under state law to be owned by both spouses. In community property states, all income earned and property acquired during marriage is marital (community) property. In other states, whether property is considered marital property depends on how it is titled and sometimes, other factors. Most states exclude inheritances from marital property.

marital settlement agreement The document that sets out the terms of a divorce settlement between two spouses. The marital settlement agreement (MSA) is usually incorporated into the final judgment issued by the judge so that it has the force of a court order.

marital termination agreement See: marital settlement agreement

marital tort A tort (civil wrong) by one spouse against the other.

maritime court A court that hears issues involving maritime law. These federal courts do not use juries and have unique rules of court. The cases are often handled by admiralty law specialists.

maritime law The laws and regulations which exclusively govern activities at sea or in any navigable waters. In the United States, the federal courts have jurisdiction over maritime law. Also called admiralty law.

mark An "X" or other writing that serves as a signature, made by a person who is too weak or does not know how to sign his or her full name.

marked for identification Documents or objects presented during a trial before testimony confirms their authenticity or relevancy. Each item is given an exhibit identification letter or number, and can then be physically marked and referred to by that letter or number. The marked exhibits can be introduced into evidence (made part of the official record) upon request of the lawyer offering the evidence and approval by the judge or by stipulation of both attorneys.

marketable title See: clear title

market value See: fair market value

marriage The legal union of two people. Once a couple is married, their rights and responsibilities toward one another concerning property and support are defined by the laws of the state in which they live. A marriage can only be terminated by a court granting a divorce or annulment.

 "The constitution does not provide for first and second class citizens."
—Wendell L. Willkie

---

marriage certificate A document that provides proof of a marriage, typically issued to the newlyweds a few weeks after they file for the certificate in a county office. Most states require both spouses, the person who officiated the marriage, and one or two witnesses to sign the marriage certificate; often this is done just after the ceremony.

marriage license A document that authorizes a couple to get married, usually available from the county clerk's office in the state where the marriage will take place. Couples pay a small fee for a marriage license, and must often wait a few days before it is issued. In addition, a few states require a short waiting period—usually not more than a day—between the time the license is issued and the time the marriage may take place. And some states still require blood tests for couples before they will issue a marriage license, though most no longer do.

marshal 1) A law enforcement officer similar to a sheriff. 2) A judicial officer who serves papers and provides other services to the court. The U.S. Marshals (also called federal Marshals) provide security and other services to the federal courts.

martial law Military control over all of a country's activities, usually during wartime or due to an emergency or widespread disaster. In the United States, martial law must be ordered by the president as commander-in-chief and must be limited to the duration of the warfare or emergency. In many foreign countries, martial law has become a method to establish and maintain dictatorships either by military leaders or politicians backed by the military. (Compare: military law)

Martin v. Hunter's Lessee (1816) A U.S. Supreme Court case in which a decision by Justice Joseph Story extended the Court's right of judicial review on the constitutionality of statutes to appeals from state and federal courts.

Massachusetts trust A legal trust set up for the purpose of doing business. Investors give management authority to a trustee and receive "trust certificates" representing their investments. Since they own only the certificates and do not participate in management, the investors are not personally liable for any debts of the trust. Similar to a "limited partnership," a Massachusetts trust does not need to be set up in Massachusetts.

mass layoff For purposes of the WARN Act, a reduction in force that results in job loss or at least a 50% hours cut at a single employment site for 1) 500 or more employees, not including part-time employees, or 2) 50 to 499 employees, not including part-time employees, if at least 33% of the employer's active workforce are laid off.

mass tort A tort that causes injury to many people. For example, if toxic emissions from a factory cause injury to a whole community, it may be a mass tort.

master 1) An outdated term for employer. Sometimes, "master and servant" law is used to refer to the field of employment law. 2) A person appointed by a court to assist with particular issues or proceedings in a case. For example, the master might hear testimony, conduct an investigation, or reach decisions on limited issues in a case. Also referred to as a "special master."

master and servant An outdated term that refers to the employment relationship and the field of employment law.

master trust A special needs trust under which a nonprofit organization operates a pooled trust on behalf of many individual beneficiaries.

material 1) Relevant and significant information—for example, material evidence as distinguished from evidence of minor importance. 2) An essential contractual condition—for example, a material provision—which, if not performed is justification for the other party to claim breach of contract and seek remedies. 3) A type of representation made to induce someone to enter into a contract to which the person would not have agreed without that assertion. If a material representation proves not to be true, the contract can be rescinded or canceled without liability.

material witness A witness who has significant information about the subject matter of a lawsuit or criminal prosecution, particularly when few, if any other witnesses have the same knowledge. Judges usually make every reasonable effort to allow such a witness to testify, including granting a continuance (delaying a trial) to accommodate the witness.

matter of record Anything in the record of the court. This may include testimony, evidence, rulings, and sometimes arguments which have been recorded by the court reporter or court clerk. It is an expression often heard in trials and legal arguments to refer to a fact recorded by the court in the course of a hearing. For example, if it was determined in cross-examination that Ms. Smith goes by another name, a lawyer might say "Ms. Smith's alias is a matter of record."

maturity 1) The date when the payment of the principal amount owed under the terms of a promissory note, bill of exchange, or bond becomes due. 2) The age when one becomes an adult, which is 18 for most purposes. (See also: age of majority)

may An expression of possibility, a permissive choice to act or not, as distinguished from "shall," which is an imperative or often mandatory course of action. (See also: shall)

mayhem Historically, injuring someone's body (particularly by depriving him of the use of his arms, legs, eyes, or other body parts), in a way that makes him less able to fight or defend himself. Modern law treats such acts as an aggravated battery. (See also: aggravated battery.)

***McCulloch v. Maryland* (1819)** A U.S. Supreme Court case in which Chief Justice John Marshall established that the federal government has "implied powers" to carry out, without state interference, any and all rights given by the Constitution. Specifically, the Court ruled that the federal government could charter a bank and a state could not tax it.

McNabb-Mallory Rule The rule that when a defendant has been detained for an unreasonably long time between arrest and a preliminary hearing, confessions obtained during that time are not admissible. This rule rarely comes into play because of the broader protections afforded by the *Miranda* rule. (See also: *Miranda* warnings)

McNaghten Rule The earliest and most common test for criminal insanity, in which a defendant in a criminal trial is judged legally insane only if the defendant, at the time of the crime: 1) did not know what he or she was physically doing, or 2) did not know what he or she was doing was wrong. For example, a delusional psychotic who believed that his assaultive acts were in response to the will of God would not be criminally responsible for his acts.

means test In bankruptcy, a formula that uses predefined income and expense categories to determine whether a debtor whose current monthly income is higher than the median family income for his or her state should be allowed to file for bankruptcy. Generally, a means test is any evaluation of inability to pay that is necessary to qualify for public assistance or another right. (See also: current monthly income)

Twelve Angry Men. (1957) The jury movie in which the arguments and emotions of the jurors make viewers feel sequestered with them. Henry Fonda, Lee J. Cobb, Ed Begley, Sr., Martin Balsam, E.G. Marshall, Jack Klugman, Jack Warden.

---

mechanic's lien A legal claim placed on real estate by someone who is owed money for labor, services, or supplies contributed to the property for the purpose of improving it. Typical lien claimants are general contractors, subcontractors, and suppliers of building materials. A mechanics' lien claimant can sue to have the real estate sold at auction and recover the debt from the proceeds. Because property with a lien on it cannot be easily sold until the lien is satisfied (paid off), owners have a great incentive to pay their bills.

median family income An annual income figure representing the point at which there are as many families earning more than that amount as there are earning less than that amount. The Census Bureau publishes median family income figures for each state each year, depending on family size. In bankruptcy, a debtor whose current monthly income yields an annual figure higher than the median family income in his or her state must pass the means test in order to file for Chapter 7 bankruptcy. If the debtor chooses to or must use Chapter 13, the debtor must propose a five-year repayment plan.

mediation A way that parties can resolve their own dispute without going to court. In mediation, a neutral third party (the mediator) meets with the opposing sides to help them find a mutually satisfactory solution. Unlike a judge or an arbitrator, the mediator has no power to impose a solution— instead, the mediator facilitates the parties' communication and helps to develop and reality-test possible solutions. No formal rules of evidence or procedure control mediation; the mediator and the parties usually agree on their own informal ways to proceed. Mediation is very commonly used in divorce cases, and is mandatory in some places when child custody is in dispute. (Compare: arbitration, trial)

mediator A person who conducts mediations, a form of dispute resolution in which the mediator acts as a neutral third party and works with parties in dispute to try to reach a resolution. (See also: mediation)

Medicaid A program established by the federal government and administered by the states to help pay medical costs for financially needy people. Need is defined by the program of the state in which the applicant resides. Medicaid operates in addition to Medicare to help pay for some of the medical costs that Medicare does not cover.

medical certification A document an employer may require an employee to provide when taking leave under the Family and Medical Leave Act (FMLA). The medical certification form must be completed by a health care provider and must include facts sufficient to demonstrate that the employee (or the employee's family member, if the employee is taking time off to care for him or her) has a serious health condition as defined by the FMLA.

Medicare A federal government program that assists older and some disabled people in paying their medical costs. The program is divided into three parts. Part A is called hospital insurance and covers most of the costs of a stay in the hospital, as well as some follow-up costs after time in the hospital. Part B, medical insurance, pays some of the cost of doctors and outpatient medical care. Part D pays for some of the cost for prescription medicine.

Medicare tax A portion of the FICA (Federal Insurance Contributions Act) tax that is 2.9% of an individual's net earned income. The employee's share of the Medicare tax is 1.45% of all wages. The employer's share of the Medicare tax is 1.45% of an employee's wages.

meet and confer A requirement of some courts that before certain types of motions or petitions are heard by the judge, the lawyers (and sometimes their clients) must meet (usually, in person or on the phone) to try to resolve the matter. This can resolve many problems and limit the amount of court time needed to resolve disagreements.

meeting of creditors A meeting the debtor must attend in a bankruptcy case with the bankruptcy trustee and any creditors who choose to attend. Typically, the trustee reviews the debtor's papers and may ask a few questions; creditors also have the opportunity to ask questions. In a Chapter 7 case, creditors rarely attend, and the meeting takes only a few minutes. In a Chapter 13 case, creditors are more likely to attend, particularly if they wish to challenge the debtor's repayment plan.

meeting of the minds An essential requirement for contract formation, when two parties to a contract have an actual and mutual understanding of the terms.

Megan's Law An informal name for federal and state laws that require convicted sex offenders to register with law enforcement authorities, who then make certain information available to the public. Registered information varies from state to state, but it often includes the offender's name, address, date of conviction, type of crime, and photograph. This information may be made available on the Internet or distributed through newspapers, pamphlets, or other means. These laws are named for seven-year-old Megan Kanka, who was kidnapped, raped, and murdered in New Jersey in 1994.

member A person or entity on the rolls of an organization, with rights and obligations. Also, the owner of a limited liability company.

memorandum Any written record, including a letter or note, that proves that a contract exists between two parties. This type of memo may be enough to validate an oral (spoken) contract that would otherwise be unenforceable because of the statute of frauds. (Under the statute of frauds, an oral contract is invalid if it can't be completed within one year from the date the contract is made.)

memorandum decision A single, very brief paragraph setting out a court's decision in a case. A memorandum decision does not usually include the court's reasons for reaching its result; those details may appear later in a comprehensive written opinion.

mens rea (menz-**ray**-ah) The mental component of criminal liability. To be guilty of most crimes, a defendant must have committed the criminal act in a certain mental state (the mens rea). The mens rea of robbery, for example, is the intent to permanently deprive the owner of his property. (Compare: actus reus)

mental anguish A type of suffering that can be compensated in a personal injury case, generally meaning significant mental suffering that may include fright, feelings of distress, anxiety, depression, trauma, or grief.

mental competence See: competence

mental cruelty An archaic term that in some states remains a ground for divorce, or a factor in division of marital property.

mental suffering See: mental anguish

mercantile law See: commercial law

merchantable Of a high enough quality to be fit for sale. To be merchantable, an article for sale must be usable for the purpose it is made. It must be of average worth in the marketplace and must not be broken, unworkable, damaged, contaminated, or flawed.

mercy killing See: euthanasia

merger 1) In corporate law, the joining together of two corporations in which one corporation transfers all of its assets to the other. In effect, one corporation "swallows" the other. The shareholders of the swallowed company receive shares of the surviving corporation. Distinguished from a "consolidation," in which both companies join together to create a new corporation. 2) In real property law, when an owner of an interest in property acquires a greater or lesser interest in the same property, the two interests become one. 3) In real property law, when a person acquires two parcels of land that had been previously subdivided and that are substandard size, the buyer who acquires title in the two lots may find that they are "merged" into one lot.

mesne (meen) From old French for intermediate, the middle point between two extremes. Seldom used, except in the phrase "mesne profits."

mesne profits (meen) Profits or value of land during the time someone was wrongfully occupying the land. For example, if someone farmed a plot of land without permission, any profit from that activity would be owed to the actual landowner. Similarly, a tenant who stays on after a court has issued a judgment for possession to the landlord owes the landlord the value of the time spent there without permission.

metes and bounds From an old term meaning measures and directions, a method of coming up with a "legal description" of a parcel of real estate that is much more precise than a street address or parcel number. The description exactly describes the perimeter of the property, using carefully measured distances, angles, and directions. The description must start at an identifiable point and end there as well. It is recorded in the county land records office in the county where the property is located.

"The Constitution of the United States forms a government, not a league."

—Andrew Jackson

mileage log A record of miles traveled in a vehicle used for business, used to substantiate deductions for vehicle use by the business.

military law Regulations governing the conduct of men and women in the armed services in relation to their military (not civilian) activities. (Compare: martial law)

millage The tax rate on real estate, used to calculate property tax. One "mill" equals a tenth of a cent. To calculate

property tax, divide the millage by 1,000 and multiply it by the property's assessed taxable value. For example, if the millage rate is 20, and the taxable value of your house is $200,000, the property tax is 0.020 x $200,000 or $4,000.

mineral rights An ownership interest in the minerals contained in a particular parcel of land, with or without ownership of the surface of the land. The owner of mineral rights is usually entitled to either take the minerals from the land or receive a royalty from the party that actually extracts the minerals.

minimum contacts A legal requirement that for a lawsuit to go forward against a nonresident defendant of a given state, the defendant must have some connections with that state. For example, advertising or having business offices within a state may provide minimum contacts between a company and the state, even if the company is based elsewhere.

mining claim The right to use a portion of public lands to excavate metal ore or minerals. A request for a mining claim describing the property must be made with the appropriate federal, state, or local agency.

ministerial act An act performed by a government employee following explicit instructions in a statute or other legal authority, or directions given from a superior, without exercising any discretion or independent judgment.

minor Someone under legal age, which is generally 18, except for certain purposes such as drinking alcoholic beverages.

minority 1) In voting, a side with less than half the votes. 2) A term for people in a predominantly Caucasian country who are not Caucasian, including African Americans, Hispanics, Asians, indigenous Americans (Indians), and other people "of color." 3) The period of life under legal age.

minutes 1) The written record of meetings, particularly of boards of directors or shareholders of corporations, kept by the secretary of the corporation or organization. 2) The record of courtroom proceedings, such as the start and recess of hearings and trials, names of attorneys, witnesses, and rulings of the court, kept by the clerk of the court or the judge.

Miranda v. Arizona (1966) A U.S. Supreme Court case in which the Court established the rights of a criminal suspect who has been arrested or is otherwise not free to leave. These rights are the right to remain silent, the right to have a lawyer present during questioning, the right to a court-appointed attorney if the suspect cannot afford one, and the warning that anything the suspect says can be used in court. To use a confession or admission in court, the prosecution must prove the suspect knowingly waived those rights, and thus the rights should be read or recited to the suspect. These became known as the *Miranda* rights or *Miranda* warnings.

Miranda warnings The warnings that law enforcement must give anyone who is in custody and about to be questioned by the police, if the police desire to use any resulting statements against the person questioned. Custodial suspects must be told that they have the right to remain silent; that they have the right to have a lawyer present during questioning; that they have the right to a court-appointed attorney if they cannot afford one; and that statements may be used against them in court.

mirror wills See: mutual wills

misappropriation The intentional, illegal use of the property or funds of another person for one's own use or other unauthorized purpose, particularly by a public official, a trustee of a trust, an executor or administrator of a deceased person's estate, or by any person with a responsibility to care for and protect another's assets.

misdemeanor A crime, less serious than a felony, punishable by no more than one year in jail. Petty theft (of articles worth less than a certain amount), first-time drunk driving, and leaving the scene of an accident are all common misdemeanors.

misfeasance Performing a legal action in an improper way. This term is frequently used when a professional or public official does his job in a way that is not technically illegal, but is nevertheless mistaken or wrong. Here are some examples of misfeasance in a professional context: a lawyer who is mistaken about a deadline and files an important legal document too late, an accountant who makes unintentional errors on a client's tax return, or a doctor who writes a prescription and accidentally includes the wrong dosage. (Compare: malfeasance; nonfeasance)

misjoinder The improper inclusion of parties (plaintiffs or defendants) or causes of action (legal claims) in a single lawsuit. (See also: joinder)

misprision of a felony Taking affirmative steps to hide the fact of another's felony. Merely remaining silent when one knows of a felony is not a misprision, but hiding evidence or intentionally misleading law enforcement could be.

misrepresentation A misstatement of facts to obtain money, goods, or benefits to which the person making the misrepresentation is not entitled. In some circumstances misrepresentation can be prosecuted as a crime. Examples include falsely claiming to represent a charity to obtain money for personal benefit, or entering into a marriage when already married (thereby misrepresenting the legal ability to marry).

mistake 1) An error which causes one party or both parties to enter into a contract without understanding the obligations or results. Such a mistake can entitle one party or both parties to a rescission (cancellation) of the contract. A mistaken understanding of the law (as distinguished from facts) by one party only is usually not a basis for rescission. 2) An error as to facts or law made by a judge. Such errors may be harmless (not meriting a reversal) or material (a reversible error).

mistrial A trial that ends prematurely and without a judgment, due either to a mistake that jeopardizes a right to a fair trial or to a jury that can't agree on a verdict (a "hung jury"). If a judge declares a mistrial in a civil case, he or she will direct that the case be set for a new trial at a future date. Mistrials in criminal cases can result in a retrial, a plea bargain, or a dismissal of the charges.

misunderstanding A mistake by both parties to a contract resulting in a failure of meeting of minds. A misunderstanding between spouses at the time of marriage can serve as grounds for an annulment. For example, if one spouse went into the marriage wanting children while the other did not, they have a misunderstanding that might be judged serious enough for a court to annul the marriage.

mitigating circumstances Information about the defendant that does not justify or excuse a criminal act or civil wrong, but that may reduce the defendant's degree of culpability. In criminal law, juries consider mitigating circumstances when deciding whether to impose the death sentence in a capital case, and judges may consider them when selecting a sentence. In civil cases, mitigating circumstances may reduce the amount of damages awarded to the plaintiff.

mitigation of damages The requirement that someone injured by another's negligence or breach of contract must take reasonable steps to reduce the damages, injury, or cost, and to prevent them from getting worse. If a tenant breaks a lease and moves out without legal justification, a landlord must try to rerent the property reasonably quickly and keep his or losses to a minimum—that, is to mitigate

damages. In another context, a person claiming to have been injured by another motorist should seek medical help and not let the problem worsen.

MLS See: multiple listing service

***M'Naughten* Rule** See: *McNaughten* Rule

M.O. See: modus operandi

Model Rules of Professional Conduct A set of professional standards prescribing legal ethics and professional responsibility for attorneys in the United States. Developed by the American Bar Association (ABA) to replace the Code of Professional Responsibility, most states have adopted the rules in whole or in part.

The People v. Ohara. (1951) A lawyer with a shady past has to clean up his act to save a client. Spencer Tracy, Pat O'Brien, Diana Lynn, John Hodiak.

modification 1) A change in an existing court order or judgment, commonly sought in family law cases where a spouse paying support asks for a modification of the amount based on a change in circumstances since the original order was made. 2) A physical change to a legally disabled tenant's living space, made because the alteration is necessary for the tenant to live safely and comfortably on the premises. Normally, tenants pay for the modifications and can be asked to undo them when they leave.

modus operandi (**mode**-us ah-purr-**and**-eye or ah-purr-**and**-ee) A criminal investigation term for "way of operating," which may prove the accused has a pattern of repeating the same criminal acts using the same method. Examples: a repeat offender always pretended to be a telephone repairman to gain entrance.

moiety Half of something—for example, half of the property in an estate. Seldom used today.

molestation The crime of sexual acts with children up to the age of 18, including touching of private parts, exposure of genitalia, taking of pornographic pictures, rape, inducement of sexual acts with the molester or with other children, and variations of these acts. Molestation also applies to incest by a relative with a minor family member, and any unwanted sexual acts with adults short of rape.

money order A draft for a specified amount of money, purchased from a post office, bank, telegraph office, or other authorized entity. The purchaser must prepay the amount shown on the money order, making it a trustworthy method of payment. Unlike a check, a money order cannot bounce.

monopoly When a business controls so much of the production or sale of a product or service to control the market, including prices and distribution. Business practices and/or acquisitions that tend to create a monopoly may violate various federal statutes that regulate or prohibit business trusts and monopolies or prohibit restraint of trade, such as the Clayton Act. Public utilities such as electric, gas, and water companies may hold a monopoly in a particular geographic area since it is the only practical way to provide the public service; they are regulated by state public utility commissions.

month-to-month Refers to a tenancy in which the tenant pays monthly rent and has no fixed-term lease; the tenancy can be terminated by the landlord at any time, typically on 30 days notice (subject to local rent control regulations).

month-to-month tenancy A rental agreement that provides for a one-month tenancy that automatically renews each month unless either tenant or landlord gives the other the proper amount of written notice (usually 30 days) to terminate the agreement. Some landlords prefer to use a month-to-month tenancy because it gives them the right to raise the rent after giving proper notice. This type of rental also provides a landlord with an easy way to get rid of troublesome tenants, because in most states (subject to rent control regulations) month-to-month tenancies can be terminated for any reason.

monument 1) A permanent landmark established to make it possible for surveyors to to ascertain boundaries and create legal descriptions of real estate parcels. A monument can be a natural or an artificial object—for example, a metal marker, a river, or a tree. 2) A legal document.

moonlighting Holding more than one job at a time. Moonlighting refers to working two jobs at the same time, or to working for one employer while on leave from another.

moot 1) Unsettled, open to argument, or debatable. 2) Without practical significance; hypothetical or academic. (See also: moot point, moot court)

moot court A fictitious court held in law school where students argue both sides of a hypothetical case, usually at the appellate level.

moot point 1) An unsettled or debatable question. 2) An issue with no practical or relevant value. (See also: moot)

moral certainty In a criminal trial, the reasonable belief (but short of absolute certainty) of the trier of the fact (the jury or judge sitting without a jury) that the evidence shows the defendant is guilty. Moral certainty is another way of saying "beyond a reasonable doubt." Because there is no exact measure of moral certainty, it is always somewhat subjective and based on the reasonable opinions of the judge and/or jury. (See also: reasonable doubt)

moral rights Certain rights of authors, recognized primarily in European countries, beyond those traditionally granted under copyright law. Moral rights include the right to proclaim authorship of a work, disclaim authorship of a work, and object to any modification or use of the work that would be injurious to the author's reputation.

moral turpitude A description of conduct that is shamefully wicked, an extreme departure from ordinary standards of morality, justice, or ethics; a base, vile, or depraved frame of mind. Used as a test of a criminal act when judging a violation of law.

moratorium 1) An authorized period of delay in paying a debt or performing an obligation. 2) A suspension of activity.

mortality charge A monthly deduction from a universal life insurance policy that increases as the policyholder ages.

mortgage An arrangement under which a borrower puts up the title to real estate as security (collateral) for a loan to buy the real estate. the borrower typically agrees to make regular payments of principal and interest to repay the loan. If the borrower falls behind (defaults) on the payments, the lender can foreclose on the real estate and have it sold to pay off the loan. (Compare: trust deed)

mortgage-backed security A kind of investment backed by mortgage loans that have been packaged into pools in the secondary mortgage market. Payments on the mortgages generate the return on investment for the people who invest in these securities.

It was widely reported that Sir William Blackstone, who wrote the *Commentaries on the Law of England*, the bible on the common law, sipped from a bottle of port while writing. When the bottle was empty, the day's work was done.

mortgage broker See: loan broker

mortgagee The person or business making a loan that is secured by the real property of the person (mortgagor) who owes the individual or business money. (See also: mortgage)

mortgage rate buydown A subsidy on the interest rate a homebuyer pays on a loan; often used (usually by developers) as an incentive to encourage homebuyers to purchase a particular home or loan. For example, if the homebuyer's interest rate is 6%, a developer might offer to pay 2% of that the first year and 1% the second year, to lower the buyer's monthly payment.

mortgage servicer A business that mortgage issuers pay to administer their mortgages. The servicer typically accepts and records mortgage payments, handles workout negotiations if the homeowner defaults, and may supervise the foreclosure process if negotiations fail.

mortgagor The person who has borrowed money and pledged his or her real property as security for the mortgagee (the person or business making the loan). (See also: mortgage)

mortmain (**mort**-maine) French for "deadhand," mortmain refers to lands that are permanently held by a church or other corporation.

motion A formal request that a judge enter a particular order or ruling in a lawsuit. An oral motion may be made during trial—for example, to strike the testimony of a witness or admit an exhibit. Often, motions are made in writing, accompanied by a written statement explaining the legal reasons why court should grant the motion. The other party has an opportunity to file a written response, and then the court decides whether to grant or deny the motion. The court may hold a hearing where each party can argue its side, or may decide the issue without a hearing.

motion for new trial A request made by a party, after a judgment is entered in a lawsuit, that the judge vacate that judgment and order a new trial. Typically, a motion for new trial argues that the judge made a significant legal error or that there was insufficient evidence to support the jury's verdict. In many jurisdictions, a party must make a motion for new trial to reserve the right to make the same arguments on appeal.

motion for summary judgment See: summary judgment

motion in limine A motion made before a trial begins, asking the court to decide whether particular evidence will be admissible. A motion in limine is most often made to exclude evidence by a party who believes that evidence would prejudice the jury against him or her. For example, a defendant in a criminal trial might make a motion in limine to exclude evidence of previous crimes.

motion to dismiss A motion asking the judge to throw out one or more claims or an entire lawsuit. Sometimes, the plaintiff or a prosecutor makes a motion to dismiss a case because it has been settled out of court. Sometimes, the defendant files a motion to dismiss claiming that the plaintiff or prosecutor has committed some procedural error that prevents the court from hearing the case or that, even if all of the facts in the complaint are true, the plaintiff or prosecutor cannot win the case (this type of motion to dismiss is called a demurrer in some courts).

motion to strike 1) A request that the judge eliminate all or part of the other party's pleading. 2) A request that the judge order evidence deleted from the court record and instruct the jury to disregard it. Typically, this request is made regarding testimony by a witness in court.

motion to suppress A request made by a defendant in a criminal trial that the court refuse to allow a particular piece of evidence to be admitted at trial, because that evidence was obtained illegally or in violation of the defendant's rights.

motive The probable reason a person committed a crime, as when one acts out of jealousy, greed, or revenge. While evidence of a motive may be admissible at trial, proof of motive is not necessary to prove a crime.

mouthpiece Slang for an attorney.

movant The party in a lawsuit or other legal proceeding who makes a motion (application for a court order or judgment).

move To make a motion in court applying for judicial action, such as an order or judgment.

moving party See: movant

mugging 1) To be robbed by force or threat, usually outdoors. 2) To have a "mug shot" or photo taken during booking.

Muller v. Oregon **(1908)** U.S. Supreme Court decision in which a state law setting a maximum number of working hours for women was upheld, with future Justice Louis D. Brandeis arguing for the state.

multiple listing service A computer-based service, commonly referred to as MLS, that provides real estate professionals with detailed listings of most homes currently on the market. The public can now access much of the information through websites like www.realtor.com.

multiplicity of actions More than one lawsuit raising the same issue(s) against the same defendant. Generally, multi-plicity of actions is to be avoided because it could lead to inconsistent results.

municipal Pertaining to a city or town government—for example, a municipal park.

municipal court A court that typically has authority over minor criminal matters, traffic tickets, and civil law-suits where a relatively small amount of money is at stake. The rules vary from state to state; in some states, courts that handle minor local matters have other names.

muniment of title 1) Written evidence of title to real estate. Examples might include a deed, a contract, or the death certificate of a co-owner if property was held in joint tenancy. 2) In Texas, a procedure to transfer real estate left by will that is simpler than regular probate.

murder The killing of a human being by a sane person, with intent or malice aforethought, and with no legal excuse or authority. Many states make killings in which there is torture, movement of the person (kidnapping) before the killing, or death of a police officer or prison guard first degree murders with or without premeditation, with malice presumed. A killing that happens during the course of specified crimes (known as felony murder) may also be first degree murder. (See also: first degree murder, second degree murder)

mutual Anything in which both parties have reciprocal rights, understanding, or agreement.

mutual wills Wills made by spouses or an unmarried couple that have identical or nearly identical provisions. For example, a husband and wife might make mutual wills that leave each person's property to the other or to the couple's children. Also called mirror wills and reciprocal wills.

mystic will A will that is completed, signed, and sealed in secret. The will maker delivers the sealed document to a notary public along with a signed statement that the document is a valid will. In front of witnesses, the notary records on the envelope the circumstances of the transaction, then the notary and witnesses sign the envelope. Mystic wills are valid only in the state of Louisiana under certain circumstances. Also called a secret will, sealed will, or closed will.

N

naked option An opportunity to buy stock at a fixed price, offered by a seller who does not own the stock to back up the promise. If the buyer wants to exercise the option, the seller must purchase the stock at market price to make good on the offer.

narcotics Drugs that dull the senses or alter perception. Popularly used to describe drugs that cannot be legally possessed, sold, or transported except for medicinal uses for which a physician or dentist's prescription is required. Among these "controlled substances" are heroin, cocaine, L.S.D., opium, methamphetamine ("speed"), angel dust, hashish, and numerous chemically-designed hallucinogenics, as well as drugs with a legitimate medical use such as morphine. Dealing in any of these narcotics is a felony (subject to a prison term) under both state and federal laws, although mere use may be a misdemeanor. Marijuana is also an illicit narcotic, but possession of small amounts for personal use is a misdemeanor in most states.

National Credit Union Administration (NCUA) A federal agency that charters and supervises federal credit unions.

The NCUA insures savings in federal and most state-chartered credit unions across the country through the National Credit Union Share Insurance Fund (NCUSIF).

National Credit Union Share Insurance Fund (NCUSIF) A federal fund backed by the full faith and credit of the U.S. government that provides deposit insurance for credit unions in much the same way as the FDIC provides insurance for banks.

National Labor Relations Board (NLRB) An independent agency created by Congress in 1935 to administer the National Labor Relations Act. The NLRB's purposes are to remedy unfair labor practices by unions or employers, and to hold elections to determine whether a particular group of employees wants to be represented by a particular union. NLRB refers both to the agency as a whole and to five members who sit as a court and issue decisions in labor disputes. These decisions can be appealed to the U.S. Court of Appeals.

National Visa Center (NVC) The NVC is run by a private company under contract with the U.S. Department of State. Federal immigration agencies send all approved green card petitions and green card lottery registrations to the NVC. It acts as an intermediary, corresponding with the applicant and ultimately forwarding the case to a U.S. consulate in another country for final processing.

naturalization The process by which a foreign person becomes a U.S. citizen. Eligibility is, in almost all cases, dependent first and foremost on having held a green card for several years. Applicants must also meet other testing and residence requirements. A naturalized U.S. citizen has virtually the same rights as a native-born U.S. citizen.

natural law Principles considered to come from nature and to bind human society in the absence of or in addition to human-made (positive) law. For example, the Declaration of Independence's statement that "all men are created equal, that they are endowed by their Creator with certain unalienable Rights, that among these are Life, Liberty and the pursuit of Happiness…." is an assertion of natural law.

natural person A living, breathing human being, as opposed to a legal entity such as a corporation. Different rules and protections apply to natural persons and corporations, such as the Fifth Amendment right against self-incrimination, which applies only to natural persons.

***Near v. Minnesota* (1931)** A U.S. Supreme Court case in which the Court ruled that prior restraint on publications is a violation of free speech and free press. In so doing, the Court struck down a state law that allowed the police to confiscate publications that were malicious, scandalous, or obscene. The case involved a virulently anti-Semitic pamphlet.

necessaries Things that are essential to a person's ordinary life, considering their individual circumstances. For most people, this includes what is needed for health and comfort and excludes things that only provide pleasure.

necessary inference A conclusion that is dictated by a fact or premise. If the underlying fact or premise is true, then the necessary inference is an unavoidable conclusion that must be drawn.

necessary party A person or entity whose interests will be affected by the outcome of a lawsuit and whose absence from the case prevents a judgment on all issues, but who cannot be joined in the lawsuit because that would deny jurisdiction to the court hearing the case.

necessities See: necessaries

negative amortization See: capitalized interest

negative income See: loss

negative pregnant A denial of wrong-doing that implies the opposite by denying only a qualification of the allegation, not the allegation itself. For example, if a defendant who is accused of embezzling a million dollars in 2007 denies the allegation by saying, "I did not embezzle a million dollars in 2007," the denial is pregnant with the possibility that the defendant may have embezzled a different sum of money in a different year.

negligence Failure to exercise the care toward others that a reasonable or prudent person would use in the same circumstances, or taking action that such a reasonable person would not, resulting in unintentional harm to another. Negligence forms a common basis for civil litigation, with plaintiffs suing for damages based on a variety of injuries, from physical or property damage to business errors and miscalculations. The injured party (plaintiff) must prove: 1) that the allegedly negligent defendant had a duty to the injured party or to the general public, 2) that the defendant's action (or failure to act) was not what a reasonably prudent person would have done, and 3) that the damages were directly ("proximately") caused by the negligence. An added factor in the formula for determining negligence is whether the damages were "reasonably foreseeable" at the time of the alleged carelessness. (See also: contributory negligence, comparative negligence, foreseeable risk, damages, negligence per se, gross negligence, family purpose doctrine, joint tortfeasors, tortfeasor, tort, liability, res ipsa loquitur)

President George Washington appointed the most Supreme Court justices (11), with President Franklin Roosevelt coming in second (9).

negligence per se Negligence due to the violation of a law meant to protect the public, such as a speed limit or building code. Unlike ordinary negligence, a plaintiff alleging negligence per se need not prove that a reasonable person should have acted differently—the conduct is automatically considered negligent, and the focus of the suit will be over whether it proximately caused damage to the plaintiff.

negligent See: negligence

negligent tort A tort that occurs when a tortfeasor does not give the proper duty of care. (See also: negligence)

negotiable instrument A written document that represents an unconditional promise to pay a specified amount of money upon the demand of its owner. Examples include checks and promissory notes. Negotiable instruments can be transferred from one person to another, as when you write "pay to the order of" on the back of a check and turn it over to someone else.

negotiation 1) A give-and-take discussion that attempts to reach an agreement or settle a dispute. Negotiation is a form of alternative dispute resolution. 2) The transfer of a check, promissory note, bill of exchange, or other negotiable instrument to another in exchange for money, goods, services, or other benefit. (See also: negotiable instrument)

net The amount of money or value remaining after all costs, taxes, depreciation of value, losses, and other expenses and deductions have been subtracted. The term is used in net profit, net income, net loss, net worth, and net estate.

net earnings For an employee, earnings left after mandatory withholdings and deductions, such as state and federal income tax and Social Security contributions; sometimes referred to as take-home pay. For a business, earnings less expenses, taxes, and deductions.

net estate The value of all property owned at death less liabilities or debts.

net income Gross income minus allowed business expenses.

net lease A commercial real estate lease in which the tenant regularly pays not only for the space (as he does with a gross lease) but for a portion of the landlord's operating costs as well. When all three of the usual costs—taxes, maintenance, and insurance—are passed on, the arrangement is known as a "triple net lease." Because these costs are variable and almost never decrease, a net lease favors the landlord. Accordingly, it may be possible for a tenant to bargain for a net lease with caps or ceilings, which limit the amount of rent the tenant must pay. For example, a net lease with caps may specify that an increase in taxes beyond a certain point (or any new taxes) will be paid by the landlord. The same kind of protection can be designed to cover increased insurance premiums and maintenance expenses.

net loss See: net operating loss

net operating loss (NOL) An annual net loss from a business operation. An NOL may be used to offset the income of unincorporated business owners from other sources of income in the year of the loss. An NOL may also be carried back two years to reduce tax liabilities or secure refunds of taxes. (See also: carryover)

new matter New facts raised in a pleading that go beyond just denying the allegations and present new issues.

***New York Times v. Sullivan* (1964)** A landmark Supreme Court decision in the field of libel, which ruled that the commercial press was shielded from lawsuits by public officials (later extended to public figures) for libel unless the public official could show the defamatory statement (even though false) was motivated by malice, meaning the defamer knew it was false or made it with reckless disregard for whether or not it was false. The theory was that political libel suits would otherwise put a chill on media reporting.

next friend A person, usually a relative, who appears in court on behalf of a minor or incompetent plaintiff, but who is not a party to the lawsuit. For example, children are often represented in court by their parents as next friends.

next of kin The closest relatives, as defined by state law, of a deceased person. Most states recognize the spouse or registered domestic partner and the nearest blood relatives as next of kin.

nihil Latin for nothing.

nil Latin for nothing or zero.

90-day letter Official notice from the IRS that a taxpayer has 90 days to contest an IRS audit by filing a Petition to the United States Tax Court.

nisi prius The original lower level or trial court where a case was first heard by the judge and the jury, irrespective of where it is heard now. "Court of original jurisdiction" is often substituted for the term nisi prius which is Latin for "unless before."

no contest A criminal defendant's plea in court that the defendant will not contest the charge of a particular crime, also called "nolo contendere." While technically not an admission of guilt for commission of the crime, a plea of "no contest" will be treated for sentencing purposes by a judge as an admission of responsibility. A no contest plea is often made in cases in which there is also a possible lawsuit for damages by a person injured by the criminal conduct (such as reckless driving, assault with a deadly weapon, aggravated assault), because it cannot be used in the civil lawsuit as an admission of fault. (See also: nolo contendere)

no-contest clause A clause intended to keep a person from doing something or not doing something. In a will, a no-contest clause is intended to keep beneficiaries of the will from challenging its terms. Such clauses usually state that if a beneficiary challenges the will and loses, that beneficiary will receive nothing under the will. Under some states' laws, no-contest clauses are unenforceable. Also called in terrorem clause, noncontest clause, terrorem clause, anticontest clause, and forfeiture clause.

no fault 1) A type of divorce, now available in all states, in which neither party must prove that the other party is at fault in order to obtain a divorce. 2) A type of automobile insurance required of car owners by law in 19 states and the District of Columbia, in which the persons injured in an accident are paid only basic damages, limited to certain categories of actual harm, by the company that insured the vehicle in which they were riding or by which they were hit. 3) Popular shorthand for a no-fault insurance statute.

no-fault divorce Any divorce in which the spouse who wants to end the marriage is not required to accuse the other of wrongdoing, but can simply state that the couple no longer gets along. Every state now has no-fault divorce. In the past, a party seeking a divorce had to prove that the other spouse was at fault for the marriage not working. No-fault divorces are usually granted for reasons such as incompatibility, irreconcilable differences, or irretrievable or irremediable breakdown of the marriage. (Compare: fault divorce)

"The law is only a memorandum."
—Ralph Waldo Emerson

no-fault insurance Car insurance laws that require the insurance companies of each person in an accident to pay for medical bills and lost wages of their insured, up to a certain amount, regardless of who was at fault.

nolle prosequi (**nol**-ee pros-**ee**-kwee) Latin for "we shall no longer prosecute." At trial, this is an entry made on the record by a prosecutor in a criminal case or a plaintiff in a civil case stating that he will no longer pursue the matter. In a criminal case, the statement is an admission that the charges cannot be proved or that evidence has demonstrated either innocence or a fatal flaw in the prosecution's claim. An entry of nolle prosequi may be made at any time after charges are brought and before a verdict is returned or a plea entered.

Most of the time, prosecutors need a judge's permission to "nol-pros" a case.

nolo Latin for "I choose not to." (See also: no contest)

nolo contendere (no-**low** kon-**ten**-der-ee) See: no contest

nol. pros. See: nolle prosequi

nominal damages A term used when a judge or jury finds in favor of one party to a lawsuit—often because a law requires them to do so—but concludes that no real harm was done and therefore awards a very small amount of money (for example, $1.00).

nominal party A plaintiff or defendant in a lawsuit who may not have any actual interest or responsibility in a lawsuit but who is included because of technical reasons—for example, an escrow company (temporarily holding title to property) may be named in a lawsuit over a real property sale. Without the nominal party, the court is unable to render the judgment to transfer the property. (See also: necessary party, party)

nominee 1) A person or entity who is requested or named to act for another, such as an agent or trustee. 2) A potential successor to another's rights under a contract. For example, in a real estate purchase agreement, Bob Smith might purchase the property but agree that ownership will be granted to "Bob Smith or nominee." 3) A person chosen by convention, petition, or primary election to be a candidate for public office.

noncompete See: noncompetition agreement

noncompetition agreement An agreement where one party agrees not to compete with the other party for a specific period of time and within a particular area. Salespeople, for example, often sign noncompetition agreements that prevent them from using the contacts gained by one employer to benefit another employer, from selling within a particular area, or even working in the same type of business. Noncompetes are also used in the context of a contract for the acquiring sale of a business: The selling owner may agree not to compete with the acquiring business for a certain period of time. In some states, such as California, courts view noncompetition agreements with disfavor and will not enforce them against employees or contractors unless the restrictions are very narrow. In other states, courts routinely uphold them.

non compos mentis (nahn **calm**-piss **men**-tiss) Latin for not master of one's own mind. Legally insane or not competent to manage one's own affairs or go to trial.

nonconforming use The existing use (for example, residential, commercial, agricultural, light industrial) of a parcel of real estate that is now zoned for other kind of use. Generally, a nonconforming use is permitted only if the use was legally established but now violates a zoning ordinance because the property was rezoned or the law was changed. For example, a corner parcel that has been used for a gasoline station for years might lie in an area now zoned for residential use only. The nonconforming use will be allowed ("grandfathered in"), but if the station were torn down or abandoned for a certain period of time, only residential use would be allowed going forward.

noncontestability clause An insurance policy provision that requires an insurance company to challenge a statement made in an application for the insurance within a specific time. Thus an insurer cannot deny coverage on the basis of fraud or error if the insurer finds the allegedly fraudulent statement or error after that period of time has ended.

noncontest clause See: no-contest clause

noncontiguous Used to describe two or more parcels of real property which are not connected.

noncountable resource Property that is not considered to be a resource by the SSI and Medicaid programs for purposes of determining the owner's program eligibility.

noncustodial parent A parent who does not have sole custody or primary custody of a child following divorce. (Compare: custodial parent)

nondischargeable debts Debts that cannot be wiped out in bankruptcy, such as alimony, child support, and most income tax debts. If you file for Chapter 7 bankruptcy, you will still owe these debts when your case is over. If you file for Chapter 13 bankruptcy, you will have to pay your nondischargeable debts in full during your plan or continue to owe the remainder. (Compare: dischargeable debts)

nondisclosure agreement A legally binding contract (also known as an NDA or confidentiality agreement) in which a person or business promises to treat specific information as a trade secret and not disclose it to others without proper authorization. Nondisclosure agreements are often used when a business discloses a trade secret to another person or business for such purposes as development, marketing, evaluation, or securing financial backing. A nondisclosure agreement will not protect trade secrets if the trade secret owner has not taken reasonable steps to keep the information secret.

nondiscretionary trust A trust in which the trustee has no discretion about how to spend or invest trust funds. Also called a fixed trust.

nondisparagement clause A provision in a contract requiring one or more parties to the agreement not to make negative statements about the other(s). A nondisparagement clause is often included in a settlement agreement that resolves a dispute.

 In Michigan, it is illegal to chain an alligator to a fire hydrant.

nonexempt property A debtor's property that can be taken by the trustee and sold for the benefit of the creditors in a Chapter 7 bankruptcy case, or can be seized by creditors if they win a judgment against the debtor. (Compare: exempt property)

nonfeasance The failure to act when a duty to act existed. (Compare: misfeasance, malfeasance)

nonimmigrant People who come to the United States temporarily, with a nonimmigrant visa, for some particular purpose. A nonimmigrant must depart the U.S. within a designated length of time, and in most cases may not act with the intention of remaining in the U.S. permanently. There are many types of nonimmigrants. Students, temporary workers, and visitors are some of the most common.

nonimmigrant visa A U.S. visa, issued by a U.S. consulate or embassy, that allows its holder to come to the United States temporarily and for a limited purpose. Each nonimmigrant visa comes with a different set of privileges, such as the right to work or study. In addition to a descriptive name, a letter of the alphabet and a number identifies each type of nonimmigrant visa. Student visas, for example, are F-1 or M-1, and investor visas are E-2. Nonimmigrant visas also vary according to how long they permit the holder to stay in the United States. For example, someone on an investor visa can remain for many years, but someone on a visitor's visa can stay for only six months at a time.

nonjudicial foreclosure Foreclosure that proceeds outside of court, under a power of sale clause in a deed of trust.

nonlapse statute See: antilapse statute

nonobviousness A requirement for patent protection. A new invention must produce unexpected or surprising new results that are not anticipated by the existing technology (or prior art). A nonobvious invention is unexpected by a person with ordinary skill in the art—for example, the telephone technology created by Alexander Graham Bell was not obvious to audio and sound engineers of Bell's day. (See also: prior art)

nonprobate assets Assets left by a deceased person that do not go through probate court proceedings before being transferred to those who inherit them. Common examples are life insurance proceeds, property held in joint tenancy, community property, and property held in a living trust.

nonprobate estate See: nonprobate assets

nonprobate transfer The distribution of a deceased person's property by any means other than probate. Many types of property pass free of probate, including (in some states) property left to a surviving spouse and property left outside of a will through probate-avoidance methods such as pay-on-death designations, joint tenancy ownership, living trusts, and life insurance. Property that avoids probate is sometimes described as the "nonprobate estate."

nonprofit corporation An organization incorporated under state laws and approved by both the state's secretary of state and its taxing authority as operating for educational, charitable, social, religious, civic, or humanitarian purposes. Some nonprofit corporations qualify for a federal tax exemption under Section 501(c)(3) of the Internal Revenue Code, which makes them eligible for certain federal and state tax exemptions and the contributions they receive are tax deductible by the donors.

non sequitur (non **sek**-wi-ter) Latin for "it does not follow." A term used to indicate that one statement does not logically follow from another.

nonsolicitation agreement An agreement that restricts an ex-employee's ability to solicit clients or employees of the ex-employer.

nonsuit A court's dismissal of case because the plaintiff does not provide sufficient evidence or make an adequate legal showing for the judge to rule in the plaintiff's favor.

nontransferable ticket An airline ticket that can be used only by the passenger whose name appears on the ticket. All airlines require passengers to show ID when they check in, and an airline can confiscate a ticket if the names on the ID and on the ticket don't match.

no-par stock Shares in a corporation that are issued without a stated value per share. (Compare: par-value stock)

Norris v. Alabama (1935) A U.S. Supreme Court decision that overturned "the Scottsboro case," in which several black men were falsely charged with raping a white woman. The Court held that organized exclusion of blacks from jury panels (the pool of potential jurors) was a violation of a defendants' constitutional right to due process.

notarize Certification by a notary public to establish the authenticity of a signature on a legal document. Many legal documents, such as deeds and powers of attorney, must be notarized.

notary See: notary public

notary public A licensed public officer who administers oaths, certifies documents, and performs other specified functions. Notaries public are usually licensed through the Secretary of State's office in the state where the notary lives. A notary public's signature and seal is required to authenticate the signatures on many legal documents.

note See: promissory note

not guilty A plea entered by a defendant in a criminal case. Often erroneously confused with a claim of innocence, technically a plea of not guilty simply compels the prosecution to prove every element of the offense beyond a reasonable doubt. When the jury (or a judge sitting without a jury) acquits a defendant after trial, they return a verdict of "not guilty," which indicates their conclusion that the prosecution

did not meet its burden of proving guilt beyond a reasonable doubt. (See also: reasonable doubt)

not guilty by reason of insanity A plea entered by a defendant in a criminal trial, in which the defendant claims that he or she was so mentally disturbed or incapacitated at the time of the offense that he or she could not have intended to commit the crime. A jury that agrees with this plea may find the defendant not guilty by reason of insanity, but usually the defendant faces civil commitment proceedings if the defendant is judged to be dangerous in a subsequent hearing. (See also: insanity defense)

notice Information that one person gives to another, alerting the other party of the first party's intentions. Notice of a lawsuit or petition for a court order begins with personal service on the defendants (delivery of notice to the person) of the complaint or petition, together with a summons or order to appear (or file an answer) in court. In a noncourt setting, notice can simply be a written statement of intentions, as when a landlord terminates a tenancy by serving a termination notice on the tenant.

notice of default A statement, usually written, from one party to a contract to another, advising the recipient that he or she has failed to live up to a term or condition of the contract. Although defaults are most common in real estate, they can happen in any contract situation. A notice of default can result when a homeowner fails to pay as required under his mortgage or deed of trust. In a lease situation, a notice of default can be sent by either the landlord or tenant, claiming that one of them has violated a condition of the lease. If the defaulting party fails to correct, or cure, the default, the other side may declare the contract to be over, by instituting foreclosure proceedings, an eviction, or taking any other act, depending on the nature of the contract, that ends the contractual relationship.

notice of deficiency See: ninety-day letter

notice of tax lien See: tax lien notice

notice to quit A legal termination notice that a landlord gives a tenant to leave (quit) the premises or to pay overdue rent or correct (cure) some other lease violation, such as bringing in an unauthorized pet or roommate, within a short time (such as three days). State rules specify details of these notices, such as how and when they may be used, the amount of time the tenant has to leave (and whether the tenant has the chance to correct or cure the violation), the delivery and timing of the notice,

and what steps a landlord must take before filing an unlawful detainer or eviction lawsuit.

"Justice delayed is justice denied."
—Anonymous, often quoted

notorious possession Possession or control of property that can be observed by others—not a hidden or secret possession. For example, if neighbors can see that a person is living in and taking care of a house, it can be said that the person has notorious possession of it.

NOV (non obstante veredicto) Shorthand acronym for the phrase non obstante veredicto (nahn ahb-**stan**-teh very-**dick**-toe), meaning "notwithstanding the verdict," referring to a decision of a judge to set aside a jury's decision when the judge is convinced the verdict is not reasonably supported by the facts or the law. The result is called a "judgment NOV."

novation The voluntary substitution of a new contract for an old one, usually to change the parties, duties, or payment terms.

novelty A requirement for obtaining a patent. To be novel, all material elements of an invention cannot have been disclosed in any previous technology or publication (prior art). (Compare: anticipation)

noxious Harmful to health; often refers to nuisances, such as fumes or smoke.

nugatory Of no force or effect; invalid. Example: a statute that is unconstitutional is a nugatory law.

nuisance Something that interferes with the use of property by being irritating, offensive, obstructive, or dangerous. Nuisances include a wide range of conditions, everything from a chemical plant's noxious odors to a neighbor's dog barking. The former would be a public nuisance, one affecting many people, while the other would be a private nuisance, limited to making your life difficult. Lawsuits may be brought to abate (remove or reduce) a nuisance. (See also: quiet enjoyment, attractive nuisance)

nuisance fees Fees charged by a credit card company or bank for using (or failing to use) its services in particular ways, such as inactivity fees, fees for not carrying a balance on a credit card, or fees for using an ATM or a teller. Sometimes used to refer to any fee a company charges that is disproportionate to the actual cost of the service provided or the activity being penalized, such as a $100 fee to change an airline seat or a $500 fee to

have real estate documents notarized when purchasing a house.

nulla bona (**nuh**-lah **bo**-nah) Latin for "no goods." If a sheriff tries to enforce a writ of execution but can't find any property in the jurisdiction that can be seized to satisfy the judgment, the sheriff returns the writ nulla bona.

nullity Something which may be treated as nothing, as if it did not exist or never happened. This can occur by court ruling or enactment of a statute. The most common example is a nullity of a marriage by a court judgment. (See also: annulment)

nunc pro tunc (**nunk** proh **tuhnk**) Latin for "now for then," meaning to cause an order or judgment to apply to an earlier date. Example: A divorce judgment is submitted to the court but, because of a mistake of the court clerk, not filed or signed by the judge. Six months later, one of the parties marries someone else. When the parties later discover the divorce was never entered, they can obtain a judgment nunc pro tunc making the judgment final as of the date they filed it, so that the remarriage is not bigamous.

nuncupative will An oral will, which is legal only in some states and in very unusual circumstances, such as when the person making the will faced imminent death.

O

oath An attestation that one will tell the truth, or a promise to fulfill a pledge, often calling upon God as a witness. The best known oath is probably the witness's pledge "to tell the truth, the whole truth, and nothing but the truth" during a legal proceeding. All witnesses are given the oath (sworn in) before testifying. In another context, a public official usually takes an "oath of office" before assuming the position, declaring that he or she will faithfully perform the job's duties.

oath of office See: oath

obiter dicta Remarks of a judge which are not necessary to reaching a decision, but are made as comments, illustrations, or thoughts. Generally, obiter dicta is simply dicta.

obiter dictum See: dictum

object See: objection

objection An attorney's formal statement protesting something that has occurred in court and seeking the judge's immediate ruling. Often, lawyers object to questions posed to a witness by an opposing attorney because the inquiries do not meet legal standards. For example, the question may be irrelevant, immaterial, call for a conclusion (seeking opinion, not facts), argumentative, assuming facts not in evidence, or compound (two or more questions asked together). The trial attorney must be alert to object before an answer is given.

obligation A legal duty to pay or do something.

obligee The person or entity to whom an obligation is owed (for example, the party to be paid on a promissory note).

obligor The person or entity that owes an obligation to another (for example, the party that must pay on a promissory note).

OBRA The federal Omnibus Budget Reconciliation Act, a law that, among other things, describes the circumstances under which property in a special needs trust may be considered the trust beneficiary's resource for the purpose of determining eligibility for SSI and Medicaid. (42 U.S.C. §§ 1395 and following.)

obscene A description of material that the average person, applying contemporary standards in their community, would find appeals to the prurient interest in sex, with no legitimate artistic, literary, or scientific purpose or value. Pictures, writings, films, or public acts that are under this standard (from the U.S. Supreme Court) is not entitled to First Amendment protection as free speech, and may be regulated or even criminalized.

obscenity Material that is obscene.

obstruction of justice An attempt to interfere with the administration of the courts, the judicial system, or law enforcement officers, including threatening witnesses, improper conversations with jurors, hiding evidence, or interfering with an arrest. Such activity is a crime.

occupancy Living in or using premises or property as a tenant or owner; includes someone who lives in or uses abandoned property with the intention of acquiring ownership.

occupancy standard A limit on the number of persons allowed per dwelling unit, based on the size of the unit, number of bedrooms and baths, and other factors, such as physical limitations of the building. Federal, state, and local laws may set either minimum occupancy standards or maximum occupancy limits (under health and safety codes).

occupant Someone living in a residence or using premises as a tenant or owner; includes someone who lives in or uses abandoned property with the intention of acquiring ownership.

occupation Fairly permanent trade, profession, employment, business, or means of livelihood.

occupational disease A disease that an employee develops as the result of exposure to particular substances, working conditions, or requirements on the job. Black lung disease from mining, mesothelioma caused by asbestos exposure, and repetitive stress disorder caused by typing or running a cash register are all examples of occupational disease.

occupational hazard A danger or risk particular to certain jobs. For example, hearing loss might be an occupational hazard for those who work around loud machinery or in a rock band.

Occupational Safety and Health Act (OSHA) The primary federal law establishing health and safety standards in the workplace. Generally, OSHA requires employers to provide a safe workplace by informing employees about potential hazards, following health and safety standards established for their industry, training employees, and recording workplace injuries.

occupy the field To preempt or monopolize an area of statutory law by a higher authority, such as federal preemption over state laws on issues affecting interstate commerce, and state statutes or state constitutions prevailing over laws of cities and counties on certain topics.

of counsel An attorney who is affiliated with a law firm, but not employed as a partner or associate. This designation often identifies a semiretired partner, an attorney who occasionally uses the office for a few clients, or one who only consults on certain matters.

off calendar Refers to a court order to take a lawsuit, petition, or motion off the list of pending proceedings. The reasons might be that the lawyers agreed (stipulated) to drop or postpone the case, the moving party's lawyer failed to appear, the suit has been settled pending final documentation, or some other reason that the case should not proceed at that time. The matter can in most instances be put back "on calendar" by stipulation of the lawyers or upon motion of either party.

offender A quasi-legal term that refers to someone who has been convicted of a crime, as in "repeat offender."

offense A violation of the law, a crime. Often used when describing lesser crimes, as when the jury convicts the defendant of a "lesser offense" than the one charged.

offensive collateral estoppel A doctrine asserted by a plaintiff (the person in the offensive position) that prevents a defendant from relitigating an issue that was previously decided against that defendant in a case with a different plaintiff.

offer An element required in the creation of an enforceable contract. An offer is a proposal to enter into an agreement and must express the intent of the person making the offer to form a contract, must contain the essential terms—including the price and subject matter of the contract—and must be communicated by the person making the offer. A legally valid acceptance of the offer will create a binding contract.

offeree The person or entity to whom an offer is made, usually to enter into a contract.

offer in compromise A proposal to the IRS (on an IRS tax form) to settle a tax debt for less than the amount owed.

offer of proof At trial, an explanation to a judge by a party or the party's attorney as to how a proposed line of questioning, or a certain item of physical evidence, would be relevant to its case and admissible under the rules of evidence. Offers of proof arise when a party begins a line of questioning that the other side objects to as calling for irrelevant or inadmissible information. If the judge thinks that the questions might lead to proper evidence, the questioner will be give a chance to show how the expected answers will be both relevant and admissible. This explanation is usually presented out of the jury's hearing, but it does become part of the trial record.

offeror The person or entity that makes an offer, usually to enter into a contract.

officer A person elected by a profit or nonprofit corporation's board of directors, or by the members or managers of a limited liability company, to manage the day-to-day operations of the organization. Officers generally hold titles such as president, secretary, or treasurer. Many states and most corporate bylaws or LLC operating agreements require a corporation or LLC to have a president, secretary, and treasurer. Election of a vice president may be required by state law.

officer of the court Any person who has an obligation to promote justice and uphold the law, including judges, clerks, court personnel, police officers, and attorneys (who must be truthful in court and obey court rules).

official 1) An act, document, product, or anything else sanctioned or authorized by a public officer or public agency. Examples might include an Official Boy Scout knife or emblem, or an official warranty, membership card, or set of rules. 2) A public officer or government employee who is empowered to exercise judgment. 3) An officer of a corporation or business.

official misconduct When a public official acts improperly or illegally in connection with his or her duties.

 "The police must obey the law while enforcing the law."

—Chief Justice Earl Warren

officious intermeddler A person who does something to benefit another without being requested or legally obligated to do so, and is therefore not entitled to seek compensation for his or her actions. For example, someone who decides to wash all of the cars on the block would not be entitled to demand payment from each car's owner.

offset See: setoff

offshore corporation A corporation chartered under the laws of a country other than the U.S. that does not conduct substantial business in its country of incorporation. Some countries (particularly in the Caribbean) are popular nations of incorporation since they have little corporate regulation or taxes and only moderate management fees. Reasons to use an offshore corporation may include avoidance of taxes, ease of international operations, freedom from state regulation, and placement of funds in accounts out of the country.

Older Workers Benefit Protection Act (OWBPA) An amendment to the Age Discrimination in Employment Act (ADEA), the OWBPA is a federal law that requires employers to offer older workers (those who are at least 40 years old) benefits that are equal to or, in some cases, cost the employer as much as, the benefits it offers to younger workers. The OWBPA also sets minimum standards for an employee waiver of the right to sue for age discrimination, designed to ensure that the waiver is knowing and voluntary.

omission 1) Failure to perform an act agreed to, especially if there was a duty to perform. 2) Leaving out a word, phrase, or other language from a written document. If the parties agree that an omission was due to a mutual mistake, the document may be reformed.

omitted heir See: pretermitted heir

omnibus clause 1) A clause in a vehicle insurance policy that provides coverage for anyone driving the car with the insured person's express or implied consent. 2) A clause in a will or probate court order that disposes of property that was not otherwise specifically disposed of in the will. For example, it might say "I leave all other property not specifically mentioned in this will to Jane."

on all fours Slang for a case or other precedent which shares near-identical facts or issues. (See also: precedent)

on demand In a promissory note, a requirement that the amount due must be paid when the person or company to whom the funds are owed demands payment (rather than upon a certain date or in installments). Such a note is called a demand note.

one-bite rule A legal rule, still in force in many states, that makes a dog owner legally responsible for injury caused by the dog only if the owner knew (or should have known) that the dog was likely to cause that kind of injury. The injured person must show that the owner had this knowledge.

one-person, one-vote rule See: *Reynolds v. Sims*

one-year rule A rule that requires a patent application to be filed within one year of: 1) any public use of the invention by the inventor, 2) a sale of the invention, 3) an offer to sell the invention, or 4) any description of the invention by the inventor in a published document. Failure to file a patent application within this one-year period results in the invention's passing into the public domain, where it is no longer eligible for a patent. The application of the one-year rule to sales is sometimes referred to as the on-sale bar.

on or about A phrase used in a civil complaint or criminal charge that refers to a date or place. It is used to protect the person making the allegations of fact from being challenged as inaccurate. Thus, a complaint will read "On or about July 11, 2009, Defendant drove his vehicle negligently and without due care on or about the corner of Sunset and Vine Streets."

on or before A phrase usually found in a contract or promissory note requiring payment or performance by a particular date or prior to that date.

on the merits Referring to a judgment, decision, or ruling of a court based upon the facts presented in evidence and the law applied to that evidence.

on the stand A phrase used to describe a witness who is testifying under oath during a trial. The witness almost always sits in a chair beside the judge's bench, often raised above the floor level of the courtroom, and behind a knee-high panel.

open adoption An adoption in which the adopting parents and birth parents are in contact before the birth and agree on some level of contact after the child is born. Contact may range from sending the birth parent(s) a photograph of the child once a year to including the birth parent(s) in family events.

open court Judicial proceedings of a court in session that the public may attend. Certain proceedings, such as hearings on evidence that might prejudice the jury or reveal sensitive information that should not be made public, are not held in open court, but instead are held "in camera" (in the judge's chambers or after the courtroom has been cleared).

open-ended loan A loan that does not have a definite term or end date—for example, a credit card account or personal line of credit.

opening statement A statement made by an attorney or self-represented party at the beginning of a trial before evidence is introduced. The opening statement outlines the party's legal position and previews the evidence that will be introduced later. The purpose of an opening statement is to familiarize the jury with what it will hear—and why it will hear it—not to present an argument as to why the speaker's side should win; that comes after all evidence is presented as part of the closing argument.

operating agreement An agreement signed by the members (owners) of a limited liability company that structures the members' financial rights and responsibilities, each member's percentage of ownership in the LLC and share of profits (or losses), the LLC's procedures for holding meetings, and what will happen to the business when a member leaves.

operation of law A way in which someone acquires certain rights or responsibilities automatically under the law, without taking individual action or being the subject of a court order. For example, when one joint tenant dies, any surviving joint tenants obtain title to the jointly owned property; when someone dies without a will, the person's legal heirs automatically become entitled to inherit property from the estate.

opinion A court's written explanation of a judgment, usually including a summary of the facts, an explanation of the law on the issue, and the court's analysis for applying the law to those facts and coming to a conclusion. The opinions of appellate courts (courts that review the decisions of trial courts, the highest appellate court being the Supreme Court) are frequently published and create rules for future litigants to follow. Appellate judges who disagree with a majority opinion may file dissenting opinions.

"We come now to analyze a law. In the first place, it is declaratory; in the second it is remedial; and in the fourth, it is vindicatory."

—Gilbert Abbot A. Beckett, *The Comic Blackstone*

---

option An agreement that conveys the right to purchase property or engage in a transaction in the future upon agreed-upon terms. An option is paid for as part of a contract, but must be "exercised" in order for the property to be purchased or the transaction to be completed.

Option ARM A type of adjustable rate mortgage that allows the borrower to choose the payment amount, each month, usually from the following four options: a minimum payment based on the borrower's initial interest rate, a payment that covers the interest that has accrued that month, a fully amortizing 30-year payment, or a fully amortizing 15-year payment.

O.R. Short for "own recognizance." A person who is charged with a criminal offense may be released without having to post bail if the judge is convinced that the person will honor his obligation to show up at future court appearances. Defendants who are good candidates for "O.R. release" are those who are unlikely to flee, namely, those with substantial ties to the community (property owners) and people with close and supportive family nearby.

oral contract An agreement based on spoken words that is valid and enforceable, provided that it is provable, meets the condition of contract formation, and is not in violation of statutes that prohibit oral agreements—for example state statutes that require sales of real property and agreements whose performance takes more than one year, must be in writing.

order A decision issued by a court. It can be a simple command—for example, ordering a recalcitrant witness to answer a proper question—or it can be a complicated and reasoned decision made after a hearing, directing that a party either do or refrain from some act. For example, following a hearing, the court may order that evidence gathered by the police not be introduced at trial; or a judge may issue a temporary restraining order. This term usually does not describe the final decision in a case, which most often is called a judgment.

order of examination A hearing in which a judgment debtor must answer questions under oath about his or her assets, income, bank accounts, and other financial information. The judgment creditor is entitled to request this information to find a source from which he or she can collect the judgment.

order to show cause An order from a judge that directs a party to come to court and convince the judge why the judge shouldn't grant an action proposed by the other side or, occasionally, by the judge. For example, in a divorce, at the request of one parent a judge might issue an order directing the other parent to appear in court on a particular date and time to show cause why the first parent should not be given sole physical custody of the children.

ordinance A law adopted by a town or city council, county board of supervisors, or other municipal governing board. Typically, local governments issue ordinances establishing zoning and parking rules, and regulating noise, garbage removal, and the operation of parks and other areas within the locality's borders.

ordinary course of business Conduct of business within normal commercial customs and practices. This term is used to determine the legitimacy of certain transactions.

original jurisdiction The authority of a court to hear and decide a matter before it can be reviewed by another court. (Compare: appellate jurisdiction)

original work of authorship A standard for copyright protection. Under copyright law, a work is considered original, if it owes its origin to the author—that is, it is the result of independent effort, and not the result of copying.

origination fee A fee paid to a lender to process a loan application. Commonly called "points" and calculated as a percentage of a loan amount.

orphan A person, particularly a minor, whose parents are dead. In some cases, such as whether a child is eligible for public financial assistance, "orphan" can mean a child who has lost one parent.

orphan works Works protected under copyright whose owners are difficult to locate—for example, a photograph taken of Elvis Presley as a teenager, or a newspaper column from a 1950s newspaper.

O.S.C. See: order to show cause

OSHA See: Occupational Safety and Health Act

ostensible agent One who has the apparent authority to act for another. (See also: apparent authority)

ostensible authority See: apparent authority

ouster 1) Wrongfully excluding someone from property, as when a cotenant changes the locks, preventing another cotenant's entry. 2) The removal of a public official from office.

outbuilding A structure not connected with the primary residence on a parcel of property. This may include a shed, garage, barn, cabana, pool house, or cottage.

outlaw A popular term for anyone who commits serious crimes and acts outside the law.

out of court Actions, including negotiations between parties or their attorneys, without any direct involvement of a judge or the judicial system. Most commonly it refers to an out-of-court settlement in which the parties work out a settlement agreement, which they may present to the court for inclusion in a judgment.

out-of-pocket expense An expense paid from an individual's own funds.

output contract An agreement in which a seller agrees to sell its entire production to the buyer, who in turn agrees to purchase the entire output.

overbooking A common practice whereby an airline, hotel, or other company accepts more reservations than it has seats or rooms available, on the presumption that a certain percentage of people will not show up. Airlines have a legal right to overbook, while hotels do not. A hotel must find a room for everyone who has a reservation and shows up on time. An airline may be required to offer compensation for people involuntarily bumped from a flight, depending on several factors, including how long they must wait for another flight.

The Trial of Mary Dugan. (1929) The first courtroom movie in sound. A woman accused of murdering her lover is deserted by her lawyer and then saved by new counsel. Norma Shearer, Lewis Stone, H.B. Warner, Raymond Hackett.

---

overcharge 1) To charge more than a posted or advertised price. 2) To file a criminal complaint for more serious crimes than the known facts support, most often to intimidate the accused into accepting a plea bargain.

overrule 1) A trial judge's decision to reject a party's objection—often, to a question for a witness or the admission of evidence. By overruling the objection, the judge allows the question or evidence in court. 2) An appellate court's decision that a prior appellate decision was incorrect, and is therefore no longer a valid precedent on the legal issue in question.

overt act In criminal law, an action that might be innocent by itself, but when part of the preparation and active furtherance of a crime, is evidence of a defendant's participation in the crime. For example, when the first World Trade Center defendants were put on trial, evidence of their renting a van, buying explosives, obtaining a map of downtown New York City, and going back and forth to the World Trade Center was admitted to establish overt acts that proved their complicity in the bombing.

owelty Under common law, an amount that one co-owner must pay to another after a lawsuit to partition real estate, so that each co-owner receives equal value from the property.

owner One who has legal title or right to something. (See also: ownership)

owners' agreement See: buy-sell agreement

ownership Having the legal right to use, possess, and give away property.

(See also: joint ownership, conditional ownership)

ownership in common Right of ownership shared by two or more people, where at the death of one owner his or her interest in the property passes to his or her heirs. This is in contrast to joint ownership, where that interest would pass to the remaining owner or owners.

own recognizance (O.R.) A way the defendant can get out of jail pending trial on the charges, without paying bail, by promising to appear in court when next required to be there. Sometimes called "personal recognizance." Only those with strong ties to the community, such as a steady job, local family, and no history of failing to appear in court are good candidates for "OR" release. If the charge is very serious, however, OR may not be an option.

P

pain and suffering The physical or emotional distress resulting from an injury. Though the concept is somewhat abstract, the injured person (the plaintiff) can seek compensation in the form of cold, hard cash. How much the defendant owes for pain and suffering is calculated separately from the amount owing for more direct expenses, such as medical bills or time lost from work—although sometimes these amounts are considered to arrive at a logical figure.

palimony A nonlegal term coined by journalists to describe the division of property or an order for support—in the nature of alimony—paid by one member of an unmarried couple to the other after they break up.

palliative care Medical care designed to keep a patient comfortable and pain-free while also providing psychological and spiritual support. Rather than focusing on curing an illness, palliative care emphasizes quality of life for both the patient and the patient's family members. Used negatively, it may mean the provision of only perfunctory medical care when an illness could be cured.

pander 1) To solicit customers for a prostitute. 2) A pimp, who procures customers for a prostitute or lures a woman into prostitution for the pimp's own profit. 3) To cater to special interests without principle.

panderer A person who panders or solicits for a prostitute.

panel The list of people selected to appear for jury duty.

paper hanger A slang expression for someone who writes bad checks.

par The face value of a stock or bond, which is the amount the original purchaser paid the issuing corporation. (See also: par-value stock)

paralegal A person who does legal work but is not licensed to practice law or give legal advice. Paralegals employed by a law office often handle the routine tasks and paperwork of a law practice. Independent paralegals (those who work directly with the public, not for lawyers) assist their customers by providing forms, helping people fill them out correctly, and filing them with the proper court.

paramount title The original title, or a title that prevails over any other claim of title.

parcel A defined piece of real estate.

pardon To use the executive power of a governor or president to forgive a person charged with a crime or convicted of a crime, thus preventing any prosecution and removing any remaining penalties or punishments. A pardon is distinguished from "a commutation of sentence," which cuts short the term; "a reprieve," which is a temporary halt to punishment, particularly the death penalty, pending appeal or determination of whether the penalty should be reduced; "amnesty," which is a blanket forgiving of possible criminal charges due to a change in public circumstances (such as the end of a war or the draft system); or a "reduction in sentence," which shortens a sentence and can be granted by a judge or an executive. Sometimes called a commutation.

parens patriae (**par**-ens **pa**-tree-ee) Latin for "parent of his or her country." The power of the state to act as guardian for those who are unable to care for themselves, such as children or disabled individuals. For example, under this doctrine a judge may change custody, child support, or other rulings affecting a child's well-being, regardless of what the parents may have agreed to.

parent The legal or natural father or mother of a person; the relationship can be established by birth or by adoption.

 "The laws, if they are to be observed, have need of good morals."

—Niccolo Machiavelli

Parental Kidnapping Prevention Act (PKPA) A federal law that seeks to control and prevent parental kidnapping by requiring states to ensure parents are in compliance with the terms of the PKPA before the court will make a custody order, and to refuse to enforce child custody orders made in another state when the parent obtaining the order did not have legal custody of the child.

parental neglect A crime consisting of acts or omissions of a parent (including a stepparent, adoptive parent, or someone who, in practical terms, serves in a parent's role) which endangers the health and life of a child or fails to take steps necessary to the proper raising of a child. The neglect can include leaving a child alone when he or she needs protection, failure to provide food, clothing, medical attention, or education to a child, or placing the child in dangerous or harmful circumstances, including exposing the child to a violent, abusive, or sexually predatory person.

parenting plan In a divorce, a document that sets out the parents' agreements about how they will share time with their children.

pari delicto See: in pari delicto

parish 1) An area served by a particular church; an ecclesiastical district. 2) In Louisiana, the governmental equivalent of a county.

parody When an author or artist ridicules a well-known work by imitating it in a comedic way. To the extent that the parodist copies material protected by copyright, the publication may be considered a copyright infringement unless excused by the fair use defense. The key factor for a parody to qualify as fair use is whether the parody is transformative—it adds something new, with a further purpose or different character altering the copied work with new expression, meaning, or message.

parol Oral. (See also: parol evidence rule)

parol evidence rule If there is a written contract, the terms of the contract cannot be altered by evidence of oral (parol) agreements purporting to change, explain, or contradict the written document. (See also: extrinsic evidence)

parole The release of a convicted criminal defendant after that person has completed part of his or her prison sentence, based on the concept that during the period of parole, the released criminal can prove he or she is rehabilitated and can "make good" in society. A parole generally has a specific period and terms, such as reporting to a parole officer, not associating with other ex-convicts, and staying out of trouble. Violation of the terms may result in revocation of parole and a return to prison to complete his or her sentence. (Compare: probation)

partial breach A failure to satisfy or meet a term of a contract which is so minimal that it does not cause the contract to fail; also referred to as an immaterial breach. A partial breach is remedied by payment or other adjustment—for example if a landlord rents a furnished apartment and fails to supply a bed, the landlord may lower the rent temporarily until the bed is provided.

partial disability The result of an injury that permanently reduces a worker's ability to function, but still permits the worker to do some gainful activity.

partially secured debt A debt that is secured by collateral that is worth less than the debt—for example, a $12,000 car loan that is secured by a car that's now worth only $10,000.

partial verdict In a criminal trial in which the defendant is charged with more than one crime, the jury's verdict that the defendant is guilty of one or more of the charges, but not guilty of the others.

participate To invest and in exchange, receive a part or share in business profits, payments on a promissory note, title to land, or as one of the beneficiaries of the estate of a person who has died.

partition A court-ordered sale or physical division of property, usually real estate, that's owned by more than one person as tenants in common or joint tenancy. Any co-owner has the right to demand a partition.

partner One of the co-owners and investors in a partnership. Each partner claims a share of the the business's income or losses on the partner's individual tax return. General partners are responsible for the debts, contracts, and actions of all the partners in the business. Limited partners do not share responsibility for partnership debts and cannot share in management decisions.

partnership Refers to a legal structure for a business of two or more individuals; called a general partnership when used without a qualifier such as "limited" or "limited liability." Each owner (partner) is personally liable for all debts of the business, and each partner claims a share of the the business's income or losses on the partner's individual tax

return. To form a partnership, each partner normally contributes money, property, or labor in exchange for an ownership interest in the partnership. Most partnerships are created by a formal written partnership agreement, although they may be based on an oral agreement or just a handshake. (See also: limited partnership, limited liability partnership)

party 1) A person, business, or other legal entity that files a lawsuit (the plaintiff or petitioner) or defends against one (the defendant or respondent). 2) A person or other legal entity that enters into an agreement.

party of the first part Antiquated language used to identify one of the parties to an agreement. Modern contract practice is to identify parties with abbreviations, or by an identifier such as buyer, seller, lessee, lessor, licensee, or licensor.

party of the second part See: party of the first part

party wall A wall that is shared by two adjoining premises, either residential or business, and that is on the property line.

par value The face value of a stock, assigned by a corporation at the time the stock is issued. The par value is often printed on the stock certificate, but the market value of the stock may be much more than par value. Most common stocks issued today do not have par values, except in states that require it. In some states, shares with a par value cannot be issued at a price less than the par value.

par-value stock Shares in a corporation that were given a stated share price (par value) when issued. (Compare: no-par stock)

passenger A rider on a train, bus, airline, taxi, ship, ferry, automobile, or other carrier in the business of transporting people for a fee (a common carrier). A passenger is owed a duty of care by such a carrier.

passive Being inactive. For tax purposes, "passive income" includes income produced without active effort or management, such as bank interest, stock dividends, trust profits, and rent (when there is no management involvement). In estate planning, a "passive trustee" is one who has no responsibilities other than to hold title or wait for an event that would activate the trust.

pass-through taxation The taxation method applied to sole proprietorships, partnerships, and limited liability companies, where the owners pay taxes on all business profits on their individual tax returns (the business income "passes through" the business to the owners' tax returns). In contrast, a corporation, or a business that elects corporate-style taxation, is taxed directly on all business profits.

pat-down See: frisk

Legal Eagles. (1986) Opposing lawyers in a murder case, Robert Redford and Debra Winger fall in love. With Daryl Hannah, Brian Dennehy, Terence Stamp.

patent A grant by the U.S. Patent and Trademark Office (USPTO) that allows the patent owner to maintain a monopoly for a limited period of time on the use and development of a new innovation. The USPTO grants three types of patents: utility patents for useful, new, inventions that are not obvious to those in the field; design patents for new and original designs that ornament a manufactured product; and plant patents for new, asexually or sexually reproducible plants.

patent ambiguity See: ambiguity

Patent and Trademark Office (PTO) See: U.S. Patent and Trademark Office

patent claim The portion of a patent that establishes the legal boundaries of the invention—that is, the exclusive rights of the owner. Patent claims are written in a formal style and precise terminology, and they serve as the basis for any determination of patent infringement. During the application process, patent claims are often the subject of intense negotiation between the applicant and the U.S. Patent and Trademark Office (USPTO).

patent claims Statements included in a patent that describe (or "recite") the structure of an invention in precise and exact terms, using a long-established formal style and precise terminology. Claims form the boundaries of an invention much like a deed describes the boundaries of real property. They may be broad or narrow in terms of the scope of the invention they address. The greater the scope of the invention defined in the claims (that is, the broader the claims), the wider the reach of the patent.

patent deed The official document (sometimes referred to as letters patent) that is sent to an applicant by the U.S. Patent and Trademark Office when the applicant's patent issues.

patent defect An obvious flaw in a product or a document (such as leaving out the property description in a deed). (Compare: latent defect)

patent drawing Visual representations of an invention that are included in a patent. Patent drawings show all the features of the invention described in the application, including those features that distinguish it from prior art. (See also: prior art)

patent infringement See: infringement (of utility patent)

patent pending The status of an invention between the time when: a utility patent application has been filed and when it is issued or rejected, or the time between when a provisional patent application has been submitted and when a subsequent patent application is issued or rejected. Inventors mark their devices patent pending in order to place others on notice that they claim priority. Patent pending status does not bestow any legal right to stop copying.

patent search A search of all existing or publicly available information to determine whether an invention is new (novel) and whether persons with ordinary skill in the field could have deduced it (nonobvious). A patent search usually begins with a review of previously issued patents, and progresses to other types of documents, such as journal articles and scientific papers describing unpatented inventions. The most thorough patent searches are performed by professional patent searchers at the U.S. Patent and Trademark Office. (See also: prior art, nonobviousness, novelty)

patent troll Disparaging term for someone who sues for patent infringement but who does not make or sell any product using the patented technology.

paternity suit A lawsuit to determine the identity of the father of a child born outside of marriage. A paternity suit may be brought either by the mother or by the father himself if the mother is denying his paternity, and is usually proved by genetic testing. Once paternity is established, the father has all the rights and obligations of parenthood, including the duty to support the child and the right to petition for custody or visitation.

Patriot Act Shorthand label for a lengthy and complex package of federal anti-terrorism and general crime control laws signed into law less than two months after the September 11, 2001 terrorist attacks on the World Trade Center and the Pentagon. (The legislation's formal name is the "Uniting and Strengthening America by Providing Appropriate Tools Required to Intercept and Obstruct Terrorism Act.") The Patriot Act was reenacted in 2006. Some sections of the original law were deleted or amended. Some provisions, including the authority for roving wiretaps, expire in 2009 unless they are reenacted. Under the Patriot Act, it is a federal crime to commit dangerous and illegal acts on U.S. soil with the intent to intimidate or coerce the government or a civilian population. It is also a federal crime to hack into government computers, give financial assistance to terrorists, and to possess substances that can be used for biological or chemical weapons for nonpeaceful purposes.

pawn To pledge an item of personal property as security for a loan, with the property left with the pawnbroker. The interest rates are on the high side, the amount of the loan is well below the value of the pledged property, and the broker has the right to sell the item without further notice if the loan is not paid. Pawnbrokers are licensed by the state. (See also: pledge)

pawnbroker One who lends money in exchange for items pledged as collateral.

payable See: accounts payable

payable-on-death designation A way to avoid probate for bank accounts, government bonds, securities, individual retirement accounts, and, in some states, real estate or cars. To create a pay-on-death designation, you simply name someone on the ownership document (such as the registration card for a bank account) to inherit the property at your death. You retain complete control of your property while you are alive, and you can change the beneficiary (payee) at any time. At your death, the property is transferred directly to the beneficiary, free of probate.

payable on demand A debt on a promissory note or bill of exchange which must be paid when demanded by the payee (the party to whom the debt is owed).

"The fine for peering into your neighbor's house without permission is one cow."

—Irish Laws, collected by
Mary Dowling Daley

payback provision A provision in a special needs trust requiring that, after the beneficiary dies, the trustee must use any property left in the trust to reimburse Medicaid for benefits the beneficiary received. Special needs trusts containing property originally belonging to the beneficiary (self-settled trusts) must have a payback provision to avoid having the property considered the beneficiary's resource for program eligibility purposes. Third-party trusts do not have a payback provision.

payee The one named on a check or promissory note to receive payment.

payment in due course Payment of funds to the holder of a promissory note or other negotiable instrument made without knowledge that the document had been acquired by fraud or that the

holder did not have valid title. The true owner of the note cannot also demand payment, but must look to the recipient of the funds.

payment in full The giving of all funds due to another. This language is often inserted on the back of check above the place for endorsement to prove that the payee accepts the payment as complete.

payment into court 1) Money or property that is given to the court clerk to be distributed after a lawsuit is concluded. Typically, the person making payment into court is not involved in the lawsuit, but owes money or property to which the parties dispute ownership. For example, a customer might make payment into court for money owed a business partnership, if the partnership has dissolved and one partner is suing the other for ownership of the business's assets. 2) In landlord-tenant law, rent money that a tenant deposits with a court during a dispute with the landlord, often to avoid eviction.

payor The person or entity that is responsible for payment on a promissory note or bill. May also be spelled payer.

pay or quit The type of written notice given to a tenant by a landlord, when the tenant is late with the rent. The notice tells the tenant to pay the rent, sometimes within a specified number of days, or leave the premises. If the tenant does neither, the landlord may file an eviction lawsuit.

payroll taxes The income taxes withheld from an employee's paycheck plus unemployment contributions and FICA contributions—including both Social Security and Medicare—that must be deposited into an IRS account.

PBGC See: Pension Benefit Guaranty Corporation

peaceable possession In real estate, holding property without any adverse claim to possession or title by another. (See also: adverse possession)

peace bond An amount the court requires someone to pay as a guarantee that he or she will not threaten or bother a particular person or otherwise commit a breach of the peace. If the protected party is bothered or injured, the bond amount is forfeited to the party or his or her survivors.

peculation Misappropriation of government funds or property.

pecuniary Relating to money. For example, a pecuniary award as an award of money.

pedophilia An abnormal obsession with children as sex objects. A person who acts upon this obsession, by molesting a child, taking explicit photographs, and

performing other acts specified by law, is guilty of a crime.

peeping Tom A person who stealthily peeks into windows, holes in restroom walls, or other openings with the purpose of seeing people undressed or couples making love. The term comes from the legendary Tom who peeked when Lady Godiva rode her horse naked through the streets of Coventry to protest taxes. Being a peeping Tom is treated as a crime based on sexual deviancy, and a victim may sue a peeping Tom for invasion of privacy.

peer 1) An equal. (See also: jury of one's peers) 2) A member of the nobility in Great Britain.

peer review An evaluation of someone's work by a group of people in the same profession or field. A peer-reviewed or "refereed" journal, for example, publishes submissions that have been read and selected by an editorial board of experts in the field. Hospitals, schools, and other institutions often have peer-review boards or committees who evaluate the work of their colleagues, sometimes in response to allegations of poor performance or malpractice.

penal Relating to crime, as in "penal code" (the laws specifying crimes and punishment) or "penal institution" (a state prison or penitentiary confining convicted felons).

penalty Punishment upon conviction of a crime, generally in the form of a monetary fine, forfeiture of property, or imprisonment.

penalty clause A contract clause that imposes an excessive monetary penalty in the event a party defaults. Courts generally don't enforce penalty clauses when the amount imposed is unrelated to the damages incurred.

pendente lite (pen-**den**-tay **lee**-tay) Latin for "while the action is pending" or "during litigation." Often used to describe a court order that is in effect only until the end of a lawsuit, such as an order for temporary child support pending the resolution of a divorce proceeding.

pendent jurisdiction In federal procedure, a federal court's right to decide a claim it would not ordinarily have a right to decide, because that claim arises out of the same incident as a claim that is properly before the court. Federal courts are courts of limited jurisdiction, and they generally don't have the right to decide issues of state law between residents of the same state. If, however, a plaintiff sued and alleged both federal and state law claims, the federal court could decide the state law claims under the doctrine of pendent jurisdiction.

penitentiary A state or federal prison for convicted criminals.

pen register A device that makes a record of the phone numbers called from a particular phone. When a court authorizes it, a law enforcement agency may use a pen register in a criminal investigation.

pension A retirement fund for employees paid for or contributed to by some employers as part of a package of compensation for the employees' work. Pensions became widespread during the Second World War, when they were commonly used as lures because there were more jobs than workers.

Pension Benefit Guaranty Corporation (PBGC) A federal insurance fund that pays pension benefits to retirees whose pension plans have ended, generally because the plans cannot meet their financial obligations. The PBGC is funded by insurance premiums paid by employers that sponsor covered plans. The PBGC covers only defined benefit plans and only up to a maximum monthly amount.

people The designation for the government in a criminal prosecution, as in *People v. Capone*. These cases may also be captioned *State v. Davis* (in a state prosecution) or *United States v. Miller* (in federal prosecutions).

per 1) For each or every—for example, "She spends five dollars per day." 2) According to—for example "Per the judge's direction, the defendant took the stand."

per capita Latin for "by head," meaning to be determined by the number of people. Under a will, this is the most common method of determining what share of property each beneficiary gets when one of the beneficiaries dies before the will maker, leaving children of his or her own. For example, Fred leaves his house jointly to his son Alan and his daughter Julie. But Alan dies before Fred does, leaving two young children. If Fred's will states that heirs of a deceased beneficiary are to receive the property per capita, Julie and the two grandchildren will each take a third. If, on the other hand, Fred's will states that heirs of a deceased beneficiary are to receive the property per stirpes, Julie will receive one-half of the property, and Alan's two children will share his half in equal shares (through Alan by right of representation).

percipient witness A witness who testifies about things she or he actually perceived. For example, an eyewitness.

per curiam By the court. It usually refers to a decision made by the court as a whole, rather than by a specific judge.

per diem (per **dee**-um) Latin for "per day," per diem refers to payment of a set amount for each day's expenses for an employee or agent. Typically, a per diem is available only for travel away from home. For example, someone who goes on an overnight business trip for an employer might receive a per diem of $50 to cover meals and incidentals on the trip.

Lizzie Borden, known in song and story for hatcheting her parents to death, was actually acquitted of murder charges.

peremptory 1) Final and absolute. 2) Not requiring any showing of cause. (See also: peremptory challenge)

peremptory challenge The right to dismiss or excuse a potential juror during jury selection without having to give a reason. Each party to a lawsuit gets a set number of peremptory challenges. (Compare: challenge for cause)

peremptory norm See: jus cogens

peremptory writ of mandate (or mandamus) A court order to any governmental body, government official, or a lower court requiring that the body, official, or court perform an act the court finds is an official duty required by law. (Compare: alternative writ of mandate)

perfect (per-**fect**) To take all required steps to achieve a legal result. For example a mechanic's lien is perfected by filing a lawsuit and obtaining a judgment.

perfected Having completed all necessary legal steps to achieve a result, such as completing and filing the necessary documents to record a security interest. (See also: perfect)

perform To fulfill one's obligations under a contract.

performance Fulfillment of an obligation required by contract. Performance of a contract may be demanded in a lawsuit (specific performance) and it may also be short of full performance (part or partial performance).

perjurer A person who intentionally lies while under an oath administered by a notary public, court clerk, or other official, and thus commits the crime of perjury. A perjurer may commit perjury in oral testimony or by signing or acknowledging a written legal document (such as an affidavit, declaration under penalty of perjury, deed, license application, or tax return) knowing the document contains false information. (See also: perjury)

perjury The crime of intentionally lying after being duly sworn to tell the truth by a notary public, court clerk, or other official. This false statement may be made in testimony in court, administrative hearings, depositions, or answers to interrogatories, as well as by signing or acknowledging a written legal document (such as an affidavit, declaration under penalty of perjury, deed, license application, or tax return) known to contain false information.

PERM Stands for Program Electronic Review Management, also known as labor certification.

permanent disability A physical or mental disability that indefinitely impairs a worker's ability to perform the duties or normal activities that the worker performed before the accident or serious illness.

permanent injunction A court order that a person or entity take certain actions or refrain from certain activities. A permanent injunction is typically issued once a lawsuit over the underlying activity is resolved, as distinguished from a preliminary injunction, which is issued while the lawsuit is pending.

permanent injury Physical or mental damage that will indefinitely restrict the employment or other normal activities of an individual. In a lawsuit to recover damages caused by the negligence or intentional wrongful act of another, a permanent injury can be a major element in an award of general damages.

permanent resident See: lawful permanent resident (LPR)

permit A license or other document given by an authorized public official or agency—for example, a building inspector or the department of motor vehicles—that allows a person or business to perform certain acts. Permits are intended to guarantee that laws and regulations are obeyed, but they also are a source of public revenue.

perpetuity Forever. See also: rule against perpetuities

per se Latin for "by itself," meaning inherently. Thus, a published writing which falsely accuses another of being a convicted felon is libel per se, without further explanation of the meaning of the statement.

person 1) A human being. 2) A corporation treated as having the rights and obligations of a person. Counties and cities can be treated as a person in the same manner as a corporation. However, corporations, counties, and cities cannot have the emotions of humans, such as malice, and therefore are not liable for punitive damages.

personal effects An expression often found in wills to refer to the personal property that the will maker owns at death. For example, "I leave my personal effects to my daughter Jane."

personal financial responsibility counseling A class intended to teach budgeting and debt management skills to those who have filed for bankruptcy. Under the 2005 bankruptcy law, someone who files for bankruptcy must get personal financial responsibility counseling before he or she can receive a bankruptcy discharge.

personal guardian See: guardian of the person

personal injury An injury not to property, but to the body, mind, or emotions. For example, if you slip and fall on a banana peel in the grocery store, personal injury covers any actual physical harm (broken leg and bruises) you suffered in the fall as well as the humiliation of falling in public, but not the harm of shattering your watch.

personal injury recovery The amount that comes from a lawsuit or insurance settlement to compensate someone for physical and mental suffering, including injury to body, injury to reputation, or both.

personal property All property other than land and buildings attached to land. Cars, bank accounts, wages, securities, a small business, furniture, insurance policies, jewelry, patents, pets, and season baseball tickets are all examples of personal property. Personal property may also be called personal effects, movable property, goods and chattel, and personalty. (Compare: real estate)

personal representative An alternative term for the executor or administrator of an estate, commonly used in states that have adopted a law called the Uniform Probate Code.

personal service A method for the formal delivery of court papers in which the papers are placed directly into the hands of the person to be served. (Compare: substituted service)

personal services In contract law, the talents of a person such as an artist or actor that are unusual, special, or unique and cannot be performed exactly the same by another person. The value of personal services is greater than general labor; for instance, woodcarving is personal service and carpentry is general labor.

personalty See: personal property

per stirpes Under a will, a method of determining who inherits property when a beneficiary has died before the will maker, leaving living children

of his or her own. For example, Fred leaves his house jointly to his son Alan and his daughter Julie. But Alan dies before Fred, leaving two young children. If Fred's will states that heirs of a deceased beneficiary are to receive the property "per stirpes," Julie will receive one-half of the property, and Alan's two children will share his half in equal shares (through Alan by right of representation). If, on the other hand, Fred's will states that the property is to be divided per capita, Julie and the two grandchildren will each take a third.

 "It is not desirable to cultivate a respect for the law, so much as for the right."

—Henry David Thoreau

---

petition 1) A formal request for something, submitted to an authority such as a court or a government agency. For example, the party who loses a court case might petition to appeal. 2) Making a formal request of a court or presenting a written request to an organization's governing body signed by one or more members.

petitioner 1) A person who signs a petition. 2) Sometimes a synonym for plaintiff, used almost universally in some states and in others for certain types of lawsuits, most commonly divorce and other family law cases. 3) Someone who sponsors an immigrant or non-immigrant for a green card or visa.

petit jury An old-fashioned name for the jury sitting to hear a lawsuit or criminal prosecution, called petit (small) to distinguish it from a grand jury, which has other duties.

pet trust A trust set up to benefit one or more pets. Allowed by law in most states, these trusts typically name a trustee to handle the money left for the pets and a caregiver to provide day-to-day care.

petty larceny A term used in many states for theft of a small amount of money or objects of little value (such as less than $500). It is distinguished from grand larceny which is theft of property of greater worth, which is a felony punishable by a term in state prison. Petty larceny is a misdemeanor punishable at maximum with a term in the county jail.

phishing A form of Internet fraud in which a fake website or email is made to resemble a legitimate one, in order to steal valuable information such as credit cards, Social Security numbers, user IDs, and passwords. "Spear phishing" is a fraudulent email targeted at a specific group, often employees of a large company or users of a networking website.

physical custody The right of a parent to have a child live with him or her. In a divorce, physical custody may be either "sole" or "joint." (Compare: legal custody)

physical incapacity The inability of a spouse to engage in sexual intercourse with the other spouse. In some states, physical incapacity is a ground for an annulment or fault divorce, assuming the incapacity was not disclosed to the other spouse before the marriage.

physician-assisted suicide See: assisted suicide

physician-patient privilege The right to withhold evidence in a trial or other legal proceeding on the basis that any information disclosed by a patient to a doctor for the purpose of diagnosis or treatment is confidential (unless the patient consents to disclosure).

picketing Protesting, typically by standing outside of a business or workplace to publicize a dispute or incident occurring there. Sometimes, picketers want to persuade others not to enter the place they are picketing (as might be the case with workers on strike or antiabortion protesters outside of an abortion clinic). Picketing may also happen online, as when IBM's campus on the Second Life website was picketed by avatars of IBM employees.

piercing the corporate veil See: piercing the veil

piercing the veil A judicial doctrine that allows a plaintiff to hold otherwise immune corporate shareholders personally liable for the debts of or damages caused by a corporation under their control. The corporate veil can be pierced when shareholders have acted intentionally and illegally, when the corporation has neglected corporate formalities, and/or when the corporation is found to be a mere alter ego of the shareholders (a shield set up to defraud creditors). This doctrine applies to limited liability companies as well. Also known as disregarding the corporate entity.

pilferage The act of theft. Also used to refer to the items stolen—for example, "He hid the pilferage in his car."

pimp A person who procures a prostitute for customers or vice versa, usually sharing the profits of the prostitute's activities. A pimp commits the crime of pandering.

pink slip 1) Slang for notice from an employer that one is being fired or laid off. 2) Slang for the official title certificate to a vehicle, because in some states the document is or was pink. This is the source of the phrase "racing for pinks," when the winner of a car race wins ownership of the loser's car.

piracy 1) Crimes of robbery, kidnapping, and similar activities on the high seas. The trial and punishment of such pirates may be under international law or under the laws of the particular nation where the pirate has been captured. 2) A colloquial term without legal significance often used to describe willful copyright, patent, and trademark infringement.

PITI Abbreviation for the major expenses that make up a mortgage payment: principal (the amount borrowed), interest, (property) taxes, and (home-owners') insurance.

PKPA See: Parental Kidnaping Prevention Act

plagiarism Deliberately passing off somebody else's original expression or creative ideas as one's own. Plagiarism can be a violation of law if copyrighted expression is taken. Often, however, plagiarism does not violate any law but marks the plagiarist as an unethical person in the political, academic, or scientific community where the plagiarism occurs.

plain error When a trial court makes an error that is so obvious and substantial that the appellate court should address it, even though the parties failed to object to the error at the time it was made.

plaintiff The person, corporation, or other legal entity that initiates a lawsuit seeking damages, enforcement of a contract, or a court determination of rights. In certain states and for some types of lawsuits, the term petitioner is used instead of plaintiff.

plaintiff's attorney A lawyer who regularly represents people who are suing for damages.

plain view doctrine The rule that allows a law enforcement officer to seize evidence of a crime, without obtaining a search warrant, when that evidence is in plain sight. For example, a policeman who stops a motorist for a minor traffic violation and sees a handgun on the back seat may conclude that the driver is unlawfully in possession of the gun, and may enter the car to seize it.

Plan for Achieving Self-Support (PASS) A plan approved by SSI that allows an SSI recipient to own otherwise countable resources as part of an effort to become self-supporting.

plant patent A patent issued for new strains of asexually reproducing plants. Plant patents last for 20 years from the date the patent is filed. Certain sexually reproduced plants also may be protected under the Plant Variety Protection Act of 1970 for periods ranging from 18 to 25 years.

plea An accused defendant's formal answer to criminal charges. Typically defendants enter one of the following pleas: guilty, not guilty, or nolo contendere. A plea is usually entered when charges are formally brought (at arraignment). (See also: nolo contendere)

"The ardor and stress of conflict are not favorable to abstract considerations of justice."

—Chief Justice Harlan F. Stone

plea bargain A negotiation between the defense, prosecution, and the judge that settles a criminal case short of trial. The defendant typically pleads guilty to a lesser crime or fewer charges than originally charged, in exchange for a guaranteed sentence that is shorter than what the defendant would face if convicted at trial. The prosecution gets the certainty of a conviction and a known sentence; the defendant avoids the risk of a higher sentence; and the judge gets to move on to other cases.

plead 1) In civil lawsuits and petitions, the filing of any document (pleading) or the act of making an assertion or allegation in a legal proceeding. 2) In criminal law, the entry of plea of a defendant in response to each charge of criminal conduct.

pleading Any legal document filed in a lawsuit, including the complaint, petition, answer, demurrer, motion, declaration, and memorandum of points and authorities (written argument citing precedents and statutes).

plea in abatement A pleading by the defendant, as a response to a plaintiff's claim, where the defendant does not dispute the plaintiff's claims but objects to its form or the time or place where it is asserted, thereby having an excuse which a judge should consider because it could affect the judge's sentence.

pledge To deposit personal property as security for a personal loan of money. If the loan is not repaid when due, the personal property pledged shall be forfeit to the lender. The property is known as collateral. (See also: pawn)

plenary Full, complete, covering all matters, often referring to an order, hearing, or trial.

***Plessy v. Ferguson* (1896)** U.S. Supreme Court decision in which the Court ruled, despite a vigorous dissent by Justice John Harlan, that "separate but equal" facilities for blacks were constitutional, which remained the rule until *Brown v. Board of Education* (1954).

PMI See: private mortgage insurance

POD See: payable-on-death designation

points and authorities The legal and factual basis for an argument in a lawsuit. A party who wants the judge to rule a particular way on a motion often must submit a memorandum of points and authorities, in which the party argues that the facts, statutes, and relevant precedents support that party's position.

poison pill A defensive strategy for avoiding a hostile takeover in which a company offers low-price stock to its current shareholders in order to dilute the shares and make it more expensive for another company to buy them out.

police court A court that handles minor criminal offenses, and that conducts hearings for more serious criminal cases, to determine whether there is enough evidence to send the case to a higher court for trial.

police powers The fundamental right of a government to make all necessary laws. In the United States, state police power comes from the Tenth Amendment to the Constitution, which gives states the rights and powers "not delegated to the United States." States are thus granted the power to establish and enforce laws protecting the welfare, safety, and health of the public.

political question A question that a court declines to consider because it more properly belongs before the legislative or executive branch of the federal or state government.

poll 1) The process of casting and recording votes in an election. Also the results of an election. 2) To receive votes—for example, a candidate is said to "poll" a certain number of votes. 3) The place where votes are cast and recorded in an election. Often referred to as "the polls." 4) A survey of individual opinions on a given topic. Also, the process of collecting these opinions.

poll book A list of all the registered voters in a voting district.

polygamy Having more than one wife or husband at the same time, usually more than just two (which is bigamy). It is a crime in all states.

polygraph A lie detector device that tests a person's physiological response (for example, changes in blood pressure and respiration) to questioning. The test's reliability is a matter of ongoing controversy, and in most U.S. states polygraph test results are not admissible in court.

POMS Program Operations Manual System, a set of guidelines issued by the Social Security Administration to help lower-level employees interpret the federal statutes and regulations that govern the SSI and Medicaid programs.

Ponzi scheme A crooked investment arrangement by which investors, lured by the promise of outsized returns, are paid from money contributed by new investors, not from the profits earned by their investments. A Ponzi scheme is the same as a pyramid scheme. The term "Ponzi scheme" is used primarily in the United States, where it was named after Charles Ponzi, who used a pyramid scheme to take millions of dollars from investors in 1920.

pooled trust A special needs trust operated by a nonprofit organization for the benefit of several beneficiaries. Assets are jointly managed and invested. SSI does not consider pooled trust funds donated by a third party for a beneficiary to be a resource available to the beneficiary.

pornography Photographs, films, books, or other material depicting erotic or sexual acts designed to cause sexual arousal. Pornography is protected by the First Amendment free speech provisions unless it is found to be obscene.

positive law Statutory man-made law, as compared to natural law, that is purportedly based on universally accepted moral principles or derived from nature and reason.

posse comitatus (**pah**-see kom-i-**tah**-tuhs) Latin for "power of the county." The power of the sheriff to call upon any able-bodied citizens to help keep the peace or apprehend a criminal.

possess To own, have title to, occupy, physically hold, or have under exclusive control. In describing the estate of a deceased, wills sometimes use the phrase "of which I die possessed."

possession Any article, object, asset, or property which one owns, occupies, holds, or has under control.

 "America is the paradise of lawyers."
—Justice David J. Brewer

---

possession of stolen goods The crime of possession of goods which one knows or which any reasonable person would realize were stolen. It is generally a felony.

possessory interest In real estate, the right of a person to occupy and/or exercise control over a particular plot of land; distinguished from an ownership interest. For example, a tenant with a long term lease has a possessory interest, but not an ownership interest.

possibility of a reverter The potential that the title to a real property interest will return to the original grantor. For example, a gift of a building to a hospital on condition that it be used

forever for health care. If the building is no longer used for that purpose, the property will revert to the estate of the original grantor.

post 1) To place a notice prominently. For example, employers are required to post notices about employee rights in a conspicuous location. 2) To mail. 3) To record a payment on a particular date. For example, when you pay a credit card bill, your next statement will show you the date payment was "posted to your account."

postdated check A check that is dated in the future, so it cannot be cashed until that date.

post hoc The phrase represents the faulty logic of assuming that one thing was caused by another merely because it followed that prior event in time. From the Latin phrase post hoc, ergo propter hoc, which means "after this, therefore because of this."

posthumous child A child born after the death of his or her father.

posting The act of entering financial transactions into bookkeeping records or transferring data to a general ledger.

postjudgment interest Interest on a court judgment that a creditor can collect from the time the judgment is entered in the court clerk's record until it is paid.

post mortem Latin for "after death," an examination of a dead body to determine cause of death, generally called an autopsy.

pot Slang for marijuana.

pot trust A trust for children in which the trustee decides how to spend money on each child, taking money out of the trust to meet each child's specific needs. One important advantage of a pot trust over separate trusts is that it allows the trustee to provide for one child's unforeseen need, such as a medical emergency. But a pot trust can also make the trustee's life difficult by requiring choices about disbursing funds to the various children. Most pot trusts end when the youngest child reaches a certain age, usually 18 or 21.

pour-over will A will that "pours over" property into a trust when the will maker dies. A pour-over will is intended to guarantee that any assets which somehow were not included in the trust become assets of the trust upon the party's death. Property left through the will must go through probate before it goes into the trust.

power of acceptance The legal ability to consent to an offer and create a binding contract.

power of appointment The legal authority to decide who will receive someone else's property, usually property held in a trust. Most trustees can distribute the income from a trust only according to the terms of the trust, but a trustee with a power of appointment can choose the beneficiaries, sometimes from a list of candidates specified by the grantor. For example, Karin creates a trust with power of appointment to benefit either the local art museum, symphony, library, or park, depending on the trustee's assessment of need.

power of attorney A document that gives another person legal authority to act on your behalf. If you create such a document, you are called the principal, and the person to whom you give this authority is called your agent or attorney-in-fact. If you make a durable power of attorney, the document will continue in effect even if you become incapacitated. (See also: durable power of attorney for finances, durable power of attorney for health care, general power of attorney, limited power of attorney, special power of attorney)

PPA See: provisional patent application

practicable When something can be done or performed.

practice 1) Custom or habit—for example, "It is the practice in the industry to confirm orders before shipping." 2) A legal business—for example, "Her law practice is located on 4th Street."

praecipe (**pree**-suh-pee or **pres**-uh-pee)
1) A written order (also called a writ)
that commands a defendant to do
something or to show why it should not
be done. 2) A written request for court
action—for example, setting a trial date
or entering a judgment.

pray To formally request judicial judgment, relief, or damages at the end of a
pleading.

prayer for relief What the plaintiff in a
lawsuit asks of the court—for example,
monetary damages, an injunction to
make the defendant stop a certain
activity, or both. The plaintiff usually
makes a "special prayer" for specific
relief (for example, a monetary amount
to recover for an injury), and then
follows with an unspecific "general
prayer" to recover any additional
amount not specified that a court
decides is appropriate.

precatory Suggested or recommended,
but not binding. For example, language
in a will or trust that says "I hope my
daughter will keep the house in the
family" is precatory and not legally
binding on the daughter who inherits
the house.

precedent An opinion of a federal or
state court of appeals establishing a
legal principle or rule that must be
followed by lower courts when faced
with similar legal issues. For example,

once the California Supreme Court
decided that employers may fire an
employee who fails a drug test because
of his use of medical marijuana, all
lower courts in California must follow
this rule.

predatory lending Any type of unscrup-
ulous lending practice where a lender
takes advantage of a borrower. It
usually involves borrowers taking on
high-cost loans they cannot afford to
pay over time because the loans were
based on the borrowers' assets and not
on their ability to repay the debt. Low-
income, elderly, or otherwise vulnerable
people are often the target of this type
of lending. While there are laws against
certain specific types of predatory lending practices, the term is often used as
a catchall for any fraudulent, abusive,
discriminatory, or deceptive lending
practice.

predecease To die before someone else.
For example, in a will: "If Harry should
predecease me, I leave his share of my
estate to his son, Eugene."

predeceased spouse In the law of wills, a
spouse who dies before the will maker
while still married to him or her.

pre-dup The equivalent of a prenuptial
agreement, sometimes abbreviated to
"prenup," for couples registering as
domestic partners in states that allow it.

preemption 1) The principal that a federal law supersedes a state law (and a state law supersedes a local law) where both governments have made laws on the same subject and the laws conflict. 2) The right of purchasing before others (for example, a preemptive right).

preemptive right The right of a shareholder in a corporation to have the first opportunity to purchase a new issue of stock of that corporation in proportion to the amount of stock already owned by the shareholder.

preference In bankruptcy, a debtor's payment to a creditor within a defined period of time before filing for bankruptcy—three months for regular commercial creditors and one year for insider creditors, such as friends, family members, and business associates. Because a preference gives that creditor an edge over other creditors in the bankruptcy case, the bankruptcy trustee can get the preference back and distribute it among all of the creditors.

preference relative An immigration term for certain people who may be eligible for U.S. permanent residence (a "green card") based on family relationships. Preference relatives include the married children of U.S. citizens, children over 21 of U.S. citizens, the spouses or children of U.S. green card holders, and brothers and sisters of U.S. citizens where the U.S. citizen is at least 21 years old. Preference relatives must usually wait to get a green card, because only around 480,000 are available to them in total each year. They must wait in line based on their priority date, which is the date when their U.S. citizen or permanent resident petitioner first filed a visa petition indicating willingness to sponsor the immigrant.

preferred dividend A payment of a corporation's profits to holders of preferred shares of stock. (See also: preferred stock)

preferred stock A class of stock giving its holders priority in receiving dividends and a share of assets upon liquidation of the corporation, but no voting rights. (Compare: common stock)

Pregnancy Discrimination Act A federal law that prohibits discrimination against employees based on the basis of pregnancy, childbirth, or related medical conditions.

prejudgment interest The interest a creditor is entitled to collect under a loan agreement or by law before going to court and obtaining a judgment against the debtor.

preliminary hearing In criminal law, a hearing to determine if a person charged with a felony (a serious crime punishable by a term in the state prison) should be tried for the crime charged. To bind the defendant over for trial, the judge must decide that there is substantial evidence that the defendant committed the offense.

Anatomy of a Murder. (1959) Classic courtroom thriller (and good legal research) written by a justice of the Michigan supreme court. Jimmy Stewart, Lee Remick, Ben Gazzara, Arthur O'Connell, Eve Arden, George C. Scott.

---

preliminary injunction A court order early in a lawsuit that prohibits the parties from taking a disputed action until the court can decide the merits of the case. For example, if a lawsuit is filed challenging the validity of a new government regulation, the court might issue a preliminary injunction preventing the government from enforcing the regulation until the court can decide whether the regulation is valid. Generally, the party seeking a preliminary injunction must show a substantial likelihood of success on the merits of the lawsuit and a substantial threat of irreparable harm if the injunction is not granted.

premarital agreement See: prenuptial agreement

premeditation Planning, plotting, or deliberating before doing something.

Premeditation is an element in first degree murder and shows intent to commit that crime. (See also: malice aforethought, murder, first degree murder)

premises A real estate term for land and the improvements on it, including a building, store, apartment, or other designated structure.

premium 1) An extra payment for an act, option, or priority. 2) Payment for insurance coverage either in a lump sum or by installments.

prenatal tort A tort involving injury to an unborn person.

prenuptial agreement An agreement made by a couple before marriage that controls certain aspects of their relationship, usually the management and ownership of property, and sometimes whether alimony will be paid if the couple later divorces. Courts usually honor premarital agreements unless one person shows that the agreement was likely to promote divorce, was written with the intention of divorcing, or was entered into unfairly. A prenuptial agreement may also be known as a premarital agreement, antenuptial agreement, or simply a "prenup," for short.

prepayment penalty A fee imposed on a borrower who pays off a loan (usually a mortgage) before its due date. Lenders impose this kind of fee to encourage borrowers to hold a debt—and keep paying interest on it—for the whole term of the loan.

preponderance of the evidence The burden of proof required in a civil (non-criminal) action to convince the court that a given proposition is true. The plaintiff must convince the judge or jury by a preponderance of the evidence that the plaintiff's version is true—that is, over 50% of the believable evidence is in the plaintiff's favor. (Compare: reasonable doubt)

preregistration agreement The equivalent of a prenuptial agreement for couples (mostly same-sex) in states that allow registration as domestic partners or civil union partners.

prerogative writ An antiquated term for any writ (court order) directed to government agencies, public officials, or another court. (See: mandamus)

prescription The method of acquiring an interest in real property by continuous and open use, in opposition to the rights of the owner. (See also: adverse possession, easement by prescription)

prescriptive easement A right to use property, acquired by open and obvious use, without the owner's permission, over a minimum period of time established by state law. For example, if hikers have been using a trail through your backyard for ten years and you've never complained, they probably have an easement by prescription through your yard to the trail.

presenteeism When employees come to work despite illness or injury that should have kept them home.

presentment 1) A demand for payment of a promissory note when it is due. 2) A formal written accusation to a court by a grand jury, made on its own initiative without a request or presentation of evidence by the local prosecutor.

presiding judge In most courts, the judge who directs the management of the courts, including making policy decisions for the court, making assignments of judges to specialized courts, overseeing the calendar, and facilitating meetings of the judges.

presumed abuse In a Chapter 7 bankruptcy, when the debtor's current monthly income exceeds the family median income for his or her state, and the debtor cannot pass the means test, the court will presume that the debtor has enough income to fund a Chapter 13 plan. In this situation, the debtor will not be allowed to proceed with a Chapter 7 bankruptcy unless the debtor can prove that he or she is not abusing the Chapter 7 bankruptcy remedy.

presumed maximum value (PMV) The presumed value of food or shelter provided to an SSI recipient by a third party. The PMV is the amount of the federal portion of the SSI grant plus $20. The recipient can prove that the value is in fact less.

presumption A rule of law that permits a court to assume a fact is true until such time as there is a preponderance of evidence which disproves or outweighs the presumption. A presumption shifts the burden to the opposing party to prove that the assumption is untrue.

presumption of innocence One of the most sacred principles in the American criminal justice system, holding that a defendant is innocent until proven guilty. In other words, the prosecution must prove, beyond a reasonable doubt, each essential element of the crime charged.

pretermitted heir A child who is not mentioned in a will and whom the court believes was accidentally overlooked by the person who made the will. For example, a child born or adopted after the will is made may be deemed a pretermitted heir. If the court determines that an heir was accidentally omitted, that heir is entitled to receive the same share of the estate as he or she would have if the deceased had died without a will. A pretermitted heir is sometimes called an omitted heir.

pretrial discovery See: discovery

prevailing party The winner in a lawsuit.

price fixing A criminal violation of federal antitrust statutes, in which several competing businesses agree to set prices for their products to prevent real competition and keep the public from benefiting from price competition. (See also: antitrust laws)

prima facie (**pree**-mah **fey**-shah) Latin for "at first look" or "on its face." A prima facie case is one that at first glance presents sufficient evidence for the plaintiff to win. The defendant must refute the case in some way for him to have a chance of prevailing at trial. For example, if you can show that someone intentionally touched you in a harmful or offensive way and caused some injury to you, you have established a prima facie case of battery. However, this does not mean that you automatically win your case. The defendant would win if he could show that you consented to the harmful or offensive touching

prima facie case See: prima facie

prime suspect The person whom law enforcement officers believe most probably committed a crime being investigated.

primogeniture Latin for "first born." Feudal England (and many other places) practiced male primogeniture, the practice of giving the oldest son the entire estate of his parents (or nearest ancestor). If there was no male heir, the daughters inherited the property in equal shares. The intent was to preserve large properties from being broken up into small holdings, which might weaken the power of nobles.

principal 1) In commercial law, the total amount of a loan, not including any capitalized fees or interest. 2) When creating a power of attorney or other legal document, the person who appoints an attorney-in-fact or agent to act on his or her behalf. 3) In the law of trusts, the property of the trust, as opposed to the income generated by that property. The principal is also known as the trust corpus (that's Latin for "body"). 4) In criminal law, the main perpetrator of a crime.

principal place of business The office of a business where the books and records are kept and where executives manage the company.

Principal Register The primary list on which trademarks that meet certain federal filing standards are placed. The benefits of getting a mark placed on the Principal Register include the notice to potential copiers that your mark is valid and protected, the right to sue to stop copying, and the right to have the mark considered immune from legal challenge after five years of continuous use.

prior(s) Slang for past convictions. A defendant with "priors" may face an enhanced sentence for a current offense, as happens when a defendant convicted of driving under the influence reoffends, thus earning the mandatory jail sentence provided for repeat offenders. In order to impose an enhanced sentence in a current case, the prosecutor must plead, or allege, the past conviction, and prove that it happened.

prior art In patent law, all technology and publications available before the date of invention or anything available about the invention more than one year prior to filing the application. A patent will not issue if prior art is uncovered by a patent examiner that demonstrates somebody already came up with the same idea—that is, all of the significant elements in the applicant's innovation were embodied in an existing innovation.

priority The right to be ahead of the rights or claims of others. In bankruptcy law, the right to collect before other creditors is given to taxing authorities, the holders of court judgments, secured creditors, bankruptcy trustees, and bankruptcy attorneys.

The right can also apply to mortgages, deeds of trusts, or liens, which are given priority in the order they were recorded.

priority date An immigration law term meaning the date on which a petition for immigration or a labor certification is first filed. The priority date is used to mark the intending immigrant's place in the green card waiting list (a list that tends to exist in every green card category that's subject to an annual numerical limit). Each month, the U.S. Department of State publishes a "Visa Bulletin" with an updated list of priority dates, meaning that anyone with a date that matches or is earlier than the dates on that list can stop waiting and continue with their application for a green card.

priority debt A type of debt that is paid first if any creditors are paid in a Chapter 7 bankruptcy case, and must be paid in full in a Chapter 13 bankruptcy case. Priority debts include alimony and child support, wages owed to employees, and fees owed to the trustee and the debtor's bankruptcy attorney.

prior restraint Government action that prevents a publication or broadcast. Prior restraints are considered a violation of the First Amendment and are rarely permitted except in cases in which the publication is obscene,

defamatory, or represents a clear and present danger—a theory articulated by the U.S. Supreme Court in *Near v. Minnesota* (1931).

privacy The right to be free of unnecessary public scrutiny, or to be let alone.

private annuity An arrangement under which a parent transfers assets to a trust for children or grandchildren and in return gets regular lifetime payments (an annuity). Under certain circumstances, the trust assets won't be subject to estate tax when the parent dies.

private carrier A business that transports goods or services for a fee but is under no obligation to do business with the general public. (Compare: common carrier)

private mortgage insurance Insurance that reimburses a mortgage lender if the buyer defaults on the loan and the foreclosure sale price is less than the amount owed the lender (the mortgage plus the costs of the sale). A home buyer who makes less than a 20% down payment may have to purchase private mortgage insurance, commonly referred to as PMI.

private nuisance An activity or thing that interferes with the use of property by an individual (or a few individuals) by being irritating, offensive, or obstructive. Nuisances can include everything from noise and illegal gambling to posting indecent signs and misdirecting water on to other property. Conditions that affect an entire community are a public nuisance. Lawsuits may be brought to abate (remove or reduce) a nuisance.

"Common sense often makes good law."
—Justice William O. Douglas

---

private property Land that is not owned by the government or dedicated to public use. The owner of private property has the right to manage and control it—for example, by using, selling, mortgaging, or exchanging it.

private road A road or driveway on privately owned property, limited to the use of the owner or a group of owners who share the use and maintain the road without help from the town, city, county, or state. (See also: public easement)

privilege A special benefit, exemption from a duty, or immunity from penalty, given to a particular person, a group, or a class of people.

privilege against self-incrimination A witness's right to refuse to testify in court if the testimony might result in the witness revealing criminal activity and/or being criminally prosecuted. This right is guaranteed in the Fifth Amendment to the Constitution, but is waivable under certain circumstances.

privileged communication See: confidential communication

Privileges and Immunities Clause A provision found in Article IV of the U.S. Constitution that prohibits states from discriminating against those who are not state citizens or from favoring its own citizens over citizens of other states. The Privileges and Immunities Clause has been interpreted to create a right to travel, in that it allows citizens of one state to go to another state and enjoy the same privileges and immunities as that state's citizens.

privity A legal relationship between two parties based on contract, estate, or other lawful status, that confers certain rights or remedies. For example, parties that are in privity of contract can enforce the contract or obtain remedies based on it.

probable cause The amount and quality of information police must have before they can search or arrest without a warrant. Most of the time, police must present their probable cause to a judge or magistrate, whom they ask for a search or arrest warrant. Information is reliable if it shows that it's more likely than not that a crime has occurred and the evidence sought exists at the place named in the search warrant, or that the suspect named in the arrest warrant has committed a crime.

probate The court-supervised process following a person's death that includes proving the authenticity of the deceased person's will, appointing someone to handle the deceased person's affairs, identifying and inventorying the deceased person's property, paying debts and taxes, identifying heirs, and distributing the deceased person's property according to the will or, if there is no will, according to state law. Formal probate is a costly, time-consuming process that is best avoided if possible. Most states now offer simplified probate procedures for estates of relatively small value. (See also: administrator, executor, personal representative)

probate court A specialized court or division of a state trial court that considers cases concerning the distribution of deceased persons' property and the appointment of guardians for children or adults who need care and supervision. Called "surrogate's court" in New York and several other states, this court normally examines the authenticity of a will or, if a person dies without a will (intestate),

figures out who inherits under state law. It then oversees a procedure to pay the deceased person's debts and to distribute the assets to the proper inheritors. (See also: probate)

probate estate Property of a deceased person that goes through probate court proceedings before being distributed to those who inherit it.

probation A type of sentence for a criminal offense. The probationer (convicted person) is sentenced to jail, but that sentence is suspended for a period of months or years while the probationer is released into the community subject to certain conditions of behavior. Common conditions of probation include performing public service work, paying a fine, maintaining good behavior, receiving therapeutic services, paying restitution to a victim, and reporting regularly to a probation officer. If the probationer fails to comply with the conditions of probation, the probation office may have the person arrested and brought before a judge for a probation hearing. A judge who finds that probation conditions have not been met can revoke probation and impose the original sentence. (Compare: parole)

probative Tending to prove something. Courts can exclude evidence that is not probative (does not prove anything).

probative facts See: probative

probative value The term used to describe the weight of evidence submitted to prove something. Courts may exclude evidence when its probative value is outweighed by the prejudice the evidence may cause. For example, a prosecutor in a criminal case may wish to introduce the previous criminal conduct of a defendant to show a propensity to commit the crime at issue, but that must be weighed against the right of the accused to be tried on the facts of the present case.

pro bono Short for pro bono publico, Latin "for the public good," legal work performed by lawyers without pay, often to help those without financial resources to pay for services, or to support social causes such as environmental, youth, battered women, or other educational organizations or charities.

procedural law Law that establishes the rules of the court and the methods used to ensure the rights of individuals in the court system. In particular, laws that provide how the business of the court is to be conducted. (Compare: substantive law)

procedure 1) A method or act that furthers a legal process. Procedures include filing complaints, serving documents, setting hearings, and conducting trials. 2) The established rule or series of steps that governs a civil lawsuit or criminal prosecution. (See also: civil procedure, criminal procedure)

proceeding 1) The ordinary process of a lawsuit or criminal prosecution, from the first filing to the final decision. 2) A procedure through which one seeks redress from a court or agency. 3) A filing, hearing, or other step that is part of a larger action. 4) A particular matter that arises and is dealt with in a bankruptcy case.

proceeds for damaged exempt property In bankruptcy, money received through insurance coverage, arbitration, mediation, settlement, or a lawsuit to pay for exempt property that has been damaged or destroyed. For example, if a debtor had the right to use a $30,000 homestead exemption, but his or her home was destroyed by fire, the debtor may instead exempt $30,000 of the insurance proceeds.

process 1) The legal means by which a person is given notice of a legal proceeding or required to appear in court. (See also: service of process) 2) Proceedings in a legal matter.

process server A person who delivers papers informing another person or business of a pending lawsuit or requirement to appear in court. (See also: process, service of process)

proctor A term in admiralty law, referring to a lawyer.

product liability The responsibility of manufacturers, distributors, and sellers of products to the public, to deliver products free of defects that harm someone and to make good on that responsibility if the products are defective. Defective products might include faulty auto brakes, contaminated baby food, exploding bottles of beer, flammable children's pajamas, or products that lack proper label warnings. A key feature of product liability law is that a person who suffers harm need not prove negligence, because the negligence is presumed and the result is strict liability (absolute responsibility) on the seller, distributor, and manufacturer.

professional corporation A type of corporation authorized by state law for a fairly narrow list of licensed professions, including lawyers, doctors, accountants, many types of higher-level health providers, and sometimes architects. A professional corporation does not free an owner from personal liability for his or her own negligence or malpractice, but owners are not personally liable for the malpractice of other owners. In some states, limited liability partnerships offer this same benefit and may be more desirable for other reasons.

professional negligence See: malpractice

proffer To offer evidence for admission at trial.

profit and loss statement A spreadsheet showing a business's gross income and expenses, used to determine the net profit or loss for a specific period.

 "Law is a bottomless pit."
—John Arbuthnot

---

profit margin See: margin

pro forma Latin for "as a matter of form." In the courts, a ruling made as a formality, intended to move matters along.

pro hac vice (proh hock-**vee**-chay) Latin meaning "for this one particular occasion." The phrase usually refers to an out-of-state lawyer who has been granted special permission to participate in a particular case, even though the lawyer is not licensed to practice in the state where the case is being tried.

prohibition See: writ of prohibition

promise 1) A firm commitment to perform an act, refrain from acting, or make a payment or delivery. 2) In contract law, something of value provided in return for the other party's promise (both of which are referred to as consideration). Failure to fulfill a contractual promise is a breach, for which the other party may seek legal remedies such as performance and damages.

promissory estoppel A legal principle that prevents a person who made a promise from reneging when someone else has reasonably relied on the promise and will suffer a loss if the promise is broken. (See also: estoppel)

promissory note A written promise by one party (called maker, obligor, payor, or promisor) to pay a specific amount of money (called principal) to another party (called payee, obligee, or promisee), which often includes a specified amount of interest on the unpaid principal amount and penalties for failure to pay according to its terms.

promoter A person who puts together a new business, particularly a corporation, including the financing; an organizer of a new venture. Usually the promoter is the principal shareholder and receives shares of promotional stock for organizing the corporation.

promotional stock Shares issued by a newly formed corporation to a promoter (organizer) of the corporation in payment for putting the company together and locating shareholders or other funding. Some states limit the amount of promotional stock the promoter can receive to an amount reasonable for the effort, since it is supported by labor alone and not by assets or cash.

proof Factual evidence that helps to establish that an event occurred or a statement is true. When someone is accused of a crime, the government must prove every element, or aspect, of the crime, such as who physically committed the act and whether that person did so with the intent to commit the crime. Unless all elements of the charged crime are proved, the prosecution will not prevail. In civil cases, too, the plaintiff must prove every aspect of the complaint. (See also: burden of proof)

pro per A term derived from the Latin "in propria persona," meaning "for one's self," used in some states to describe a person who handles his or her own case, without a lawyer. In other states, the term pro se is used. When a nonlawyer files his or her own legal papers, that party is expected to write "in pro per" under his or her name in the heading on the first page.

proper party A person or entity who has an interest in the subject matter of a lawsuit and, therefore, can join in the lawsuit or may be brought into the suit by one of the parties to the legal action. A proper party is distinguished from a "necessary party" who the court will order joined (brought into) the suit. Example: Marianne and Issac both use the road on Allen's property to reach their vacation cabins. Marianne brings a lawsuit to establish the right to use the road. Issac could join the lawsuit as a proper party.

property Anything that is owned by a person or entity. (See also: community property, personal property, public property, real property, separate property)

property control trust Any trust that imposes limits or controls over the rights of trust beneficiaries. These trusts include 1) special needs trusts designed to assist people who have special physical, emotional, or other requirements; 2) spendthrift trusts designed to prevent a beneficiary from wasting the trust principal; and 3) sprinkling trusts that allow the trustee to decide how to distribute trust income or principal among the beneficiaries.

property damage Injury to real or personal property through another's negligence, willful destruction, or by an act of nature. In lawsuits for damages caused by negligence or a willful act, property damage is distinguished from personal injury. Property damage may

include harm to an automobile, a fence, a tree, a home, or any other possession.

property guardian See: guardian of the estate

property tax A tax on the value of property (usually real estate, but sometimes personal property as well) levied by a local government. The property's value is usually established by a public assessor. Local government entities may also impose special taxes for particular public property improvements such as sidewalks, tree planting, or storm drains that benefit property owners. (See also: ad valorem tax, millage)

property tort A tort involving damage to property.

propria persona See: pro per

proprietary Refers to ownership.

proprietary interest Total or partial ownership in a company.

proprietary lease An agreement that gives a co-op owner the right to occupy a specific residential unit.

proprietary rights Rights that come with ownership of a business or real property.

proprietor The owner of a business operated by that individual as a sole proprietorship.

proprietorship See: sole proprietorship

pro rata (proh **rat**-ah or proh **ray**-tah) From Latin for "in proportion," refers to a share to be received or an amount to be paid based on the fractional share of ownership, responsibility, or time used. For example, a buyer of rental property will pay his or her pro rata share of the property taxes for that portion of the year in which he or she holds title.

pro se (proh **say**) A Latin phrase meaning "for oneself" or "on one's own behalf." This phrase describes a party to a lawsuit who represents himself or herself, without a lawyer. It is used in some states in place of in pro per (or in propria persona) and has the same meaning.

prosecute When a local District Attorney, state Attorney General, or federal United States Attorney brings a criminal case against a defendant.

Prosecuting Attorney See: District Attorney, prosecutor

prosecution 1) In criminal law, the government attorney charging and trying the case against a person accused of a crime. 2) A common term for the government's side in a criminal case, as in "The prosecution will present five witnesses," or "The prosecution rests" (completed its case).

prosecutor A lawyer who works for the local, state, or federal government to bring and litigate criminal cases.

Witness for the Prosecution. (1957) An Agatha Christie courtroom thriller with Charles Laughton as a defense barrister fighting back from disastrous testimony by Marlene Dietrich against his client (Tyrone Power). With Elsa Lanchester, Una O'Connor, Ian Wolfe.

---

prospectus A detailed statement by a corporation used to describe an issuance (offer) of stock to the general public. A prospectus includes the corporation's financial statements, information about its directors and officers, its business plans, any litigation in progress, its recent performance, and other matters that would assist a potential investor or investment adviser to evaluate the stock and the prospects of the company for profit, loss, or growth. The Federal Securities Act requires the filing of the prospectus with the Securities and Exchange Commission before any major stock issuance. State laws generally require similar documentation for some issuances of stock within the state.

prostitute A person who receives payment for sexual intercourse or other sexual acts, generally as a regular occupation.

prostitution The profession of performing sexual acts for money. Prostitution is a crime throughout the United States, except for a few counties in the State of Nevada. Soliciting acts of prostitution is also a crime, called pandering or simply, soliciting.

pro tanto (proh **tan**-toh) Latin for "for so much" or "to that extent." Often used to refer to partial payment on a claim (for example, the debt is pro tanto discharged).

protected characteristic In employment law, a trait that may not be the basis of employment decisions. Under federal law, protected characteristics include race, color, national origin, religion, gender (including pregnancy), disability, age (if the employee is at least 40 years old), and citizenship status.

protected class A group of people protected by law from discrimination or harassment based on their membership in the group. For example, under federal law, race, national origin, sex, and age are examples of protected classes.

protective custody The confinement of a person by the government, when the authorities think it's necessary for that person's own security or well-being. A witness who is being threatened may

be placed in protective custody, as may a child or other person who may harm others.

pro tem Temporarily or for the time being. A judge pro tem normally refers to a judge who is sitting temporarily for another judge or to an attorney who has been appointed to serve as a judge as a substitute for a regular judge.

pro tempore (proh **temp**-oh-ray) See: pro tem

protest 1) To complain in a public way about an act, such as sending troops overseas, use of the death penalty, or adoption of a regulation or law. 2) To dispute the amount of property taxes, the assessed evaluation of property for tax purposes, or an import duty. 3) A written demand for payment of the amount owed on a promissory note that has not been paid or on a check that was refused by a bank.

prove In a legal proceeding, to present evidence or logic that makes a fact seem certain.

proving a will Convincing a probate court that a document is truly the deceased person's will. Usually this is a simple formality that the executor or administrator easily satisfies by showing that the will was signed and dated by the deceased person in front of two witnesses. When the will is holographic—that is, completely handwritten by the deceased and not witnessed, it is still valid in many states if the executor can produce relatives and friends to testify that the handwriting is that of the deceased.

provisional ballot A paper ballot used by a voter when there is some problem in establishing a voter's eligibility. The ballot will be counted only if election officials determine that the person was in fact entitled to vote.

provisional patent application (PPA) An interim patent application (also called a PPA) that contains only a portion of the information required in a regular patent application. If the PPA sufficiently discloses the invention, and a regular patent application is filed within one year of the PPA's filing date, the inventor gets the benefit of the PPA filing date. In addition, the inventor gets the full 20-year patent term from the date the regular application is filed.

provisional remedy Any temporary order of a court to protect a party from irreparable damage while a lawsuit or petition is pending. (See also: temporary restraining order, interlocutory decree, temporary injunction)

proviso A term or condition in a contract or title document, which sometimes begins with the phrase "provided that"

followed by a condition or requirement of the agreement.

provocation The act of inciting another person to do a particular thing. In a fault divorce, provocation may constitute a defense to the divorce, preventing it from going through. For example, if a wife suing for divorce claims that her husband abandoned her, the husband might defend the suit on the grounds that she provoked the abandonment by driving him out of the house. In criminal law, provocation can be a defense that justifies an acquittal, mitigated sentence, or reduction of conviction to a lesser charge (for instance, from murder to manslaughter).

proximate cause See: direct and proximate cause

proxy 1) Someone who is authorized to serve in one's place at a meeting, and particularly to cast a vote. 2) The written authority given to someone to act or vote in someone's place. A proxy is commonly given to cast a shareholder's vote at a meeting of shareholders.

prudent person rule The requirement that a trustee, a city or county treasurer, a manager of pension funds, or any fiduciary (a trusted agent) must invest funds with discretion, care, and intelligence. Investments that are generally within the prudent man rule include solid "blue chip" securities, secured loans, federally guaranteed mortgages, treasury certificates, and other conservative investments providing a reasonable return. Some states have statutes that list the types of investments allowable under this rule.

PTO See: U.S. Patent and Trademark Office

public 1) The body politic, or the people of a state, nation, or municipality. 2) Under the authority of the government or belonging and available to the people; not private. It may refer to an entity, agency, or activity. For example, there are both public and private schools, public and private utilities, public and private hospitals, public and private lands, and public and private roads.

public administrator Someone hired by a probate court to administer a deceased person's estate if no relatives or creditors are available to do it. Some states have public administrators who are responsible for temporarily preserving the assets of an estate if there are disputes about specific provisions in the will or about who will be appointed the regular administrator.

publication 1) Information conveyed or made generally known to the public regardless of the media or method

of communication. 2) A method of providing legal notice, usually by means of an approved newspaper in the appropriate county or district. 3) In defamation (libel and slander), the communication of an untrue statement to anyone other than the victim of the falsehood. 4) In copyright law, the act of making copies of a work available to the public on an unrestricted basis. (See also: published work)

"Mercy bears richer fruits than strict justice."

—Abraham Lincoln

public benefit corporation A public benefit corporation is usually a corporation created by the government that performs a specific function for the benefit of the public, such as a public library or an adult day center. More broadly, a public benefit corporation can mean any corporation created for a charitable purpose, though these are usually called nonprofit or not-for profit corporations if they are not created by the government. Some states (California for example) define any charitable corporation as a public benefit corporation.

public charge A general term for a person who is in economic distress and who must be cared for at public expense.

public corporation 1) A corporation whose shares are traded to the general public on a stock exchange. Also known as a publicly held corporation. 2) A corporation created to perform a governmental function, such as a municipal water company or hospital. A public corporation may operate under government control or be financially independent.

public defender A lawyer appointed by the court and paid by the county, state, or federal government to represent clients who are charged with violations of criminal law and are unable to pay for their own defense.

public domain The status of any creative work, invention, or device that is not protected by copyright law. Such items are available for use without permission. Often, works enter the public domain after patent, copyright, or trademark rights have expired or been abandoned.

public domain lands Land or interest in land owned by the United States and administered by the Secretary of the Interior through the Bureau of Land Management. (Compare: public domain)

public easement The right of the general public to use certain streets, highways, paths, or airspace, even though the areas are owned by others.

public figure A person of great public interest or familiarity, such as a government official, politician, celebrity, business leader, movie star, or sports hero. Incorrect harmful statements published about a public figure cannot be the basis of a lawsuit for defamation unless there is proof that the writer or publisher intentionally defamed the person with malice (hate).

public nuisance An activity or thing that affects the health, safety, or morals of a community. It is distinguished from a private nuisance, which harms only a neighbor or a few individuals. For example, a factory that spews out clouds of noxious fumes is a public nuisance, but playing drums at three in the morning is a private nuisance bothering only the immediate neighbors.

public property Property owned by the government or one of its agencies, divisions, or entities. Commonly a reference to parks, playgrounds, streets, sidewalks, schools, libraries, and other property regularly used by the general public.

public record Any information, minutes, files, accounts, or other records which a governmental body is required to maintain, and which must be accessible to scrutiny by the public.

public trust doctrine The principle that certain natural and cultural resources are preserved for public use, and that the government owns and must protect and maintain these resources for the public's use. For example, under this doctrine, the government holds title to all submerged land under navigable waters. Thus, any use or sale of such land must be in the public interest.

public use The right of the public to use property taken by the government through the exercise of its power of eminent domain. Any property taken by eminent domain must be for a public use. Some jurisdictions define public use broadly to mean a public benefit, while other jurisdictions limit its meaning to only actual use by the public.

public utility Any organization which provides services to the general public, although it may be privately owned. Public utilities include electric, gas, telephone, water, and television cable systems, as well as streetcar and bus lines. Public utilities are allowed certain monopoly rights because of the practical need to service entire geographic areas with one system, but they are regulated by state, county, and city public utility commissions under state laws.

publish See: publication

published work When copies of a copyrighted work are made available to the public on an unrestricted basis. Both published and unpublished works are entitled to copyright protection, but some of the rules differ. For example, the duration of a copyright in an unpublished work made for an employer (a work made for hire), or an anonymous or pseudonymous work, can last up to 25 years longer than if the work were published.

When future president John Adams came to court in Boston to be sworn in as an attorney he forgot to bring his lawyer sponsor to attest to his skill and honesty. Another attorney stepped forward and swore to Adams's talent, saving the young man further embarrassment.

---

puffery See: puffing

puffing The practice of exaggerating the value of a product, a business, or property for promotional purposes. Sellers are not generally held liable for exaggerations that are considered puffing. But they can be liable for misrepresenting the facts of a product. (See also: fraud)

punitive damages See: exemplary damages

pur autre vie (**per o-**tra **vee**) Legal French meaning "for another's life." It is a phrase used to describe the duration of a property interest. For example, if Bob is given use of the family house for as long as his mother lives, he has possession of the house pur autre vie.

putative Commonly believed, supposed, or claimed. For example, a putative father is one believed to be the father unless proved otherwise; a putative marriage is one that is accepted as legal when in reality it was not lawful (for example, due to failure to complete a prior divorce).

put option An option to sell a particular commodity or security at a certain time for a certain price. Sometimes simply called a "put." (Compare: call option)

pyramid scheme A crooked investment arrangement by which investors, lured by the promise of outsized returns, are paid from money contributed by new investors, not from the profits earned by their investments. (See also: Ponzi scheme)

QDOT A qualified domestic trust. This type of trust is used to postpone estate taxes when more than the amount of the personal federal estate tax exemption is left to a non-U.S. citizen spouse by the other spouse.

QDRO See: Qualified Domestic Relations Order

QMSCO See: Qualified Medical Child Support Order

QTIP trust A type of trust for married couples that allows a surviving spouse to postpone estate taxes. A QTIP trust allows the surviving spouse to make use of the trust property tax-free. Taxes are deferred until the surviving spouse dies and the trust property is received by the final trust beneficiaries, who were named by the first spouse to die.

Qualified Domestic Relations Order (QDRO) A court order based on the division of a party's pension or retirement benefits as part of a divorce. The QDRO orders the administrator of the pension plan to distribute a specified share of benefits to the nonemployee spouse at the time that the employee spouse begins receiving benefits. This special order is necessary to comply

with federal law governing retirement pay.

qualified domestic trust See: QDOT

qualified endorsement An endorsement that passes title to a negotiable instrument with certain restrictions. For example, writing "without recourse" on the back of the check would create a qualified endorsement. (Compare: blank endorsement)

qualified individual with a disability Under the Americans with Disabilities Act, an individual with a disability who has the necessary skill, education, experience and other job-related requirements to perform the essential functions of a position.

qualified intermediary In a 1031 exchange, a neutral third party who holds the proceeds of the sale of a relinquished property until replacement property is purchased with these funds. This prevents the investor from receiving the funds during the 1031 transaction, and so avoids taxes.

Qualified Medical Child Support Order (QMSCO) A court order that directs an insurance company to continue providing health coverage for the child of a noncustodial parent under that parent's group health plan.

qualified ownership Ownership with limitations or conditions. For example, if your grandmother leaves you a plot of land, but requires that you never build on it.

qualified personal residence trust (QPRT) A trust designed to save on estate tax by moving a residence (or vacation home, if certain conditions in the tax code are met) out of the owner's taxable estate. The owner transfers ownership of the property to the trust but keeps the right to live there for a number of years. QPRTs are most popular when real estate values are going up rapidly.

qualified plan See: qualified retirement plan

qualified retirement plan A retirement plan that meets certain requirements under the Internal Revenue Code and is thus eligible for special tax considerations and benefits. Often, the plan allows employers to make tax deductible contributions on behalf of eligible employees. Employees generally do not have to pay tax on the plan earnings until they withdraw the money.

qualified small business stock Certain small business corporation stock which receives a special tax break that is designed to help qualifying small C corporations raise capital. It does this by allowing qualifying investors in original issue stock to exclude 50% of their gains on the sale of the stock if a five-year holding period is met.

qualified witness A witness who helps lay a foundation for admission of evidence under the business exception to the hearsay rule by explaining how a business keeps its records.

quantum meruit Latin for "as much as he deserved." A principle used to award the reasonable value of services performed by the victim of a broken contract.

quash To annul or set aside. A motion to quash asks the judge for an order setting aside or nullifying an action, such as quashing a service of summons when the wrong person was served.

quasi (**kwah**-zee, **kway**-zeye) From the Latin for "as if," almost, somewhat, to a degree. Quasi is always used in combination with another word and refers to things and actions which are not exactly or fully what they might appear, but are treated "as if" they were. (See, for example: quasi-community property, quasi contract, quasi corporation, quasi-criminal, quasi in rem, quasi-judicial)

quasi-community property A form of property owned by a married couple. If a couple moves to a community property state from a non-community property state, property they acquired together in the non-community property state may be considered quasi-community property. Quasi-community property is treated just like community property when one spouse dies or if the couple divorces.

The Rainmaker. (1997) Francis Ford Coppola directed this adaptation of John Grisham's novel about a young attorney (Matt Damon) who brings a class action lawsuit against big tobacco. Jon Voight plays an icily slick corporate attorney for the defense. With Danny DeVito, Claire Danes.

---

quasi contract An arrangement created and enforced by a court to prevent one party from being unjustly enriched by another; also known as an implied-in-law contract. (See also: implied contract, unjust enrichment)

quasi-corporation A business that operates as a corporation but has not completed the legal requirements, often in the period just before formal incorporation.

quasi-criminal A reference to a court's right to punish for actions or omissions as if they were criminal. The most common example is finding a parent who is delinquent in child support in contempt of court and penalizing him or her with a jail sentence. When a hearing is quasi-criminal, the quasi-defendant is entitled to all due process protections afforded a criminal defendant.

quasi in rem Latin for "as if against a thing," referring to a legal action that involves determining the legal rights of a person with an interest in a property within a court's jurisdiction.

quasi-judicial 1) A description of decisions or actions of an administrative or executive government agency that are similar to a court proceeding. For example, the National Labor Relations Board is a quasi-judicial body that decides labor dispute cases based on the written record of evidence heard and decisions reached by administrative law judges. 2) Sometimes used more generally to refer to adjudicative procedures that occur outside of courts. For example, arbitration is often referred to as a quasi-judicial proceeding.

quasi-personalty Property that is considered to be personal property, even though it is actually (a fixture) or legally (a lease) attached to real property.

Queen's Bench The highest court in Great Britain during the reign of a queen, so that opinions are identified as a volume of Queen's Bench (QB).

question of fact A question that involves factual matters. In a legal proceeding, a jury (if there is one) will determine issues of fact, while only a judge can decide questions of law. For example, whether a defendant was present at the scene of a crime is a question of fact; whether mere presence meets the legal definition of a crime is a question of law.

question of law An issue arising in a lawsuit or criminal prosecution which only relates to determination of what the law is, how it is applied to the facts in the case, and other purely legal points in contention. All "questions of law" arising before, during, and sometimes after a trial are to be determined solely by the judge and not by the jury. (See also: question of fact)

QUID See: qualified individual with a disability

quid pro quo (**kwid** pro **kwoh**) Latin for "this for that." A quid pro quo is what each person in a deal expects to get from the other. In employment law, quid pro quo sometimes refers to a type of sexual harassment in which workplace rewards are explicitly linked to the victim's willingness to submit to unwanted sexual advances. ("If you agree to go out with me, you'll be first in line for promotion.")

quiet enjoyment The right of a property owner or tenant to enjoy his or her property without interference. Disruption of quiet enjoyment may constitute a legal nuisance. Leases and rental agreements often contain a "covenant of quiet enjoyment," expressly obligating the landlord to ensure that tenants live undisturbed.

quiet title action A lawsuit to determine who owns a piece of real estate and so "quiet" any disputes over the title. Such a suit arises when there is some question about title—for example, uncertainty about the boundary, claims by a lienholder, a question about an old mortgage, or an easement that's been used for years without a recorded description. A quiet title lawsuit names as defendants anyone who might have an interest (including descendants—known or unknown—of prior owners). Notice of the action must be posted on the property and published in an approved local newspaper. If the court rules that the plaintiff is the rightful owner, it will grant a quiet title judgment, which can be recorded and will settle the issue of ownership. Quiet title actions are a common example of "friendly" lawsuits in which often there is no opposition. (See also: cloud on title)

quit To leave, used in a written notice to a tenant to leave the premises (called a notice to quit).

qui tam action (**kwee**-tam) Latin for "who as well," a lawsuit brought by a private citizen but brought for "the government as well as the plaintiff." This type of action is generally based on significant legal violations which involve fraudulent or criminal acts, and not technical violations or errors. If successful, the plaintiff will be entitled to a percentage of the recovery of the penalty as a reward for exposing the wrongdoing and recovering funds for the government.

quitclaim deed A deed that transfers whatever ownership interest the transferor has in a particular property. The deed does not guarantee anything about what is being transferred, however. For example, a divorcing husband might quitclaim his interest in certain real estate to his former wife, officially giving up any legal interest he may have in the property. Quitclaim deeds are used primarily among family members or others familiar with the property and each other. (Compare: grant deed, warranty deed)

quorum The number of people required to be present at a meeting before a vote can be taken. A quorum is usually a majority of directors, shareholders, or members, but a different quorum may be set in the bylaws or operating agreement of the business or association.

quotient verdict An award of money damages in a lawsuit obtained by averaging the amounts of damages awarded by jurors when they disagree as to what the award should be. A quotient verdict is not legal since it is not based on a rational discussion of the facts, and such a verdict will be set aside and a mistrial will be declared by the judge.

quo warranto (kwoh wahr-**rahn**-toe) Latin for "by what warrant." The name for a writ (order) used to challenge another's right to either public or corporate office or to challenge actions that are not authorized by a corporation charter (articles of incorporation).

R

Racketeer Influenced and Corrupt Organizations Act (RICO) A federal law, passed in 1970, that allows prosecution and civil penalties for certain acts (including illegal gambling, bribery, kidnapping, murder, and money laundering) performed as part of an ongoing criminal enterprise. RICO has been used to prosecute members of the mafia, the Hells Angels motorcycle gang, and Operation Rescue, an anti-abortion group, among others.

racketeering Certain illegal activities, such as bribery, money laundering, prostitution, or extortion, committed as part of an ongoing criminal enterprise.

rainmaker An employee who creates a lot of new business for a company by bringing in new clients.

ransom 1) As a noun, money paid to, or demanded by, someone in exchange for the release of a kidnapped person or stolen property. 2) As a verb, ransom may refer to either end of the transaction—that is, it may mean to demand payment for release of a person held captive, or it may mean to pay money in exchange for the release of the person held captive.

rape The crime of having sexual intercourse with another person without consent. Common law defined rape as unlawful intercourse by a man against a woman who is not his wife by force or threat and against her will. However, modernly, states have broadened the definition so that marriage, gender, and force are not relevant—lack of consent is the crucial element. Statutory rape occurs when the victim is under the legal age of consent even if the intercourse is consensual.

ratable Capable of being appraised or apportioned. Also taxable according to value, such as an estate or property.

ratification See: ratify

ratify Approval or confirmation of a previous contract or other act that would not otherwise be binding in the absence of such approval. If an employer ratifies the unauthorized acts of an employee, those actions become binding on the employer. A person who is under the legal age to enter into a contract may ratify (and thereby adopt) the contract when he or she reaches majority, or may refuse to honor the contract without obligation.

rational basis See: rational basis test

rational basis test A legal standard to determine the constitutionality of a statute. To determine whether a statute passes the test, a court considers whether it has a reasonable connection to achieving a legitimate objective. (See also: strict scrutiny, intermediate scrutiny)

read on In patent law, to literally describe an element of an invention. Thus, a patent is infringed if the patent's claims read on (literally describe) all the elements of the infringing device.

ready, willing, and able Fully prepared to act, as in prepared to perform the services required under a contract.

reaffirmation An agreement that a debtor and a creditor enter into after a debtor has filed for bankruptcy, in which the debtor agrees to repay all or part of an existing debt after the bankruptcy case is over. For instance, a debtor might make a reaffirmation agreement with the holder of a car note that the debtor can keep the car and must continue to pay the debt after bankruptcy.

real covenant See: covenant that runs with the land

real estate Land and things permanently attached to it, such as buildings, houses, stationary mobile homes, fences and trees. Real estate is also called real property. Anything that isn't real estate is personal property.

real estate agent A foot soldier of the real estate business who shows houses and does most of the other nitty-gritty tasks associated with selling real estate. An agent must have a state license and be supervised by a real estate broker. Most agents are completely dependent upon commissions from sellers for their income, so it pays to find out which side the agent represents (buyer, seller, or both) before placing too much trust in the agent's opinion.

real estate broker A real estate professional licensed to negotiate the purchase and sale of real estate for a commission or fee. One step up from a real estate agent, a broker has more training and can supervise agents.

real estate investment trust (REIT) A business that invests in real estate. Investors buy shares in a REIT to invest in real estate in much the same way as they might buy shares in a mutual fund to invest in stocks. A REIT is set up to minimize or avoid corporate income taxes.

real party in interest The person or entity who will benefit from a lawsuit or petition even though the plaintiff (the person filing the suit) is someone else (often called a "nominal" plaintiff). For example, a trustee files a suit against a person who damaged a building owned by the trust; the real party in the interest is the beneficiary of the trust.

real property See: real estate

realty See: real estate

"There is no distinctly native American criminal class except Congress."

—Mark Twain

reasonable Just, rational, appropriate, ordinary, or usual in the circumstances. It may refer to care, cause, compensation, doubt (in a criminal trial), and a host of other actions or activities. In the law of negligence, for example, the reasonable person standard is the standard of care that a reasonably prudent person would observe under a given set of circumstances. An individual who subscribes to such standards can avoid liability for negligence.

reasonable accommodation Any adjustment to a work environment or job that allows a qualified worker to perform the job in question. Employers subject to federal employment laws must offer reasonable accommodations to employees with disabilities (for example, providing a TDD telephone to an employee with a hearing impairment) or based on religious beliefs (such as not assigning an employee to a shift on his Sabbath), as long as those accommodations do not create an undue burden for the employer.

reasonable care The degree of caution and attention to possible dangers that an ordinarily prudent and rational person would use in similar circumstances. This is a subjective test of determining whether a person is negligent and therefore liable.

reasonable doubt The standard of proof used in criminal trials to find a defendant guilty of a crime. When a criminal defendant is prosecuted, the prosecutor must prove the defendant's guilt "beyond a reasonable doubt." A reasonable doubt exists when a juror cannot say with moral certainty that a person is guilty. (Compare: preponderance of the evidence)

reasonable reliance A legal standard based upon what a prudent person would believe. If reliance is not reasonable, a defendant in certain situations may not seek redress. For example, someone who invested in a machine that allegedly turned rocks into gold could not recover damages for fraud if it could be shown that a prudent person would not have reasonably relied on such claims.

reasonable speed The speed at which it is safe to drive an automobile considering road conditions and other circumstances, such as rain, ice, heavy traffic, the vehicle's condition, or visibility. Reasonable speed may be less than the posted speed limit. Drivers who exceed reasonable speed can be cited for speeding or may be found to be negligent even if they were driving within the posted speed limit.

reasonable time A vague, and disfavored, contractual qualifier used to connote a period by which an act should be performed. (Compare: time is of the essence)

reasonable wear and tear Damage or loss to an item (such as a table) or element of a room (such as the floor) resulting from ordinary use and exposure over time. The term is commonly used in leases to limit the tenant's responsibility to repair damage, repaint the walls, or replace items when moving out. The term is subjective, but more wear and tear can be expected the longer the occupancy or the worse the condition of the premises when the tenant moved in. This is often a source of conflict between landlord and tenant, particularly when there is a deposit for any damages beyond reasonable (sometimes called normal or ordinary) wear and tear.

rebate 1) A discount or deduction on sales price. A secret rebate given by a subcontractor to a contractor is illegal. 2) To give a discount or deduction.

rebuttable presumption An assumption of fact accepted by the court to be true unless someone proves it to be untrue. A rebuttable presumption is often drawn from prima facie evidence.

rebuttal 1) Evidence or argument introduced to counter, disprove, or contradict the opposing party's evidence or argument. 2) Legal arguments presented in a reply brief.

rebuttal witness A witness who is called to rebut testimony already presented.

recapture In tax law, the requirement that a taxpayer—upon the sale of property—pay the amount of tax savings from past years due to accelerated depreciation or deferred capital gains.

receipt A written and signed acknowledgement by the recipient of payment for goods, money in payment of a debt, or receiving assets from the estate of someone who has died.

receiver 1) In a lawsuit, a neutral person (often a professional trustee) appointed by a judge to take charge of the property and business of a party to the lawsuit, and receive the rents and profits due to the party, while the lawsuit is being decided. A receiver is appointed if requested by the other party to the suit and if there is a strong showing that the property would not be available when the lawsuit concludes. 2) In debt and bankruptcy law, a person appointed to receive rents and profits coming to a debtor either while a bankruptcy is being processed or while an arrangement is being worked out to pay creditors. 3) In criminal law, shorthand for one who commits the crime of receiving stolen goods knowing they were obtained illegally.

receivership The process of appointment by a court of a receiver to take custody of the property, business, rents and profits 1) of a party to a lawsuit pending a final decision or 2) an agreement that a receiver control the financial receipts of a debtor for the benefit of creditors.

recess A break in a trial or other court proceedings or a legislative session until a date and time certain. Recess is not to be confused with adjournment, which winds up the proceedings.

recidivist A repeat criminal offender, who is convicted of a crime after having been previously convicted for another.

reciprocal beneficiaries Any two people who register under Hawaii's reciprocal beneficiary laws. Reciprocal beneficiaries have hospital visitation rights, the right to inherit from each other in the absence of a will, and certain other limited rights under Hawaii state law. Reciprocal beneficiaries may be of the same or opposite sex and may be related—there is no requirement that the two people be in an intimate relationship.

reciprocal discovery Also known as "reverse *Jencks* material," (named after the U.S. Supreme Court decision that established the principle, *Jencks v. United States*), the duty of the defense to give the prosecution copies of any pretrial statements that a defense witness may have given. The prosecution has a similar duty, to supply the defense with any written or recorded pretrial statement that the defendant may have given. (See also: *Brady* material)

reciprocity 1) The condition of being reciprocal. 2) The mutual exchange of privileges between states, nations, businesses, or individuals for commercial or diplomatic purposes.

reckless Behavior that is so careless that it is considered an extreme departure from the care a reasonable person would exercise in similar circumstances.

reckless disregard Grossly negligent without concern for injury to others.

reckless driving Operating an automobile in a dangerous manner under the circumstances, including speeding (or going too fast for the conditions, even if within the posted speed limit) and other careless and dangerous driving behavior. Reckless driving is a misdemeanor.

reconveyance The transfer of title to real estate from a lender to the buyer when a loan secured by the property is paid off. A trustee (commonly a title or escrow company) usually holds title for the lender and handles the reconveyance when the loan is fully paid back. (See also: trust deed)

"Facts are stubborn things; and whatever may be our wishes, our inclinations, or the dictates of our passions, they cannot alter the state of facts and evidence."

—John Adams, while defending soldiers accused of the Boston Massacre

---

record 1) To file a copy of a deed or other document concerning real estate with the land records office (often called the county recorder, registry of deeds, or something similar) for the county in which the land is located. 2) The official transcript of a trial or public hearing, including in the case of a trial all evidence introduced.

recording The process of filing a copy of a deed or other document concerning real estate with the land records office for the county in which the land is located. Recording creates a public record of changes in ownership (including liens) of all property in the state. (See also: chain of title)

recording acts State statutes that establish a system to keep records of land ownership in an office in each county, commonly called the county recorder, register of deeds, or recorder of deeds. The laws provide for the recording of deeds, liens, mortgages, decrees of distribution from estates, and other documents that affect ownership of land. By making land records public, recording gives everyone notice of ownership and interests in land.

record keeping The listing of financial transactions, including inflows (income) and outflows (payment of expenses) for a business.

records In business, tangible evidence, usually in writing, of the income, expenses, and financial transactions of a business or individual.

recoupment 1) The reduction of a successful plaintiff's judgment by an amount the plaintiff owes the defendant arising from the same transaction. For example, if a landlord wins an action against a tenant for failing to pay rent, the tenant might be entitled to recoupment for periods of time when the property was uninhabitable and, therefore, the tenant was not obligated to pay rent. 2) Generally, the recovery or collection of money that was paid out.

recourse The right to demand payment to the writer of a check or bill of exchange.

recover To receive a money judgment in a lawsuit.

recoverable Capable of being recovered in a lawsuit. Refers to the amount of money to which a plaintiff (the party suing) is entitled. (See also: damages)

recovery The amount of money and any other right or property awarded to or received by a plaintiff in a lawsuit.

recusal A situation in which a judge or prosecutor is removed or voluntarily steps down from a legal case. This often happens when the judge or prosecutor has a conflict of interest—for example, a prior business relationship or close relationship with one of the parties.

recuse See: recusal

redaction The act of going over a document with a fine-toothed comb in order to find any ambiguities or areas that are not to your advantage.

redeem To buy back property, as when a homeowner pays off a mortgage. (This typically happens when the homeowner faces foreclosure and pays off the original mortgage by refinancing or when someone in bankruptcy pays off a loan to keep an item of property.) A person who has pawned a possession may redeem the item by paying the loan and interest to the pawnbroker. (See also: redemption)

redemption 1) In Chapter 7 bankruptcy, when the debtor obtains legal title to collateral for a debt by paying the creditor the replacement value of the collateral in a lump sum. For example, a debtor may redeem a car note by paying the lender the amount a retail vendor would charge for the car, considering its age and condition. 2) In foreclosure, the homeowner's right (usually granted by state statute), for a certain period of time, to redeem the mortgage and keep the house by refinancing and paying off the original mortgage.

red herring A legal or factual issue that is irrelevant and is used to divert attention away from the main issues of a case. (The term is derived from the practice of training hunting dogs by dragging cured herrings across the scent trail of a fox.)

reentry Taking back, or literally reentering, property that belongs to the person entering the property but that, until a specific event has happened, was lawfully occupied by another. A landlord properly reenters property that a tenant has clearly abandoned; and a bank reenters when it has foreclosed upon a mortgage or deed of trust.

referee A person whom a judge appoints to handle certain parts of a case, such as taking testimony or reviewing written evidence. Sometimes, the referee makes written findings and submits them to the judge to use in deciding the case.

referendum The process by which the repeal or approval of an existing statute or state constitutional provision is voted upon. Many states allow for referenda which are placed on the ballot by a required number of voter signatures on a petition filed.

reformation The act of changing a written contract when one of the parties can prove that the actual agreement was different than what's written down. Reformation is usually made by a court, for example, when both parties overlooked a mistake in the document, or when one party has deceived the other.

refresh one's recollection To show a witness a document in an effort to help the witness remember something. A party may try to refresh a witness's recollection only after demonstrating that the witness does not remember. The party may then show the document to the witness, ask the witness to read it silently, and then ask whether the document refreshes the witness's recollection. If the witness answers in the affirmative, the party then takes the document away from the witness and asks the witness to answer the question that led to the failure of memory. The testimony the witness gives after reviewing the document is sometimes referred to as "present recollection refreshed."

refugee In the context of U.S. immigration law, people who have been allowed to live in the United States indefinitely to protect them from persecution in their home countries. Refugees get their status before coming to the U.S. and may, after one year, apply for U.S. green cards. (See also: asylum)

***Regents of the University of California v. Bakke* (1978)** A U.S. Supreme Court case in which the Court ruled that a white applicant for a medical school that received federal funding could not be excluded because of his race (there was a limited quota for whites under the school's admission plan) due to the nondiscrimination provisions of the 1964 Civil Rights Act.

register In corporations, the record of shareholders, including information on the issuance and transfer of shares.

registered agent See: agent for service of process

Register of Deeds A county government office where you file documents in the public records. Most register of deeds offices record documents related to real estate, including deeds, land contracts, mortgages, liens, and lease agreements. Some also accept vital records such as birth, death, and marriage certificates. In many locations, the register of deeds office is known as the county recorder's office.

registration statement A detailed report to be filed with the Securities and Exchange Commission (SEC) by a corporation making an issuance of shares to be advertised and sold to the general public in more than one state, which must be approved by the SEC before it will approve the stock issuance.

registry of deeds See: Register of Deeds

regulation A rule, adopted under authority granted by a statute, issued by a municipal, county, state, or federal agency. Although not laws, they have the force of law and often include penalties for violations. Regulations are not generally published in the books that contain state statutes or federal laws, but often must be obtained from the agency. To adopt a regulation, an agency usually drafts the rule, publishes it in governmental journals intended to give public notice, holds hearings, and then adopts a final, revised regulation. The process is best known to industries

and groups concerned with the subject matter. Federal regulations are adopted under the procedure set out in the federal Administrative Procedure Act (APA); states usually follow similar procedures.

Vice President Aaron Burr shot and killed former Secretary of Treasury Alexander Hamilton in a duel on July 11, 1804, despite the fact that these two lawyers had been co-counsel on several lawsuits.

rehearing Conducting a hearing again based on the motion of one of the parties to a lawsuit, petition, or criminal prosecution, usually by the court or agency which originally heard the matter. Rehearings are usually requested due to newly discovered evidence, an unfortunate and possibly unintended result of the original order, a change of circumstance, or a simple claim that the judge or agency was just wrong.

REIT See: real estate investment trust

release 1) To give up a right, as releasing one from the obligation to perform under a contract, or relinquishing an interest in property. 2) To give freedom, as letting out of prison. 3) The written document that establishes or grants a release.

release on one's own recognizance A judge's decision to allow a person charged with a crime to remain at liberty pending the trial, without having to post bail. Likely candidates for such release are those with strong roots in the community, regular employment, and the recommendation of the prosecutor. The type of crime charged may also play a role. Often called "O.R." or "R.O.R.," it is granted routinely in traffic matters, minor and technical crimes, and to people with no criminal record who display stability. (See also: O.R.)

relevant Having some reasonable connection with, and in regard to evidence in trial, having some value or tendency to prove a matter of fact significant to the case. A common objection to testimony or physical evidence is that it is irrelevant.

reliance Dependence on another person's (or entity's) statements or actions. Reasonable reliance on another person's statements may, in some cases, lead to a claim of fraud. (See also: reasonable reliance)

reliction The increase in land caused by the gradual recession or shrinkage of a body of water (such as a lake or sea) which gives the owner of the property more dry land.

relief The generic term for a benefit which an order or judgment of court can give a party to a lawsuit, including a money award, injunction, return of property, property title, alimony, and many others.

relinquished property In a 1031 exchange, the property the investor is selling. Instead of receiving the funds, the investor has them held in trust (usually, with a neutral trustee), until he or she uses the funds to purchase a replacement property.

remainder A future interest that will become available when another estate ends. For example, Patricia deeds Happy Acres Ranch to Sally for life, and upon Sally's death to Charla or to Charla's children if Charla does not survive. Charla has a remainder, and her children have a contingent remainder, which they will receive if Charla dies before Sally.

remainderman Someone who will inherit property in the future—usually as a result of the end of a life estate. For instance, if someone dies and leaves his home "to Alma for life, and then to Barry," Barry is a remainderman because he will inherit the home in the future, after Alma dies.

remainder subject to a condition precedent See: contingent remainder

remainder subject to divestment See: defeasible remainder

remainder subject to open A vested remainder that will go to a group containing an undetermined number of people. For example, "to Adam for life, and then to his children." The remainder left to the children is subject to open because it is unknown how many children (if any) Adam will have at his death.

remand To send back. For example, an appeals court might reverse a lower court's decision and send a matter back to that court for a new trial. Or a judge might remand into custody a person accused of a crime, if there appears to be a legal reason to hold the person for trial.

remedy The means of redressing an injury or enforcing a right in a legal action. Remedies may be ordered by the court, granted by judgment after trial or hearing, by agreement between the parties, and by the automatic operation of law. Some remedies require that certain acts be performed or prohibited, others involve payment of money, and still others require a court's declaration of the rights of the parties and an order to honor them.

remise To give up a claim to something; a term sometimes used in quitclaim deeds conveying property.

remittitur Latin for "it is sent back." 1) A judge's order reducing a judgment awarded by a jury. 2) An appellate court's transmittal of a case back to the trial court so that the case can be retried, or an order can be entered consistent with the appellate court's decision (such as dismissing the plaintiff's case or awarding costs to the winning party on appeal).

removal 1) The change of a legal case from one court to another, as from a state court to federal court or vice versa based on a motion by one of the parties stating that the other jurisdiction is more appropriate for the case. 2) An immigration legal proceeding, formerly known as "deportation," conducted before an immigration judge to decide whether or not an immigrant will be allowed to enter or remain in the United States. Generally speaking, a person who is already in the U.S. cannot be expelled without first going through a removal hearing, while someone arriving at the border or a port of entry can be removed without a hearing or ever seeing a judge (called "summary" or "expedited" removal). Those who are deported or removed are barred from returning to the United States for at least five years unless U.S. Citizenship and Immigration Services (USCIS) grants a special waiver.

renewal Keeping an existing agreement in force for an additional period of time, such as a lease, a promissory note, insurance policy, or any other contract. Renewal usually requires a writing or some action which evidences the new term.

rent Monetary amount a tenant pays a landlord (typically on a monthly basis) for occupying premises for a set period of time or an open-ended term.

Presumed Innocent. (1990) Film adaptation of Scott Turow's best-seller in which a lawyer is under suspicion for the murder of his colleague and mistress. Harrison Ford, Brian Dennehy, Raul Julia, Bonnie Bedelia, Paul Winnfield, Greta Scacchi.

rental agreement A contract (oral or written) between a landlord and tenant that provides for a tenancy for a short period of time, such as one month; it automatically renews at the end of this period, unless the landlord or tenant give each other the proper amount of notice (which usually must be written) to terminate the contract.

rental value The amount which someone would pay for rental of similar property in the same condition in the same area. Evidence of rental value becomes important in lawsuits in which loss of use of real property or equipment is an issue, and the rental value is the measure of damages. In divorce cases in which one of the spouses stays in the family residence, the use of the property may have rental value which is considered in balancing the income of the parties, determining division of property, or setting the amount of alimony to be paid.

rent control Laws that limit the amount of rent landlords may charge, and that state when and by how much the rent can be raised. Most rent control laws also require a landlord to provide a good reason, such as repeatedly paying rent late, for evicting a tenant. Rent control exists in some cities and counties in California, Maryland, New Jersey, New York, and Washington, DC. Also called rent stabilization, maximum rent regulation, or a similar term.

rent withholding A residential tenant's refusal to pay the rent, based on the landlord's unjustified refusal or failure to fix a defect in the rental that renders it unlivable or seriously unsafe. Rent withholding is legal only if a state statute provides for it, and often the tenant must deposit the rent in court or in an escrow account, pending the landlord's repairs. (See also: implied warranty of habitability)

renunciation 1) The act of forfeiting a right. For example, in wills and estates, if a beneficiary does not want to take an inheritance, the beneficiary can make a renunciation of that inheritance. 2) In criminal law, renunciation is abandoning a crime before it takes place.

reorganization 1) The implementation of a business plan to restructure a corporation, which may include transfers of stock between shareholders of two corporations in a merger. 2) In bankruptcy, a corporation in deep financial trouble may be given time to restructure itself while protected from creditors by the bankruptcy court. The theory is that if the business is able to get on its feet and either survive or be able to sell itself for a good price, the creditors will eventually collect. (See also: Chapter 11 bankruptcy)

repair and deduct A residential tenant's repair of a serious defect or problem in the rental, making it unlivable or significantly unsafe, followed by deducting the cost of the repair from the next month's rent. Proper use of the remedy, which may be invoked only if state law provides for it, requires notice to the landlord and allowing the landlord a reasonable time to fix the problem.

repeal To annul an existing law by passage of a repealing statute or by public vote on a referendum. Repeal of Constitutional provisions require an amendment.

replacement property In a 1031 exchange, the property the investor purchases with the proceeds of the sale of the original property (called the relinquished property). Under current IRS rules, replacement property must be identified within 45 days of the sale of the relinquished property, and the sale must close within 180 days of the sale.

replacement value The amount you would have to pay, at the present time, to replace a particular item, taking into consideration the item's age and condition.

replevin A type of legal action where the owner of movable goods is given the right to recover them from someone who shouldn't have them. Replevin is often used in disputes between buyers and sellers—for example, a seller might bring a replevin action to reclaim goods from a buyer who failed to pay for them.

reply brief When a case is appealed to a higher court, the written legal argument of the respondent (the party who won in trial court), submitted in answer to the "opening brief" of an appellant (the party who lost at trial and has appealed to the appellate court).

reports A published volume of federal, state, or regional judicial decisions. Examples include *California Appellate Reports* and *Supreme Court Reporter*. (See also: advance sheets)

repossess To take back property that has been pledged as collateral for a loan. (See also: repossession)

repossession A creditor's taking of property that has been pledged as collateral for a loan. Vehicles are the type of property most often repossessed: Lenders will repossess cars when the owner has missed loan or lease payments and has not attempted to work with the lender to resolve the problem. The loan contract or lease and state law dictate what a repossessor can and cannot do, but usually a repossessor cannot use force to take a car. A repossession of property will appear on the car owner's credit report for seven years, and he or she will owe the costs of repossession and attorney's fees, as well as the difference between what the lender can sell the car for and what was owed on the loan or lease.

represent 1) To act as the agent for another. 2) To serve—for example, as a member of a legislative body after an election. 3) To act as a client's attorney. 4) To state something as a fact, such as "This horse is only four years old."

representation 1) The act of representing—for example, by serving as agent for another or acting as an attorney for a client. 2) A statement of alleged fact either in negotiations or in court. 3) A process by which an heir inherits in place of a predecessor, called right of representation.

representative 1) An agent or other individual who stands in for another. 2) Someone who serves a constituency, such as a member of the House of Representatives. 3) The executor or administrator of the estate of a person who has died, sometimes called a personal representative.

representative payee Typically, a person authorized by a government agency such as the Social Security Administration to receive benefits such as SSI payments on behalf of a recipient who is not competent to handle his or her own money.

reprieve A temporary delay in imposition of the death penalty by order of the state's governor. Reasons for reprieves include the possibility of newly discovered evidence, awaiting the result of a last-minute appeal, or the governor's concern that there might have been some error in the record that should be examined. On occasion a reprieve has saved someone who was later found to be innocent. A reprieve is only a delay, not a pardon or reduction or commutation of the sentence. When the reprieve expires, the date for execution can be reset.

repudiation Actions demonstrating that one party to a contract refuses to perform an obligation. (See also: anticipatory breach)

reputation What the community thinks of a person; a factor in determining liability and damages in suits for defamation, because damage to reputation is the principal injury.

reputed Information based on public belief, whether or not correct.

request When a party asks the court to act (such as a request for reconsideration), demands a right (such as request for production of documents from an opposing party), or asks a question.

request for admission A discovery procedure, authorized by the Federal Rules of Civil Procedure and the court rules of most states, in which one party asks an opposing party to admit that certain facts are true. If the opponent admits the facts or fails to respond in a timely manner, the facts will be deemed true for purposes of trial. A request for admission is called a "request to admit" in many states.

request to admit See: request for admission

requirements contract A contract between a supplier or manufacturer and a buyer, where the seller agrees to sell all the particular products that the buyer needs, and the buyer agrees to purchase the goods exclusively from the supplier. (Compare: output contract)

res Latin for "thing" or "matter."

res adjudicata See: res judicata

 "No man is above the law, and none is below it."

—Theodore Roosevelt

---

resale Selling again, particularly at retail (a retail product is sold once to the retail store and again to the final customer). In many states, a resale license, resale number, or seller's permit is required so that the state can monitor the collection of sales tax on retail sales.

rescind To cancel a contract by mutual agreement of the parties, putting them the positions they would have occupied had the contract not existed.

rescission Cancellation of a contract by mutual agreement of the parties.

rescue doctrine A rule in tort law that states that when a wrongdoer (tortfeasor) has negligently endangered the safety of another, the wrongdoer can be held liable for injuries suffered by a third person who attempts to rescue the person in danger.

reservation A provision in a deed which keeps (reserves) to the grantor some right or portion of the property. The language might read: "Sarah Sims reserves to herself an easement of access to lots 6, 7, and 8."

reserve fund The fund of money that covers maintenance, repairs, or unexpected expenses of a business or a multiunit housing development (often condominiums or a housing cooperative), managed by a homeowners' association or other governing body.

res gestae (rayz **jest**-eye) All circumstances surrounding and connected with a happening. Thus, the res gestae of a crime includes the immediate area and all occurrences and statements immediately before and after the crime.

res gestae witness (rayz **jest**-eye) A witness who has experienced an event firsthand and can therefore testify about what happened.

residence 1) The place where one makes his or her home. (Compare: domicile) 2) In corporation law, a business's state of incorporation.

resident A person who lives in a particular place.

residuary beneficiary A person who receives any property by a will or trust that is not specifically left to another designated beneficiary. For example, if Antonio makes a will leaving his home to Edwina and the remainder of his property to Elmo, then Elmo is the residuary beneficiary.

residuary bequest In a will, the gift of whatever is left over after all specific and general gifts are given. For example, John gives his house and his stocks to his wife, and leaves everything else to his daughter—the gift of "everything else" is the residuary bequest.

residuary estate The property that remains in a deceased person's estate after all specific gifts are made, and all debts, taxes, administrative fees, probate costs, and court costs are paid. The residuary estate also includes any specific gifts under a will that fail or lapse. For example, Connie's will leaves her house and all its furnishings to Andrew, her VW bug to her friend Carl, and the remainder of her property (the residuary estate) to her sister Sara. She doesn't name any alternate beneficiaries. Carl dies before Connie. The VW bug becomes part of the residuary estate and passes to Sara, along with all of Connie's property other than the house and furnishings.

Also called the residual estate or residue.

residue See: residuary estate

res ipsa loquitur (ray-**sip**-sah **loh**-quit-er) Latin for "the thing speaks for itself"; a legal presumption that a defendant acted negligently even though there may be no direct evidence of liability. For example, a construction company is presumed to be negligent if a load of bricks under its control falls off a roof and injures a pedestrian, even though nobody witnessed the accident. The presumption arises only if 1) the thing that caused the accident was under the defendant's control, 2) the accident could happen only as a result of a careless act, and 3) the injured plaintiff's behavior did not contribute to the accident. Lawyers also refer to this doctrine as "res ips" or "res ipsa."

resisting arrest The crime of using physical force (no matter how slight in the eyes of most law enforcement officers) to prevent arrest, handcuffing, or taking the accused to jail. It is also called "resisting an officer" (which can include interfering with a peace officer's attempt to keep the peace) and is sometimes referred to merely as "resisting."

res judicata Latin for a legal issue that has been finally decided by a court, between the same parties, and cannot be ruled on again. For example, if a court rules that John is the father of Betty's child, John cannot raise the issue again in another court. (He could appeal the court's ruling to a higher court, but he could not raise the paternity issue again in another lawsuit.) Sometimes called res adjudicata. (See also: collateral estoppel)

res nova Latin for "a new thing," used by courts to describe an issue of law or case that has not previously been decided.

resolution 1) In business, an approval of an action or determination of policy of a corporation or limited liability company by the vote of its members, managers, or board of directors. 2) In government, a statement of policy, belief, or appreciation passed by a legislative body.

respondeat superior (ruh-**spon**-dee-at soo-**peer**-ee-**or**) Latin for "let the master answer." A legal doctrine that holds the employer or principal responsible for the acts of its employees or agents committed within the scope of employment.

respondent A term used instead of defendant or appellee in some states—especially for divorce and other family law cases—to identify the party who is sued and must respond to the petitioner's complaint.

response See: answer

responsible 1) Legally liable or accountable. 2) Having the ability to pay or perform.

responsive pleading See: answer

Restatement of the Law A series of legal treatises that set out basic U.S. law on a variety of subjects, written and updated by legal scholars and published by the American Law Institutes. While not having the force of statutes or court rulings, the *Restatements* (as lawyers generally call them) are prestigious and can carry some weight in a legal argument. Topics covered include agency, contracts, property, torts, trusts, and more.

restitution Returning property or its monetary value to the rightful owner. The losing party in a negligence or contracts case may be ordered to make restitution, such as restoring ruined landscaping. A criminal defendant may also be ordered to make restitution, such as returning stolen goods or paying the victim for harm caused. Restitution may be imposed as a condition of probation or a shorter-than-normal sentence.

restraining order An order from a court directing one person not to do something, such as make contact with another person, enter the family home, or remove a child from the state. Restraining orders are often issued in cases in which spousal abuse, stalking, or other immediate harm is feared. A restraining order is always temporary and is also commonly referred to as a temporary restraining order or TRO.

The youngest Supreme Court justice ever was Joseph Story. He was 32 when he joined the Court in 1811 and he served for 33 years.

restraint of trade Any activity (including agreements among competitors or companies doing business with each other) that tends to limit trade, sales, and transportation in interstate commerce or has a substantial impact on interstate commerce. Most restraints of trade are illegal under various antitrust statutes. Some state laws also outlaw local restraints on competitive business activity. (See also: monopoly)

restraint on alienation A provision in a deed or will that attempts to restrict the sale or transfer of the property forever or for an extremely long period of time—for example, selling your house to your daughter with the provision that it never be sold to anyone outside the family. These provisions are usually unenforceable on the grounds that a present owner should not be allowed to tie the hands of future generations. The maximum period of time for limiting transfer is generally "lives in being, plus 21 years." (This is known as the rule against perpetuities.) Restraints on alienation (restrictive covenants) based on race ("only Caucasians may hold title") were declared unconstitutional in 1949.

restriction Any limitation on activity, by statute, regulation, or contract provision. In multiunit real estate developments, condominiums, and cooperative housing projects, the homeowners' associations or similar organizations that manage these developments are usually required to impose restrictions on use. The restrictions are part of the "covenants, conditions, and restrictions" ("CC&Rs") intended to protect and enhance the property. They are part of each owner's deed.

restrictive covenant An agreement (covenant) in a deed to real estate that restricts future use of the property. Example: "No fence may be built on the property except of dark wood and not more six feet high, no tennis court or swimming pool may be constructed within 30 feet of the property line, and no structure can be built within 20 feet of the frontage street." Also called "covenant running with the land" if it's enforceable against future owners. Restrictive covenants based on race (for example, "the property may be occupied only by Caucasians") were declared unconstitutional in 1949.

restrictive endorsement An endorsement signed on the back of a check, note, or bill of exchange that restricts to whom the paper may be transferred—for example, "for transfer only to Frank Lowry." Also spelled "indorsement."

resulting trust A trust implied by law, as determined by a court. Under this type of trust, the person who holds title to or has possession of property is considered a trustee for the proper owner, who is considered the beneficiary. The resulting trust is a legal fiction that forces a property holder to honor the beneficiary's property rights. For example, Mahalia leaves $100,000 with her friend, Albert, while she is on a trip to Europe, asking him "to buy the old Barsallo place if it comes on the market." Albert buys the property, but has title put in his own name, which the court will find is held in a resulting trust for Mahalia. A resulting trust differs from a "constructive trust," which comes about when someone gains possession of another's property by accident, misunderstanding, or dishonesty.

resumé inflation To include false or misleading information on one's resumé to make oneself a more attractive candidate for a job. Examples include adding degrees or awards one never received or positions one never held.

retained earnings The accumulated profits of a corporation that are not paid out as dividends. Instead, the money is reinvested in the core business or used to pay off debt. Also called accumulated earnings or earned surplus.

retainer A fee paid in advance to a lawyer to secure the lawyer's services. It acts as a down payment, ensuring that the lawyer won't get stiffed and that the client will be represented. If the amount is significant, some states require the lawyer and client to sign an agreement.

retaliation Punishment of an employee by an employer for engaging in legally protected activity such as making a complaint of harassment or participating in workplace investigations. Retaliation can include any negative job action, such as demotion, discipline, firing, salary reduction, or job or shift reassignment.

retaliatory eviction An eviction of a tenant by a landlord that is motivated, in whole or in part, by the tenant's exercise of a legal right, such as complaining in good faith to the health department, using a tenant remedy such as rent withholding, or organizing tenants in response to rental conditions. Not all states recognize retaliation as a defense to an eviction, and of those that

do, each state defines retaliation, and how to prove it, differently.

retirement benefits Benefits provided by the Social Security Administration to persons of retirement age (which varies depending on the year you were born) who have accumulated sufficient work credits to be eligible. Retirement benefits may also be provided by an individual's private pension or other retirement plan.

retraction To disavow or take back. This may include: 1) withdrawing a confession or legal document in a lawsuit or other proceeding; 2) withdrawing a promise or offer of contract; or 3) correcting any untruth published or broadcast in the media, usually upon the demand of the person about whom the damaging false statement was made. A clear and complete retraction will usually end the right of the defamed party to go forward with a libel lawsuit. In most states the plaintiff must request a retraction before filing suit, in order to give the defendant a chance to cure the problem without litigation.

retrial A new trial (by the same court as made the decision in the first trial), granted upon the motion of the losing party, based on obvious error, bias, or newly discovered evidence.

retroactive A law or court decision that takes away or impairs a previously vested right, imposes new duties or obligations, or changes or effects past transactions or legal actions. Retroactive (or retrospective) laws are not favored and, unless it is expressly stated, it is usually presumed that legislation is not intended to apply retroactively. In criminal law, statutes which would increase penalties or make activities which had been previously legal criminal are prohibited by the Constitutional ban on ex post facto laws.

Class Action. (1991) Father and daughter lawyers battle in court over injuries caused by a defective automobile, roughly based on the controversy over the Ford Pinto. Starring Gene Hackman and Mary Elizabeth Mastrantonio.

---

return of service Written confirmation under oath by a process server declaring that there was service of legal documents (such as a summons and complaint).

revenue agent An IRS employee who performs audits in the field; for example, at a business, a taxpayer's home, or an attorney's office.

revenue ruling A published opinion of the Internal Revenue Service stating what it would rule on future tax questions based on the same circumstances. These rulings are of general use to taxpayers, tax preparers, accountants, and attorneys in anticipating tax treatment by the IRS. They have the force of law until otherwise determined by the federal tax court or a new revenue ruling.

reversal The decision of a court of appeal ruling that the judgment of a lower court was incorrect and is reversed. The result is that the lower court which tried the case is instructed to dismiss the original action, retry the case, or is ordered to change its judgment.

reverse engineering Disassembly and examination of products that are available to the public.

reverse mortgage A loan for homeowners 62 years of age or older who have considerable equity in their houses. Typically, borrowers make no payments during their lifetimes; the loan is paid off at their death, when the house is sold.

reversible error A legal mistake at the trial court level that is so significant (resulted in an improper judgment) that the judgment must be reversed by the appellate court. A reversible error is distinguished from an error which is minor or did not contribute to the judgment at the trial.

reversion The return to an original owner, or to that person's heirs, of real estate after all interests in the property given to others have terminated. Example: George deeds property to the local hospital district for "use for health facilities only." Eventually, the hospital is torn down, and the property is now vacant. The property reverts to George's descendants. Also called reverter.

reverter See: reversion

review The judicial consideration of a lower court judgment by an appellate court, determining if there were legal errors sufficient to require reversal. In reviewing a lower court decision or order, appellate courts focus on errors of a legal nature and will usually not disturb factual findings.

revival 1) Requesting a court to reinstate the force of an old judgment. 2) Reinstating a contract or debt by a new agreement after the right to demand performance or collect has expired under the statute of limitations.

revocable living trust A trust set up during life that can be revoked at any time before death. Revocable living trusts are a common and excellent way to avoid the cost and hassle of probate, because the property held in the trust during the trust maker's life passes directly to the trust beneficiaries after death, without probate court proceedings. The successor trustee—the person appointed to handle the trust after the trust maker's death—simply transfers ownership to the beneficiaries named in the trust. Certain revocable living trusts can also reduce federal estate tax. Also called "inter vivos trust." (Compare: living trust, living will, testamentary trust)

revocation Annulment or cancellation of a statement, document, or offer not yet accepted, or cancellation of a contract by the parties to it. For example, a person can revoke a will or revoke an offer to enter into a contract, and a government agency can revoke a license. (Compare: rescission)

revoke To annul or cancel an act, particularly a statement, document, or promise, as if it no longer existed. For example, a person can revoke a will or revoke an offer to enter into a contract, and a government agency can revoke a license.

***Reynolds v. Sims* (1964)** A U.S. Supreme Court case in which the Court ruled that the voting districts of state legislatures must have roughly equal populations. The decision was based on the Equal Protection Clause of the U.S. Constitution and is sometimes known as the "one-person, one-vote" rule.

rhadamanthine (rad-a-**man**-then) Strict and inflexible in the application of the law; sometimes used to describe a judge.

RICO See: Racketeer Influenced and Corrupt Organizations Act.

rider 1) An attachment to a document that adds to or amends it. Typical is an added provision to an insurance policy, such as additional coverage for a valuable item or temporary insurance to cover a public event. 2) An amendment tacked on to a legislative bill that has little or no connection to the main purpose of the legislation, as a way to get the amendment passed.

right 1) Just, fair, correct. 2) An entitlement to something, whether to a concept like justice or due process, or to a legally enforceable claim or interest—for example, an ownership interest in property.

right of representation See: per stirpes

right of survivorship The right of a surviving co-owner to take ownership of a deceased owner's share of the property. Forms of ownership that come with a right of survivorship include joint tenancy, tenancy by the entirety, and community property with right of survivorship.

right of way 1) The right to pass over or through property owned by someone else, usually based upon an easement. There may be a specific path that must be taken, or the right may be more general. The mere right to cross without a specific description is a "floating" easement. A right of way may be granted for a particular purpose—for example, to repair power lines or to make deliveries to the back door of a business. 2) In traffic law, the right to proceed, which must be granted to a driver by other drivers under certain circumstances. A driver who fails to yield the right of way when it is required by law may be ticketed. The failure to yield can also be evidence of negligence if an accident results and there is a lawsuit.

right to cancel (a contract) See: cooling-off rule

right to counsel The right of criminal defendants to have a lawyer appointed by the court to represent them if the defendants cannot afford to hire one. The Sixth Amendment of the U.S. Constitution guarantees this right to those charged with federal crimes; the U.S. Supreme Court case of *Gideon v. Wainright* extended this right to those charged with state offenses. The right to counsel applies only where the defendant faces the possibility of imprisonment, and only at trial and through the first appeal, if the defendant is convicted. Juveniles are also entitled to counsel.

right to privacy 1) The right not to have one's personal matters disclosed or publicized; the right to be left alone. 2) The right against undue government intrusion into fundamental personal issues and decisions. Although the U.S. Constitution does not explicitly state that there is a right to privacy, Supreme Court decisions have found an implicit constitutional right to privacy in striking down laws that criminalize sodomy, the use of contraceptives, and abortion.

right to work state A state that has a law prohibiting union security agreements.

rights 1) Plural of right. 2) Slang for the information which must be given by law enforcement officers to a person who is under arrest or otherwise not free to leave. (See also: *Miranda* warning)

riot 1) A turbulent and violent disturbance of peace by three or more people acting together. 2) An assemblage of people who are out of control, causing injury, or endangering the physical safety of others or themselves, causing or threatening damage to property, and often violating various laws both individually and as a group. The common thread is that the people in a riot have the power through violence to break the public peace and safety, requiring police action.

riparian Referring to land adjoining a river or stream.

riparian rights Rights of the owner of land adjacent to a river or stream to use the water for certain purposes. State laws vary on the extent of the rights given riparian landowners. A riparian landowner may not, however, interfere with the rights of other riparian land-owners farther downstream—which means no damming or diversion of a stream.

ripe Referring to a claim for relief that is ready for a court's review because an injury has occurred or will occur, and is not just hypothetical or speculative.

risk The probability of danger or loss, particularly of property covered by an insurance policy. (See also: assumption of risk)

risk of loss The responsibility a carrier, borrower, or user of property or goods assumes, or an insurance company agrees to cover, if there is damage or loss.

roadside test See: field sobriety test

robbery The crime of directly taking property (including money) from a person (victim) through force, threat, or intimidation. Robbery is a felony, punishable by a term in state or federal prison. Armed robbery involves the use of gun or other weapon, such as a knife or club, and under most state laws carries a stiffer penalty than robbery by merely taking. (Compare: burglary, embezzlement, shoplifting)

Roe v. Wade (1973) A U.S. Supreme Court case in which the Court ruled that abortions (previously limited to those necessary to save a woman's life) are legal, and any state law that denied the right of a woman to have an abortion in the first trimester (three months) of pregnancy was a denial of her right to privacy under the due process guarantee in the Fourteenth Amendment. Until this ruling, every state had laws making an elective abortion a crime.

rogatory letters See: letter of request

roll over 1) To reinvest funds from a tax-deferred account or maturing security into a similar account or security. For example, moving money from one individual retirement account (IRA) to another IRA, or from a qualified retirement plan into an IRA. 2) To defer or postpone payment of an obligation, such as a loan that gives the borrower the option to renew the terms on maturity.

Roth v. United States (1957) A U.S. Supreme Court case in which the Court denied free speech and free press protection to obscene material which was utterly without redeeming social value.

royalty 1) A form of compensation based on a percentage of revenue or unit sales generated under an agreement, typically a patent or copyright licensing contract. 2) A compulsory payment required under statute in exchange for the right to use or sell certain property—for example, a statutory royalty that is paid by the sellers of musical ringtones to the copyright owners of the underlying songs.

rule 1) To decide a legal question, as when at the end of a lawsuit a court announces: "This court rules that the plaintiff is entitled to the goods and damages for delay in the sum of $10,000." 2) A regulation issued by a court or government agency. 3) A legal principle set by a court's written decision in an appellate case, as "the rule in the case of *Murray v. Crampton* is ...." (See also: rules of court, local rules)

rule against perpetuities An exceedingly complex legal doctrine that limits the amount of time that property can be controlled after death by a person's instructions in a will. The maximum period for which title to real property may be held without being transferred to another is "lives in being plus 21 years." For example, a provision in a deed or will that reads "Title shall be held by David Smith and, upon his death, title may be held only by his descendants until the year 2200, when it shall vest in the Trinity Episcopal Church" is invalid. But a provision stating that "the property will be held by my son George for his life, and thereafter by his son, Thomas, and for 20 years by the Trinity Episcopal Church, before it may be conveyed" is acceptable under the rule.

rule of doubt The rule under which the U.S. Copyright Office allows software object code to be deposited in connection with a computer program registration. Under the rule there is an express understanding that doubt exists as to whether the code qualifies for copyright protection should litigation later occur. In essence, the Copyright Office is saying, "We will let you deposit object code, but since we can't read or understand it, we won't commit ourselves as to its copyrightability." If the registration is accomplished under the rule of doubt, the copyright owner may be unable to claim the presumption of ownership—an important benefit of registration—should the issue end up in court because of an alleged copyright infringement.

rules of court A set of procedural rules adopted by local, state, or federal courts that instruct parties and attorneys what the court's mandatory procedures are about things like the time allowed to file papers, format of documents, filing procedures and fees, basis for calculating alimony and child support.

ruling Any decision a judge makes during the course of a lawsuit.

running at large 1) A reference to an animal that is roaming free, such as cattle that have escaped an enclosure or a dog that has slipped its leash. The owner of an animal running at large is generally liable for any damage it causes. 2) A reference to a candidate who is campaigning for an office elected by an entire city, county, or state, rather than from a particular political district within that larger region.

running with the land A phrase used in real estate law to describe a right or duty that remains with a piece of real estate no matter who owns it. For example, the duty to allow a public path across beachfront property would most likely pass from one owner of the property to the next.

S

sale The transfer of ownership (title) to property in return for money (or another thing of value) on terms agreed upon between buyer and seller.

sales tax A state or local tax imposed on sales of retail products based on a percentage of the price.

salvage 1) To save goods. 2) Payment to a person or group that saves cargo from a shipwreck.

same-sex marriage Marriage between two people of the same sex, currently available only in Connecticut and Massachusetts. (See also: domestic partners, civil union, reciprocal beneficiaries)

sample ballot A document sent to registered voters to help them prepare for an election. A sample ballot usually provides the voter's polling place and hours, and contains an image of what the actual ballot will look like, including candidates, questions, and instructions for voting.

sanction 1) A financial penalty imposed by a judge on a party or attorney—or the act of imposing such a penalty. 2) In international law, to impose economic constraints on trade against a country that violates international law or commits human rights violations. 3) To allow or approve.

Sarbanes-Oxley Act A law enacted in 2002 in response to several corporate and accounting scandals, requiring publicly traded companies to disclose information to shareholders, protecting whistleblowers, and requiring stringent audit practices.

 "If the law supposes that," said Mr. Bumble ... "the law is a ass, a idiot."
—Charles Dickens, *Oliver Twist*

---

satisfaction Receiving payment or performance of what is due under a contract.

satisfaction of judgment A document signed by the party who is owed money under a court judgment (called the judgment creditor) stating that the full amount due on the judgment has been paid. If the judgment creditor has a lien on real property belonging to the judgment debtor, then the judgment debtor may demand that the judgment creditor record the satisfaction of judgment with the County Recorder (or Recorder of Deeds).

satisfaction of mortgage 1) Payment in full on a mortgage. 2) The document a mortgage holder signs to indicate that a mortgage has been fully paid and the mortgage lien has been released.

save harmless See: hold harmless

savings and loan A banking and lending institution chartered either by a state government or the federal government. Savings and loans institutions take savings deposits, upon which they pay interest slightly higher than that paid by most banks, and they make mortgage loans on residential properties from the deposits.

Schecter Poultry Corp. v. United States (1931) A U.S. Supreme Court case in which the Court struck down the National Industrial Recovery Act (a key measure of the New Deal) on the basis that the government had improperly delegated authority to make rules governing industries in interstate commerce. The decision by an aging Court (called "nine old men" by its critics) and other rulings that the New Deal was unconstitutional prompted President Franklin D. Roosevelt to launch his ill-fated effort to pack the Supreme Court by adding an additional justice for each one who would not

retire at 70, Death and resignation soon gave Roosevelt vacancies to fill on the Court.

schedule 1) An IRS form on which taxpayers report details about an item or a business and which is attached to the main tax return. 2) A list of assets held in a trust, attached to the trust document.

Schenk v. United States (1919) U.S. Supreme Court decision sustaining the Espionage Act of 1917. The Court ruled that freedom of speech and freedom of the press could be limited if the words in the circumstances created "a clear and present danger."

scienter (si-**en**-ter) Latin for "knowingly." In criminal law, it refers to the knowledge by a defendant that makes him or her responsible for the crime. In some, but not all crimes, scienter is a requirement—that is, the crime must be done knowingly.

scintilla A little bit, from the Latin for "spark." The term is commonly used to refer to evidence—for example in a lawyer's argument that there is not a "scintilla of evidence" (at least a faint spark) to support one of the other side's claims.

scope of employment The actions or activities an employee might reasonably undertake as part of his or her job.

An employer is responsible for actions an employee takes within the scope of employment, which means the employer can be liable to third parties who are injured by the employee's conduct. For example, an employer would be liable for harm to a pedestrian caused by its delivery driver while driving a route; the employer most likely would not be liable for harm the same driver caused if he or she hit a pedestrian while using the delivery van as the getaway car in a bank robbery. (See also: respondeat superior)

S corporation A term that describes a profit-making corporation whose shareholders have applied for and received subchapter S corporation status from the Internal Revenue Service (IRS). Electing to do business as an S corporation lets shareholders enjoy limited liability status, as would be true of any corporation, but be taxed as a pass-through tax entity, where income taxes are reported and paid by the owners, like a partnership or sole proprietor. (A regular, or C, corporation is taxed as a separate entity from its owners.) To qualify as an S corporation, a number of IRS rules must be met, such as a limit of 100 shareholders and U.S. citizenship for all shareholders.

scrivener A person who writes a document for another, usually for a fee. If a lawyer merely writes out the terms of a lease or contract exactly as requested by the client, without giving legal advice, then the lawyer is just a scrivener and is probably not responsible for legal errors (unless they were so obvious as to warrant comment). A nonlawyer may act as a scrivener without getting in trouble for practicing law without a license.

seal 1) A device that creates an impression upon paper, used by corporations, LLCs, and notaries public to show that the document is executed or acknowledged by the signer. Corporate and LLC seals include the name of the corporation and the date and state of incorporation. Notaries increasingly use a rubber stamp instead of a seal, since their print is easier to microfilm for official recording. 2) To conceal from public record. In some instances, for example, a person's arrest or criminal records may be sealed, meaning without a court order to inspect them they may not be viewed. (See also: expunge)

sealed verdict The decision of a jury when there is a delay in announcing the result, such as when court is not in session. The verdict is kept in a sealed envelope until handed to the judge when court reconvenes.

sealing of records The requirement that trial records and court decisions must be kept under seal, in contrast to most other court records, which are available for public review. The records most commonly sealed are criminal records of underage offenders; cases might also be sealed if they involve inventions, proprietary business information, or national security.

search 1) In criminal law, to examine another's premises (including a vehicle) or person to look for evidence of criminal activity. It is unconstitutional under the Fourth and Fourteenth Amendments for law enforcement officers to conduct a search without a "search warrant" issued by a judge, or without facts that give the officer "probable cause" to believe evidence of a specific crime is present and there is not enough time to obtain a search warrant. 2) In civil law, to trace the records of ownership of real property in what is commonly called a "title search."

search and seizure In criminal law, the phrase that describes law enforcement's gathering of evidence of a crime. Under the Fourth and Fourteenth Amendments to the U.S. Constitution, any search of a person or his premises (including a vehicle), and any seizure of tangible evidence, must be reasonable. Normally, law enforcement must obtain a search warrant from a judge, specifying where and whom they may search, and what they may seize, though in emergency circumstances, they may dispense with the warrant requirement.

Canada's first two women judges, appointed in 1916 and 1917, were not lawyers but writers of legislation and advocates of the legal rights of women and children.

search warrant An order signed by a judge that directs owners of private property to allow the police to enter and search for items named in the warrant. Judges won't issue a warrant unless they have been convinced by the police that there is probable cause for the search—that reliable evidence shows that it's more likely than not that a crime has occurred and that the items sought by the police are connected with it and will be found at the location named in the warrant. In limited situations, the police may search without a warrant, but they cannot use what they find at trial if the defense can show that they had no probable cause for the search.

secondary boycott An attempt to stop others from purchasing products from, performing services for, or otherwise doing business with a company that does business with another company that is in the midst of a labor dispute.

For example, if a grocery chain's clerks are on strike, and their union discourages a delivery drivers' union from moving the products of the chain's largest food supply companies, that would be a secondary boycott. The purpose of the secondary boycott is typically to exert indirect pressure on the employer to resolve the labor dispute by causing its business connections to suffer as a result of the dispute. Secondary boycotts are illegal under the National Labor Relations Act.

secondary meaning When a trademark that is not distinctive acquires a meaning within the marketplace such that consumers associate it with the product or service. For example, though first names are not generally considered distinctive, Ben & Jerry's Ice Cream has become so well known that it has acquired secondary meaning and is entitled to trademark protection. Proving secondary meaning requires evidence of public recognition through use and exposure in the marketplace.

second degree murder An unpremeditated killing, resulting from an assault in which death of the victim was a distinct possibility. Second degree murder is different from first degree murder, which is a premeditated, intentional killing; or results from a vicious crime such as arson, rape, or armed robbery. Exact distinctions on degree vary by state.

secret rebate A kickback of money by a business to a "preferred" customer, not offered to the public, or by a subcontractor to a contractor, but not shown on a job estimate. Both practices are illegal in most states as unfair business practices and may result in criminal penalties or refusal of a court to enforce a contract (written or oral) in which there is such a secret rebate.

secret warranty program A program under which a car manufacturer will make repairs for free on vehicles with persistent problems, even after the warranty has expired, in order to avoid a recall and the accompanying bad press. Secret warranties are rarely advertised by the manufacturer, so consumers must pursue the manufacturer to discover and take advantage of them. A few states require manufacturers to notify car buyers when they adopt secret warranty programs.

Section 8 The name of a federally financed housing assistance program, in which the government helps low-income tenants with rent payments. Typically, the government pays about one-third of the rent, and the tenant pays the balance. Landlords who choose to participate in the Section 8 program must have their properties inspected, and must agree to use the lease addendum issued by HUD, which obligates the landlord to a rental term of no less than one year, and specifies allowable reasons for termination.

Section 1244 Stock Stock issued by eligible small corporations under Section 1244 of the Internal Revenue Code which allows the shareholders to treat up to $50,000 of losses ($100,000 if married and filing jointly) from the sale of the stock as ordinary losses instead of capital losses.

Section 1981 A shorthand reference to the Civil Rights Act of 1866, which declares African Americans to be citizens entitled to a series of rights previously reserved to white men. Among the rights conferred by Section 1981 are the right to sue or be sued in court, to give evidence in a lawsuit, to purchase property, and to make and enforce contracts, which courts have interpreted to prohibit racial discrimination in employment.

secured debt A debt that gives the creditor the right to take property pledged as security for the debt (collateral) if the debtor does not pay. For example, a creditor can repossess a car if the debtor defaults on the car loan. (Compare: unsecured debt)

secured transaction An arrangement in which a lender or buyer pledges property as collateral for a loan or sale. (See: secured debt)

securities A generic term for shares of stock, bonds, and debentures issued by corporations and governments to evidence ownership and terms of payment of dividends or final payoff. They are called securities because the assets or profits of the corporation or the credit of the government stand as security for payment. However, unlike secured transactions in which specific property is pledged, securities are only as good as the future profitability of the corporation or the management of the governmental agency. Most securities are traded on various stock or bond markets.

security deposit A payment required by a landlord to ensure that a tenant pays rent on time and keeps the rental unit in good condition. If the tenant damages the property or leaves owing rent, the landlord can use the security deposit to cover what the tenant owes. The laws of most states limit the size of a deposit, dictate its use, and set specific rules for when and how landlords must return the deposit.

security interest A claim against property that secures a debt.

sedition The federal crime of advocating insurrection against the government through speeches and publications. Sedition charges are rare because freedom of speech, press, and assembly are guaranteed by the Bill of Rights, and because treason or espionage charges can be made for overt acts against the nation's security.

seduction The use of charm, promises, and flattery to induce another person to have sexual intercourse outside of marriage, without any use of force or intimidation. At one time, seduction was a crime in many states, but seduction is no longer criminal (unless the seduced person is underage or otherwise unable to consent). However, seduction does linger in the criminal codes of some states.

seised See: seized

seisin See: seizin

seized Having ownership and possession of something. This term is not used much these days, but it may turn up in an old will ("I leave all the property of which I die seized as follows: ….") or other document. Also spelled "seised."

seizin Ownership of real estate; in the old sense of the term, both ownership and possession. This term is not used in modern real estate transactions, but appears in some old deeds.

seizure The taking of physical evidence or property by law enforcement officials. Seized evidence can include taking blood for a drug test to impounding a car used in a robbery. In most cases,

the police must obtain a search warrant before they can seize personal property.

self-dealing Taking part in a transaction or business deal that benefits oneself rather than a person or company to whom one owes a fiduciary duty. For instance, a director of a corporation owes a duty to the corporation not to engage in transactions that benefit the director rather than the corporation. Self-dealing can also apply to owners of a partnership or limited liability company who do not inform their co-owners of business opportunities that should belong to the company.

self-defense The use of reasonable force to protect oneself from an aggressor. Self-defense shields a person from criminal liability for the harm inflicted on the aggressor. For example, a robbery victim who takes the robber's weapon and uses it against the robber during a struggle won't be liable for assault and battery if he can show that his action was reasonably necessary to protect himself from imminent harm.

self-employed Owning and working in a business other than a corporation, as opposed to working for an employer.

self-employment tax Social Security and Medicare taxes on net self-employment income that is a percentage of an individual's earned income up to a certain limit (called the Social Security

Wage Base) that increases each year, and then a lower percentage of wages without limit. The tax is reported on Schedule SE of the individual's income tax return.

self-executing Immediately effective without further action, legislation, or legal steps.

self-help Obtaining relief or enforcing one's rights outside of the normal legal process. Examples include repossessing a car when payments have not been made, retrieving borrowed or stolen goods, demanding and receiving payment, or abating a nuisance (such as digging a ditch to divert flooding from someone else's property). Self-help is legal as long as it does not "break the public peace" or violate some other law (although brief trespass is common).

self-incrimination The making of statements that might expose the maker to criminal prosecution, either now or in the future. The Fifth Amendment of the U.S. Constitution prohibits the government from forcing a person to provide evidence (as in answering questions) that might lead to prosecution for a crime.

self-proving will A will that is created in a way that allows a probate court to easily accept it as the true will of the person who has died. In some states, a will is self-proving when two witnesses sign under penalty of perjury that they observed the will maker sign it and that he told them it was his will. If no one contests the validity of the will, the probate court will accept the will without hearing the testimony of the witnesses or other evidence. In other states, the will maker and one or more witnesses must sign an affidavit (sworn statement) before a notary public certifying that the will is genuine and that all will making formalities were observed.

self-serving Refers to a statement or answer to a question that serves no purpose and provides no evidence, but only argues or reinforces the legal position of a particular party in a lawsuit. An example would be a lawyer asking his own client: "Are you the sort of person who would never do anything dishonest?" A judge may disallow this kind of question unless there is some evidentiary value.

self-settled trust A special needs trust funded with property belonging to the beneficiary, such as a direct inheritance, recovery in a personal injury lawsuit, or gift.

sell To transfer possession and ownership of goods or other property for money or something of equivalent value.

seller An individual or entity that sells goods or other property to a buyer.

senior lien The first lien or security interest placed on property at a time before all other liens, called junior liens.

sentence Punishment in a criminal case. A sentence can range from a fine and community service to life imprisonment or death. For most crimes, the sentence is chosen by the trial judge; the jury chooses the sentence only in a capital case, when it must choose between life in prison without parole and death.

"No, no," said the Queen. "Sentence first, verdict afterwards."

—Lewis Carroll, *Alice in Wonderland*

SEP See: simplified employee pension plan

separate property In community property states, property owned and controlled entirely by one spouse in a marriage. At divorce, separate property is not divided under the state's property division laws, but is kept by the spouse who owns it. Separate property includes all property that a spouse obtained before marriage, through inheritance, or as a gift. It also includes any property that is traceable to separate property—for example, cash from the sale of a vintage car owned by one spouse before marriage—and any property that the spouses agree is separate property. (See also: community property, equitable distribution)

separation In the context of marriage, the state of living apart. Spouses are said to be separated if they no longer live in the same dwelling, even though they may continue their relationship. They may also be considered separated while living in the same house, if they no longer share a bedroom and each live their separate lives. A legal separation results when the parties separate and a court rules on the division of property, alimony (spousal support) or child support, and child custody, but does not grant a divorce.

separation agreement An agreement between two married people to live apart indefinitely. Similar to a marital settlement agreement, a separation agreement may define the spouses' rights with regard to property, custody, and support.

SEP-IRA An individual retirement account set up to receive contributions from a simplified employee pension plan.

sequester 1) To isolate, separate, or keep a person or people apart from others. For example, a jury in a highly publicized trial may be sequestered to prevent them from reading or hearing anything about the case. A sequestered jury may have to live apart from their families for the duration of the trial. A witness who is sequestered is required to leave the courtroom so he or she does not hear the testimony of other witnesses. 2) For a court to take custody of property that is the subject of a dispute, pending the outcome of a legal proceeding to determine ownership.

sequestration 1) The act of isolating a jury or witness. 2) The act of a court taking property that is a subject of a legal dispute pending the outcome of a lawsuit to determine ownership. (See also: sequester)

seriatim Latin for one after another, as in a series. For example, issues or facts might be discussed seriatim (or "ad seriatim"), meaning one by one in order.

serious health condition Under the Family and Medical Leave Act (FMLA), eligible employees may take leave for their own serious health condition or to care for a family member with a serious health condition. A serious health condition is an illness, injury, impairment, or physical or mental condition that involves 1) inpatient care; 2) incapacity for more than three full days with continuing treatment by a health care provider; 3) incapacity due to pregnancy or prenatal care; 4) incapacity due to, or treatment for, a chronic serious health condition; 5) permanent or long-term incapacity for a condition for which treatment may not be effective, such as a terminal illness; or (6) absence for multiple treatments for either restorative surgery following an injury or accident, or a condition that would require an absence of more than three days if not treated.

servant An outdated term for employee.

service 1) Delivering legal papers to a defendant or a plaintiff in a lawsuit. 2) Delivering written notification of the sender's intent to invoke a legal or contractual right. (See also: service of process, personal service, substituted service)

service business An enterprise that derives income primarily from providing personal services, rather than goods. Examples include plumbers, contractors, consultants, physicians, and accountants.

service by fax Using a fax machine to deliver legal documents, which otherwise would be sent with a process server or served by mail. Service by fax is often specifically allowed by statute, and is followed by mailing an original (hard copy) of the document.

service by mail Mailing legal pleadings to opposing attorneys or parties, while filing the original with the court clerk, along with a declaration stating that the copy was mailed to a particular person at a specific address.

service by publication Serving a summons or other legal document in a lawsuit on a defendant by publishing the document in an advertisement in a newspaper of general circulation. Service by publication is used to attempt to notify a defendant who is intentionally absent, in hiding, or at an unknown address. It's allowed only after a judge has been convinced, based on a sworn declaration, of the serving party's inability to find the defendant after trying hard. Service by publication is commonly used in a divorce action to serve a spouse who has disappeared without a leaving a forwarding address or to give notice to people who might have a right to object to a "quiet title" action to clear title to real estate.

service mark A word, phrase, logo, symbol, color, sound, or other device used by a business to identify a service and distinguish it from those of its competitors. In practice, the legal rights and protections for trademarks and service marks are identical.

service of process The delivery of copies of legal documents such as summons, complaint, subpena, order to show cause (order to appear and argue against a proposed order), writs, notice to quit the premises, and certain other documents, usually by personal delivery to the defendant or other person to whom the documents are directed. In certain cases of absent or unknown defendants, the court will allow service by publication in a newspaper. Once all parties have filed a complaint, answer, or any pleading in a lawsuit, further documents usually can be served by mail or even fax. (See also: personal service, substituted service)

servient estate A parcel of land that is subject to an easement that benefits another parcel of real estate, called a dominant estate. For example, one parcel (the servient estate) might be subject to a right of way that provides access to another parcel (the dominant estate). (See also: running with the land)

servient tenement See: servient estate

session 1) A meeting of a court, legislature, or other government body to carry out business. For courts, this is also called sitting. 2) The period of time during which such a body is gathered together and working, as in "the spring term," or "the court is in session."

set To schedule, as to "set a case for trial."

set aside 1) As a verb, to vacate or annul a court order or judgment. For example, the losing party in a trial might file a motion asking the judge to set aside the verdict. 2) As a noun, something (often money) that is to be used for a particular purpose. For example, funds that are earmarked for a specific program might be described as a set-aside.

"Good men must not obey the laws too well."

—Ralph Waldo Emerson

---

setback The distance between a property boundary and a building. Local zoning laws usually require minimum setbacks.

setoff A claim made by someone who allegedly owes money, that the amount should be reduced because the other person owes him or her money. This is often raised in a counterclaim filed by a defendant in a lawsuit. By claiming a setoff, the defendant does not necessarily deny the plaintiff's original demand, but seeks to reduce the amount of money owed to the plaintiff by the amount that the plaintiff owes to the defendant.

setting 1) The scheduling of a particular legal proceeding, such as a hearing or trial. 2) The date and time when a particular hearing or trial is scheduled to take place.

settle To resolve a lawsuit before going to trial.

settlement 1) The resolution of a dispute or lawsuit. 2) Payment or adjustment. For example, a debtor might settle an account by paying the full amount owed, or an insurance company might settle a property damage claim by paying the insured for the covered damage. 3) The distribution of property and wrapping up of a decedent's affairs by the executor. 4) The transfer of real property from the seller to the buyer (and new owner); closing.

settlor The person who creates a trust by a written trust declaration. Called a "trustor" in many (particularly western) states and is sometimes referred to as a "grantor" or "donor." The settlor usually transfers the original assets into the trust. (Compare: grantor)

707(b) action An action filed by the U.S. Trustee, the bankruptcy trustee, or any creditor, under authority of Section 707(b) of the Bankruptcy Code, to dismiss a debtor's Chapter 7 bankruptcy case on the ground of abuse.

severability clause A provision in a contract that preserves the rest of the contract if a portion of it is invalidated by a court. Without a severability clause, a decision by the court finding one part of the contract unenforceable would invalidate the entire document.

severable contract A contract which is comprised of several separate contracts such that the breach of one does not necessarily mean the breach of the remainder—for example, a sales agreement for several pieces of equipment each with its own payment schedules.

several liability When a party is responsible for his or her own obligation (separately from another's liability), so that the plaintiff may bring a separate action against that party without suing other responsible parties. (Compare: joint liability)

severance 1) Separation of legal claims by court order to allow the claims to be tried separately. For example, a judge might sever the trials of two defendants accused of the same crime. 2) Money paid or benefits provided to an employee who is fired, laid off, or agrees to leave. (See also: severance pay)

severance pay Money paid to an employee who is laid off, fired, or leaves by mutual agreement. Employers are not generally required to offer severance pay, although a few states require some severance pay for employees who lose their job in a plant closing or large

layoff. Employers may also be obligated to provide severance pay if they promised to do so in an employment contract or employee handbook.

sex offender A generic term for persons convicted of crimes involving sex, including rape, molestation, sexual harassment, and pornography production or distribution.

sexual harassment Offensive and unwelcome sexual conduct that is so severe or pervasive that it affects the terms and conditions of the victim's employment, either because the victim's submission or failure to submit to the behavior is the basis for job-related decisions (like firing or demotion) or because the victim reasonably finds the workplace abusive or hostile as a result of the harassment.

shall an imperative, usually indicating that certain actions are mandatory, not permissive. (Compare: may)

share 1) A portion of a benefit from a trust, estate, claim, or business. 2) A portion of ownership interest in a corporation, represented by a stock certificate.

shared custody After a divorce or separation between parents, the sharing of parenting responsibilities for children born to the parents. (See also: joint custody)

shared equity mortgage A mortgage in which the lender gets a share of the equity of the home in exchange for providing a portion of the down payment. When the property is later sold, the lender is entitled to a portion of the proceeds.

shareholder An owner of a corporation whose ownership interest is represented by shares of stock in the corporation. The benefits of being a shareholder include the right to vote for members of the board of directors, to receive dividends if approved by the board of directors, to participate in a division of assets the upon dissolution and winding up of the corporation, and to bring a derivative action (lawsuit) if the corporation is poorly managed. A shareholder's rights may be limited by a buy-sell agreement. Also called a stockholder.

shareholders' agreement An agreement among the shareholders of a corporation that can cover buy-sell rights, restrictions on transferring shares, voting rights, and/or the employment of a shareholder. (See also: buy-sell agreement)

shareholder's derivative action See: derivative action

shareholders' meeting A meeting of all or most shareholders of a corporation to hear reports on the company's business situation. Shareholders usually elect members of the board of directors at an annual shareholders' meeting, often by proxies.

sharp practice Questionable or unethical actions, especially by a lawyer. Sharp practice may include making misleading statements or threats, ignoring agreements, improperly using process, or employing other tricky and/or dishonorable means barely within the law. A consistent pattern of sharp practice may lead to discipline by a court or state bar association.

Shelley v. Kraemer (1948) A U.S. Supreme Court case in which the Court declared so-called restrictive covenants in real property deeds that prohibited the sale of property to non-Caucasians to be unconstitutional and in violation of the equal protection provision of the Fourteenth Amendment. Where such covenants remain in the text of deeds they must be ignored.

sheltered workshop A place of employment designed and managed to accommodate the needs of people with disabilities.

Shepardize A method of locating the subsequent history of a case using a book or computerized version of *Shepard's Citations*. This process can locate a list of decisions which either follow, distinguish, or overrule any case.

sheriff The top law enforcement officer for a county, usually elected, who is responsible for police protection outside of incorporated cities, management of the county jail, and providing bailiffs for protection of the courts. A sheriff also handles civil activities like serving summons, subpenas, and writs, conducting judgment sales, and fulfilling various functions ordered by the courts.

sheriff's sale A sale of property seized by the sheriff pursuant to a court order in order to satisfy a judgment against the property's owner.

Sherman Antitrust Act A federal anti-trust law, enacted in 1890, that prohibits direct or indirect interference with interstate trade. This Act was amended by the Clayton Act in 1914.

shield laws Statutes in some states that make communications between news reporters and informants confidential and privileged, freeing journalists of the obligation to testify about them in court. This is similar to the doctor-patient, lawyer-client, or priest-parishioner privilege. The goal is to let journalists gather news without being ordered to reveal sources and notes of conversations. In states that have no shield law, many judges have found reporters in contempt of court (and given them jail terms) for refusing to name informants or reveal information gathered on the promise of confidentiality.

Suspect. (1987) Public Defender Cher represents deaf homeless vet Liam Neeson and gets help from juror Dennis Quaid, with more fun than logic. With John Mahoney, Philip Bosco.

shifting the burden of proof In a lawsuit, the transfer of the obligation to prove particular facts from one party to the other. For example, the person who sued (the plaintiff) initially bears the burden of proving facts that, if no rebutting evidence is presented, would allow that party to win the case. The burden may then shift to the defendant to prove one or more defenses to the plaintiff's case.

shoplifting The crime of stealing goods from a retail store by a customer or someone posing as a customer.

short cause A lawsuit that is estimated to take no more than one day. A short cause case may get priority for court-room space because it can fill a time-slot between bigger cases. However, if a supposed "short cause" lasts beyond one day the judge is authorized to declare a mistrial and the case will be reset later as a "long cause."

shortening time A court order allowing a motion or other legal matter to be set at a time shorter than provided by law or court rules. Shortening time is usually granted when the time for trial or some other court action is approaching and a hearing must be heard promptly by the judge. Example: Local rules require that a party give the other side ten days' notice before a hearing. If the trial is set to begin in nine days, a court might shorten the time to schedule a hearing to five days, provided the notice is served within 24 hours.

short sale A sale of a house in which the proceeds fall short of what the owner still owes on the mortgage. Short sales usually occur when the homeowner is facing foreclosure. Many lenders will agree accept the proceeds of a short sale and forgive the rest of what is owed on the mortgage when the owner cannot make the mortgage payments. By accepting a short sale, the lender can avoid a lengthy and costly foreclosure, and the owner is able to pay off the loan for less than what is owed. (See also: deed in lieu of foreclosure)

shotgun charge See: dynamite charge

show cause order See: order to show cause

sick leave Time off work due to illness or injury.

sickness benefits See: disability benefits

sidebar 1) An area in front of or next to a judge's bench (the raised desk in front of the judge) away from the witness stand and the jury box, where lawyers are called to speak confidentially with the judge out of earshot of the jury. 2) A discussion between the judge and attorneys at the bench off the record and outside the hearing of the jurors or spectators.

sideline business A small business activity carried on in addition to an individual's full-time employment or principal trade or business.

signature guarantee Verification from a bank or broker that a signature is genuine. It's similar to notarization, but notarization is not a substitute for a guarantee.

silent partner An investor who puts money into a business and in exchange receives a share in the profits, but takes no part in management and may be unknown to the public or customers. A silent partner may be liable for business debts and judgments unless designated as a limited partner in a limited partnership agreement.

similarly situated Alike in all relevant ways for purposes of a particular decision or issue. This term is often used in discrimination cases, in which the plaintiff may seek to show that he or she was treated differently from others who are similarly situated except for the alleged basis of discrimination. For example, a plaintiff who claims that she was not promoted because she is a woman would seek to show that similarly situated men—that is, men with similar qualifications, experience, and tenure with the company—were promoted. This term is also used to define the group of people on whose behalf a class action may be brought: Everyone in the group must be similarly situated as to the issue(s) litigated. For example, in a case alleging that a credit card company charged improper fees, only people who had a credit card with that company during the time when the improper fees were imposed could be members of the class.

simple trust See: discretionary trust

simplified employee pension plan A pension plan allowing self-employed business owners to make contributions toward their own retirement plans and to their employees' retirement plans. Contributions are made directly to an individual retirement account set up for each employee (a SEP-IRA) and there the contributions accumulate tax-deferred until withdrawn.

simultaneous death act A statute in effect in most states that helps determine inheritance among beneficiaries who die at the same time. The statutes provide that if spouses, siblings, or other beneficiaries die simultaneously, or if it cannot be determined who died first, then it is presumed that each died before the other.

sine qua non Latin for "without which it could not be," an indispensable action or condition. Example: if Charlie had not left the keys in the ignition, his ten-year-old son could not have started the car and backed it over Polly's bike. So Charlie's act was the sine qua non of the damage to Polly's bike.

single-entry accounting A system of tracking business income and expenses that requires each item of income or expense to be recorded just once. (Compare: double-entry accounting)

situs Latin for location. Used to refer to the site of a crime or accident or where a building stands.

skip person Someone who receives property (by gift or inheritance) from another person who is at least two generations older—most commonly, a grandparent. Transferring assets to a skip person can trigger the federal generation-skipping transfer tax (GSTT).

slander An untruthful oral (spoken) statement about a person that harms the person's reputation or standing in the community. Because slander is a tort (a civil wrong), the injured person can bring a lawsuit against the person who made the false statement. If the statement is made via broadcast media—for example, over the radio or on TV—it is considered libel, rather than slander, because the statement has the potential to reach a very wide audience. Both libel and slander are forms of defamation. (See also: defamation)

SLAPP suit A Strategic Lawsuit Against Public Participation, in which a corporation, business, or developer sues an organization in an attempt to scare it into dropping protests against its actions. SLAPP suits typically involve the environment—for example, a developer might sue local residents, who are petitioning to change zoning laws to prevent a real estate development, for interference with the developer's business interests. Many states have "anti-SLAPP suit" statutes that protect citizens' rights to free speech and to petition the government.

Slaughter House Cases **(1873)** U.S. Supreme Court decision that upheld, by a vote of 5-4, the contract rights of an owner of a monopoly on slaughter houses granted by the "carpet bagger" government of Louisiana. In so doing, the Court ruled that the "privileges and immunities" protections of the Constitution applies to the states through the Fourteenth Amendment.

 "Legal process is an essential part of the democratic process."

—Justice Felix Frankfurter

---

small claims court A state court that resolves disputes involving relatively small amounts of money—usually between $2,000 and $10,000, depending on the state. Adversaries usually appear without lawyers—in fact, some states forbid lawyers in small claims court—and recount their side of the dispute in plain English. Evidence, including the testimony of eyewitnesses and expert witnesses, is relatively easy to present because small claims courts do not follow the formal rules of evidence that govern regular trial cases. A small claims judgment has the same force as does the judgment of any other state court, meaning that if the loser—now called the "judgment debtor"—fails to pay the judgment voluntarily, it can be collected using normal collection techniques, such as property liens and wage garnishments.

small entity Status of a patent applicant that entitles the applicant to pay reduced application, issuance, and maintenance fees. Small entities are any for-profit company with 500 or fewer employees, any nonprofit organization, or an independent inventor.

small estate An estate that contains property with a value small enough to be eligible, under state law, for simplified probate procedures or out-of-court transfers of the deceased person's property.

smoking gun Slang for evidence that decisively proves a case.

Social Security The general term that describes a number of related programs, including retirement, disability, dependents, and survivors benefits. These programs provide workers and their families with some monthly income when their normal flow of income shrinks because of retirement, disability, or death. These programs are administered by the Social Security Administration.

Social Security Administration The Social Security Administration (SSA) is an independent federal agency that administers the Social Security program, which includes retirement, disability, dependents, and survivors benefits.

Social Security statement An accounting of each worker's earnings and work

credits for purposes of calculating the amount of Social Security retirement, disability, survivors, or dependents benefits to which an individual is entitled. Social Security statements are generally mailed out each year to people age 40 and older. You can request your statement from the Social Security Administration.

Social Security tax A portion of the FICA (Federal Insurance Contributions Act) tax that is 12.4% of an individual's net earned income. The employee's share of the Medicare tax is 6.2% of wages up to a certain limit (called the Social Security Wage Base) that increases each year. The employer's share of the Medicare tax is 6.2% of an employee's wages up to that limit.

sodomy Anal copulation by a man inserting his penis in the anus either of another man or a woman. If accomplished by force, without consent, or with someone incapable of consent, sodomy is a felony in all states in the same way that rape is. Homosexual (male to male) consensual sodomy between consenting adults has traditionally been a felony, but increasingly is either decriminalized or seldom prosecuted. Sodomy with a consenting adult female is virtually never prosecuted even in those states in which it remains on the books as a criminal offense.

sole custody A custody arrangement under which one parent is the only one to have either legal or physical custody or both. A parent with sole physical custody has the right to live with the child, while the other parent has visitation rights. A parent with sole legal custody has the right to make all decisions affecting the child, including decisions about education, religion, and medical care.

sole proprietorship A business owned by an individual that has not been registered as a limited liability company, a corporation, or any other type of legal tax entity. For IRS purposes, the owner (sole proprietor) and the business are one tax entity, meaning that business profits are reported and taxed on the owner's personal tax return. The main downside of a sole proprietorship is that its owner is personally liable for all business debts.

solicitation 1) The crime of encouraging or inducing another to commit a crime. 2) The crime of paying or requesting money in exchange for sex; prostitution. 3) The act of requesting something from others, such as asking others to donate to a particular charity, purchase products, or patronize a certain business.

solicitor In the United Kingdom, an attorney who may provide all legal services except representing a client in court. Only a specially trained attorney, called a barrister, makes court appearances. The United States does not make this distinction among attorneys.

Solicitor General The chief trial attorney in the U.S. Department of Justice, who is responsible for arguing cases before the Supreme Court. The Solicitor General is the second-highest ranking attorney in the Department of Justice, behind the Attorney General.

solitary confinement The placement of a prisoner in a cell away from other prisoners, usually as a form of internal discipline, but occasionally to protect the convict from other prisoners or to prevent the prisoner from causing trouble.

solvency 1) Having sufficient funds or other assets to pay debts. 2) Having more assets than liabilities (debts). (Compare: insolvency)

sound mind and memory When making a will, the ability to understand in general what one owns, one's family relationships, and the meaning and effect of the will.

sound recording A type of copyrighted work resulting from the fixation of a series of musical or other sounds (including narration or spoken words) in some medium. The result is known as a phonorecord. A sound recording copyright protects the way that the composition is performed. The performer, producer, or recording company usually claims copyright in a sound recording. (Compare: musical works copyright)

sounds in Referring to an underlying legal basis or cause of action—such as a contract or tort (civil wrong)—in a lawsuit. For example: "Plaintiff's first cause of action against defendant sounds in tort, and his second cause of action sounds in contract."

sovereign immunity A legal principal making governmental bodies and employees immune from being sued in their own courts without governmental consent. The legislature can, and often does, carve out areas where this immunity will be waived (canceled).

spam Internet slang for unsolicited bulk email, primarily unsolicited commercial email (UCE). Spam has been linked with fraudulent business schemes, chain letters, and offensive sexual and political messages

speaking demurrer An attempt to introduce new evidence during a hearing on a demurrer. Because a demurrer is an argument that assumes all of the facts in the challenged pleading are correct, evidence outside of the pleading may not be considered, and speaking demurrers are therefore not allowed. (See also: demurrer)

spear phishing See: phishing

special administrator 1) A person appointed by a court to take charge of only a designated portion of an estate during probate. For example, a special administrator with particular expertise on art might be appointed to oversee the probate of a wealthy person's art collection, but not the entire estate. 2) A person appointed to be responsible for a deceased person's property for a limited time or during an emergency, such as a challenge to the will or to the qualifications of the named executor. In such cases, the special administrator's duty is to maintain and preserve the estate, not necessarily to take control of the probate process. (See also: administrator, administrator pendente lite, administrator ad litem)

special appearance 1) The personal attendance in court of a party or attorney for the sole purpose of arguing that the court does not have personal jurisdiction over that party. If the party or attorney instead makes a "general" appearance in court, that party is presumed to have waived the right to contest the court's jurisdiction. 2) A one-time court appearance by an attorney for a party who either is represented by another attorney or is not represented at the time. Quite often an attorney will make a "special appearance" to protect the interests of a potential client, but before a fee has been paid or arranged.

special circumstances In criminal cases, particularly homicides, actions of the accused or the situation under which the crime was committed for which state statutes allow or require imposition of a more severe punishment. "Special circumstances" in murder cases may well result in the imposition of the death penalty (in states with capital punishment). Such circumstances may include: rape, kidnapping or maiming prior to the killing, multiple deaths, killing a police officer or prison guard, or actions showing wanton disregard for life such as throwing a bomb into a restaurant. (See also: capital punishment)

special damages Damages that compensate the plaintiff for quantifiable monetary losses such as medical bills and the cost to repair damaged property (direct losses) and lost earnings (consequential damages). Distinguished from general damages, for which there is no exact dollar value to the plaintiff's losses.

special education The broad term used to describe the educational system available for children (ages three to 21) with disabilities, including physical, mental, and learning disabilities (See also: individualized education program)

Special Immigrant A catchall category of people made eligible to apply for U.S. green cards by specially passed laws. Commonly used special immigrant types include workers for recognized religions, former U.S. government workers, and foreign doctors who have been practicing medicine in the United States for many years.

special master A person appointed by the court to carry out an order of the court, such as selling property or mediating child custody cases. (See also: master)

special needs The needs of a person with disabilities for things and services other than food and shelter, which SSI provides.

special needs trust A trust designed to hold and disburse property for the benefit of an SSI recipient so that SSI and Medicaid won't consider the trust property or disbursements to be a resource or income. To accomplish this purpose, the trust typically gives the trustee sole discretion over trust disbursements and bars the trustee from making disbursements that would impair the beneficiary's eligibility for SSI and Medicaid. In addition, the trust must be for the beneficiary's sole benefit and bar creditors from going after trust assets. A special needs trust funded with the beneficiary's own property (a self-settled trust) is subject to additional restrictions. Also called a supplemental needs trust.

special power of attorney See: limited power of attorney

🔊 *"There are not enough jails, not enough policemen, not enough courts to enforce a law not supported by the people."*

—Senator and Vice President Hubert H. Humphrey

---

special prosecutor An attorney from outside of the government selected by the Attorney General or Congress to investigate and possibly prosecute a federal government official for wrongdoing in office. The theory behind appointing a special prosecutor is that there is a built-in conflict of interest between the Department of Justice and officials who may have political or governmental connections with that department.

specials See: special damages

special verdict The jury's decisions or findings of fact with the application of the law to those facts left up to the judge, who will then render the final verdict. This type of limited verdict is used when the legal issues to be applied are complex or require difficult computation.

specification The narrative portion of a patent application that describes the purpose, structure, and operation of the invention, as well as any relevant prior technology (prior art). The specification must provide enough information about the invention so that a person proficient in the field of invention can build and operate it.

specific bequest A specific item of property that is left to a named beneficiary under a will. (See also: ademption)

specific devise A gift of a specific piece of property through a will. (See also: devise)

specific finding A decision on a fact made by a jury in its verdict at the judge's request. Often the judge gives a jury a list of decisions to be made on specific findings of fact to help the jurors focus on the issues. For example, a judge may ask the jury to answer the specific question, "Was the defendant exceeding the speed limit?"

specific intent A person's intent to produce the precise consequences of that person's act, including the intent to do the physical act itself. For example, larceny is taking the personal property of another with the intent to permanently deprive the other person of it. A person is not guilty of larceny just because he took someone else's property; the prosecutor must prove that the defendant intended to take the property, and that he took it in order to keep it permanently.

specific legacy A gift of a specific piece of property through a will. (See also: legacy)

specific performance A contract remedy provided by a court that orders the losing side to perform its part of an agreement rather than, or possibly in addition to, paying money damages to the winner. Generally required in cases of unique goods, for example artwork or antiques.

speculative damages Possible financial loss or expenses claimed by a plaintiff that are contingent upon a future occurrence, purely conjectural, or highly improbable. These damages should not be awarded. For example, a plaintiff may claim that in ten years, as he ages, he may begin to feel pain from a healed fracture caused by a defendant (even though no doctor has testified this is likely to happen), and should therefore recover money from the defendant now.

speedy trial In criminal prosecutions, the right of a defendant to have a trial within a short time, premised on the Fifth Amendment's guarantee of due process. Each state has a statute or constitutional provision limiting the time an accused person may be held before trial (for example, 45 days). Charges must be dismissed and the defendant released if the period expires without trial. However, defendants often waive the right to a speedy trial in order to prepare a stronger defense or negotiate a plea to a lesser offense.

spend down To spend resources on medical needs when an applicant for certain Medicaid benefits has resources over the resource limit. When the applicant's resources are sufficiently reduced, he or she will qualify for Medicaid.

spendthrift clause A provision in a trust that restricts a beneficiary's ability to transfer rights to future payments of income or capital under the trust to a third party. In effect, the clause prevents "spendthrift" beneficiaries from squandering inheritance before they receive it and it also protects a beneficiary's inheritance from creditors.

spendthrift trust A trust created for a beneficiary who may be irresponsible with money. The trustee keeps control of the trust income, doling out money to the beneficiary as needed, and sometimes paying third parties (creditors, for example) on the beneficiary's behalf, bypassing the beneficiary completely. Spendthrift trusts typically contain a provision prohibiting creditors from seizing the trust fund to satisfy the beneficiary's debts. These trusts are legal in most states. (See also: property control trust)

spite fence An unsightly fence erected for no other purpose than to irritate a neighbor. Such a fence may be illegal under local fence height and appearance regulations or state laws that specifically bar spite fences. Even if it doesn't violate regulation or laws, the fence may still be illegal if it was built with malicious intent.

split custody A custody arrangement that involves multiple children and awards sole custody of one child to one parent and sole custody of another child to the other parent. This arrangement is generally disfavored by judges because it's generally not considered beneficial to split up siblings.

sponsor See: petitioner (immigration)

spontaneous exclamation A sudden statement (also known as an "excited utterance") made by someone who has seen a surprising, startling, or shocking event (such as an accident or a death), or has suffered an injury. For example, "Oh my God, that blue car hit the little girl!" Spontaneous exclamations are often introduced at trial as evidence of the speaker's state of mind or the truth of the matter being spoken about, and will be admitted if the judge decides that the circumstances surrounding the statement make it likely that the speaker was telling the truth. Without this determination, the statement is simply hearsay; that is, a statement made out of court and offered for the truth of the matter it deals with. (See also: hearsay)

spot zoning Zoning a parcel of land differently from the parcels around it. For example, a school might be allowed in a residential zone if the local zoning authority decides it benefits the public welfare and is consistent with the city's general land use plan. If a particular instance of spot zoning is challenged in court, the court might find it illegal if it violates the general plan, allows development that is very different from the current surrounding uses, or appears to favor an individual property owner to the detriment of the public. (Compare: variance)

spousal privilege See: marital privilege

spousal share See: elective share

spousal support Monetary support paid by one former spouse to another, usually for a specified period of time, pursuant to a divorce agreement or court order. In many states, it's called alimony.

springing durable power of attorney A durable power of attorney that takes effect only when and if the principal becomes incapacitated.

springing interest An interest in property that will take effect in the future, at a specific time or when a specific event occurs. For example, a will or deed might give someone the right to use property for life and direct that ownership of the property then pass to someone else.

sprinkling trust A trust that gives the person managing it—the trustee—the discretion to disburse its funds among the beneficiaries in any way the trustee sees fit. It is a type of property control trust. (See also: pot trust)

SSA See: Social Security Administration

SSDI Social Security Disability Insurance. This federal program provides monthly cash payments to disabled persons who qualify because they have paid enough Social Security taxes. There are no resource or income ceilings.

SSI Supplemental Security Income, a federal program that provides cash payments to persons of limited income and resources who are disabled (according to federal standards), over age 65, or blind. SSI is the main form of government support for people who aren't eligible for Social Security retirement or disability benefits and who meet the program's income and resources requirements.

stakeholder 1) In law, a person holding money or property in which he or she has no right or title while awaiting the outcome of a dispute between two or more claimants to the money or property is settled. Once the right to legal possession is established by judgment or agreement, the stakeholder has a duty to deliver to the owner the money or property. (See also: escrow agent) 2) In business, a person or company that can be affected by an organization's actions and therefore has an interest in the outcome of a project or activity.

standard deduction An annual fixed tax deduction granted to each taxpayer who chooses not to itemize their deductions. The amount of the standard deduction is based on a taxpayer's filing status, age, and whether he or she is blind or is claimed as a dependent on someone else's tax return.

standard mileage rate The dollar amount per mile that the Internal Revenue Service sets annually for small businesses and self-employed people to calculate their vehicle expenses for tax deduction purposes.

standard of care The degree of care (watchfulness, attention, caution, and prudence) that a reasonable person should exercise under the circumstances. If a person does not meet the standard of care, he or she may be liable to a third party for negligence.

***Standard Oil Co. of New Jersey v. United States* (1911)** U.S. Supreme Court decision confirming the dissolution of the Standard Oil Trust, because its monopoly position was an unreasonable restraint on trade under the Sherman Antitrust Act.

standing The right to file a lawsuit or make a particular legal claim. Only a person or entity that has suffered actual injury has standing to seek redress in court. For example, an advocacy group may not file a lawsuit challenging the constitutionality of a statute on its own; there must be a plaintiff who has actually been harmed by the statute.

star chamber proceedings Proceedings of any court or other government body that are held in secret and produce arbitrary results. This derogatory term takes its name from an English court, whose members were appointed by the crown, that met in the 15th to 17th centuries. That court, which met in a room that was apparently decorated with gilt stars, decided guilt and punishment of people accused of violating the monarch's orders.

Its practices made "star chamber" synonymous with any unfair and secretive proceedings.

stare decisis (**stah**-ry dee-**sigh**-sis) Latin for "let the decision stand," a doctrine requiring that judges apply the same reasoning to lawsuits as has been used in prior similar cases.

***Starker* exchange** See: 1031 exchange

state 1) A body of people that is politically organized, especially one that occupies a clearly defined territory and is sovereign. 2) The political system that governs such a body of people. 3) One of the constituent parts of a nation, as in any of the 50 states.

state action The involvement of a government in a particular activity. Certain constitutional claims prohibit only state action, not private activities. For example, the right to free speech enshrined in the First Amendment of the U.S. Constitution gives people a right against laws that restrict their speech, not against private efforts to restrict speech (for example, by a private employer).

state court A court in the state judicial system, rather than the federal judicial system, that decides cases involving state law or the state constitution. State courts are often divided according to the dollar amount of the claims they can hear. Depending on the state, small claims, justice, municipal, or city courts usually hear smaller cases, while district, circuit, superior, or county courts (or in New York, supreme court) have jurisdiction over larger cases. State courts may also be divided according to subject matter, such as criminal court, family court, and probate court.

state's attorney See: district attorney

status Under immigration law, the name of the visa category a person has been assigned and the group of privileges received upon becoming either a permanent resident or a nonimmigrant (temporary visa holder). For example, a green card shows that the holder has the status of a permanent resident and the privilege of living and working in the United States on a permanent basis. An F-1 or M-1 visa indicates that the holder has the status of a student and the privilege of attending school in the United States until the study program is completed.

status conference A meeting of the judge and the lawyers (or unrepresented parties) in a pending legal matter, to determine how the case is progressing. At the status conference, the judge may ask about what discovery has been conducted, whether and how the parties have tried to settle the case, and other pretrial matters. The judge may

also schedule dates for pretrial motions, completion of discovery, and trial. Often, court rules require the parties to file paperwork before the conference answering questions about the issues to be discussed at the conference.

"Judicial decrees may not change the heart, but they can restrain the heartless."

—Martin Luther King, Jr.

---

statute A written law passed by Congress or a state legislature and signed into law by the president or a state governor. (In fairly rare circumstances, a legislative act can become law without the approval of the head of the executive branch of government.) Statutes are often gathered into compilations called "codes," large sets of books that can be found in many public and all law libraries and on the Internet.

statute of frauds A law in every state that requires certain types of documents to be in writing and signed by the party to be charged (usually, the defendant in a lawsuit). Examples include: real estate transfers (conveyances), leases for more than a year, wills, and some types of contracts.

statute of limitations The legally prescribed time limit in which a lawsuit must be filed. Statutes of limitation differ depending on the type of legal claim and on state law. For example, many states require that a personal injury lawsuit be filed within one year from the date of injury—or in some instances, from the date when it should reasonably have been discovered—but some allow two years. Similarly, claims based on a written contract must be filed in court within four years from the date the contract was broken in some states and five years in others. Statute of limitations rules apply to cases filed in all courts, including federal court.

statutory damages Predetermined payments established by law to compensate for certain injuries. Statutory damages are sometimes made available because it is too difficult to calculate actual damages.

statutory offer of settlement A written offer of a specific sum of money made by a defendant to a plaintiff, which will settle the lawsuit if accepted within a short time. The offer may be filed with the court. If the eventual judgment for the plaintiff is less than the offer, the plaintiff will not be able to claim the court costs usually awarded to the prevailing party.

statutory rape Sexual intercourse with a person who has not yet reached the age of consent (determined by state law), whether or not the sexual act is against that person's will. In many states, "Romeo and Juliet" trysts, in which the male and female are young and there is little or no difference in age between them, are punished less severely than when the victim is significantly younger than the perpetrator. When the victim is not only below the age of consent, but also a child (as defined by state law), the offense may be rape or child molestation.

statutory share See: elective share

statutory subject matter A requirement for utility patent rights. To qualify, an invention must fit into at least one of five categories: compositions of matter (compounds such as a drug or glue); articles of manufacture (simple devices such as screwdrivers and rakes); machines (devices with moving parts, such as an auto engine); processes (a method of doing something such as an implant procedure); and new and useful improvements of any of the above categories.

stay A court order that suspends or stops certain proceedings. (See also: automatic stay)

stayaway order A court order prohibiting one party from coming near or contacting another. Most common in divorce actions and cases of stalking.

stay of execution A court-ordered delay in carrying out the death penalty.

stepchild A child born to or legally adopted by your spouse before your marriage whom you have not legally adopted. If you adopt the child, your parent-child relationship is the same as if the child were biologically related to you.

stepparent The spouse of a parent, who becomes the stepparent of that parent's child upon marriage. Stepparents are not legal parents of their spouse's children unless they complete a stepparent adoption, which requires the consent of the other legal parent or the termination of that parent's rights. (See also: stepparent adoption)

stepparent adoption The formal, legal adoption of a child by a stepparent who is married to a legal parent or in a marriage-equivalent relationship like a domestic partnership or civil union. Most states have special provisions making stepparent adoptions relatively easy if the child's noncustodial parent gives consent, is dead or missing, or has abandoned the child.

stepped-up basis An increased basis (value that is used to determine taxable profit or loss when property is sold) given to inherited property that went up in value after the deceased person acquired it but before the new owner inherited it. The basis of the new owner is "stepped up" to the market value of the property at the time of death. The stepped-up basis means that when the property is eventually sold, there will be less taxable capital gain.

stipulation 1) An agreement between the parties to a lawsuit. For example, if the parties enter into a stipulation of facts, neither party will have to prove those facts: The stipulation will be presented to the jury, who will be told to accept them as undisputed evidence in the case. 2) A representation or statement, typically by a party to a contract.

stirpes A term used in wills that refers to distribution of property to descendants of a common ancestor or branch of a family. (See also: per stirpes)

stock 1) A proportional ownership interest of a corporation's capital, represented by shares (equal units of ownership). 2) Inventory (goods) of a business meant for sale.

stock certificate A printed document proving ownership of shares of a corporation. A certificate states the name of the corporation, the state and date of incorporation, the number of shares of stock that the certificate represents, the registered number of the certificate, the name of the shareholder, and the date of issuance. The certificate is signed by authorized officers of the corporation.

stock dividend See: dividend

stockholder See: shareholder

stockholder's derivative action See: derivative action

stock in trade The inventory held by a business for sale.

stock option The right to purchase stock in the future at a price set at the time the option is granted (by sale or as compensation by the corporation). To actually obtain the shares of stock the owner of the option must exercise the option by paying the agreed upon price and requesting issuance of the shares.

stop and frisk A law enforcement officer's brief detention, questioning, and search for a concealed weapon when the officer has reason to believe that the detainee has committed or is about to commit a crime. Any further search requires either a search warrant or probable cause to believe the suspect will commit or has committed a crime (including carrying a concealed weapon, which itself is a crime).

straight-line depreciation A method of deducting the cost of a business asset by deductions in equal annual amounts. The period of time is specified by the Internal Revenue Code for different categories of assets, typically from three to 39 years.

straw man 1) A person to whom title to property or a business is transferred (sometimes known as a "front") for the sole purpose of concealing the true owner—for example, a person is listed as the owner of a bar in order to conceal a criminal who cannot obtain a liquor license. 2) A fallacious argument intended to distract.

street A roadway in an urban area, owned and maintained by the municipality for public use. A private road cannot be a street.

strict construction Interpreting a legal provision (usually a constitutional protection) narrowly. Strict constructionists often look only at the literal meaning of the words in question, or at their historical meaning at the time the law was written. Also referred to as "strict interpretation" or "original intent," because a person who follows the doctrine of strict construction of the Constitution tries to ascertain the intent of the framers at the time the document was written by considering what the language they used meant at that time.

strict liability Automatic responsibility for damages due to manufacture or use of equipment or materials that are inherently dangerous, such as explosives, animals, poisonous snakes, or assault weapons. A person injured by such equipment or materials does not have to prove the manufacturer or operator was negligent in order to recover money damages.

strict scrutiny A legal standard to determine the constitutionality of a statute, used when the statute implicates a fundamental right or relates to a suspect classification under the equal protection clause (such as race). To determine if a statute passes the test, a court considers whether the government has a compelling interest in creating the law, whether the statute is "narrowly tailored" to meet the government's objectives, and whether there are less restrictive means of accomplishing the same thing. (See also: rational basis)

strike 1) An organized work stoppage by employees, intended to pressure the employer to meet the employees' demands (for example, for higher pay, better benefits, or safer working conditions). 2) For the judge to order that all or part of a party's pleading be removed or disregarded, typically after a motion by the opposing party. 3) For the judge to order evidence deleted from the court record and instruct the jury to disregard it. Typically, this order is made regarding testimony by a witness in court.

structure anything built on land, from a shed to a high rise.

sua sponte (**sooh**-uh **spahn**-tay) Latin for "of one's own accord," most commonly used to describe a decision by a judge that neither party to a lawsuit has requested.

subchapter S corporation See: S corporation

> "There is no country (like the United States) in the world in which the doing of justice is burdened by such heavy overhead charges or in which so great a force is maintained for a given amount of litigation."
>
> —Elihu Root

subcontractor A person or business that contracts with an independent contractor to perform some portion of the work or services on a project which the independent contractor has agreed to perform. In building construction, subcontractors may include such trades as plumbing, electrical, roofing, cement work, and plastering.

sublease A rental agreement or lease between a tenant and a new tenant (called a subtenant or sublessee) who will either share the rental or take over from the first tenant. The sublessee pays rent directly to the tenant. The tenant is still completely responsible to the landlord for the rent and for any damage, including that caused by the sublessee. Most landlords prohibit subleases unless they have given prior written consent. (Compare: assign)

submit To finish presenting evidence or an argument in a hearing or trial and give the matter over to the judge for a decision.

subordination The process by which a creditor holding a priority debt agrees to accept a lower priority for the collection of its debt in a deference to a new debt. (See also: subordination agreement)

subordination agreement A written contract in which a lender who has secured a loan by a mortgage or deed of trust agrees with the property owner to subordinate its loan (accept a lower priority for the collection of its debt), thus giving the new loan priority in any foreclosure or payoff. The agreement must be acknowledged by a notary so that it can be recorded in the official county records. (See also: subordination)

subornation of perjury The crime of encouraging, inducing, or assisting another in the commission of perjury, which is knowingly telling an untruth under oath. Example: Lawyer Frank is interviewing a witness in an accident case who says that Frank's client was jaywalking outside the crosswalk when struck by the defendant's car. Frank tells the witness to help his client by saying the accident occurred in the crosswalk and the witness so testifies in court. Frank is guilty of subornation of the witness's perjury.

subpena (subpoena) A court order issued at the request of a party requiring a witness to testify, produce specified evidence, or both. A subpena can be used to obtain testimony from a witness at both depositions (testimony under oath taken outside of court) and at trial. Failure to comply with the subpena can be punished as contempt of court.

subpena duces tecum A type of subpena, usually issued at the request of a party, by which a court orders a witness to produce certain documents at a deposition or trial.

subpoena See: subpena

subprime loan A loan to a borrower who does not qualify for a loan at the best market rates (the prime rate) because of a weak credit history, inadequate assets to secure the loan, or an income too low to guarantee payments. These loans are offered at a higher interest rate because of the increased risk to the lender. Not all lenders engage in subprime lending and the rates and terms of the loans vary from institution to institution.

subprime mortgage See: subprime loan

subrogation A taking on of the legal rights of someone whose debts or expenses have been paid. For example, subrogation occurs when an insurance company that has paid off its injured claimant takes the legal rights the claimant has against a third party that caused the injury, and sues that third party.

subrogee The insurance company that assumes the legal right to collect the claim of an injured claimant (the subrogor) against the third party that caused the injury, in return for paying the other's expenses in advance. (See also: subrogation)

subrogor An injured claimant who, after being compensated by an insurance company (the subrogee), gives the insurance company the right to collect a claim against the third party that caused the injury. (See also: subrogation)

subscribe 1) To sign at the end of a document. The courts have been flexible in recognizing signatures elsewhere on a contract or will, on the theory that a document should be found valid if possible. 2) To order and agree to pay for an issue of stock, bonds, limited partnership interest, investment, or periodical magazine or newspaper.

subscribing witness A person who signs a document indicating that they have witnessed a signature. For example, a person who witnesses the signing of a will is a subscribing witness.

subsidiary A corporation or other limited liability entity that operates under the legal authority of a larger "parent" corporation. Typically, a parent corporation owns a controlling interest in the shares of a subsidiary corporation, giving the parent the votes necessary to control who is appointed to the subsidiary's board of directors.

substantial performance When a party to a contract, through no fault of that party, performs in a manner that varies slightly from the contract's obligations. In cases of substantial performance, a court may determine that it would be unfair to deny compensation. (See also: specific performance)

substantive law Statutory or written law that governs the rights and obligations of everyone within its jurisdiction. It defines crimes and punishments, as well as civil rights and responsibilities. (Compare: procedural law)

substituted service A method for the formal delivery of court papers that takes the place of personal service. Personal service means that the papers are placed directly into the hands of the person to be served. Substituted service, on the other hand, may be accomplished by leaving the documents with a designated agent, with another adult in the recipient's home, with the recipient's manager at work, or by posting a notice in a prominent place and then using certified mail to send copies of the documents to the recipient.

substitution Putting one person or thing in the place of another. For example, a substitution of parties takes place when a new party is named to take the place of a party who has died or is otherwise unable to continue as a party. Or, one attorney might substitute into a case to replace the attorney of record if, for example, the client fired the first attorney.

substitution of attorney A document in which a party to a lawsuit states that his or her attorney is being replaced by another attorney or by the party acting in propria persona. (See also: substitution)

substitution of parties A replacement of one of the parties in a lawsuit because of events that prevent the party from continuing with the trial. For example, substitution of parties may occur when

one party dies or, in the case of a public official, when that public official is replaced or removed from office.

subtenant See: sublease

success billing A method for lawyers to bill clients that is based on how the lawyer solves the client's problem, instead of the number of hours the lawyer spends working on it. For example, if a lawyer represents a company that's being sued, they might agree that the client will pay a certain fee if the lawyer settles the case for an amount that the client's insurance policy will cover.

succession The passing of property or legal rights after death. The word commonly refers to the distribution of property under a state's intestate succession laws, which determine who inherits property when someone dies without a valid will. When used in connection with real estate, the word refers to the passing of property by will or inheritance, as opposed to gift, grant, or purchase.

successive sentences In criminal law, when a defendant has been convicted of more than one crime, the judge's ruling that the sentences for each conviction will be served one after the other, rather than at the same time (concurrent sentences).

successor trustee The person or institution who takes over the management of living trust property when the original trustee has died or become incapacitated.

suffering The pain, hurt, inconvenience, embarrassment, and inability to perform normal activities as a result of injury, for which a person injured by another's negligence or wrongdoing may recover general damages. Usually in the combination "pain and suffering."

sufficient cause See: good cause

suicide The intentional killing of oneself.

suicide clause Standard clause in life insurance policies that limits payments made to survivors of a policyholder who commits suicide within a certain period after purchasing the policy.

sui generis (**soo**-ee **jen**-ris) Latin for of its own kind, and used to describe a form of legal protection that exists outside typical legal protections—that is, something that is unique or different. In intellectual property law, for example, ship hull designs have achieved a unique category of protection and are "sui generis" within copyright law.

suit See: lawsuit

sum certain An amount that is directly stated in a contract or negotiable instrument (like a promissory note) at the time the document is written. For example, "I agree to pay you $500 for painting my living room."

summary adjudication A court order ruling that certain factual issues are already determined prior to trial, based on a motion by one of the parties, supported by evidence, contending that these issues are settled and need not be tried. For example, in a car accident case there might be overwhelming and uncontradicted evidence of the defendant's carelessness, but conflicting evidence as to the extent of the plaintiff's injuries. The plaintiff might ask for summary adjudication on the issue of carelessness, but go to trial on the question of injuries. If there is any question as to whether there is conflict on the facts on an issue, the summary adjudication must be denied regarding that matter.

summary judgment A final decision by a judge, upon a party's motion, that resolves a lawsuit before there is a trial. The party making the motion marshals all the evidence in its favor, compares it to the other side's evidence, and argues that there are no "triable issues of fact." Summary judgment is awarded if the undisputed facts and the law make it clear that it would be impossible for the opposing party to prevail if the matter were to proceed to trial.

summary probate A relatively simple probate proceeding available for "small estates," as that term is defined by state law. Every state's definition is different, and many are complicated, but a few states include estates worth $100,000 or more. Some states allow summary probate whenever the value of property in the estate doesn't exceed what is needed to pay a family allowance and certain creditors.

summation The final argument of an attorney at the close of a trial in which he or she attempts to convince the judge or jury of the virtues of the client's case. (See also: closing argument)

Jimmy Carter is the only U.S. President who served a single full four-year term and never had the opportunity to appoint a Supreme Court justice.

summons A form prepared by the plaintiff and issued by a court that informs the defendant that he or she has been sued. The summons requires that the defendant file a response with the court—or in many small claims courts, simply appear in person on an appointed day—within a given time period or risk losing the case under the terms of a default judgment.

sunset law A law that automatically terminates the agency or program it establishes unless the legislature expressly renews it. For example, a state law creating and funding a new drug rehabilitation program within state prisons may provide that the program will shut down in two years unless it is reviewed and approved by the state legislature.

sunshine laws Statutes that provide public access to government agency meetings and records.

superior court The main county trial court in many states, mostly in the West. (See also: state court)

supernumerary witness A witness beyond the required number of witnesses. For example, the third witness where only two are needed to witness the signing of a will.

supersedeas (soo-per-**seed**-es) Latin for "you shall desist," an order (writ) by an appeals court commanding a lower court not to enforce or proceed with a judgment or sentence pending the decision on the appeal or until further order of the appeals court.

superseding cause See: intervening cause

supervening cause See: intervening cause

supplemental Completing or making an addition to, particularly to a document—for example, a supplemental complaint, supplemental claim, or supplemental proceeding.

supplemental needs trust See: special needs trust

Supplemental Register A secondary list of trademarks and service marks maintained by the U.S. Patent and Trademark Office. The Supplemental Register provides limited trademark rights and benefits and consists of marks that do not qualify for the Principal Register, usually because they are nondistinctive and consumers do not associate these terms with a specific source. (In trademark terminology, they lack secondary meaning.) Descriptive marks, surnames, and marks consisting primarily of geographical terms are commonly placed on the Supplemental Register. (See also: secondary meaning, Principal Register)

suppression of evidence 1) A judge's order that certain evidence may not be admitted at trial because it was obtained illegally, such as an involuntary confession or drugs discovered in an illegal search. 2) For a prosecutor in a criminal case to improperly hide or withhold evidence that he or she is legally required to provide to the defense.

supra (**soo**-prah) Latin for "above." In legal briefs and decisions, it is used to refer the reader to an earlier cited authority.

supremacy clause Provision under Article IV, Section 2 of the U.S. Constitution, providing that federal law is superior to and overrides state law when they conflict.

Supreme Court America's highest court, which has the final power to decide cases based on federal statutes or the U.S. Constitution, cases in which the U.S. government is a party, or in certain lawsuits between parties in different states. The U.S. Supreme Court has nine justices—one of whom is the Chief Justice—who are appointed for life by the president and must be confirmed by the U.S. senate. Most states also have a supreme court, which is the final arbiter of the state's constitution and state laws. However, in several states, the highest state court uses a different name.

surcharge An additional charge of money made because it was omitted in the original calculation or as a penalty, such as for paying a bill late.

surety A person who agrees to be responsible for another's debt or obligation, such as a bonding company that posts a bond for a building contractor. Unlike a guarantor (who is liable to creditors only if the debtor fails to perform) a surety is directly liable.

surplusage Language in a legal document that is irrelevant or has no legal effect and therefore can be ignored.

surrebuttal In written or oral legal argument, the moving party's response to the responding party's rebuttal to the initial argument.

surrender value The amount of money an insurance policyholder would get from selling the policy back to the insurance company Only some kinds of life insurance policies, such as whole life policies, have a surrender value. Term life insurance has no surrender value. (See also: avails)

surrogate 1) A person acting on behalf of another or a substitute, including a woman who gives birth to a baby of a mother who is unable to carry the child. 2) A judge in some states responsible only for probates, estates, and adoptions.

surrogate court See: probate court

surveillance The act of observing persons or groups either with notice or their knowledge (overt surveillance) or without their knowledge (covert surveillance). Intrusive surveillance by private citizens may give rise to claims of invasion of privacy. Police officers, as long as they are in a place they have a right to be, can use virtually any type of surveillance device to observe property. Police cannot use specialized heat-scanning surveillance devices to obtain evidence of criminal activity inside a home. Law enforcement officials acquired additional surveillance capability following enactment of The Patriot Act.

surviving spouse A widow or widower.

surviving spouse's trust When a couple creates a bypass (AB) trust, the revocable trust of the surviving spouse after one spouse has died.

survivor A person who outlives another. The term is often used in wills and trust documents. For example a will might leave property "to my sons, Arnold and Zeke, or the survivor." If only one son is alive at the time the property is distributed, it would all go to him.

survivors benefits An amount of money available to a deceased worker's surviving spouse and minor or disabled children, if the deceased worker qualified for Social Security retirement or disability benefits.

survivorship See: right of survivorship

suspect classification In constitutional law, a group that meets certain qualifications that make the group likely subjects of discrimination. Suspect classifications include those based on race, national origin, and alienage.

suspended sentence A criminal sentence that is not enforced unless the defendant fails to meet conditions imposed by the judge (such as a requirement to make restitution to victims or perform certain services) or commits another crime.

suspension of deportation An immigration remedy that is no longer available (with rare exceptions), it allowed undocumented immigrants placed into deportation proceedings to request permanent resident status on the basis of 1) continuous physical presence in the United States for at least seven years; 2) good moral character during this period; and 3) that the applicant's departure from the U.S. would cause "extreme hardship" to the applicant or any qualifying U.S. citizen or lawful permanent resident relatives, including spouse, parents, or children. The nearest remedy available now is called "cancellation of removal."

sustain To agree with or rule in favor of a party in court. For example, if a judge agrees with an attorney's objection to a question at trial, the judge will say "objection sustained."

swear 1) To declare under oath that one will tell the truth, (sometimes "the truth, the whole truth, and nothing but the truth"). Failure to tell the truth, and to do so knowingly, is the crime of perjury. 2) To administer an oath to a witness that he or she will tell the truth, which is done by a notary public, a court clerk, a court reporter, or anyone authorized by law to administer oaths. 3) To install into office by administering an oath.

swearing match A case that turns on the word of one witness versus another. The outcome of a swearing match usually depends on whom the jury finds most trustworthy.

sweat equity An ownership interest in property that results from the hard labor a person puts into improving it. For example, Jenny gave her brother James a share of her new business in exchange for the hundreds of hours he worked to help her start it up.

swift witness See: zealous witness

swindle To cheat through trick, device, false statements, or other fraudulent methods with the intent to acquire money or property from another to which the swindler is not entitled. (See also: fraud, theft)

syndicate A joint venture among individuals or corporations to accomplish a particular business goal, such as the purchase, development, and sale of real estate, followed by division of the profits. A syndicate is similar to a partnership, but it has a specific objective or purpose after the completion of which it will dissolve.

T

tainted evidence In a criminal trial, information that was obtained by illegal means, including evidence that would not have been discovered but for an illegal search or seizure. This evidence is called "the fruit of the poisonous tree," and is usually not admissible in court.

take To gain or obtain possession. For example, when beneficiary is named in a will to receive a gift, that person takes the gift under the will. In criminal law, stealing is an unlawful taking.

taking See: eminent domain

taking against the will The choice of a surviving spouse to not accept whatever was left to him or her in the deceased spouse's will and to instead claim the share of the estate that is allowed by state law. (See also: elective share)

taking the Fifth A popular phrase that refers to a witness's refusal to testify on the ground that the testimony might incriminate the witness in a crime. The principle is based on the Fifth Amendment to the U.S. Constitution, which provides that "No person … shall be compelled to be a witness against himself," and is applied to state courts by the Fourteenth Amendment. (See also: self-incrimination)

tangible employment action An actual change that has an actual adverse effect on the job or working conditions, such as a firing, demotion, or suspension. When an employee claims to have been discriminated against or harassed by a supervisor, a tangible employment action supports the employee's case (and may be required to be proved).

tangible personal property Personal property that can be felt or touched. Examples include furniture, cars, jewelry, and artwork. In contrast, cash and checking accounts are not tangible personal property. The law is unsettled as to whether computer data is tangible personal property. (Compare: intangible property)

target witness A witness whom the grand jury seeks to indict, or a witness who has specific information sought by the grand jury.

tax A governmental assessment upon property value, transactions (transfers and sales), licenses granting a right, and income. A tax levied directly on income or property is a direct tax. A tax levied on the price of goods or services is an indirect tax. The government uses tax revenues to finance public services and goods, such as building highways and schools.

taxable income An individual's or business's gross income minus all allowable deductions, adjustments, and exemptions.

tax attorney A lawyer who specializes in taxes and has a special degree in tax law or certification from a state bar association.

tax auditor An IRS employee who analyzes tax returns for correctness.

tax basis See: basis

tax bracket The percentage rate at which an individual's or business's last dollar of income is taxed. In a graduated tax system like that of the United States, this rate is the highest rate the person or business pays, because the the first dollars of income are taxed at a lower rate than subsequent dollars. For example, the first $20,000 of annual income might be taxed at 15%, and the next $40,000 at 18%. Also called marginal tax rate.

tax costs A motion to contest a claim for court costs submitted by a prevailing party in a lawsuit. It is called a "Motion to Tax Costs" and asks the judge to deny or reduce claimed costs.

tax court A federal court which hears taxpayers' appeals from decisions of the Internal Revenue Service. Tax courts hear taxpayer appeals "de novo" (as a trial rather than an appeal), and taxpayers do not have to pay the amount claimed by the IRS before their case is heard by the tax court. Tax court decisions may be appealed to the Federal District Court of Appeals.

tax deduction See: deduction

tax-deferred exchange See: 1031 exchange

tax evasion The intentional and fraudulent attempt to escape payment of taxes in whole or in part. If proved to be intentional and not just an error or difference of opinion, tax evasion can be a federal crime. Evasion is distinguished from attempts to use interpretation of tax laws or imaginative accounting to reduce the amount of payable tax.

tax examiner See: tax auditor

tax-exempt income Income that is specifically made exempt from taxation by Congress, such as certain Social Security benefits, tax-exempt interest, welfare benefits, nontaxable life insurance proceeds, and nontaxable pension income.

tax fraud A willful act done with the intent to cheat in the assessment or payment of any tax liability. Examples include keeping two sets of books or using a false Social Secutiry number.

tax lien notice An IRS announcement of a tax debt recorded at a government record's office in the county where the debtor resides or the business is located.

tax loss carryover See: carryover

taxpayer bill of rights Federal tax laws that restrict IRS conduct and establish taxpayer rights in dealing with the IRS.

taxpayer identification number (TIN) A number assigned by the IRS or the SSA to be used for tax administration. Taxpayer identification numbers include Social Security numbers, employer identification numbers, and individual taxpayer identification numbers.

tax registration certificate See: business license

tax return The form taxpayers must file with the taxing authority which details the taxpayer's income, expenses, exemptions, deductions, and calculation of taxes.

tax sale An auction sale of a taxpayer's property conducted by the federal government to collect unpaid taxes.

tax withholding See: withholding

temporary injunction See: preliminary injunction

temporary insanity In a criminal case, a defense by the accused that he or she was briefly insane at the time the crime was committed and therefore was incapable of knowing the nature of the alleged criminal act.

 "The income tax has made more liars out of the American people than golf has."

—Will Rogers

Temporary Protected Status (TPS) The U.S. government may grant Temporary Protected Status (TPS) to persons already in the United States who came from certain countries experiencing conditions of war or natural disasters. TPS allows a person to live and work in the United States for a specific time period, but it does not lead to U.S. permanent residence (a green card).

temporary restraining order (TRO) An order that tells one person to stop harassing or harming another, issued after the person being harassed appears before a judge or submits appropriate paperwork. A few days or weeks after the TRO is issued, the court holds a second hearing where the person being restrained can argue to the judge and the court can decide whether to make the TRO permanent by issuing an injunction. In domestic violence situations, the police tend to be more willing to intervene if there's a TRO in place and the abused spouse can show the other spouse is violating it.

tenancy The right to occupy real property for a specific term, such as under a one-year lease, for a series of periods until cancelled, (such as month-to-month rental agreement), or at will (which may be terminated at any time).

tenancy at sufferance A description of the nature of the tenancy that is created after a lease has expired, but before the landlord has demanded that the tenant quit (vacate) the premises. During a tenancy at sufferance the tenant is bound by the terms of the lease (including payment of rent) that existed before it expired. Also known as a "holdover tenancy."

tenancy at will A tenancy that is created when the landlord allows the tenant to occupy the premises, but no formal terms of the tenancy exist. A tenancy at will may be terminated by proper notice from either landlord or tenant.

tenancy by the entireties See: tenancy by the entirety

tenancy by the entirety A special kind of ownership that's similar to joint tenancy but is only for married couples and, in a few states, same-sex couples who have registered with the state. It is available in about half the states. Both spouses have the right to enjoy the entire property. Neither one can unilaterally end the tenancy, and creditors of one spouse cannot force a sale of the property to collect on a debt. When one dies, the survivor automatically gets title to the entire property without a probate court proceeding. Also called "tenancy by the entireties." (Compare: joint tenancy)

tenancy in common A way two or more people can own property together, in unequal shares. Each has an undivided interest in the property, an equal right to use the property, and the right to leave his or her interest upon death to chosen beneficiaries instead of to the other owners (as is required with joint tenancy). In some states, two people are presumed to own property as tenants in common unless they've agreed otherwise in writing.

tenant 1) Anyone, including a corporation, who occupies or possesses land by right or title. 2) A person or corporation who rents real property, with or without a house or structure, from the owner landlord.

tenants in common See: tenancy in common

tender 1) To present to another person an unconditional offer to enter into a contract; a request for bids. 2) To present payment to another.

Hoagy Carmichael, songwriter, singer and actor, who wrote "Stardust" and other popular songs, was a lawyer.

tender back rule A legal principle requiring a party who seeks to invalidate a contract to return whatever that party received under the contract's terms. For example, a former employee who receives a severance package in exchange for agreeing not to sue a former employer for wrongful termination must tender back the money if he or she decides to sue and claim that the release is invalid. There is an exception to the tender back rule for age discrimination claims brought under the Age Discrimination in Employment Act: Those suing for age discrimination despite having signed a release do not have to tender back the money they received for signing (although they may have to reimburse the employer for that money if they win the lawsuit).

tender offer A public offer to purchase stock at a specified price per share, usually done to gain a controlling interest in a corporation.

tenement 1) A term found in older deeds or in antiquated deed language, referring to any structure on real property. 2) Old run-down urban apartment buildings with several floors reached by stairways.

tentative trust See: Totten trust

1031 exchange A method of selling business or investment property but deferring payment of capital gains taxes by reinvesting the proceeds of the sale in another business or investment property.

tenure 1) The right to occupy or hold property, sometimes only for a set period of time. 2) The right to hold a position indefinitely, absent serious misconduct or inability to perform the duties of the position. For example, federal judges have lifetime tenure, and professors who are granted tenure generally have indefinite job security. 3) The length of time for which a person has held a particular position. For example, "During my tenure on the Board of Directors, the company has doubled in size."

term 1) In contracts or leases, a period of time, such as one year, in which a contract or lease will be in force. 2) In contracts or leases, a specified condition, often also called a clause, such as a provision that prohibits tenants from keeping pets. 3) A period of time for which a court sits or a legislature will be in session.

term life insurance No-frills life insurance, with neither cash surrender value nor loan value (an amount that can be used as collateral for a loan). Term life insurance provides a pre-set amount of coverage if the policyholder dies during the period of time specified in the policy. Policyholders usually have the option to renew at the end of the term for the period of years specified in the policy. Unlike whole life insurance, premiums generally increase as the insured person gets older and the risk of death increases.

terrorem clause See: no-contest clause

testacy The condition of dying with a valid will. (Compare: intestacy)

testamentary Pertaining to a will.

testamentary capacity The mental competency to execute a will at the time the will was signed and witnessed. Generally, the will maker must understand nature of making a will, have a general idea of what he or she possesses, and know who his beneficiaries are.

testamentary disposition Leaving property at one's death, most often though a will. The person making the disposition retains ownership of the property until his or her death, at which time the property is transferred to the beneficiary.

testamentary trust A trust created by a will, effective only upon the death of the will maker. (Compare: living trust)

testate The circumstance of dying after making a valid will. A person who dies with a will is said to have died testate. (Compare: intestate)

testate succession Distribution of rights and property through a will. (Compare: intestate succession)

testator Someone who makes a will.

testatrix A female will maker. However, modernly, the word testator is used for both men and women.

testify To provide oral evidence under oath at a trial or at a deposition.

testimony Evidence given under oath by a witness either at trial or in an affidavit or deposition.

TFRP See: trust fund recovery penalty

theft The generic term for all crimes in which a person intentionally takes personal property of another without permission or consent and with the intent to convert it to the taker's use (including potential sale). In many states, when the value of the property taken is low (for example, less than $500) the crime is "petty theft" and a misdemeanor; but it is "grand theft" and a felony for larger amounts. Theft is synonymous with "larceny." Although robbery (taking by force), burglary (taking after entering unlawfully), and embezzlement (stealing from an employer) are all commonly thought of as theft, they are distinguished by the means and methods used, and are separately designated as specific types of crimes in criminal charges and statutory punishments. (See also: larceny, robbery, burglary, embezzlement)

third degree instruction See: dynamite charge

third party A person who is not a party to a contract or a transaction, but who has an involvement. The third party normally has no legal rights in the matter, unless the contract was made specifically for the third party's benefit. (See also: third-party beneficiary)

third-party beneficiary A person who is not a party to a contract, but has legal rights to enforce the contract or share in proceeds because the contract was specifically intended for that person's benefit. For example, a grandparent contracts to buy a car for a grandchild. If the seller refuses to go through with the deal after receiving payment, the grandchild may sue, even though not a party to the contract. (Compare: incidental beneficiary)

third-party trust A special needs trust funded exclusively with property given by people other than the beneficiary. (Compare: self-settled trust)

30-day notice In a month-to-month tenancy or tenancy at will, the notice from a landlord to a tenant to leave the premises within 30 days; or the notice by a landlord advising of a change in tenancy terms (such as a rent increase) that will take effect in 30 days; or the notice from a tenant to a landlord that the tenant intends to leave in 30 days. The landlord's notice does not need to state a reason for the landlord's action, although it must typically meet specific state (and sometimes rent control) rules as to preparing and serving notice. The landlord's service of the notice and the tenant's failure to vacate at the end of 30 days provides the basis for a lawsuit for an unlawful detainer or eviction lawsuit and a court judgment ordering the tenant to leave.

three-day notice A notice from a landlord to a tenant to pay delinquent rent within three days or quit (leave or vacate) the premises. State laws typically set specific rules for preparing and serving three-day notices. A landlord may file an eviction lawsuit for unpaid rent against a tenant who fails to pay or vacate within three days. While the three-day notice period is common, it does not apply in all states or in all circumstances, such as property covered by local rent control ordinances.

341 meeting See: meeting of creditors

341 notice A notice sent to the debtor and creditors in a bankruptcy case, which announces the date, time, and location of the first meeting of creditors. The 341 notice is sent along with the notice of bankruptcy filing and information about important deadlines by which creditors have to take certain actions to preserve their rights in the case.

342 notice A notice the court clerk is required to give debtors in a bankruptcy case, pursuant to Section 342 of the Bankruptcy Code, to inform them of their obligations and the consequences of not being completely honest in their bankruptcy case.

three-of-five test A rebuttable IRS presumption that a business venture that does not make a profit in three out of five consecutive years of operation is a hobby and not a business for tax purposes. Not meeting this test has significant tax consequences because businesses can take advantage of many tax benefits and advantages that hobbies do not get.

three strikes A state statute requiring a harsher sentence, especially life imprisonment, for a repeat offender's third felony conviction.

tidelands 1) Land between the high and low tides that is uncovered each day by tidal action. It belongs to the owner of the land that fronts on the sea at that point. 2) Land that is submerged below the low-tide point of the sea but is still the territory of a state or nation.

"The constitution is what the judges say it is."

—Chief Justice Charles Evans Hughes (before he was appointed to the Supreme Court)

TILA See: Truth in Lending Act

time is of the essence A phrase often used in contracts to emphasize that any delays will be grounds for termination.

timely Within the time required by statute, court rules, or contract. For example, if a notice of appeal must be filed within 60 days of the entry of judgment, a notice filed on the 61st day would not be timely.

time served At the time a criminal defendant is sentenced, the amount of time the defendant has already spent in jail awaiting trial or a plea of guilty. When a judge sentences a defendant to "time served," the sentence is the same as the time the defendant has spent in jail, and the defendant is set free.

title Ownership of real estate or personal property. With real estate, title is evidenced by a deed (or sometimes, another document) recorded in the county land records office.

Title VII A federal law (Title VII of the Civil Rights Act of 1964) that prohibits employment discrimination based on race, color, religion, sex (including pregnancy), national origin, and genetic information.

Title X The name of a federal law ("Title Ten," the Residential Lead-Based Paint Hazard Reduction Act) passed in 1992, aimed at helping residential landlords evaluate the risk of lead poisoning in each housing situation. Among other things, Title X requires landlords to disclose the presence of known lead paint hazards to prospective and current tenants, to give them an informational booklet, and to warn again if renovations will disturb lead paint. Home sellers must also disclose known hazards. (See also: lead based hazard)

title abstract See: abstract of title

title company A company that performs title searches and issues title insurance when real estate is sold. (See also: escrow)

title insurance Insurance issued by a title insurance company that protects a property buyer against loss if it is later discovered that title is imperfect—that is, that someone else has a claim to the property or that the description on the deed is erroneous. (See also: title search)

title report The written analysis of a real estate title search, including a property description, names of titleholders and how title is held (joint tenancy, for example), tax rate, encumbrances (mortgages, liens, deeds of trust, recorded judgments), and real estate taxes due. A title report is needed before a lender will agree to finance purchase of the property. A title report is prepared by a title company, an abstracter, an attorney, or an escrow company, depending on local practice.

title search A search of the local public land records, usually made by a title insurance company before a purchase of a parcel of real estate, to see whether the current owner of the real estate actually has good title to the land. The search should turn up any easements, mortgages, tax liens, or other liens on the property. If the title search reveals a problem ("cloud on the title"), such as a break in the chain of title, inaccurate property description in a previous deed, or some old secured loan which has not been released, the problem will have to be cleared up before the sale can go through. (See also: chain of title, title insurance, title report)

TOD Abbreviation for "transfer on death."

TOD deed See: transfer-on-death deed

toll 1) To stop or suspend the operation of a statute. Most often, this term is used in reference to statutes of limitations, which set the time limits for bringing a lawsuit or criminal prosecution on particular types of legal claims. For example, the statute of limitations for filing a lawsuit may be tolled if the plaintiff didn't realize he or she had been injured by the defendant's actions until after the time period to sue had run out. 2) A fee charged to use something, such as a bridge, turnpike, or ferry.

tontine An agreement in which investors receive annuity payments, with the special provision that when one participant dies, his or her share goes to the others (increasing the payments to the survivors). Generally, the last to die receives the remaining funds. They are illegal in the United States.

tools of the trade The items a person needs to pursue his or her occupation. Many state laws provide that tools of the trade are exempt property—that is, they may not be seized by creditors or by the trustee in a bankruptcy case—

either entirely or up to a certain dollar amount. (See also: exempt property)

tort An injury to one person for which the person who caused the injury is legally responsible. A tort can be intentional—for example, an angry punch in the nose—but is far more likely to result from carelessness (called "negligence"), such as riding your bicycle on the sidewalk and colliding with a pedestrian. While the injury that forms the basis of a tort is usually physical, this is not a requirement—libel, slander, and the "intentional infliction of mental distress" are on a good-sized list of torts not based on a physical injury. A tort is a civil wrong, as opposed to a criminal wrong. (Compare: crime)

tort claims act A federal or state law that waives the government's sovereign immunity under certain conditions, allowing lawsuits by people who claim they have been harmed by negligent or intentional torts (wrongful acts) by a government agency or its employees. Before the enactment of tort claims acts, governmental bodies could not be sued without the specific permission of the government. The federal version is the Federal Tort Claims Act.

tortfeasor A person who commits a tort (civil wrong), either intentionally or through negligence.

tortious Constituting a tort (civil wrong), referring to an act that is a tort.

tortious interference Causing harm by intentionally 1) disrupting a contractual relationship, for example by preventing one party from delivering goods on time, or 2) harming a business relationship or activity, for example, by spreading lies about a competitor to one of its clients.

> "I cannot agree that it should be the declared public policy of Illinois that a cat visiting a neighbor's yard or crossing the highway is a public nuisance."
>
> —Adlai E. Stevenson, vetoing a bill requiring that cats be restrained from leaving their owners' property.

Totten trust A bank account that's held in trust for a beneficiary, who inherits any money in the account when the account holder dies. Probate proceedings are not necessary to transfer the money. A Totten trust works just like a payable-on-death bank account.

to wit A term that means "that is to say" or "namely." Example: "The passengers in the vehicle, to wit: Arlene Jones, Betty Bumgartner, and Sherry Younger, were uninjured."

toxic mold A popular phrase often used incorrectly to refer to any mold that appears in a residence or workplace. Some molds produce toxins (a substance that prevents other molds from growing nearby), and some people are sensitive to them, but the majority of molds are merely unsightly and destructive to property and do not cause health problems.

toxic tort A personal injury caused by exposure to a toxic substance, such as asbestos or hazardous waste. Victims can sue for medical expenses, lost wages, and pain and suffering.

trade dress Various design elements used to promote a product or service. For example, trade dress includes the unique shape of a bottle, the color of a pill, or the decorative elements within a chain restaurant. Trade dress can be protected under trademark law if it is distinctive and a showing can be made that the average consumer would likely be confused as to product origin if another product had a similar appearance.

trade fixture A piece of equipment placed on or attached to commercial real estate, which is used in the tenant's trade or business. Trade fixtures differ from other fixtures in that they may be removed from the real estate (even if attached) at the end of the tenancy, while ordinary fixtures attached to the real estate become part of it.

trademark A word, phrase, logo, graphic symbol, or other device that is used to identify the source of a product or service and to distinguish it from competitors. Some examples of trademarks are Ford (cars and trucks), Betty Crocker (food products), and Microsoft (software). For all practical purposes, a service mark is the same as a trademark—except that trademarks promote products while service marks promote services. Some familiar service marks include McDonald's (food services), FedEx (delivery services), and Fidelity (financial services).

trademark owner The person or entity who retains legal control over all (or some) of the rights granted under trademark law, usually the first business to use a distinctive trademark on goods or services in commerce. Federal registration is not a prerequisite of trademark ownership but it offers the trademark owner certain benefits. (See also: trademark registration)

trademark registration A grant by a state or the federal government indicating that a trademark has met certain statutory requirements. Federal trademark registration makes it easier for the owner to protect against would-be copiers and puts the rest of the country on notice that the mark is already taken. Registration will not occur until a mark has been used in commerce.

trademark search An investigation to discover any potential conflicts between a proposed trademark and existing ones, and preferably done before a new trademark is used in commerce. A trademark search reduces the possibility of inadvertently infringing a mark belonging to someone else. A business can conduct a preliminary search using the U.S. Patent and Trademark Office's online trademark database. The most thorough trademark searches are accomplished by professional search firms.

trade name The formal or official name of a business—that is, the name the business uses on its letterhead and bank account. A trade name may serve as a company's trademark if it is used to market the company's goods or services. For example, "Dell" is the trade name for Dell, Inc. It is also a trademark used by the company for personal computers, servers, software, and certain computer-related services. (Compare: trademark)

trade secret Any formula, pattern, device, or compilation of information that is used in business, that is not generally known, and that gives the owner an opportunity to obtain an advantage over competitors who do not know it. A trade secret must also be the subject of efforts that are reasonable under the circumstances to maintain its secrecy.

transaction An event associated with the transfer of an amount of money (debit or credit) in the operation of a business.

transcript The official written record of all proceedings in a trial, hearing, or deposition, taken down by the court reporter. In most appeals a copy of the trial transcript is required so that the court of appeals can review the entire proceedings in the trial court.

transfer To move ownership or possession of an asset (or an interest in an asset) from one party to another. The term encompasses all methods for disposing of an asset, including by gift, sale, release, lease, and so on.

transfer agent The person or company that handles the paperwork when shares of a corporation's stock are transferred to a new owner.

transfer in contemplation of death A gift made by a person who believes that he or she will soon die. Also called gift causa mortis. Recovery of health may void the gift.

transfer-on-death (TOD) Refers to the right to name a beneficiary in a document of title which allows the beneficiary to receive the property quickly, outside of probate. In most states, securities can be registered in TOD form. In some states, you can register vehicles in this way or create transfer-on-death deeds for real estate.

transfer-on-death deed A real estate deed that takes effect at death and allows a property owner to leave property in a way that avoids probate court proceedings after death. It is allowed in only some states. Sometimes called a beneficiary deed.

transferred intent Intent to commit a criminal or civil wrong against one person that instead harms a different person. In this situation, the intent necessary to convict or find the wrongdoer liable transfers from the intended act to the committed act. For example, someone who intends to shoot and kill one person, but misses and kills a bystander may be convicted of murder; the perpetrator had the necessary criminal intent even though he or she didn't intend to kill the bystander.

transgender The state of a person's gender identity (self-identification as male or female) not matching their assigned sex at birth. (See also: transsexual)

transsexual A person who identifies with a sex different from the physical or genetic sex with which the person was born. Often, transsexuals undergo surgery to bring their physical sex into conformity with their experienced gender identity.

treason The crime of betraying one's country. Treason requires overt acts and includes attempts to make war against the state, sharing govenment secrets with other countries, espionage, or materially supporting the enemies of one's country.

treasury bill A promissory note issued in multiples of $10,000 by the U.S. Treasury with a maturity date of not more than one year. (See also: treasury bond, treasury note)

treasury bond A long-term bond issued by the U.S. Treasury. (See also: treasury bill, treasury note)

treasury note A promissory note issued by the U.S. Treasury for a period of one to five years. (See also: treasury bill, treasury bond)

treasury stock Stock of a private corporation that was issued and then bought back or otherwise reacquired by the corporation.

treatise A legal reference book, usually covering an entire legal subject.

treaty A pact between nations that, if entered into by the United States through its Executive Branch, must be approved by two-thirds of the Senate under Article II, Section 2 of the Constitution. Presidents sometimes get around this requirement by entering into "Executive Agreements" with leaders of other countries; these are mutual understandings rather than enforceable treaties.

Judgment at Nuremberg. (1961) Nazi war crimes trial with an Academy Award winning screenplay. The star-studded cast includes Spencer Tracy, Burt Lancaster, Maximilian Schell (who also won an Oscar), Marlene Dietrich, Judy Garland, Richard Widmark, and Montgomery Clift.

treble damages Tripling the amount of actual damages to be paid to a prevailing party in a lawsuit. Treble damages are sometimes provided by law in order to punish intentional or willful behavior of the losing party.

trespass The act of entering someone's property without permission or authority. (Although it usually refers to real estate, trespass can apply to personal property as well.) Trespassing can be a tort (a civil wrong, which the property owner can sue over) and can be a crime if it's done willfully. Examples of trespass include erecting a fence on another's property or dumping debris on another's real estate.

trial The examination of facts and law presided over by a judge, magistrate, or other person with authority to hear the matter (such as a lawyer appointed to hear the case). Trials begin with the selection of a jury (unless the case will be heard without one), followed by opening statements by each side if they choose to give them. (The defense may also give an opening statement just before it presents its case.) The plaintiff (in a civil case) or the prosecution (in a criminal case) presents its side, then the defense puts on its case. Sometimes the plaintiff or prosecution presents more evidence, called rebuttal evidence, as does the defense. Following closing arguments, the jury (if there is one) is instructed by the judge on the law they must apply when deciding whether the plaintiff or prosecution adequately proved their case. The trial ends when the jury reaches a verdict, or when they fail to do so and the judge declares a mistrial.

trial court The court that has original jurisdiction and holds the original trial where all the evidence is first received and considered. (Compare: appellate court)

trial de novo A trial held on appeal, in which the appeals court holds a trial as if no prior trial had been held, considering the evidence anew rather than reviewing the lower court's decision for correctness. A trial de novo is common on appeals from small claims court judgments.

tribunal Any court, judicial body, or board which has judicial or quasi-judicial functions (such as a public utilities board that sets rates or a planning commission that can allow variances from zoning regulations).

trier of fact The jury responsible for deciding factual issues in a trial, if there is a jury. If there is no jury the judge is the trier of fact as well as the trier of the law. In administrative hearings, an administrative law judge, a board, commission, or referee may be the trier of fact.

triple net lease See: net lease

TRO See: temporary restraining order

true bill The name for the decision by a grand jury that the evidence presented to it, contained in the prosecutor's indictment, justifies charging the defendant with a crime. This decision results in the indictment being sent to the trial court. (See also: grand jury, indictment)

trust An arrangement under which one person, a trustee, manages property for a beneficiary. The person who creates the trust is called the settlor, trustor, or grantor. There are many kinds of trusts, some created during the settlor's lifetime and some at death. Trusts are used for, among other things, avoiding probate court proceedings, saving on estate tax, providing quality management of assets, and keeping money out of the hands of spendthrift beneficiaries. (See also: living trust, testamentary trust)

trust administration The trustee's management of trust property according to the trust's terms and for the benefit of the beneficiaries.

trust corpus Latin for "the body" of the trust. This term refers to all the property transferred to a trust. For example, if a trust is established (funded) with $250,000, that money is the corpus. Also called the trust res.

trust declaration See: declaration of trust

trust deed The most common instrument of financing real estate purchases in California and some other states (most states use mortgages). The trust deed transfers the title to the property to a trustee—often a title company—who holds it as security for a loan. When the loan is paid off, the title is transferred (reconveyed) to the borrower. The trustee will not become involved in the arrangement unless the borrower defaults on the loan. At that point, the trustee can generally sell the property in a nonjudicial foreclosure and pay the lender from the proceeds.

trustee The person (or business) who manages assets held in trust, under the terms of the trust document. A trustee's purpose is to invest trust assets and distribute trust income or principal to beneficiaries as directed in the trust document. With a simple probate-avoidance living trust, the person who creates the trust is also the original trustee. (See also: successor trustee)

trustee in bankruptcy See: bankruptcy trustee

trustee powers The provisions in a trust document defining what the trustee may and may not do.

trust fund The principal, or corpus, of a trust.

trust fund recovery penalty (TFRP) A penalty from the IRS for not paying "trust fund" taxes, which are taxes a company withholds from an employee's paycheck, including Social Security and Medicare taxes and federal income (withholding) taxes. This penalty can be assessed against any owner, officer, or company employee whose job is related to accounts payable, payroll, or the financial operations of the business.

trust fund taxes Taxes a company withholds from an employee's paycheck, including Social Security and Medicare taxes and federal income (withholding) taxes. A trust fund recovery penalty can be assessed when a business doesn't pay these taxes to the Internal Revenue Service.

trust instrument See: declaration of trust

trust merger Under a trust, the situation that occurs when the sole trustee and the sole beneficiary are the same person or institution. Then, there's no longer the separation between the trustee's legal ownership of trust property from the beneficiary's interest. The trust "merges" and ceases to exist.

trustor See: settlor

trust protector A person or company with the job of keeping an eye on a trustee and making sure the trust's purposes are fulfilled. The trust protector's powers, which are set out in the document that creates the trust, may include helping the trustee with legal, investment, and tax matters. The trust protector may also have authority to settle disputes among trustees or beneficiaries and may be able to appoint a new trustee if the original one isn't following the terms of the trust.

trust res See: trust corpus

Truth in Lending Act (TILA) A federal law that requires lenders to disclose the true cost of credit transactions by providing certain information to borrowers, including the terms of a loan, interest rates, and the number, amount, and due dates of all payments necessary to pay off the loan.

turncoat witness A witness who was expected to be a friendly witness, but who becomes a hostile witness during the course of the trial.

turn state's evidence The decision by a person charged with a crime, or suspected of a crime, to cooperate with the prosecution and testify against another participant in the criminal activity. In exchange for giving information or testifying, the person who has "turned" gets some sort of lenient treatment, such as a reduced charge, a plea bargain to a lesser charge, or a promise that the prosecution will recommend a light sentence.

"Twinkie" defense Slang for a claim by criminal defendants that at the time of the crime, they were suffering from a mental impairment (short of insanity) caused by intoxication, disease, or trauma, which prevented them from having the mental state required to hold them responsible for the crime. The phrase arose from the defense argued successfully by Dan White, charged with murdering San Francisco Mayor George Moscone and Supervisor Harvey Milk. White claimed that the sugar high resulting from eating "Twinkie" cupcakes made it impossible for him to form the intent necessary for a murder conviction. White was convicted of manslaughter instead of murder. (See also: manslaughter, insanity)

typosquatting The process of acquiring misspellings of a domain name in the hopes of catching and exploiting traffic intended for another website. For example, a typosquatter might purchase domain names such as www.lnadsend. com and www.landswnd.com and then demand money for referring customers under the Land's End affiliate program. Typosquatting is a variation of cybersquatting, an illegal practice in which a domain name is acquired in bad faith.

U

UBO Short for unincorporated business organization. (See: Massachusetts trust)

UCC See: uniform commercial code

UCC-1 Form See: UCC financing statement

UCC Financing Statement A standardized form that a lender files with a state agency (usually a Secretary of State) to secure an interest in personal property that the borrower used as collateral for a loan. Also called a UCC-1 Form.

UCCJEA See: Uniform Child Custody Jurisdiction and Enforcement Act

ultimate fact In a trial, a fact that is essential to the case.

ultrahazardous activity An action or process that is so inherently dangerous that there is strict liability for the person or entity conducting the activity. Examples: working with high explosives or conducting a professional auto race on public streets.

ultra vires (**uhl**-trah **vey**-rehz) Latin for "beyond powers." It refers to conduct by a corporation or its officers that exceeds the powers granted by law.

unbundled legal services The provision of legal services by an attorney who does not represent the client or take over the entire case, but performs specific services such as appearing at one hearing, preparing a legal brief, or negotiating a settlement after the client has prepared the case as a self-represented party. Most common in divorce cases.

unclean hands See: clean hands doctrine

unconscionability See: unconscionable

unconscionable When one party to a contract takes advantage of the other due to unequal bargaining positions, perhaps because of the disadvantaged party's recent trauma, physical infirmity, ignorance, inability to read, or inability to understand the language. A contract will be terminated as unconscionable if the unfairness is so severe that it is shocking to the average person.

unconstitutional In opposition to the constitution. Used to describe to a statute, governmental conduct, court decision, or private contract that violates one or more provisions of the constitution. Can be used in reference to the federal constitution or a state constitution.

uncontested divorce A divorce in which the parties are able to agree on how to divide their property and share custody of their children, and join together in filing the appropriate paperwork to have the divorce granted. (See also: default divorce)

undercapitalization A situation in which a company does not have enough cash available to carry on its business.

undersecured debt A debt secured by collateral that is worth less than the debtor owes. A $500,000 mortgage on a house worth $450,000 is undersecured, for example.

under the influence Phrase used to describe a person who is intoxicated, affected by the use of alcohol or drugs, or a combination of both. (See also: driving under the influence)

underwater Slang for a situation in which a homeowner owes more on the mortgage than the current value of the property.

underwrite 1) To agree to pay an obligation which may arise from an insurance policy. 2) To guarantee purchase of all shares of stock or bonds being issued by a corporation, including an agreement to purchase by the underwriter if the public does not buy all the shares or bonds. 3) To guarantee by investment in a business or project.

underwriter Another term for an insurer who assumes the risk of another's loss and compensates for the loss under the terms of an insurance policy.

 "Ignorance of the law excuses no man."
—John Selden

undisclosed principal A person whose identity is hidden either because an agent refuses to disclose the identity, or because the agent deliberately misleads third parties into believing that the agent *is* the principal. In either case, the third party does not know how to pursue the real principal in the event of a dispute.

undivided interest Ownership right to use and possess property that is shared by two or more co-owners. No individual co-owner has an exclusive right to any portion of the property. (See also: joint tenants, tenants in common, tenants by the entirety)

undocumented immigrant A foreign-born person who lacks a right to be in the United States, having either entered without inspection (and not subsequently obtained any right to remain) or stayed beyond the expiration date of a visa or other status.

undue burden In the field of reproductive rights, having the purpose or effect of placing a substantial obstacle in the path of a woman seeking an abortion of a fetus that is not yet viable. Laws that impose an undue burden on a fundamental right are unconstitutional under current Supreme Court cases.

undue hardship 1) An action to accommodate an employee or applicant with a disability that would require significant difficulty or expense when considered in light of factors such as an employer's size, financial resources, and the nature and structure of its operation. An employer need not provide an accommodation that would impose an undue hardship. (See: reasonable accommodation) 2) The circumstances in which a debtor may discharge a student loan in bankruptcy. For example, a debtor who has no income and little chance of earning enough in the future to pay off the loan may be able to show that repayment would be an undue hardship.

undue influence Improper influence over someone who is making financial decisions, commonly about making gifts, leaving property at death, or signing a contract. Typically, it occurs when the person is susceptible to pressure because of illness or emotional state, and is taken advantage of by someone he or she depends on for guidance—for example, a lawyer or family member. Undue influence is a ground for challenging the validity of a will or other document in court. (See also: will contest)

unearned income Income from investments, such as interest, dividends, or capital gains, or any other income that isn't compensation for services.

unemployment insurance (UI) A joint state and federal program that provides some wage replacement for up to 26 weeks to employees who have lost their jobs through no fault of their own. Most employees who are laid off or fired may collect unemployment, unless they were fired for willful misconduct.

unfair competition Any commercial behavior or activity that is legally unjust or deceptive. It includes such diverse activities as trademark infringement, false advertising, and theft of trade secrets but can include any illegal dirty tricks within the marketplace. If a court finds that an activity constitutes unfair competition, it will prevent that activity from occurring in the future and may award money damages to the person or company harmed by the activity.

unified estate and gift tax See: estate tax, gift tax

Uniform Anatomical Gift Act A uniform law adopted by every state that governs organ and body donations. It covers such matters as how anatomical gifts can be made and offers a suggested form for making donations. It also provides a list of relatives who can authorize organ donation in the absence of donation arrangements made before death. States are free to adopt the act as written or to modify it through the state's legislative process.

Uniform Child Custody Jurisdiction and Enforcement Act A law in every state that determines which court has jurisdiction over custody matters involving children—in other words, where a custody action can be brought if the children have lived in different places in the period just before the custody action begins.

Uniform Commercial Code A set of laws that govern commercial transactions (such as sales, warranties, negotiable instruments, loans secured by personal property, and other commercial matters) that has been adopted in some form in every state.

Uniform Gifts to Minors Act (UGMA) A uniform law, adopted by many states, that allows an adult to give money or securities to a child but have the assets managed by someone of the donor's choosing, called a custodian. The gift is made during the donor's lifetime, not at death. The custodianship ends, and the property goes to the beneficiary outright, at an age set by state law, usually 18 or 21. (Compare: Uniform Transfers to Minors Act)

uniform law A law written by legal scholars and adopted (often with modifications) by individual states.

Uniform Premarital Agreement Act A law crafted by national lawmakers to promote consistency in prenuptial agreements from state to state. The UPAA governs such matters as what a premarital agreement can include and what will render an agreement unenforceable. The UPAA has been adopted in some form by most states.

Uniform Principal and Interest Act A uniform statute, adopted by most states, that in its most recent version allows some trustees to make adjustments that were not formerly allowed. For example, a trustee could distribute principal to income beneficiaries if it were necessary to carry out the purpose of the trust.

Uniform Probate Code A standard comprehensive set of laws, adopted in whole or in part by various states, that regulate the administration of estates, including wills and trusts.

Uniform Prudent Investor Act A uniform statute that sets out guidelines for trustees to follow when investing trust assets.

Uniform Resource Locator (URL) The address of a specific location on the Web. URLs commonly contain a domain name and a description of the material sought. For example, http://www.nolo.com/patents.html is the URL for an article on patents on Nolo's website.

Uniform Simultaneous Death Act A standard set of laws, enacted by some U.S. states, to deal with inheritance in the case that two people die simultaneously. The Act says that if two (or more) people die within 120 hours of each other, each is considered to have predeceased the other unless a will or other document specifies otherwise.

Uniform Transfer-on-Death Securities Registration Act A statute that allows people to name a beneficiary to inherit stocks or bonds without probate. This is called registering the securities in beneficiary or transfer-on-death form. The owner of the securities can register them with a broker using a simple form that names a person to receive the property after the owner's death. Every state but Texas has adopted the statute.

Uniform Transfers to Minors Act (UTMA) A statute, adopted by almost all states, that provides a method for transferring property to minors and arranging for an adult to manage it until the child is old enough to receive it.

"The law embodies the story of a nation's development through many centuries, and it cannot be dealt with as if it contained only the axioms and corollaries of a book of numbers."

—Justice Oliver Wendell Holmes, Jr.

Uniformed Services Employment and Reemployment Rights Act (USERRA) A federal law that guarantees certain employment rights to employees who serve in the Army, Navy, Marine Corps, Air Force, Coast Guard, Reserves, Army or Air National Guard, or the Commissioned Corps of the Public Health Service. USERRA prohibits discrimination against these employees, requires employers to reinstate them to the position they would have held if not for serving in the military, requires employers to restore their benefits on return from military service, and prohibits employers from firing them, except for cause, for up to one year after they return from military service.

unilateral contract An agreement to pay in exchange for performance, if the potential performer chooses to act. An example would be if you promise to pay someone $1,000 if they bring your car from Cleveland to San Francisco. Bringing the car is acceptance (and performance) of the agreement. (Compare: bilateral contract)

unincorporated business organization (UBO) Any business that is not incorporated. (See: corporation)

uninsured motorist clause A clause in an automobile insurance policy that provides that if the owner or a passenger suffers any injury because of the actions of a driver of another vehicle who does not have liability insurance, the insurance company will pay its insured's actual damages.

union security agreement A contract between an employer and a union requiring workers to make certain payments (called "agency fees") to the union as a condition of getting or keeping a job. Although it is illegal to require an employee to join a union, workers may be required to instead pay agency fees if such an agreement is in place. Union security agreements are prohibited in right to work states.

union shop A business in which a majority of the workers have voted to name a union as their certified bargaining agent. Employers may hire nonunion workers, but these workers must join the union within a specified amount of time. (Compare: closed shop)

unissued stock A corporation's shares of stock which are authorized by its articles of incorporation, but have never been issued (sold) to anyone.

United States Attorney The prosecutor in charge of enforcing the federal criminal laws of the United States in a particular district. Each U.S. Attorney is responsible for enforcing certain federal civil statutes, such as the Civil Rights Act. U.S. Attorneys are appointed by the president and the job is considered a political plum. Typical cases brought by the U.S. Attorney and Assistant U.S. Attorneys are immigration violations, drug importation, securities fraud, and bank robberies. Any offense committed on federal property (such as a military base or national park) may be prosecuted by the U.S. Attorney.

United States Citizenship and Immigration Services (USCIS) A branch of the Department of Homeland Security (DHS). USCIS is primarily responsible for handling immigration benefits, such as applications for asylum, work permits, green cards, and citizenship.

United States Copyright Office See: Copyright Office

United States Patent and Trademark Office (USPTO) An administrative branch of the U.S. Department of Commerce charged with overseeing and implementing the federal laws on patents and trademarks. This includes examining, issuing, classifying, and maintaining records of all patents and trademarks issued by the United States.

***United Steelworkers of America v. Weber* (1979)** A U.S. Supreme Court case in which the Court ruled that the 1964 Civil Rights Act provisions for affirmative action programs to encourage minority hiring for jobs in which the minorities were previously underrepresented were constitutional.

universal life insurance A type of whole life insurance that offers some additional features and advantages. Like whole life insurance, universal life insurance accumulates cash value through investment of the premium payments. The unique feature of universal life insurance is that it has variable premiums, benefits, and payment schedules, all of which are tied to market interest rates and the performance of the investment portfolio. Also, universal life policies normally provide the insured with more consumer information. For example, an insured person is told how much of the policy payment goes for insurance company overhead expenses, reserves, and policy proceed payments, and how much is retained and invested for savings. This information isn't usually provided with whole life policies.

unjust enrichment A legal principle that if a person receives money or other property unfairly and at the expense of another—that is, by chance, mistake, or without any personal effort—the recipient should return the property to the rightful owner. In lawsuits based on unjust enrichment, courts can order that the property be returned (referred to as making restitution).

unlawful See: illegal

unlawful assembly When three or more people meet with the intention of carrying out an unlawful act to deliberately disturb the peace.

unlawful detainer A legal action to evict a tenant that involves properly terminating the tenancy before going to court and seeking possession of the property, unpaid rent, and/or damages. Also known as an eviction lawsuit.

unqualified ownership Ownership without conditions or limitations. (Compare: qualified ownership)

unreasonable search and seizure A search and seizure by a law enforcement officer without a search warrant and without probable cause to believe that evidence of a crime is present. Such a search or seizure is unconstitutional under the Fourth Amendment (applied to the states by the Fourteenth Amendment), and evidence obtained from the unlawful search may not be introduced in court. (See also: fruit of the poisonous tree)

 "Wherever law ends, tyranny begins."
—John Locke

unsecured debt A debt that doesn't give the creditor the right to take a particular item of property if the debtor doesn't pay. Examples include credit card debts and medical bills. (Compare: secured debt)

URL See: Uniform Resource Locator

use The right to enjoy the benefits of real estate or personal property (but primarily used in reference to real estate), whether the owner of the right owns the property.

useful life The number of months or years, as determined by the IRS, that depreciable business equipment or property is expected to be in use.

usefulness A requirement for obtaining a utility patent. A patented invention must have some functional purpose or utility. The purpose does not have to be groundbreaking; it can be solely for

amusement or a minor improvement on an existing invention.

use tax A tax imposed by a state to compensate for the sales tax lost when an item is purchased outside of the state, but is used within the state. For example, you buy your car in a state that has no sales tax, but you live across the border in a state that does have a sales tax. When you bring your car home and register it in your state, the state taxing authority may bill you for the sales tax it would have collected had you bought the car within the state.

usufruct The right to use property—or income from property—that is owned by another.

usurious Exceeding the maximum interest rate on a debt that is allowed by law.

usury Extending credit at an exorbitant or illegally high interest rate. States set their own maximum interest rates, and courts will not enforce payment of interest on a loan if the rate is usurious. Most credit card issuers are based in states with no usury laws or caps on credit card interest rates.

utility patent The most common type of patent; issued for useful inventions that are new (novel) and that produce results that are not expected by those working in the field of invention (nonobvious).

A utility patent lasts for 20 years from the patent application's filing date. (See also: patent, novelty, nonobvious)

UTMA See: Uniform Transfers to Minors Act

utter To speak, articulate, or issue (as in a forged document).

uxor See: et uxor

V

vacant succession Succession that occurs when there are no known heirs for an estate to pass to. In vacant succession, the estate may escheat to the state.

vacate 1) For a judge to set aside or nullify an order or judgment that he or she finds was improper. 2) To move out of real estate and cease occupancy.

vagrancy The condition, once considered a crime, of being without work or permanent home and dependent on begging. Until the 1970s police used vagrancy laws to charge (or threaten) "undesirable" persons who might be suspected of criminal activity. Since then courts have struck down vagrancy laws as unconstitutionally vague. (See also: loiter)

valuable consideration See: consideration

variable annuity An annuity that makes payments that vary in amount, depending on the performance of the investments made by the annuity company. (Compare: fixed annuity)

variable life insurance A type of whole life insurance in which the amount of death benefits varies, depending on the performance of investments. The

insurance company places some or all of the fixed premium payments into an investment account; some companies let the insured person decide how the money is invested. The policyholder bears the risk of investment losses, though there is a guaranteed minimum benefit payment. One benefit of variable insurance is that interest and dividend income from the investment account is not taxed until it is paid out to the policyholder.

variable universal life insurance A type of whole life insurance that provides greater potential for financial gain—and brings greater risks. Like universal life insurance, variable universal life insurance offers flexible premiums, payment schedules, and benefits. But variable universal life policies are riskier because the premiums are invested in stocks, rather than more predictable money market accounts and bonds. Also called universal variable life insurance.

variance 1) An exception to a zoning ordinance, usually granted by a local government. For example, if you own an oddly shaped lot that could not accommodate a house in accordance with your city's setback requirement, you could apply at the appropriate office (usually the zoning or planning department) for a variance allowing you to build closer to a boundary line. 2) In criminal cases, a discrepancy between what is alleged in the charges and what the prosecution produces as proof. If the judge or jury has nevertheless convicted the defendant, an appellate court may find that the discrepancy is a "fatal variance," requiring reversal. 3) In civil cases, the disparity between the plaintiff's claims (or allegations) and the proof that the plaintiff has produced. Modern pleading rules allow plaintiffs to amend their claims even during trial, to conform with the evidence they produce.

vehicular manslaughter A violation of traffic laws that results in a fatality. Vehicular manslaughter can be charged as a misdemeanor or a felony depending on the circumstances. Drunk driving resulting in a death is most likely treated as a felony. The death of a passenger, including a loved one or friend, can also be vehicular manslaughter. (See also: manslaughter, reckless driving)

vendee A buyer of goods, services, or something for sale.

vendor A seller of goods, services, or something for sale.

venire See: jury panel

veniremen People who are summoned to the courthouse so that they may be questioned and perhaps chosen as jurors for civil or criminal trials.

venue The appropriate location(s), according to law and court rules, for a trial. In a criminal case, the proper venue is generally the judicial district or county where the crime was committed. In civil cases, venue is generally proper in the county or district where important events related to the case took place, such as the signing or performance of a contract or the accident or other incident that led to a personal injury case. Typically, the plaintiff in a civil case may also sue in the district or county where the defendant lives or does business.

The Verdict. (1982) Broken-down alcoholic storefront lawyer takes on powerful defendants in a negligence case to gain final redemption for a wasted career. Paul Newman in the lead role, backed by Charlotte Rampling, Jack Warden, James Mason, Milo O'Shea, Edward Binns, and Lindsay Crouse.

verdict A jury's decision after a trial, which becomes final when accepted by the judge. (See also: directed verdict, special verdict)

verification A formal declaration under oath or upon penalty of perjury that a document or pleading is true.

vertical privity A legal relationship in corporate law that exists between companies in the chain of distribution of a product. This relationship creates responsibilities between the companies involved, including being liable for defects in the product. For example, vertical privity exists between the manufacturer of a car and the dealership that sells it. Therefore, both the dealer and the manufacturer are liable for defects in cars sold by the dealership.

vest To give unconditional right to title or ownership. (See also: vested)

vested An unconditional right or title. For example, if an employee must work for ten years before his pension becomes vested, then after ten years of employment he has unconditional right to that pension. During the ten years prior, his right to the pension was unvested.

vested ownership Complete, unconditional ownership. (Compare: conditional ownership)

vested remainder An unconditional right to receive property at some point in the future. A vested interest may be created by a deed or a will. For example, if Julie leaves her house in a life estate to her husband and then to her daughter when her husband dies, the daughter has a vested remainder in the house.

vexatious litigation A lawsuit that is filed when there is no legal basis, and with the purpose to bother, annoy, embarrass, and cause legal expenses to the defendant. Vexatious litigation also includes continuing a lawsuit after discovery of the facts shows it has absolutely no merit. Vexatious litigation may lead to a legal claim of malicious prosecution against the vexatious litigant. Most states allow a judge to penalize plaintiffs and attorneys for filing or continuing a frivolous legal action. (See also: frivolous lawsuit)

vicarious liability Responsibility for a civil wrong that a supervisor bears when a subordinate or associate has actually committed the acts that give rise to the liability. For example, the owner of a residential rental may be vicariously liable if the manager discriminates against tenants on the basis of their religion.

view ordinance A local law designed to protect property owners who have desirable (and valuable) views. Typically, these ordinances allow property owners to insist on the trimming of trees that have grown and now block the view, so that the original view is restored, The property owner must pay for the trimming. View ordinances generally don't cover buildings or other structures that block views.

vigilante Someone who takes the law into his or her own hands by seizing someone and attempting to convict and punish the supposed criminal.

Village of Euclid v. Amber Realty **(1926)** A U.S. Supreme Court case in which the Court ruled that zoning ordinances are a legitimate exercise of the states' police powers.

visa The literal meaning is a stamp placed in a foreign national's passport by an official at a U.S. consulate outside of the United States. All visas allow their holders to enter the United States within a certain period of time. Visas can be designated as either "immigrant visas" or "nonimmigrant visas." Immigrant visas are given to people who have earned U.S. permanent residence or a "green card." Nonimmigrant visas are given to people coming to the U.S. for a temporary stay. However, immigration law also sometimes talks about visas "becoming available," which refers not to the stamp itself, but to instances where a limited number of visas are given out each year, and people who want them must place themselves on a waiting list.

visa waiver program A program that allows nationals from certain countries to come to the United States without a visa, so long as they're planning on being tourists, and to leave within 90 days. Persons coming to the United States under this program receive green-colored I-94 cards. They are not (except in rare cases) permitted to extend their stay or change their statuses. For example, someone who enters on the visa waiver program cannot then ask to stay on as a student, but would have to leave the U.S. and apply for a student visa.

visitation rights The right to see a child regularly, typically awarded by the court to a parent who does not have primary physical custody of the child.

viz "To wit" or "namely." Example: "There were several problems, viz: leaky roof, dangerous electrical system, and broken windows."

void Status of a statute, contract, or ruling that is determined to be invalid and unenforceable. (See also: voidable)

voidable A contract that can become void, but is not necessarily so; a contract that one party can affirm or rescind at that party's option. An example might be a contract entered into by a minor that is voidable once the minor reaches the age of majority, or alternatively, which the minor may affirm.

void for vagueness A civil or criminal statute that is so unclear or ambiguous that a reasonable person of average intelligence could not determine its meaning or application. A vague criminal statute is unconstitutional on the basis that a defendant could not defend against a charge which could not be understood. (See also: due process)

voir dire (vwah-**deer**) French for "to speak the truth," this is the questioning of prospective jurors by a judge and attorneys in court to determine if any juror is biased or cannot deal with the issues fairly, or if there is cause not to allow a juror to serve (such as knowledge of the facts or acquaintanceship with one of the parties).

volenti non fit injuria (voh-**len**-ti non fit in-**joor**-ee) Latin for "to a willing person, no injury is done." This doctrine holds that a person who knowingly and willingly puts himself in a dangerous situation cannot sue for any resulting injuries.

voluntary bankruptcy A bankruptcy case filed by the debtor. In contrast, an "involuntary bankruptcy" case is filed by the debtor's creditors.

voter bill of rights A set of rules adopted by most states to protect the rights of voters in an election. These rights typically cover who can vote, how the voting process must be conducted, how votes will be counted, and how to resolve complaints about the voting process. You can usually find the voter bill of rights by contacting your Secretary of State's office.

Texas is the only state that permits residents to cast absentee ballots from space. The first to vote while in orbit was astronaut David Wolf, who cast a ballot in from the Russian space station Mir in 1997.

voting trust A trust created to combine the voting power of shareholders. The participating shareholders' shares and their accompanying voting rights are transferred to a trust for a designated period of time. A designated trustee votes to elect a board directors or vote on other important matters at a shareholders' meeting. A voting trust is usually established by current directors to ensure continued control, but occasionally a voting trust represents a person or group trying to gain control of the corporation.

wage attachment See: attachment

W

wages Compensation that a worker receives in exchange for labor.

waive To voluntarily give up a right, including not enforcing a term of a contract (such as insisting on payment on an exact date), or knowingly giving up a legal right (such as a speedy trial). (See also: waiver)

waiver The intentional and voluntary giving up of a right, either by an express statement or by conduct (such as by not enforcing a right). A waiver accomplished by conduct may be interpreted as giving up the right to enforce the same right in the future. For example, a landlord who never invokes his "no pets" rule and allows tenants to keep dogs may not be able to successfully invoke the rule at a future date. A waiver of a legal right in court, such as the right to a jury trial, must be expressed on the record.

wanton 1) Behavior that is grossly negligent and recklessly unconcerned with the safety of people or property. For example, speeding past a school while students are leaving, or firing a shotgun in a crowded public park, are wanton acts that will, if someone is killed, justify a charge of second degree murder. 2) Sexually immoral and unrestrained.

ward 1) A person (usually a minor) who has a guardian appointed by the court to care for and take responsibility for that person. Such a person is a "ward of the court" (if the custody is court-ordered) or a "ward of the state." 2) A political division of a city. (See also: guardian)

warrant See: search warrant, arrest warrant

warranty A promise or assurance that may be express, implied by the circumstances, or implied by law. A warranty might be an express or implied statement that particular facts are true (for example, that merchandise may be used for particular purposes or that the seller has clear title to real estate). A warranty might be a promise to repair property within a certain period of time, or a legal obligation incident to a contract (for example, an implied warranty that leased residential property is habitable). (See also: express warranty, extended warranty contracts, home warranty, implied warranty of habitability, implied warranty of merchantability, warranty deed)

warranty adjustment program See: secret warranty program

warranty deed A kind of real estate deed that contains express assurances about the legal validity of the title being transferred to the new owner. (See also: grant deed, quitclaim deed)

warranty of fitness See: implied warranty

warranty of merchantability See: implied warranty

wash sale The selling and repurchasing of an asset, usually stocks or bonds, within a very short time frame. People used to do this to realize a loss for tax purposes, but the IRS caught on and made such losses nondeductible for most taxpayers.

waste Damage to real estate by a tenant that lessens its value to the owner or future owner. An owner can sue for damages for waste, terminate the lease of a tenant committing waste, or obtain a court order against further waste.

watered stock Shares of stock of a corporation that were issued at a price greater than fair market value. The actual value of watered stock is less than the value carried on the books of the corporation.

weight of evidence The strength, value, and believability of evidence. (See also: preponderance of the evidence)

wet reckless A reckless driving charge that is labeled as "alcohol related." It is usually made as a result of a plea bargain in which a charge of drunk driving has been reduced. A "wet reckless" occurs when the amount of alcohol is borderline illegal, there was no accident, and the defendant has no prior record. If there is a subsequent drunk driving conviction the "wet reckless" is usually considered a "prior" drunk driving conviction and can result in a sentence required for a second conviction. (See also: drunk driving, plea bargain, DUI, DWI)

whiplash A common neck or back injury, often suffered in automobile accidents in which the head and/or upper back is snapped back and forth suddenly and violently.

whistleblogger A whistleblower who raises concerns about a company's misconduct or wrongdoing on a blog.

whistleblower An employee who raises concerns about misconduct or wrongdoing within the company where the person works.

white-collar crime A variety of non-violent financial crimes, generally committed by businesspeople or public officials, involving commercial fraud, consumer fraud, swindles, insider trading on the stock market, embezzlement, bribery, or other dishonest schemes.

🔊 *"Two skillful lawyers are like two experts at any game of skill or endurance, and the result is that the clearest case becomes at least somewhat doubtful, and the event quite problematical."*

—Irving Brown, *Legal Recreations*

---

whole life insurance Life insurance that provides coverage for the entire life of the policyholder, who pays the same fixed premium throughout his or her life. The policy builds up cash reserves that may be paid out to the policyholder when he or she surrenders or partially surrenders the policy or uses the cash reserves to fund low-interest loans. The annual increase in the cash value of the policy is not taxed. If the policyholder surrenders the policy, a portion of the payment is not taxable. Also called straight life insurance or ordinary life insurance.

widow A woman whose husband died while she was married to him and who has not remarried.

widower A man whose wife died while he was married to her and and who has not remarried.

widow's election See: elective share

wildcard exemption An exemption that allows a debtor to apply a certain dollar amount to any type of property to make it—or more of it—exempt.

will A document in which the will maker specifies who is to receive his or him property at death and names an executor. You can also use your will to name a guardian for your young children. To be valid, a will must be signed by the person who made it (called the testator), dated, and witnessed by two people. In some states the witnesses must be disinterested. A will totally in the handwriting of the testator, signed and dated but without witnesses (a "holographic will"), is valid in about half of the states.

will contest A lawsuit challenging the validity of a will or some of its terms after the person who made the will has died. Will contests are quite rare. There are just a few legal grounds for challenging a will. The most common are undue influence by someone close to the deceased person, the deceased person's lack of capacity (understanding) when the will was signed, improper execution (signing and witnessing) of the will, or fraud (forgery, for example). (See also: no-contest clause)

willful Intentional, conscious, and intended to achieve a particular result.

willful tort A harmful act that is committed in an intentional and conscious way. For example, if your neighbor builds an ugly new fence and you intentionally mow it down with your truck, that's a willful tort. But carelessly backing into the fence as you pull out of your driveway is not willful, though it's still a tort. (Compare: negligence)

winding up 1) The process of liquidating or closing down a corporation, limited liability company, or partnership. Typically this involves paying off expenses and creditors, settling accounts, and collecting and distributing (to shareholders and owners) whatever assets then remain. 2) With respect to an estate or trust, gathering assets, paying debts, and distributing property to those entitled to inherit it. (See also: personal representative)

winding up a corporation See: dissolution of corporation

wiretap Using an electronic device to listen to or record another's telephone (or electronic) communications.

wiretapping Eavesdropping on private conversations by connecting listening equipment to a telephone line. To be legal, wiretapping must be authorized by a search warrant or court order.

withdrawal In criminal law, leaving a conspiracy to commit a crime before the actual crime is committed. If the withdrawal is before any overt act, the withdrawing person may escape prosecution. (See also: overt act)

withdrawal of a corporation See: dissolution of corporation

withholding The practice of holding back a portion of money from an employee's paycheck to pay Social Security, Medicare, and income taxes.

with prejudice A final and binding decision by a judge about a legal matter that prevents further pursuit of the same matter in any court. When judges make such a decision, they dismiss the matter "with prejudice." The parties may also agree to dismiss a claim with prejudice. (See also: jurisdiction)

witness A person who testifies under oath at a deposition or trial, providing firsthand or expert evidence. The term also refers to someone who watches another person sign a document and then adds his or her name to confirm (called "attesting") that the signature is genuine.

witnesseth Legal jargon for "to take notice of," used in phrases such as "On this day I do hereby witnesseth the signing of this document."

witness stand A chair at the end of the judge's bench, on the jury box side, where a witness sits and gives testimony after being sworn to tell the truth. When called to testify, the witness "takes the stand." Most witness stands are equipped with a microphone so that everyone can hear the testimony.

wobbler A crime that can be either a misdemeanor (a conviction punishable by a small amount of jail time, typically one year or less) or a felony (a conviction punishable by time in state prison). Wobblers can be charged either way, and depending on the law of their state, judges may have the discretion to reduce a felony conviction in a wobbler case to a misdemeanor.

***Woodson v. North Carolina* (1976)** A U.S. Supreme Court case in which a mandatory death penalty for first degree murder was ruled unconstitutional because a defendant has the right to individual consideration of the facts in the case when determining the penalty.

words of art Terms used by people who specialize in a particular occupation and understood by other such specialists.

words of procreation Language in a will or deed, used to transfer property to a person and that person's descendants only. Typically, the words take the form "to A, and the heirs of his body," where A is the person inheriting the property.

work credits To receive any kind of Social Security benefit—retirement, disability, dependents, or survivors—the person on whose record the benefit is to be calculated must have accumulated enough work credits. A person can earn up to four work credits per year, and anyone who works full time, even at a very low-paying job, easily accumulates them. Ask the Social Security Administration for a copy of your Social Security Statement to see how many work credits you have accumulated.

Worker Adjustment and Retraining Notification Act (WARN) A federal law that requires employers with at least 100 employees to give workers some advance notice of an impending plant closing or mass layoff that will result in job loss or more than a 50% hours cut for a certain number or percentage of employees. (See also: mass layoff)

workers' compensation A program that provides medical care and replacement income to employees who are injured or become ill due to their jobs. Financial benefits may also extend to the survivors of workers who are killed on the job. In most circumstances, workers' compensation pays relatively modest amounts and prevents the worker or survivors from suing the employer for the injuries or death.

Erin Brockovich. (2000) Based on a true story, this is the ultimate small law firm versus big corporation film. Julia Roberts won an Academy Award for her performance as Erin, an intrepid legal clerk who convinces her crusty lawyer boss (Albert Finney) to file a difficult class action on behalf of sick and dying families against giant utility Pacific Gas & Electric, based on evidence that it knew it was contaminating groundwater in a small California town.

Workers' Compensation Acts State statutes that 1) require employers to purchase insurance to protect their workers and 2) establish the liability of employers for injuries to workers while on the job or illnesses due to the employment. Workers' compensation is not based on the negligence of the employer; benefits are granted regardless of fault and include medical coverage, a percentage of lost wages, costs of retraining, and compensation for any permanent injury. Coverage does not include general damages for pain and suffering.

work for hire See: work made for hire

work made for hire Under copyright law, a work created by an employee within the scope of employment, or a commissioned work that falls within certain categories and is the subject of a written agreement. When a work is made for hire, the hiring party is considered the author and owner, not the person who creates the work. This status—that is, whether a work is made fore hire— affects the length of copyright protection and termination rights.

workmen's compensation See: workers' compensation

workout An arrangement negotiated between a debtor and creditor a way to take care of a debt, by paying it off or through loan forgiveness. Workouts are often created to avoid bankruptcy or foreclosure proceedings.

work permit See: Employment Authorization Document (EAD)

work product The writings, notes, memoranda, reports on conversations with the client or witness, research, and confidential materials which an attorney has developed while representing a client, particularly in preparation for trial. A work product may not be demanded or subpenaed by the opposing party because it reflects the confidential strategy, tactics, and theories to be employed by the attorney.

World Court The International Court of Justice, a judicial tribunal established by the United Nations to hear disputes submitted by nations and to issue advisory opinions upon request of a United Nations organ, such as the General Assembly or Security Council. The World Court has 15 judges and sits in The Hague (Netherlands).

writ A written order from a judge requiring specific action by the person or entity to whom the writ is directed. Writs can be directed to other, lower court judges (writ of mandamus); to prison officials (writ of habeas corpus); and others.

write-off A tax-deductible expense, usually referring to depreciating the cost of an asset used in business or taking a Section 179 expense for that asset.

writ of attachment A court order directing a sheriff (or other law enforcement officer) to seize property of a defendant that will satisfy a judgment against that person.

writ of coram nobis (kor-m-**noh**-bis) A Latin term that describes a request to a judge to reopen and reconsider a matter that has already been decided. The basis for the request is a claim that the decision is based on a mistake of fact, which can now be rectified.

writ of execution A court order to a sheriff to enforce a judgment, by seizing real or personal property of a judgment debtor, in order to obtain funds to pay the winning plaintiff the judgment amount.

writ of mandate (mandamus) See: mandamus

writ of prohibition An appellate court's written order to prohibit a lower court from acting because it does not have jurisdiction to do so.

wrongful death A death caused by the wrongful act of another, either accidentally or intentionally. A claim for wrongful death is made by a family member of a deceased person to obtain compensation for having to live without that person. The compensation is intended to cover the earnings and the emotional comfort and support the deceased person would have provided.

wrongful termination A legal claim that an employee has been fired for an illegal reason, such as discrimination, breach of contract, or in violation of public policy. (See also: wrongful termination in violation of public policy)

wrongful termination in violation of public policy A legal claim that an employee has been illegally fired for reasons that most people would find morally or ethically repugnant. In many states, for example, an employee can sue for wrongful termination in violation of public policy after being fired for 1) exercising a legal right, such as voting, 2) refusing to do something illegal, such as submitting false tax returns or lying on reports

the employer is required to submit to the government, or 3) reporting illegal conduct.

W-2 form An IRS form on which wages paid to employees are reported by employers.

Y

yellow-dog contract An agreement in which an employer forbids an employee to join a labor union. Yellow-dog contracts are unenforceable.

***Youngstown Steel v. Sawyer* (1952)** A U.S. Supreme Court case in which the Court ruled that President Harry S. Truman's seizure of strike-bound steel plants in order to provide materials for the Korean War could not be based on inherent presidential powers, but had to be authorized by statute. Truman immediately halted the takeover.

youthful offender Someone under the age of 18 accused of a crime, who is processed through a juvenile court and juvenile detention or prison facilities instead of regular court, jail, and prison. Courts may have the latitude to try some young defendants as adults, particularly those who are repeat offenders, appear to be beyond rehabilitation, or are involved in major crimes like murder, manslaughter, armed robbery, rape, or aggravated assault. (See also: juvenile delinquent)

Z

zealous witness A witness who gives testimony clearly biased toward the party that called him or her to testify.

zero tape A tape that is printed out when a voting machine is first set up at a polling place. It is called a zero tape because it should register zero votes for each candidate or question.

zoning The local laws dividing cities or counties into different zones according to allowed uses, from single-family residential to commercial to industrial. Mixed-use zones are also used. Zoning ordinances control the size, location, and use of buildings within these different areas and have a profound effect on traffic, health, and livability.

The Constitution of the United States of America

We the people of the United States, in order to form a more perfect union, establish justice, insure domestic tranquility, provide for the common defense, promote the general welfare, and secure the blessings of liberty to ourselves and our posterity, do ordain and establish this Constitution for the United States of America.

Article I

Section 1. All legislative powers herein granted shall be vested in a Congress of the United States, which shall consist of a Senate and House of Representatives.

Section 2. The House of Representatives shall be composed of members chosen every second year by the people of the several states, and the electors in each state shall have the qualifications requisite for electors of the most numerous branch of the state legislature.

No person shall be a Representative who shall not have attained to the age of twenty five years, and been seven years a citizen of the United States, and who shall not, when elected, be an inhabitant of that state in which he shall be chosen.

Representatives and direct taxes shall be apportioned among the several states which may be included within this union, according to their respective numbers, which shall be determined by adding to the whole number of free persons, including those bound to service for a term of years, and excluding Indians not taxed, three fifths of all other persons. [The preceding provision was superseded by Amendment IV, Section 2.] The actual enumeration shall be made within three years after the first meeting of the Congress of the United States, and within every subsequent term of ten years, in such manner as they shall by law direct. The number of Representatives shall not exceed one for every thirty thousand, but each state shall have at least one Representative; and until such enumeration shall be made, the State of New Hampshire shall be entitled to choose three, Massachusetts eight, Rhode Island and Providence Plantations one, Connecticut five, New York six, New Jersey four, Pennsylvania eight, Delaware one, Maryland six, Virginia ten, North Carolina five, South Carolina five, and Georgia three.

When vacancies happen in the representation from any state, the executive authority thereof shall issue writs of election to fill such vacancies.

The House of Representatives shall choose their speaker and other officers; and shall have the sole power of impeachment.

Section 3. The Senate of the United States shall be composed of two Senators from each state, *chosen by the legislature thereof,* [The preceding provision was superseded by Amendment XVII, Section 1.] for six years; and each Senator shall have one vote.

Immediately after they shall be assembled in consequence of the first election, they shall be divided as equally as may be into three classes. The seats of the Senators of the first class shall be vacated at the expiration of the second year, of the second class at the expiration of the fourth year, and of the third class at the expiration of the sixth year, so that one third may be chosen every second year; *and if vacancies happen by resignation, or otherwise, during the recess of the legislature of any state, the executive thereof may make temporary appointments until the next meeting of the legislature, which shall then fill such vacancies.* [The preceding provision was superseded by Amendment XVII, Section 2.]

No person shall be a Senator who shall not have attained to the age of thirty years, and been nine years a citizen of the United States, and who shall not, when elected, be an inhabitant of that state for which he shall be chosen.

The Vice President of the United States shall be President of the Senate, but shall have no vote, unless they be equally divided.

The Senate shall choose their other officers, and also a President pro tempore, in the absence of the Vice President, or when he shall exercise the office of President of the United States.

The Senate shall have the sole power to try all impeachments. When sitting for that purpose, they shall be on oath or affirmation. When the President of the United States is tried, the Chief Justice shall preside: and no person shall be convicted without the concurrence of two thirds of the members present.

Judgment in cases of impeachment shall not extend further than to removal from office, and disqualification to hold and enjoy any office of honor, trust or profit under the United States: but the party convicted shall nevertheless be liable and subject to indictment, trial, judgment and punishment, according to law.

Section 4. The times, places and manner of holding elections for Senators and Representatives, shall be prescribed in each state by the legislature thereof; but the Congress may at any time by law make or alter such regulations, except as to the places of choosing Senators.

The Congress shall assemble at least once in every year, and such meeting shall *be on the first Monday in December,* [The preceding provision was superseded by Amendment XX, Section 2.] unless they shall by law appoint a different day.

Section 5. Each House shall be the judge of the elections, returns and qualifications of its own members, and a majority of each shall constitute a quorum to do business; but a smaller number may adjourn from day to day, and may be authorized to compel the attendance of absent members, in such manner, and under such penalties as each House may provide.

Each House may determine the rules of its proceedings, punish its members for disorderly behavior, and, with the concurrence of two thirds, expel a member.

Each House shall keep a journal of its proceedings, and from time to time publish the same, excepting such parts as may in their judgment require secrecy; and the yeas and nays of the members of either House on any question shall, at the desire of one fifth of those present, be entered on the journal.

Neither House, during the session of Congress, shall, without the consent of the other, adjourn for more than three days, nor to any other place than that in which the two Houses shall be sitting.

Section 6. The Senators and Representatives shall receive a compensation for their services, to be ascertained by law, and paid out of the treasury of the United States. They shall in all cases, except treason, felony and breach of the peace, be privileged from arrest during their attendance at the session of their respective Houses, and in going to and returning from the same; and for any speech or debate in either House, they shall not be questioned in any other place.

No Senator or Representative shall, during the time for which he was elected, be appointed to any civil office under the authority of the United States, which shall have been created, or the emoluments whereof shall have been increased during such time; and no person holding any office under the United States, shall be a member of either House during his continuance in office.

Section 7. All bills for raising revenue shall originate in the House of Representatives; but the Senate may propose or concur with amendments as on other bills.

Every bill which shall have passed the House of Representatives and the Senate, shall, before it become a law, be presented to the President of the United States: if he approve he shall sign it, but if not he shall return it, with his objections to that House in which it shall have originated, who shall enter the objections at large on their journal, and proceed to reconsider it. If after such reconsideration two thirds of that House shall agree to pass the bill, it shall be sent, together with the objections, to the other House, by which it shall likewise be reconsidered, and if approved by two thirds of that House, it shall become a law. But in all such cases the votes of both Houses shall be determined by yeas and nays, and the names of the persons voting for and against the bill shall be entered on the journal of each House respectively. If any bill shall not be returned by the President within ten days (Sundays excepted) after it shall have been presented to him, the same shall be a law, in like manner as if he had signed it, unless the Congress by their adjournment prevent its return, in which case it shall not be a law.

Every order, resolution, or vote to which the concurrence of the Senate and House of Representatives may be necessary (except on a question of adjournment) shall be presented to the President of the United States; and before the same shall take effect, shall be approved by him, or being disapproved by him, shall be repassed by two thirds of the Senate and House of Representatives, according to the rules and limitations prescribed in the case of a bill.

Section 8. The Congress shall have power to lay and collect taxes, duties, imposts and excises, to pay the debts and provide for the common defense and general welfare of the United States; but all duties, imposts and excises shall be uniform throughout the United States;

To borrow money on the credit of the United States;

To regulate commerce with foreign nations, and among the several states, and with the Indian tribes;

To establish an uniform rule of naturalization, and uniform laws on the subject of bankruptcies throughout the United States;

To coin money, regulate the value thereof, and of foreign coin, and fix the standard of weights and measures;

To provide for the punishment of counterfeiting the securities and current coin of the United States;

To establish post offices and post roads;

To promote the progress of science and useful arts, by securing for limited times to authors and inventors the exclusive right to their respective writings and discoveries;

To constitute tribunals inferior to the Supreme Court;

To define and punish piracies and felonies committed on the high seas, and offenses against the law of nations;

To declare war, grant letters of marque and reprisal, and make rules concerning captures on land and water;

To raise and support armies, but no appropriation of money to that use shall be for a longer term than two years;

To provide and maintain a navy;

To make rules for the government and regulation of the land and naval forces;

To provide for calling forth the militia to execute the laws of the union, suppress insurrections and repel invasions;

To provide for organizing, arming, and disciplining, the militia, and for governing such part of them as may be employed in the service of the United States, reserving to the states respectively, the appointment of the officers, and the authority of training the militia according to the discipline prescribed by Congress; To exercise exclusive legislation in all cases whatsoever, over such District (not exceeding ten miles square) as may, by cession of particular states, and the acceptance of Congress, become the seat of the government of the United States, and to exercise like authority over all places purchased by the consent of the legislature of the state in which the same shall be, for the erection of forts, magazines, arsenals, dockyards, and other needful buildings;—And

To make all laws which shall be necessary and proper for carrying into execution the foregoing powers, and all other powers vested by this Constitution in the government of the United States, or in any department or officer thereof.

Section 9. The migration or importation of such persons as any of the states now existing shall think proper to admit, shall not be prohibited by the Congress prior to the year one thousand eight hundred and eight, but a tax or duty may be imposed on such importation, not exceeding ten dollars for each person.

The privilege of the writ of habeas corpus shall not be suspended, unless when in cases of rebellion or invasion the public safety may require it.

No bill of attainder or ex post facto law shall be passed.

No capitation, or other direct, tax shall be laid, *unless in proportion to the census or enumeration herein before directed to be taken.* [The preceding provision was modified by Amendment XVI.]

No tax or duty shall be laid on articles exported from any state.

No preference shall be given by any regulation of commerce or revenue to the ports of one state over those of another; nor shall vessels bound to, or from, one state, be obliged to enter, clear, or pay duties in another.

No money shall be drawn from the treasury, but in consequence of appropriations made by law; and a regular statement and account of receipts and expenditures of all public money shall be published from time to time.

No title of nobility shall be granted by the United States: and no person holding any office of profit or trust under them, shall, without the consent of the Congress, accept of any present, emolument, office, or title, of any kind whatever, from any king, prince, or foreign state.

Section 10. No state shall enter into any treaty, alliance, or confederation; grant letters of marque and reprisal;

coin money; emit bills of credit; make anything but gold and silver coin a tender in payment of debts; pass any bill of attainder, ex post facto law, or law impairing the obligation of contracts, or grant any title of nobility.

No state shall, without the consent of the Congress, lay any imposts or duties on imports or exports, except what may be absolutely necessary for executing its inspection laws: and the net produce of all duties and imposts, laid by any state on imports or exports, shall be for the use of the treasury of the United States; and all such laws shall be subject to the revision and control of the Congress.

No state shall, without the consent of Congress, lay any duty of tonnage, keep troops, or ships of war in time of peace, enter into any agreement or compact with another state, or with a foreign power, or engage in war, unless actually invaded, or in such imminent danger as will not admit of delay.

Article II

Section 1. The executive power shall be vested in a President of the United States of America. He shall hold his office during the term of four years, and, together with the Vice President, chosen for the same term, be elected, as follows: Each state shall appoint, in such manner as the Legislature thereof may direct, a number of electors, equal to the whole number of Senators and Representatives to which the State may be entitled in the Congress: but no Senator or Representative, or person holding an office of trust or profit under the United States, shall be appointed an elector.

The electors shall meet in their respective states, and vote by ballot for two persons, of whom one at least shall not be an inhabitant of the same state with themselves. And they shall make a list of all the persons voted for, and of the number of votes for each; which list they shall sign and certify, and transmit sealed to the seat of the government of the United States, directed to the President of the Senate. The President of the Senate shall, in the presence of the Senate and House of Representatives, open all the certificates, and the votes shall then be counted. The person having the greatest number of votes shall be the President, if such number be a majority of the whole number of electors appointed; and if there be more than one who have such majority, and have an equal number of votes, then the House of Representatives shall immediately choose by ballot one of them for President; and if no person have a majority, then from the five highest on the list the said House shall in like manner choose the President. But in choosing the President, the votes shall be taken by States, the representation from each state having one vote; A quorum for this purpose shall consist of a member or members from two thirds of the states, and a majority of all the states shall be necessary to a choice. In every case, after the choice of the President, the person having the greatest number of votes of the electors shall be the Vice President. But if there should remain two or more who have equal votes, the Senate shall choose from them by ballot the Vice President. [The preceding provision was superseded by Amendment XII.]

The Congress may determine the time of choosing the electors, and the day on which they shall give their votes; which day shall be the same throughout the United States.

No person except a natural born citizen, or a citizen of the United States, at the time of the adoption of this Constitution, shall be eligible to the office of President; neither shall any person be eligible to that office who shall not have attained to the age of thirty five years, and been fourteen Years a resident within the United States. [For qualifications of the Vice President, see Amendment XII.]

In case of the removal of the President from office, or of his death, resignation, or inability to discharge the powers and duties of the said office, the same shall devolve on the Vice President, and the Congress may by law provide for the case of removal, death, resignation or inability, both of the President and Vice President, declaring what officer shall then act as President, and such officer shall act accordingly, until the disability be removed, or a President shall

be elected. [This clause was modified by Amendments XX and XXV.]

The President shall, at stated times, receive for his services, a compensation, which shall neither be increased nor diminished during the period for which he shall have been elected, and he shall not receive within that period any other emolument from the United States, or any of them.

Before he enter on the execution of his office, he shall take the following oath or affirmation:—"I do solemnly swear (or affirm) that I will faithfully execute the office of President of the United States, and will to the best of my ability, preserve, protect and defend the Constitution of the United States."

Section 2. The President shall be commander in chief of the Army and Navy of the United States, and of the militia of the several states, when called into the actual service of the United States; he may require the opinion, in writing, of the principal officer in each of the executive departments, upon any subject relating to the duties of their respective offices, and he shall have power to grant reprieves and pardons for offenses against the United States, except in cases of impeachment.

He shall have power, by and with the advice and consent of the Senate, to make treaties, provided two thirds of the Senators present concur; and he shall nominate, and by and with the advice and consent of the Senate, shall appoint ambassadors, other public ministers and consuls, judges of the Supreme Court, and all other officers of the United States, whose appointments are not herein otherwise provided for, and which shall be established by law: but the Congress may by law vest the appointment of such inferior officers, as they think proper, in the President alone, in the courts of law, or in the heads of departments.

The President shall have power to fill up all vacancies that may happen during the recess of the Senate, by granting commissions which shall expire at the end of their next session.

Section 3. He shall from time to time give to the Congress information of the state of the union, and recommend to their consideration such measures as he shall judge necessary and expedient; he may, on extraordinary occasions, convene both Houses, or either of them, and in case of disagreement between them, with respect to the time of adjournment, he may adjourn them to such time as he shall think proper; he shall receive ambassadors and other public ministers; he shall take care that the laws be faithfully executed, and shall commission all the officers of the United States.

Section 4. The President, Vice President and all civil officers of the United States, shall be removed from office on impeach-

ment for, and conviction of, treason, bribery, or other high crimes and misdemeanors.

Article III

Section 1. The judicial power of the United States, shall be vested in one Supreme Court, and in such inferior courts as the Congress may from time to time ordain and establish. The judges, both of the supreme and inferior courts, shall hold their offices during good behavior, and shall, at stated times, receive for their services, a compensation, which shall not be diminished during their continuance in office.

Section 2. The judicial power shall extend to all cases, in law and equity, arising under this Constitution, the laws of the United States, and treaties made, or which shall be made, under their authority;—to all cases affecting ambassadors, other public ministers and consuls;—to all cases of admiralty and maritime jurisdiction;—to controversies to which the United States shall be a party;—to controversies between two or more states;—*between a state and citizens of another state,* [The preceding provision was modified by Amendment XI.]—between citizens of different states,—between citizens of the same state claiming lands under grants of different states, and between a state, or the citizens thereof, and foreign states, citizens or subjects.

In all cases affecting ambassadors, other public ministers and consuls, and those in which a state shall be party, the Supreme Court shall have original jurisdiction. In all the other cases before mentioned, the Supreme Court shall have appellate jurisdiction, both as to law and fact, with such exceptions, and under such regulations as the Congress shall make.

The trial of all crimes, except in cases of impeachment, shall be by jury; and such trial shall be held in the state where the said crimes shall have been committed; but when not committed within any state, the trial shall be at such place or places as the Congress may by law have directed.

Section 3. Treason against the United States, shall consist only in levying war against them, or in adhering to their enemies, giving them aid and comfort. No person shall be convicted of treason unless on the testimony of two witnesses to the same overt act, or on confession in open court.

The Congress shall have power to declare the punishment of treason, but no attainder of treason shall work corruption of blood, or forfeiture except during the life of the person attainted.

Article IV

Section 1. Full faith and credit shall be given in each state to the public acts, records, and judicial proceedings of every other state. And the Congress may by

general laws prescribe the manner in which such acts, records and proceedings shall be proved, and the effect thereof.

Section 2. The citizens of each state shall be entitled to all privileges and immunities of citizens in the several states.

A person charged in any state with treason, felony, or other crime, who shall flee from justice, and be found in another state, shall on demand of the executive authority of the state from which he fled, be delivered up, to be removed to the state having jurisdiction of the crime.

No person held to service or labor in one state, under the laws thereof, escaping into another, shall, in consequence of any law or regulation therein, be discharged from such service or labor, but shall be delivered up on claim of the party to whom such service or labor may be due. [The previous clause was superseded by Amendment XIII.]

Section 3. New states may be admitted by the Congress into this union; but no new states shall be formed or erected within the jurisdiction of any other state; nor any state be formed by the junction of two or more states, or parts of states, without the consent of the legislatures of the states concerned as well as of the Congress.

The Congress shall have power to dispose of and make all needful rules and regulations respecting the territory or other property belonging to the United States; and nothing in this Constitution shall be so construed as to prejudice any claims of the United States, or of any particular state.

Section 4. The United States shall guarantee to every state in this union a republican form of government, and shall protect each of them against invasion; and on application of the legislature, or of the executive (when the legislature cannot be convened) against domestic violence.

Article V

The Congress, whenever two thirds of both houses shall deem it necessary, shall propose amendments to this Constitution, or, on the application of the legislatures of two thirds of the several states, shall call a convention for proposing amendments, which, in either case, shall be valid to all intents and purposes, as part of this Constitution, when ratified by the legislatures of three fourths of the several states, or by conventions in three fourths thereof, as the one or the other mode of ratification may be proposed by the Congress; provided that no amendment which may be made prior to the year one thousand eight hundred and eight shall in any manner affect the first and fourth clauses in the ninth section of the first article; and that no state, without its consent, shall be deprived of its equal suffrage in the Senate.

Article VI

All debts contracted and engagements entered into, before the adoption of this Constitution, shall be as valid against the United States under this Constitution, as under the Confederation.

This Constitution, and the laws of the United States which shall be made in pursuance thereof; and all treaties made, or which shall be made, under the authority of the United States, shall be the supreme law of the land; and the judges in every state shall be bound thereby, anything in the Constitution or laws of any State to the contrary notwithstanding.

The Senators and Representatives before mentioned, and the members of the several state legislatures, and all executive and judicial officers, both of the United States and of the several states, shall be bound by oath or affirmation, to support this Constitution; but no religious test shall ever be required as a qualification to any office or public trust under the United States.

Article VII

The ratification of the conventions of nine states, shall be sufficient for the establishment of this Constitution between the states so ratifying the same.

Done in convention by the unanimous consent of the states present the seventeenth day of September in the year of our Lord one thousand seven hundred and eighty seven and of the independence of the United States of America the twelfth. In witness whereof we have hereunto subscribed our Names,

G. Washington—Presidt and deputy from Virginia

Delaware: Geo: Read, Gunning Bedford jun, John Dickinson, Richard Bassett, Jaco: Broom

Maryland: James McHenry, Dan of St Thos. Jenifer, Danl. Carroll

Virginia: John Blair, James Madison Jr.

North Carolina: Wm. Blount, Richd. Dobbs Spaight, Hu Williamson

South Carolina: J. Rutledge, Charles Cotesworth Pinckney, Charles Pinckney, Pierce Butler

Georgia: William Few, Abr Baldwin

New Hampshire: John Langdon, Nicholas Gilman

Massachusetts: Nathaniel Gorham, Rufus King

Connecticut: Wm. Saml. Johnson, Roger Sherman

New York: Alexander Hamilton

New Jersey: Wil: Livingston, David Brearly, Wm. Paterson, Jona: Dayton

Pennsylvania: B Franklin, Thomas Mifflin, Robt. Morris, Geo. Clymer, Thos. FitzSimons, Jared Ingersoll, James Wilson, Gouv Morris

Amendments to the Constitution of the United States

[The first ten amendments known as the *Bill of Rights* were passed by Congress on September 25, 1789 and ratified by sufficient states on December 15, 1791.]

Amendment I (1791)

Congress shall make no law respecting an establishment of religion, or prohibiting the free exercise thereof; or abridging the freedom of speech, or of the press; or the right of the people peaceably to assemble, and to petition the government for a redress of grievances.

Amendment II (1791)

A well regulated militia, being necessary to the security of a free state, the right of the people to keep and bear arms, shall not be infringed.

Amendment III (1791)

No soldier shall, in time of peace be quartered in any house, without the consent of the owner, nor in time of war, but in a manner to be prescribed by law.

Amendment IV (1791)

The right of the people to be secure in their persons, houses, papers, and effects, against unreasonable searches and seizures, shall not be violated, and no warrants shall issue, but upon probable cause, supported by oath or affirmation, and particularly describing the place to be searched, and the persons or things to be seized.

Amendment V (1791)

No person shall be held to answer for a capital, or otherwise infamous crime, unless on a presentment or indictment of a grand jury, except in cases arising in the land or naval forces, or in the militia, when in actual service in time of war or public danger; nor shall any person be subject for the same offense to be twice put in jeopardy of life or limb; nor shall be compelled in any criminal case to be a witness against himself, nor be deprived of life, liberty, or property, without due process of law; nor shall private property be taken for public use, without just compensation.

Amendment VI (1791)

In all criminal prosecutions, the accused shall enjoy the right to a speedy and public trial, by an impartial jury of the state and district wherein the crime shall have been committed, which district shall have been previously ascertained by law, and to be informed of the nature and cause of the accusation; to be confronted with the witnesses against him; to have compulsory process for obtaining witnesses in his favor, and to have the assistance of counsel for his defense.

Amendment VII (1791)

In suits at common law, where the value in controversy shall exceed twenty dollars, the right of trial by jury shall be preserved, and no fact tried by a jury, shall be otherwise reexamined in any court of the United States, than according to the rules of the common law.

Amendment VIII (1791)

Excessive bail shall not be required, nor excessive fines imposed, nor cruel and unusual punishments inflicted.

Amendment IX (1791)

The enumeration in the Constitution, of certain rights, shall not be construed to deny or disparage others retained by the people.

Amendment X (1791)

The powers not delegated to the United States by the Constitution, nor prohibited by it to the states, are reserved to the states respectively, or to the people.

Amendment XI (1798)

The judicial power of the United States shall not be construed to extend to any suit in law or equity, commenced or prosecuted against one of the United States by citizens of another state, or by citizens or subjects of any foreign state.

Amendment XII (1804)

The electors shall meet in their respective states and vote by ballot for President and Vice President, one of whom, at least, shall not be an inhabitant of the same state with themselves; they shall name in their ballots the person voted for as President, and in distinct ballots the person voted for as Vice President, and they shall make distinct lists of all persons voted for as President, and of all persons voted for as Vice President, and of the number of votes for each, which lists they shall sign and certify, and transmit sealed to the seat of the government of the United States, directed to the President of the Senate;—The President of the Senate shall, in the presence of the Senate and House of Representatives, open all the certificates and the votes shall then be counted;—The person having the greatest number of votes for President, shall be the President, if such number be a majority of the whole number of electors appointed; and if no person have such majority, then from the persons having the highest numbers not exceeding three on the list of those voted for as President, the House of Representatives shall choose immediately, by ballot, the President. But in choosing the President, the votes shall be taken by states, the representation from each state having one vote; a quorum for this purpose shall consist of a member or members from two-thirds of the states, and a majority of all the states shall be necessary to a choice. *And if the House of Representatives shall not choose a President whenever the right of choice shall devolve upon them, before the fourth day of March next following, then the Vice President shall act as President, as in the case of the death or other constitutional disability of the President.* [The preceding provision was superseded by Amendment XX, Section 3.] The person having the greatest number of votes as Vice President, shall be the Vice President, if such number be a majority of the whole number of electors appointed, and if no person have a majority, then from the two highest numbers on the list, the Senate shall choose the Vice President; a quorum for the purpose shall consist of two-thirds of the whole number of Senators, and a majority of the whole number shall be necessary to a choice. But no person constitutionally ineligible to the office of President shall be eligible to that of Vice President of the United States.

Amendment XIII (1865)

Section 1. Neither slavery nor involuntary servitude, except as a punishment for crime whereof the party shall have been duly convicted, shall exist within the United States, or any place subject to their jurisdiction.

Section 2. Congress shall have power to enforce this article by appropriate legislation.

Amendment XIV (1868)

Section 1. All persons born or naturalized in the United States, and subject to the jurisdiction thereof, are citizens of the United States and of the state wherein they reside. No state shall make or enforce any law which shall abridge the privileges or immunities of citizens of the United States; nor shall any state deprive any person of life, liberty, or property, without due process of law; nor deny to any person within its jurisdiction the equal protection of the laws.

Section 2. Representatives shall be apportioned among the several states according to their respective numbers, counting the whole number of persons in each state, excluding Indians not taxed. But when the right to vote at any election for the choice of electors for President and Vice President of the United States, Representatives in Congress, the executive and judicial officers of a state, or the members of the legislature thereof, is denied to any of the male inhabitants of such state, being twenty-one years of age, [See Amendment XXVI.] and citizens of the United States, or in any way abridged, except for participation in rebellion, or other crime, the basis of representation therein shall be reduced in the proportion which the number of such male citizens shall bear to the whole number of male citizens twenty-one years of age in such state.

Section 3. No person shall be a Senator or Representative in Congress, or elector of President and Vice President, or hold any office, civil or military, under the United States, or under any state, who, having previously taken an oath, as a member of Congress, or as an officer of the United States, or as a member of any state legislature, or as an executive or judicial officer of any state, to support the Constitution of the United States, shall have engaged in insurrection or rebellion against the same, or given aid or comfort to the enemies thereof. But Congress may by a vote of two-thirds of each House, remove such disability.

Section 4. The validity of the public debt of the United States, authorized by law, including debts incurred for payment of pensions and bounties for services in suppressing insurrection or rebellion, shall not be questioned. But neither the United States nor any state shall assume or pay any debt or obligation incurred in aid of insurrection or rebellion against the United States, or any claim for the loss or emancipation of any slave; but all such

debts, obligations and claims shall be held illegal and void.

Section 5. The Congress shall have power to enforce, by appropriate legislation, the provisions of this article.

Amendment XV (1870)

Section 1. The right of citizens of the United States to vote shall not be denied or abridged by the United States or by any state on account of race, color, or previous condition of servitude.

Section 2. The Congress shall have power to enforce this article by appropriate legislation.

Amendment XVI (1913)

The Congress shall have power to lay and collect taxes on incomes, from whatever source derived, without apportionment among the several states, and without regard to any census of enumeration.

Amendment XVII (1913)

The Senate of the United States shall be composed of two Senators from each state, elected by the people thereof, for six years; and each Senator shall have one vote. The electors in each state shall have the qualifications requisite for electors of the most numerous branch of the state legislatures.

When vacancies happen in the representation of any state in the Senate, the executive authority of such state shall issue writs of election to fill such vacancies: *Provided,* That the legislature of any state may empower the executive thereof to make temporary appointments until the people fill the vacancies by election as the legislature may direct.

This amendment shall not be so construed as to affect the election or term of any Senator chosen before it becomes valid as part of the Constitution.

Amendment XVIII (1919)

Section 1. After one year from the ratification of this article the manufacture, sale, or transportation of intoxicating liquors within, the importation thereof into, or the exportation thereof from the United States and all territory subject to the jurisdiction thereof for beverage purposes is hereby prohibited.

Section 2. The Congress and the several states shall have concurrent power to enforce this article by appropriate legislation.

Section 3. This article shall be inoperative unless it shall have been ratified as an amendment to the Constitution by the legislatures of the several states, as provided in the Constitution, within seven years from the date of the submission hereof to the states by the Congress.

[Repealed by Amendment XXI, Section 1.]

Amendment XIX (1920)

The right of citizens of the United States to vote shall not be denied or abridged by the United States or by any state on account of sex.

Congress shall have power to enforce this article by appropriate legislation.

Amendment XX (1933)

Section 1. The terms of the President and Vice President shall end at noon on the 20th day of January, and the terms of Senators and Representatives at noon on the 3d day of January, of the years in which such terms would have ended if this article had not been ratified; and the terms of their successors shall then begin.

Section 2. The Congress shall assemble at least once in every year, and such meeting shall begin at noon on the 3d day of January, unless they shall by law appoint a different day.

Section 3. If, at the time fixed for the beginning of the term of the President, the President elect shall have died, the Vice President elect shall become President. If a President shall not have been chosen before the time fixed for the beginning of his term, or if the President elect shall have failed to qualify, then the Vice President elect shall act as President until a President shall have qualified; and the Congress may by law provide for the case wherein neither a President elect nor a Vice President elect shall have qualified, declaring who shall then act as President, or the manner in which one who is to act shall be selected, and such person shall act accordingly until a President or Vice President shall have qualified. [See Amendment XXV.]

Section 4. The Congress may by law provide for the case of the death of any of the persons from whom the House of Representatives may choose a President whenever the right of choice shall have devolved upon them, and for the case of the death of any of the persons from whom the Senate may choose a Vice President whenever the right of choice shall have devolved upon them.

Section 5. Sections 1 and 2 shall take effect on the 15th day of October following the ratification of this article.

Section 6. This article shall be inoperative unless it shall have been ratified as an amendment to the Constitution by the legislatures of three-fourths of the several states within seven years from the date of its submission.

Amendment XXI (1933)

Section 1. The eighteenth article of amendment to the Constitution of the United States is hereby repealed.

Section 2. The transportation or importation into any state, territory, or possession of the United States for delivery or use therein of intoxicating liquors, in violation of the laws thereof, is hereby prohibited.

Section 3. This article shall be inoperative unless it shall have been ratified as an amendment to the Constitution by conventions in the several states, as provided in the Constitution, within seven years from the date of the submission hereof to the states by the Congress.

Amendment XXII (1951)

Section 1. No person shall be elected to the office of the President more than twice, and no person who has held the office of President, or acted as President, for more than two years of a term to which some other person was elected President shall be elected to the office of the President more than once. But this article shall not apply to any person holding the office of President when this article was proposed by the Congress, and shall not prevent any person who may be holding the office of President, or acting as President, during the term within which this article becomes operative from holding the office of President or acting as President during the remainder of such term.

Section 2. This article shall be inoperative unless it shall have been ratified as an amendment to the Constitution by the legislatures of three-fourths of the several states within seven years from the date of its submission to the states by the Congress.

Amendment XXIII (1961)

Section 1. The District constituting the seat of government of the United States shall appoint in such manner as the Congress may direct:

A number of electors of President and Vice President equal to the whole number of Senators and Representatives in Congress to which the District would be entitled if it were a state, but in no event more than the least populous state; they shall be in addition to those appointed by the states, but they shall be considered, for the purposes of the election of President and Vice President, to be electors appointed by a state; and they shall meet in the District and perform such duties as provided by the twelfth article of amendment.

Section 2. The Congress shall have power to enforce this article by appropriate legislation.

Amendment XXIV (1964)

Section 1. The right of citizens of the United States to vote in any primary or other election for President or Vice President, for electors for President or Vice President, or for Senator or Representative in Congress, shall not be denied or abridged by the United States or any state by reason of failure to pay any poll tax or other tax.

Section 2. The Congress shall have power to enforce this article by appropriate legislation.

Amendment XXV (1967)

Section 1. In case of the removal of the President from office or of his death or resignation, the Vice President shall become President.

Section 2. Whenever there is a vacancy in the office of the Vice President, the President shall nominate a Vice President who shall take office upon confirmation by a majority vote of both Houses of Congress.

Section 3. Whenever the President transmits to the President pro tempore of the Senate and the Speaker of the House of Representatives his written declaration that he is unable to discharge the powers and duties of his office, and until he transmits to them a written declaration to the contrary, such powers and duties shall be discharged by the Vice President as Acting President.

Section 4. Whenever the Vice President and a majority of either the principal officers of the executive departments or of such other body as Congress may by law provide, transmit to the President pro tempore of the Senate and the Speaker of the House of Representatives their written declaration that the President is unable to discharge the powers and duties of his office, the Vice President shall immediately assume the powers and duties of the office as Acting President.

Thereafter, when the President transmits to the President pro tempore of the Senate and the Speaker of the House of Representatives his written declaration that no inability exists, he shall resume the powers and duties of his office unless the Vice President and a majority of either the principal officers of the executive department or of such other body as Congress may by law provide, transmit within four days to the President pro tempore of the Senate and the Speaker of the House of Representatives their written declaration that the President is unable to discharge the powers and duties of his office. Thereupon Congress shall decide the issue, assembling within forty-eight hours for that purpose if not in session. If the Congress, within twenty-one days after receipt of the latter written declaration, or, if Congress is not in session, within twenty-one days after Congress is required to assemble,

determines by two-thirds vote of both Houses that the President is unable to discharge the powers and duties of his office, the Vice President shall continue to discharge the same as Acting President; otherwise, the President shall resume the powers and duties of his office.

Amendment XXVI (1971)

Section 1. The right of citizens of the United States, who are 18 years of age or older, to vote, shall not be denied or abridged by the United States or any state on account of age.

Section 2. The Congress shall have the power to enforce this article by appropriate legislation.

Amendment XXVII (Passed September 25, 1789; ratified May 7, 1992)

No law, varying the compensation for the services of the Senators and Representatives, shall take effect, until an election of Representatives shall have intervened.

Get the Latest in the Law

1   **Nolo's Legal Updater**
We'll send you an email whenever a new edition of your book is published!
Sign up at **www.nolo.com/legalupdater**.

2   **Updates at Nolo.com**
Check **www.nolo.com/update** to find recent changes in the law that
affect the current edition of your book.

3   **Nolo Customer Service**
To make sure that this edition of the book is the most recent one, call us at
800-728-3555 and ask one of our friendly customer service representatives
(7:00 am to 6:00 pm PST, weekdays only). Or find out at **www.nolo.com**.

4   **Complete the Registration & Comment Card...**
...and we'll do the work for you! Just indicate your preferences below:

Registration & Comment Card

NAME _____   DATE _____

ADDRESS _____

CITY _____   STATE _____   ZIP _____

PHONE _____   EMAIL _____

COMMENTS _____

WAS THIS BOOK EASY TO USE?   (VERY EASY)   5   4   3   2   1   (VERY DIFFICULT)

☐ Yes, you can quote me in future Nolo promotional materials. *Please include phone number above.*

☐ Yes, send me **Nolo's Legal Updater** via email when a new edition of this book is available.

Yes, I want to sign up for the following email newsletters:

☐ **NoloBriefs** (monthly)
☐ **Nolo's Special Offer** (monthly)
☐ **Nolo's BizBriefs** (monthly)
☐ **Every Landlord's Quarterly** (four times a year)

☐ Yes, you can give my contact info to carefully selected
partners whose products may be of interest to me.

DICT1

NOLO

Send to: **Nolo** 950 Parker Street Berkeley, CA 94710-9867, Fax: (800) 645-0895, or include all of
the above information in an email to regcard@nolo.com with the subject line "DICT1."

The Busy Family's Guide to Money

by Sandra Block, Kathy Chu & John Waggoner • $19.99

The Busy Family's Guide to Money will help you make the most of your income, handle major one-time expenses, figure children into the budget—and much more.

The Work From Home Handbook
Flex Your Time, Improve Your Life

by Diana Fitzpatrick & Stephen Fishman • $19.99

If you're one of those people who need to (or simply want to) work from home, let this book help you come up with a plan that both you and your boss can embrace!

Retire Happy
What You Can Do NOW to Guarantee a Great Retirement

by Richard Stim & Ralph Warner • $19.99

You don't need a million dollars to retire well, but you do need friends, hobbies and an active lifestyle. This book shows how to make retirement the best time of your life.

The Essential Guide for First-Time Homeowners
Maximize Your Investment & Enjoy Your New Home

by Ilona Bray & Alayna Schroeder • $19.99

This reassuring resource is filled with crucial financial advice, real solutions and easy-to-implement ideas that can save you thousands of dollars.

Easy Ways to Lower Your Taxes
Simple Strategies Every Taxpayer Should Know

by Sandra Block & Stephen Fishman • $19.99

Provides useful insights and tactics to help lower your taxes. Learn how to boost tax-free income, get a lower tax rate, defer paying taxes, make the most of deductions—and more!

First-Time Landlord
Your Guide to Renting Out a Single-Family Home

by Attorney Janet Portman, Marcia Stewart & Michael Molinski • $19.99

From choosing tenants to handling repairs to avoiding legal trouble, this book provides the information new landlords need to make a profit and follow the law.

Stopping Identity Theft
10 Easy Steps to Security

by Scott Mitic, CEO, TrustedID, Inc. • $19.99

Don't let an emptied bank account be your first warning sign. This book offers ten strategies to help prevent the theft of personal information.

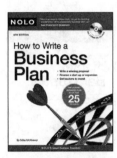

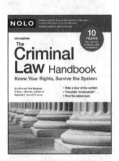

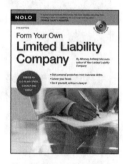
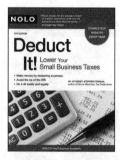

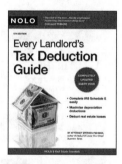